SOCIAL
REALITY

PRENTICE-HALL SOCIOLOGY SERIES

Neil J. Smelser, *Editor*

SOCIAL REALITY

edited by

Harvey A. Farberman

*State University of New York
at Stony Brook*

Erich Goode

*State University of New York
at Stony Brook*

PRENTICE-HALL, INC.   Englewood Cliffs, New Jersey

Library of Congress Cataloging in Publication Data

FARBERMAN, HARVEY A. comp.
  Social reality.

  (Prentice-Hall sociology series)
  CONTENTS: Hall, E. T. The silent language.—Horton,
J. Time and cool people.—Mead, M. The standardization
of sex temperament. [etc.]
  Includes bibliographical references.
  1. Sociology—Addresses, essays, lectures.
I. Goode, Erich, joint comp. II. Title.
HM51.F27   301   72-11694
ISBN 0-13-818245-0

Printed in the United States of America

10 9 8 7 6 5 4 3 2 1

Prentice-Hall International, Inc., London
Prentice-Hall of Australia, Pty. Ltd., Sydney
Prentice-Hall of Canada, Ltd., Toronto
Prentice-Hall of India Private Limited, New Delhi
Prentice-Hall of Japan, Inc., Tokyo

To Julia, Max, Pinu, Si, and Ruth

Contents

2

Socialization   *30*

3

Interaction   *68*

4

Formal Organizations   *115*

5

Stratification and Social Class *160*

6

Deviance and Social Control *227*

7

SOCIAL
REALITY

Introduction

American sociological thought encompasses a broad spectrum of view-points and theories. At present, the field has not crystallized into a single consistent outlook. Attempts at presenting sociology as a discipline often result in eclecticism—a hodgepodge of unrelated and even contradictory perspectives offered up between the covers of a book as if there were some-thing holding the resulting product together aside from the binding. A different approach would be to present sociology from a single point of view, omitting others which do not contribute to a consistent line of reasoning. This volume is closer to the second of these approaches than to the first. Although the topic areas covered in this anthology are traditional and well-worn, the thread of a definite point of view will run throughout the entire volume. Thus, we will deal with culture, socialization, interaction, formal organizations, stratification, and deviance, but all of the readings will emit a distinctive flavor. This distinctiveness in our approach stems from our conception of what sociology and the sociologist ought to do. As we see it, our calling is to help rip down the barriers that separate us from the people we study. We do this in order to enter their life space and understand their situations, to see through their eyes the complex network of existential circumstances constraining them, and, with compassion and humility, to work with them to transcend these constraints.

To aid us in this work, we bring to bear certain general ideas. First, that the social reality we live in and experience is constructed collectively. Second, that this collectively constructed social world is an ongoing process which is pulled this way or that way by groups who have either more or less political power and whose impact on the direction of that process is proportional to their power. Third, that those whose impact is most powerful work to channel, concretize, and reify that process so as to reflect and maximize their own interests. Fourth, that this preferential reification closes down alternative channels and forces those who are less powerful to participate in the maximization of privileged interests. Fifth, that this imposed participation is oppressive and constitutes a state of inauthenticity and alienation. Sixth, that this state of alienation can be transcended through reflection, heightened consciousness, and social action. In sum, for us, the ultimate aim and strongest justification for doing sociology is liberation.

Fundamental to our view is the assumption that the universe has no intrinsic meaning—it is, at bottom, absurd—and that the task of the sociologist is to discover the various imputed or fabricated meanings constructed by man and woman in society. Or, to put it another way, the sociologist's job is to find out *by what illusions people live.* Without these artifacts, these delicately poised fantasies, most of us would not survive. Society, as we know it, could not exist. Meaningless produces terror. And terror must be dissipated by participating in, and believing in, collective fictions. They constitute society's "noble lie," the lie that there is some sort of inherent significance in the universe. It is the job of sociology to understand the mechanisms of imputing meaning to the various aspects of life.

This view emphasizes *imputations* rather than inherent meanings. This proposition should not be taken too lightly, nor understood too quickly. It attacks centuries of folk wisdom, seeks to replace a host of taken-for-granted assumptions that even practicing sociologists accept—and it tries to destroy some of the fundamental assumptions on which much of contemporary social and behavioral science rests.

Opposed to our "imputational" view is what might be called the "immanentist" or positivistic view. This view holds that reality is "out there," external to man and independent of his cognition; the aim of science is thus to describe this reality in a neutral way. One prominent reason for our rejection of the mainstream positivistic view is our belief that these two assumptions—the independent status of reality and the possibility of neutral description—are self-contradictory and, in fact, upon examination, give more support to our view than to the mainstream view. A closer look may help to understand why.

The first, or ontological, assumption holds that reality exists as an entity independent of man *and* that it contains a network of intrinsic interconnections. The second, or epistemological, assumption holds that an observer can describe those interconnections in a neutral way. Now, with regard to these assumptions, the German philosopher-sociologist Jürgen Habermas raises the following question: What exactly does the word *neutral* refer to—the reality under observation or the observer himself? If we start with an independent pre-given reality that has intrinsic interconnections, in what sense can these interconnections be neutral or, for that matter, non-neutral? The category neutral simply doesn't apply to anything that is naturally given. Yet, mainstream sociologists would argue that it does.   They would insist that we separate what we think from how we feel, what we see from how we evaluate it, and what we reflect on from what we desire.   In other words, they would have us separate cognition from emotion, description from evaluation, and pure theory from practical interest.   Thus they would extract cognition, description, and theory and accept them as a scientifically legitimate reality.   Similarly, they would extract emotion, evaluation, and interest and reject them as scientifically illegitimate.   The contradiction now emerges. The mainstream sociologist starts with an independent reality and a detached, neutral observer; he winds up having that observer actively intervene in order to accept certain parts of reality and reject others.   In what sense then can that observer be said to be detached or neutral?   The very fact that he has chosen to accept certain aspects of reality is a value judgment and a statement of non-neutrality.

Accordingly, we believe that the key assumptions of mainstream sociology actually support the position we subscribe to, namely, that the observer *constitutes,* through a selection procedure, the very reality with which he is dealing.   Thus, reality is a social construction, and what is observed is not independent of the observer.   Put another way, there exists a *transactional* relationship between the observer and the observed, and this reality-constituting procedure is a matter to be investigated, something we cannot presume to know beforehand.   We believe, then, that there is possible *an infinity of constructions of reality* and that the mainstream scientific representation is one of them.   Reality is a kind of Rorschach ink-blot test tapping sentiment of various kinds.   One form of sentiment might be the "scientific" temper; another might be a more "mystical" bent; still a third could be a "humanistic" orientation, and so on.   Which view is correct?   Our view is that all views of reality are equally biased—or equally unbiased, depending on the vocabulary we wish to choose.   But, is there not an "objective" reality, independent of the perspective adopted?   Our view is that objectivity is an imputation, not a fact.   Society has laid down the *rules* for determining bias—which are themselves a kind of bias.   There are no immutable, stable reference points in the social universe.   We can fix reality only by adopting one or another perspective.

A key question for us, then, is, Who has the power to construct reality, and who has the power to have his construction accepted as legitimate? Howard S. Becker, a sociologist, has coined the term, "the hierarchy of credibility."   This means that some members of society, or participants within some social setting, have greater power to define what is real, what is true, than others do.   Credibility is the power to be believed by others. In any situation, the lines of power and prestige will run parallel to the lines of credibility.   The teacher will be believed, in most disputes or disagreements, over the pupil.   The policeman over the criminal.   The psychiatrist over the insane.   The politician over the public.   The *New York Times* over The *East Village Other*.   The scientist over the layman.   Societies invest such hierarchies with an enormous amount of emotion. Calling them into question calls the entire social order into question.

Moreover, by not granting legitimacy to prestigious figures an observer almost invariably elicits an accusation of "bias" from the members of the society or group in question. The irony is that by attempting to avoid bias —that is, by detaching ourselves from a society's established and arbitrary views as to who is automatically right and who is automatically wrong—we thereby and for that reason become labeled as biased. But the crucial point is that there is no necessary relationship between a society's or a group's hierarchy of credibility, and what might be seen by outside observers as "reality" or "truth."

What is, or is not, science, and what defines, or is not permitted to define, reality, are questions which have enormous ideological implications. Scientists have traditionally attempted to clothe themselves in the mantle of objectivity and detachment. And yet, all scientific work is densely implicated in political, cultural, and ideological issues. The process by which an individual scientist, or the entire scientific enterprise, attempts to convince the public that science, or a specific scientific effort, constitutes objectivity, is itself an ideological and political process. Given the immense respect most Americans have for science, it is to the advantage of any observer or commentator to have his work or views accepted as science; this will yield more legitimacy than any other tactic. In other words, science is often the crystallization of an observer's private views—or of the values of one or another social group or subculture. The realm of drug use provides an example. Many physicians, psychiatrists, psychologists, pharmacologists, or sometimes even sociologists, view the illegal use of drugs as "pathological." Terms such as "irresponsibility," "inadequate personality," "demoralizing effect," "poorly adjusted," "withdrawn from reality," "poor judgment," and so on, are put forth as if they had an "objective," scientific meaning, independent of the moral sentiment of the individual using the terms. Yet it is clear that the use of these terms is blatantly ideological, and science is being used as a strategy to achieve legitimacy. Thus, what is or is not science becomes a political question and is closely tied in with being taken seriously.

Our view of sociology assumes *diversity* among members of a society. We mean a truly *radical* diversity. Not only are groups merely different in any moderately complex society—but they are *fundamentally* different; they are different to such a degree that it is legitimate to wonder whether they belong to the same society, whether they are attached in any way above and beyond the similarity of sharing roughly the same geographical boundaries at the same point in time. Sociologists traditionally have pointed out the diversity in the norms and values of members of the various subcultures in a society. But what we wish to stress is the contradiction in views as to what is real and what is true. Different individuals and groups do not merely inhabit a different moral universe—they also inhabit a different factual universe, a different realm of reality. There may very well be almost nothing which two inhabitants of the same society share in common, which two groups will accept as legitimate, which two members of two subcultures will see as true or false.

Yet in any given society, certain systems of meanings, values, and sentiments become reified and fixed; they become concretized, inevitable, seemingly "natural." And to be captured by these reifications is to be alienated; to accept them as "real," binding, legitimate, and unyielding is to be unfree and guilty of "bad faith." A man who is thus guilty usually is not even aware of these imposed limitations—he sees them as external. He fools himself into thinking that he has no choice. The alienated man has bought the lie that society's options constitute the full range of his freedom. Instead of permitting himself the full play of acting out the multi-dimensional man that he might be, he turns himself into a "one dimensional man," to use Herbert Marcuse's phrase.

To take a case in point, most societies urge their female members to marry and raise children. The option of not marrying and not raising children (or of marrying and not raising children—or of not marrying and raising children) are not considered viable, legitimate, reasonable. Thus, by accepting the "myth of motherhood," women everywhere alienate themselves from the non-mother selves that they might be. It is society's lie that every woman is destined to be a wife and a mother, and that if she chooses otherwise, she is incomplete and unfulfilled. It is a lie to assume that motherhood is inevitable and somehow more "natural" than a life without children. The nonalienated woman considers the full range of options—marriage, or no marriage; motherhood, or not having or raising children—or any combination of these, depending on personal taste and personal choice. The alienated woman restricts herself to the single option dictated by mainstream social opinion.

Our view also, and correlatively, requires a measure of *empathy*—of understanding the world of the actor, of grasping reality from the point of view of the subject. Meaning, value, and sentiment are *contextual*—they arise out of specific situations; they can be known only by participants in these situations; they can be understood by the sociologist only by getting as close to these situations and participants as possible. The same behavior, externally the same "reality," can mean, or symbolize, radically different things. We must empathize with the participants we study in order to understand them. This may sound like a simple-minded axiom—taken-for-granted and obvious. But it is simpler still to slip into an externalistic view of man. This has been the approach of much social science in the past. The earliest students of non-Western civilizations and tribes committed the fallacy of imposing their own morality, their own interpretations, on the behavior of the peoples they visited. What was "primitive" to these Europeans was simply that which was different from their own values and beliefs. Later sociologists and anthropologists prided themselves on their "objectivity"; a closer look at some of this "value free" work has revealed that much of it contains a different variety of value imposition. We have to get inside the heads of the people we are attempting to understand.

We say again, as investigators, that we must learn to resonate with the people we study. We must help them to understand the constituted nature of social reality, its moral-political forces, the oppressive nature of reification, the inauthenticity of alienation, and the possibility of emancipation.

Culture

1

Culture is an historical product that reflects a people's way of life. It is a heritage of collectively established strategies which grow out of the perennial attempt to survive. This survival strategy passes through the hands of successive generations who modify it, add to it, and pass it on. Like a map which one group of travelers hands on to the next group of travelers, culture lays out the boundaries, routes, distances, detours, and dead ends. It is a convenience for the traveler and all he need do is pick it up. But convenience often turns into necessity and necessity into compulsion. And so what was merely a guide becomes a governance structure.

Soon the traveler follows the well-worn route and hesitates to strike out on his own; he observes the detour signs and doesn't re-explore the dead ends; he accepts the boundary lines and doesn't cross them. All too often, he relates to his culture as though it were separate and apart from himself, as though it were an entity which confronts him or stands over and against him. Eventually, he treats the culture as being autonomous and irrevocable.

One way, however, to gain some perspective on what we take as inevitably fixed is to look at the cultural map of people in other societies. This kind of comparative perspective helps us to see that even very fundamental things, such as space, time, sexual identity, and reality itself are quite relative, and that different societies or even different groups within the same society have arranged these phenomena in different ways.

In our first reading, Edward T. Hall takes us south of the border to Latin America and shows us how space is handled in a way that makes North Americans uncomfortable. Latin Americans, it seems, feel most comfortable when they can converse with other people at a physical distance of between eight and ten inches. At this distance, North Americans feel imposed upon. They quickly reach the point of panic when they discover that the Latin American also likes to touch people as he talks. In short order, the North American quickly retreats to the distance at which he feels safe— about two feet—only to discover that the Latin American closes in again to less than one foot. This advance and retreat pattern is comical but it shows clearly how different cultures use space.

A similar pattern occurs with respect to time. Punctuality is a notorious virtue among middle class white Americans. To be late is a sign of disrespect and inefficiency. But for the Latin American, rushing in and getting right down to business is to miss an opportunity to know someone. One must make friends before one does business because it is understood that only friends can be trusted. Thus *time* derives its meaning and value in relation to friendship.

But one doesn't have to go too far to find other conceptions of time. John Horton shows us that, right here in the United States, especially in low income ghetto areas, time takes on a different meaning. Its meaning there derives from the street culture emphasis on "action." When there is no action, time is "dead." Being in jail, working, going to school, or not having money kills time. Time is alive when the action is on—when there is money, women, parties. Street time is not clock time, but personal time, and it is measured by involvement or lack of involvement in action. Hours, days, weeks disappear in the face of action. Thus, what first appear as "natural" properties of the world, i.e., "space" and "time," turn out to be rigidifications of social preference, conventions which vary from people to people and derive their meaning in relation to those things that people value. So, time derives its meaning in one case from friendship, in another, from action; it is established or constituted in the course of ongoing activity. It is not an independent, absolute dimension.

Much as space and time are different in different cultures, so are sex role distinctions. Typically, men are thought to be dominant and aggressive, women, passive and submissive. Usually, these character traits are thought to be associated with the more powerful sexual drives of men and the less powerful sexual drives of women. These character types, however, are culturally specific and there is ample evidence to suggest that mere biological distinctions between male and female are in no way directly associated with personality or character type. The anthropologist Margaret Mead, in fact, describes three cultures where sexual identity and character type vary in several ways. For example, in Arapesh society *both* men and women are passive, submissive, and cooperative. In Mundugumor society, *both* men and women are cruel, violent, and aggressive. And in Tchambuli society, *women* are dominant, aggressive, and impersonal, whereas *men* are passive, dependent, and emotional. In other words, character type is not sex-linked. Just this point is being expressed trenchantly by the women's liberation movement, and the evidence in their favor, from anthropological research, is overwhelming. In fact, students might well wonder why it has taken so long for this elementary fact of *social* life to become known.

the silent language

EDWARD T. HALL

There is a great reservoir of mutual good will among the peoples of the Americas. Much of it is needlessly dissipated in the desert sands of misunderstanding because in today's troubled world good will alone is not enough. Between the people of the United States and their southern neighbors there are deep and subtle differences. What is needed is an understanding and an appreciation of each other's psychology that will help to bridge political and economic gaps when these exist. Surface differences can be seen and dealt with. What defeats all of us are the hidden elements in man's psychological make-up whose presence is all too often not even suspected.

I will use the Spanish word *ocultos*—"not seen"—in a new sense to stand for these hidden psychological patterns that stand between peoples. Like germs that can't be seen, there are many ocultos that

Reprinted from AMÉRICAS, monthly magazine published by the General Secretariat of the Organization of American States in English, Spanish, and Portuguese. Vol. 14. (Feb., 1962).

cause psychological difficulty. All one sees are the symptoms, the outward manifestation of the oculto.

One can never hope to uncover all these unsuspected patterns that influence the communication between people. Even reviewing the principal elements at work here is virtually impossible, because each country in the Americas is unique and has a unique relationship with its fellow states.

DEFINING THE OCULTO

I will particularize about three specific topics to demonstrate a principle. These are Time, Space, and Friendship. Ocultos between the U.S. Citizen and his neighbors differ in all three. One must keep in mind, however, that times are changing very fast: therefore, some of my examples no longer apply to regions where there has been a great influx of North Americans.

I first became aware of space as a patterned aspect of human behavior when I noted that people raised in other cultures handled it differently. In the Middle East I felt crowded and was often made to feel anxious. Fellow U.S. citizens, also, found it hard to adapt themselves to houses and offices arranged so differently, and often commented on how there was too little or too much space, and how much space was wasted. These spatial differences are not limited to offices and homes: towns, subway systems, and road networks usually follow patterns that appear curious to one not accustomed to the culture.

The "natural" way to describe space may be different in two cultures. For instance, I discovered in Japan that intersections of streets were named and the streets were not. Similarly, Europeans find it almost impossible to follow directions given by Arabs until a whole new system of visualizing space is learned. One reason for this is that the Arab takes so completely for granted the details of a familiar route that he thinks that if he identifies the desired destination as being near a well-known landmark, he has given adequate directions. He visualizes each area as a fixed unit, instead of focusing on the positional relationship between units.

These differing ideas of space— like the ideas of time and place— contain traps for the uninformed. A person raised in the United States is often likely to give an unintentional snub, without realizing it, to a Latin American because of the way he handles space relationships, particularly the physical distance between individuals during conversations. A Colombian or Mexican often feels that the *Norteamericano* he is talking to is cold and withdrawn.

A conversation I once observed

between a Latin and a North American began at one end of a forty-foot hall. I watched the two conversationalists until they had finally reached the other end of the hall. This maneuver had been effected by a continual series of small backward steps on the part of the North American as he unconsciously retreated, searching for a comfortable talking distance. Each time, there was an accompanying closing of the gap, as his Latin friend attempted to reestablish his own accustomed conversation distance.

In formal business conversations in North America, the "proper" distance to stand when talking to another adult male who is simply a business acquaintance you don't know well, is usually about two feet. This distance diminishes, of course, at social functions like the cocktail party, but anything under eight to ten inches is likely to irritate. An easy way to test where the hidden line is, is to watch for the first point in closeness that causes the other person to back up, or move. To the Latin, with his own ocultos, a distance of two feet seems remote and cold, sometimes even unfriendly. One of the things that gives the South American or Central American the feeling that the North American is *simpático* is when he starts to use space in a sympathetic way and is no longer made uncomfortable by closeness or being touched.

North Americans, working in offices in Latin America, may keep their local acquaintances at a distance—not the Latin American distance—by remaining behind a desk or typewriter. Even North Americans who have lived in Latin America for years have been known to use the "barricade approach" to communication, and to remain completely unaware of its cultural significance. They are aware only that *they* "feel comfortable" when not crowded, without realizing that the distance and the desk often create an oculto that distorts or gives a cold tone to virtually everything that takes place. The hold of the oculto is so strong, however, that the Latin is sometimes observed trying to "climb over" the intervening obstacles—leaning over the desk, for instance—in order to achieve a distance at which he can communicate comfortably.

The Spanish colonial house is usually built around a patio that is adjacent to the sidewalks, but hidden from outsiders behind a wall. Small architectural differences like these sometimes affect outsiders to a degree that seems out of proportion to the actual facts. North American Point Four technicians residing in Latin America often said that they felt "shut off" and "left out" of things. Many kept wondering "what went on behind those walls." When North Americans live next door to people in Latin America, they soon find that sharing of adjacent space does not always conform to their own pattern. In the United States, propinquity is the sole basis of many relationships. In the North, being a neighbor gives one certain privileges and rights as well as responsibilities. The North American is accustomed to borrowing things, including food and drink, from his neighbor, but also assumes the responsibility of taking his neighbor to the hospital in an emergency, even if they are not well acquainted or particularly congenial. In the United States, except perhaps in a big city apartment house, your neighbor has as much claim on you as a cousin, and what's more you are supposed to get along with him, and hide any unkind thoughts.

Because of this oculto, the North American usually picks his neighborhood carefully and appears to segregate himself in a golden ghetto because he knows he is going to be thrown into intimate contact with the people who live near him, and share his living space. He knows that his children will go to the same schools and that the men will belong to the same clubs, and that the wives will visit: that his life will be an open book to his neighbors.

TIME—PATTERNS OF PUNCTUALITY

As with space, there are many time ocultos that characterize each people. The North American has developed a language of time that involves much more than being prompt. He can usually tell you when his own ocultos have been violated, but not how they work. His blood pressure rises and he loses his temper when he is kept waiting; this is because time and the ego have been linked. As a rule, the longer a North American is kept waiting *in his own setting,* the greater the discrepancy between the status of the two parties. Because of their high status, important people can keep less important people waiting. Also, very important business takes precedence over less important business. Five minutes brings a mild apology; thirty minutes a very long explanation; forty-five minutes is a slap in the face. In addition, the North American has developed a pattern for seeing one person at a time.

Individual appointments aren't usually scheduled by the Latin American to the exclusion of other appointments. The Latin often enjoys seeing several people at once even if he has to talk on different matters at the same time. In this setting, the North American may feel he is not being properly treated, that his dignity is under attack, even though this simply is not true. The Latin American clock on the wall may look the same, but it tells a different sort of time.

By the U.S. clock, a consistently tardy man is considered undependable. To judge a Latin American by the same time values is to risk a major error.

This cultural error may be compounded by a further miscalculation. Suppose the *Norteamericano* has waited forty-five minutes or an hour and finally gets to see the Latin American with whom he has an appointment, only to be told, with many apologies, that "there is only five minutes—maybe a meeting can be arranged for tomorrow or next week?" At this point, the North American's schedule has been "shot." If it is important, he will have to *make the time*. What he may not understand is an oculto common in Mexico, for example, and that is that one is very likely to take one's time before doing business, in order to provide time for "getting acquainted." First meetings leave the North American with the feeling he isn't getting anywhere. If not forewarned by a friendly advisor, or by experience, he keeps trying to get down to business and stop "wasting time." This, too, turns out to be a mistake. In the United States, *discussion* is used as a means to an end: the deal. One tries to make his point with neatness and dispatch—quickly and efficiently. The North American begins by taking up major issues, leaving details for later, perhaps for technicians to work out.

Discussion, however, is to the Latin American an important part of life. It serves a different function and operates according to rules of form; it has to be done right. For the Latin American, the emphasis is on courtesy, not speed. Close friends who see each other frequently, shake hands when they meet and when they part. It is the invisible social distance that is maintained, not the physical distance. Forming a new friendship, or a business acquaintance, must be done properly. The Latin American wants to know the human values of a new acquaintance—his cultural interests, his philosophy of life—not his efficiency, before he can establish confidence. And this is all accompanied by elaborate and graceful formal verbal expressions, which people in the United States have long felt too busy to take time for. They tend to assume familiarity very quickly, to invite new acquaintances to their homes after one or two meetings. But the Latin American entertains only friends of very long standing in his home—and never for business reasons.

Of course, times are changing, and the North American can be fooled, too, because there is an increasing number of Latin businessmen who now demand punctuality even greater than in the North. However there are still a great many times when the old patterns prevail and are not understood. The hidden differences seem to center around the fact that in the North, the ego of the man is more on the surface, whereas in the South preserving institutional forms is important.

THE LANGUAGE OF FRIENDSHIP

It has been observed that in the United States, friendships may not be long lasting. People are apt to take up friends quickly and drop them just as quickly. Friendships formed during school days persist when neither party moves away, but this is unusual. A feature influencing North American friendship patterns is that people move constantly (in the twelve-year period from 1946–1958, according to U.S. census data, two thirds of those owning homes had moved, while virtually all those renting property had moved). The North American, as a rule, looks for and finds his friends next door and among those with whom he works. There are for him few well-defined, hard and fast rules governing the obligations of friendship. At just what point our friendships give way to business opportunism or pressure from above difficult to say. In this, the United States seems to differ from many other countries in the world.

In Latin America, on the other hand, while friendships are not formed as quickly or as easily as in the United States, they often go much deeper and last longer. They almost always involve real obligations. For example, it is important to stress that in Latin America your "friends" will not let you down. The fact that they, personally, are having difficulties is never an excuse for failing friends. You, in turn, are obligated to look out for their interests.

Thus, friends and family around the world—and especially in Latin America—represent a kind of social insurance that is hard to find in the United States, where friends are often a means of getting ahead—or at least, getting the job done. Frequently, friendship in the U.S. system involves a series of carefully, though silently, tabulated favors and obligations, doled out where they will do the most good. The least that North Americans expect in exchange for a favor is gratitude.

The weight of tradition presses the Latin American to do business within a circle of friends and relatives. If a product or service he needs is not available within his circle, he hesitates to go outside; if he does so, he looks for a new friend who can supply the want. Apart from the cultural need to "feel right" about a new relationship, there is the logic of the business system. One of the realities of life is that it is dangerous to enter into business with someone over whom you have no "control." The difference between the two systems lies in the controls. One is formal, personal, and depends upon family and friends. The other is technical-legal, impersonal, and depends upon courts and contracts.

SPEAKING ONE'S MIND

Europeans often comment on how candid the North American is. Being candid, he seeks this in others. What fools him is that the Latin American does not readily reciprocate. One has to be known and trusted—admitted into the circle of friendship—before this happens. Even then, what is not said may be just as important, and just as much noticed, as what is said. Much of the miscuing that takes place can be traced to the reciprocity oculto in the North American friendship pattern. North Americans tend to believe much too much of what they hear, and then are shocked when things turn out differently. The Latin American, in particular, will not speak his mind to someone involved in his own operation unless there is complete confidence.

UNCOVERING THE OCULTO CAN HELP

Latin Americans are tired of trying to find North Americans who will understand and who are *simpático*. Some have given up trying. They value the whole man, not just his skill or knowledge in one or two fields. They feel that North Americans are so engrossed in getting things done that they never take time to live. This observation is corroborated by the statistics that show how quickly U.S. men whose whole energy has been devoted to their jobs, to the exclusion of other interests and hobbies, die when forced to retire while still vigorous. These have much to learn from their southern neighbors. But there are today many people in the United States who, tired of the trapped feeling of being caught in their inflexible daily rounds, find these Latin American values deeply congenial.

Nevertheless, until we face up to the reality of the ocultos, and make them explicit, difficulties in communication are going to continue. Ocultos drain the great reservoir of good will that the people of the Americas feel in their hearts for each other.

The Latin American must help the North American to understand. And the North American must do everything in his power to reach his friends in Latin America. He must continue to inform himself about the tremendously rich heritage, and the vitality and subtlety, of Hispano-American culture.

time and cool people

JOHN HORTON

Street culture exists in every low income ghetto. It is shared by the

Reprinted by permission from John Horton, "Time and Cool People," TRANSACTION, 4 (April, 1967), 5–12. Copyright © April 1967 by Transaction, Inc., New Brunswick, New Jersey.

hustling elements of the poor, whatever their nationality or color. In Los Angeles, members of such street groups sometimes call themselves "street people," "cool people," or simply "regulars." Whatever the label, they are known the world over by outsiders as hoods or hoodlums, persons who live on and off the street. They are recognizable by their own fashions in dress, hair, gestures, and speech. The particular fashion varies with time, place, and nationality. For example, in 1963 a really sharp Los Angeles street Negro would be "conked to the bone" (have processed hair) and "togged-out" in "continentals." Today "natural" hair and variations of mod clothes are coming in style.

Street people are known also by their activities—"duking" (fighting or at least looking tough), "hustling" (any way of making money outside the "legitimate" world of work), "gigging" (partying)—and by their apparent nonactivity, "hanging" on the corner. Their individual roles are defined concretely by their success or failure in these activities. One either knows "what's happening" on the street, or he is a "lame," "out of it," "not ready" (lacks his diploma in street knowledge), a "square."

There are, of course, many variations. Negroes, in particular, have contributed much to the street tongue which has diffused into both the more hip areas of the middle class and the broader society. Such expressions as "a lame," "taking care of righteous business," "getting down to the nitty-gritty," and "soul" can be retraced to Negro street life.

The more or less organized center of street life is the "set"—meaning both the peer group and the places where it hangs out. It is the stage and central market place for activity, where to find out what's happening. My set of Negro street types contained a revolving and sometimes disappearing (when the "heat," or police pressure, was on) population of about 45 members ranging in age

from 18 to 25. These were the local "dudes," their term meaning not the fancy city slickers but simply "the boys," "fellas," the "cool people." They represented the hard core of street culture, the role models for younger teenagers. The dudes could be found when they were "laying dead"—hanging on the corner, or shooting pool and "jiving" ("goofing" or kidding around) in a local community project. Isolated from "the man" (in this context the man in power—the police, and by extension, the white man), they lived in a small section of Venice outside the central Los Angeles ghetto and were surrounded by a predominantly Mexican and Anglo population. They called their black "turf" "Ghost-town"—home of the "Ghostmen," their former gang. Whatever the origin of the word, Ghost-town was certainly the home of socially "invisible" men.

THE STREET SET

In 1965 and 1966 I had intensive interviews with 25 set members. My methods emerged in day to day observations. Identified as white, a lame, and square, I had to build up an image of being at least "legit" (not working for police). Without actually living in the area, this would have been impossible without the aid of a key fieldworker, in this case an outsider who could be accepted inside. This fieldworker, Cowboy, was a white dude of 25. He had run with "Paddy" (white), "Chicano" (Mexican) and "Blood" (Negro) sets since the age of 12 and was highly respected for having been president of a tough gang. He knew the street, how to duke, move with style, and speak the tongue. He made my entry possible. I was the underprivileged child who had to be taught slowly and sympathetically the common-sense features of street life.

Cowboy had the respect and I the toleration of several set leaders. After that, we simply waited for the opportunity to "rap." Although sometimes used synonymously with street conversation, "rap" is really a special way of talking—repartee. Street repartee at its best is a lively way of "running it down," or of "jiving" (attempting to put someone on), of trying "to blow another person's mind," forcing him "to loose his cool," to give in or give up something. For example, one needs to throw a lively rap when he is "putting the make on a broad."

Sometimes we taped individuals, sometimes "soul sessions." We asked for life histories, especially their stories about school, job, and family. We watched and asked about the details of daily surviving and attempted to construct street time schedules. We probed beyond the past and present into the future in two directions—individual plans for tomorrow and a lifetime, and individual dreams of a more decent world for whites and Negroes.

The set can be described by the social and attitudinal characteristics of its members. To the observer, these are expressed in certain realities of day to day living: not enough skill for good jobs, and the inevitable trouble brought by the problem of surviving. Of the 25 interviewed, only four had graduated from high school. Except for a younger set member who was still in school, all were dropouts, or perhaps more accurately kicked-outs. None was really able to use or write

formal language. However, many were highly verbal, both facile and effective in their use of the street tongue. Perhaps the art of conversation is most highly developed here where there is much time to talk, perhaps too much—an advantage of the *lumpen*-leisure class.

Their incomes were difficult to estimate, as "bread" or "coins" (money) came in on a very irregular basis. Of the 17 for whom I have figures, half reported that they made less than $1,400 in the last year, and the rest claimed income from $2,000–4,000 annually. Two-thirds were living with and partially dependent on their parents, often a mother. The financial strain was intensified by the fact that although 15 of 17 were single, eight had one or more children living in the area. (Having children, legitimate or not, was not a stigma but proof of masculinity.)

At the time of the interview, two-thirds of them had some full- or part-time employment—unskilled and low-paid jobs. The overall pattern was one of sporadic and—from their viewpoint—often unsatisfactory work, followed by a period of unemployment compensation, and petty hustling whenever possible and whenever necessary.

When I asked the question, "When a dude needs bread, how does he get it?" the universal response was "the hustle." Hustling is, of course, illegitimate from society's viewpoint. Street people know it is illegal, but they view it in no way as immoral or wrong. It is justified by the necessity of surviving. As might be expected, the unemployed admitted that they hustled and went so far as to say that a dude could make it better on the street than on the job: "There is a lot of money on the street, and there are many ways of getting it," or simply, "This has always been my way of life." On the other hand, the employed, the part-time hustlers, usually said, "A dude could make it better on the job than on the street." Their reasons for disapproving of hustling were not moral. Hustling meant trouble. "I don't hustle because there's no security. You eventually get busted." Others said there was not enough money on the street or that it was too difficult to "run a game" on people.

Nevertheless, hustling is the central street activity. It is the economic foundation for everyday life. Hustling and the fruit of hustling set the rhythm of social activities.

What are the major forms of hustling in Ghost-town? The best hustles were conning, stealing, gambling, and selling dope. By gambling, these street people meant dice; by dope, peddling "pills" and "pot." Pills are "reds" and "whites" barbiturates and benzedrine or dexedrine. Pot is, of course, marijuana —"grass" or "weed." To "con" means to put "the bump" on a "cat," to "run a game" on somebody, to work on his mind for goods and services.

The "woman game" was common. As one dude put it, "If I have a good lady and she's on County, there's always some money to get." In fact, there is a local expression for getting county money. When the checks come in for child support, it's "mother's day." So the hustler "burns" people for money, but he also "rips off" goods for money; he thieves, and petty thieving is always a familiar hustle. Pimping is often the hustler's dream of the good life, but it was almost unknown here

among the small-time hustlers. That was the game of the real professional and required a higher level of organization and wealth.

Hustling means bread and security but also trouble, and trouble is a major theme in street life. The dudes had a "world of trouble" (a popular song about a hustler is "I'm in a World of Trouble")—with school, jobs, women, and the police. The intensity of street life could be gauged in part by the intensity of the "heat" (police trouble). The hotter the street, the fewer the people visible on the street. On some days the set was empty. One would soon learn that there had been a "bust" (an arrest). Freddy had run amok and thrown rocks at a police car. There had been a leadership struggle; "Big Moe" had been cut up, and the "fuzz" had descended. Life was a succession of being picked up on suspicion of assault, theft, possession, "suspicion of suspicion" (an expression used by a respondent in describing his life). This was an ordinary experience for the street dude and often did lead to serious trouble. Over half of those interviewed claimed they had felony convictions.

THE STRUCTURE OF STREET TIME

Keeping cool and out of trouble, hustling bread, and looking for something interesting and exciting to do created the structure of time on the street. The rhythm of time is expressed in the high and low points in the day and week of an unemployed dude. I stress the pattern of the unemployed and full-time hustler because he is on the street all day and night and is the prototype in my interviews. The sometimes employed will also know the pattern, and he will be able to hit the street whenever released from the bondage of jail, work, and the clock. Here I describe a typical time schedule gleaned through interviews and field observation.

Characteristically the street person gets up late, hits the street in the late morning or early afternoon, and works his way to the set. This is a place for relaxed social activity. Hanging on the set with the boys is the major way of passing time and waiting until some necessary or desirable action occurs. Nevertheless, things do happen on the set. The dudes "rap" and "jive" (talk), gamble, and drink their "pluck" (usually a cheap, sweet wine). They find out what happened yesterday, what is happening today, and what will hopefully happen on the weekend—the perpetual search for the "gig," the party. Here peer socialization and reinforcement also take place. The younger dude feels a sense of pride when he can be on the set and throw a rap to an older dude. He is learning how to handle himself, show respect, take care of business, and establish his own "rep."

On the set, yesterday merges into today, and tomorrow is an emptiness to be filled in through the pursuit of bread and excitement. Bread makes possible the excitment—the high (getting loaded with wine, pills, or pot), the sharp clothes, the "broad," the fight, and all those good things which show that one knows what's happening and has "something going" for himself. The rhythm of time—of the day and of the week—is patterned by the flow of money and people.

Time is "dead" when money is tight, when people are occupied elsewhere—working or in school. Time is dead when one is in jail. One is "doing dead time" when nothing is happening, and he's got nothing going for himself.

Time is alive when and where there is action. It picks up in the evening when everyone moves on the street. During the regular school year it may pick up for an hour in the afternoon when the "broads" leave school and meet with the set at a corner taco joint. Time may pick up when a familiar car cruises by and a few dudes drive down to Johnny's for a "process" (hair straightening and styling). Time is low on Monday (as described in the popular song, "Stormy Monday"), Tuesday, Wednesday, when money is tight. Time is high on Friday nights when the "eagle flies" and the "gig" begins. On the street, time has a personal meaning only when something is happening, and something is most likely to happen at night—especially on Friday and Saturday nights. Then people are together, and there may be bread—bread to take and bread to use.

Human behavior is rational if it helps the individual to get what he wants whether it is success in school or happiness in the street. Street people sometimes get what they want. They act rationally in those situations where they are able to plan and choose because they have control, knowledge, and concern, irrationally where there are barriers to their wants and desires.

When the street dude lacks knowledge and power to manipulate time, he is indeed irrational. For the most part, he lacks the skills and power to plan a move up and out of the ghetto. He is "a lame" in the middle class world of school and work; he is not ready to operate effectively in unfamiliar organizations where his street strengths are his visible weaknesses. Though irrational in moving up and out of the street, he can be rational in day to day survival in the street. No one survives there unless he knows what's happening (that is, unless he knows what is available, where to get what he can without being burned or busted). More euphemistically, this is "taking advantage of opportunities," exactly what the rational member of the middle class does in his own setting.

To know what's happening is to know the goods and the bads, the securities, the opportunities, and the dangers of the street. Survival requires that a hustling dude know who is cool and uncool (who can be trusted); who is in power (the people who control narcotics, fences, etc.); who is the "duker" or the fighter (someone to be avoided or someone who can provide protection). When one knows what's happening he can operate in many scenes, providing that he can "hold his mud," keep cool and out of trouble.

With his diploma in street knowledge, a dude can use time efficiently and with cunning in the pursuit of goods and services—in hustling to eat and yet have enough bread left over for the pleasures of pot, the chicks, and the gig. As one respondent put it, "The good hustler has the knowhow, the ambition to better himself. He conditions his mind and must never put his guard too far down, to relax, or he'll be taken." This is street rationality. The problem is not a deficient sense of time but deficient knowledge and control

to make a fantasy future and a really better life possible.

The petty hustler more fully realizes the middle class ideal of individualistic rationality than does the middle class itself. When rationality operates in hustling, it is often on an individual basis. In a world of complex organization, the hustler defines himself as an entrepreneur; and indeed, he is the last of the competitive entrepreneurs.

The degree of organization in hustling depends frequently on the kind of hustling. Regular pimping and pushing require many trusted contacts and organization. Regular stealing requires regular fences for hot goods. But in Ghost-town when the hustler moved, he usually moved alone and on a small scale. His success was on him. He could not depend on the support of some benevolent organization. Alone, without a sure way of running the same game twice, he must continually recalculate conditions and people and find new ways of taking or be taken himself. The phrase "free enterprise for the poor and socialism for the rich" applies only too well in the streets. The political conservative should applaud all that individual initiative.

CLOCK TIME VS. PERSONAL TIME

Negro street time is built around the irrelevance of clock time, white man's time, and the relevance of street values and activities. Like anyone else, a street dude is on time by the standard clock whenever he wants to be, not on time when he does not want to be and does not have to be.

When the women in school hit the street at the lunch hour and he wants to throw them a rap, he will be there then and not one hour after they have left. But he may be kicked out of high school for truancy or lose his job for being late and unreliable. He learned at an early age that school and job were neither interesting nor salient to his way of life. A regular on the set will readily admit being crippled by a lack of formal education. Yet school was a "bum kick." It was not his school. The teachers put him down for his dress, hair, and manners. As a human being he has feelings of pride and autonomy, the very things most threatened in those institutional situations where he was or is the underdeveloped, unrespected, illiterate, and undeserving outsider. Thus whatever "respectable" society says will help him, he knows oppresses him, and he retreats to the streets for security and a larger degree of personal freedom. Here his control reaches a maximum, and he has the kind of autonomy which many middle class males might envy.

In the street, watches have a special and specific meaning. Watches are for pawning and not for telling time. When they are worn, they are decorations and ornaments of status. The street clock is informal, personal, and relaxed. It is not standardized nor easily synchronized to other clocks. In fact, a street dude may have almost infinite toleration for individual time schedules. To be on time is often meaningless, to be late an unconsciously accepted way of life. "I'll catch you later," or simply "later," are the street phrases that mean business will be taken care of, but not necessarily now.

Large areas of street life run on late time. For example, parties are not cut off by some built-in alarm clock of appointments and schedules. At least for the unemployed, standard time neither precedes nor follows the gig. Consequently, the action can take its course. It can last as long as interest is sustained and die by exhaustion or by the intrusion of some more interesting event. A gig may endure all night and well into another day. One of the reasons for the party assuming such time dimensions is purely economic. There are not enough cars and enough money for individual dates, so everyone converges in one place and takes care of as much business as possible there, that is, doing whatever is important at the time—sex, presentation of self, hustling.

COLORED PEOPLE'S TIME

Events starting late and lasting indefinitely are clearly street and class phenomena, not some special trait of Afro-Americans. Middle class Negroes who must deal with the organization and coordination of activities in church and elsewhere will jokingly and critically refer to a lack of standard time sense when they say that Mr. Jones arrived "CPT" (colored people's time). They have a word for it, because being late is a problem for people caught between two worlds and confronted with the task of meshing standard and street time. In contrast, the street dudes had no self-consciousness about being late; with few exceptions they had not heard the expression CPT. (When I questioned members of a middle class Negro fraternity, a sample matched by age to the street set, only three of the 25 interviewed could not define CPT. Some argued vehemently that CPT was the problem to be overcome.)

Personal time as expressed in parties and other street activities is not simply deficient knowledge and use of standard time. It is a positive adaption to generations of living whenever and wherever possible outside of the sound and control of the white man's clock. The personal clock is an adaptation to the chance and accidental character of events on the street and to the very positive value placed on emotion and feeling. (For a discussion of CPT which is close to some of the ideas presented here, see Jules Henry, "White People's Time, Colored People's Time," *Trans-action,* March/April 1965.)

Chance reinforces personal time. A dude must be ready on short notice to move "where the action is." His internal clock may not be running at all when he is hanging on the corner and waiting for something to do. It may suddenly speed up by chance: Someone cruises by in a car and brings a nice "stash" of "weed," a gig is organized and he looks forward to being well togged-out and throwing a rap to some "boss chick," or a lame appears and opens himself to a quick "con." Chance as a determinant of personal time can be called more accurately *uncertain predictability.* Street life is an aggregate of relatively independent events. A dude may not know exactly what or when something will happen, but from past experience he can predict a range of possibilities, and he will be ready, in position, and waiting.

In white middle class stereotypes and fears—and in reality—street action is highly expressive. A forthright yet stylized expression of emo-

tion is positively evaluated and most useful. Street control and communication are based on personal power and the direct impingement of one individual on another. Where there is little property, status in the set is determined by personal qualities of mind and brawn.

The importance of emotion and expression appears again and again in street tongue and ideology. When asked, "How does a dude make a rep on the set?" over half of the sample mentioned "style," and all could discuss the concept. Style is difficult to define as it has so many referents. It means to carry one's self well, dress well, to show class. In the ideology of the street, it may be a way of behaving. One has style if he is able to dig people as they are. He doesn't put them down for what they do. He shows toleration. But a person with style must also show respect. That means respect for a person as he is, and since there is power in the street, respect for another's superior power. Yet one must show respect in such a way that he is able to look tough and inviolate, fearless, secure, "cool."

Style may also refer to the use of gestures in conversation or in dance. It may be expressed in the loose walk, the jivey or dancing walk, the slow cool walk, the way one "chops" or "makes it" down the street. It may be the loose, relaxed hand rap or hand slap, the swinger's greeting which is used also in the hip middle class teen sets. There are many refined variations of the hand rap. As a greeting, one may simply extend his hand, palm up. Another slaps it loosely with his finger. Or, one person may be standing with his hand behind and palm up. Another taps the hand in passing, and also pays his respect verbally with the conventional greeting "What's happening, Brother." Or, in conversation, the hand may be slapped when an individual has "scored," has been "digging," has made a point, has got through to the person.

Style is a comparatively neutral value compared to "soul." Soul can be many things—a type of food (good food is "soul food," a "bowl of soul"), music, a quality of mind, a total way of acting (in eating, drinking, dancing, walking, talking, relating to others, etc.). The person who acts with soul acts directly and honestly from his heart. He feels it and tells it "like it is." One respondent identified soul with ambition and drive. He said the person with soul, once he makes up his mind, goes directly to the goal, doesn't change his mind, doesn't wait and worry about messing up a little. Another said soul was getting down to the nityy-gritty, that is, moving directly to what is basic without guise and disguise. Thus soul is the opposite of hypocrisy, deceit, and phoniness, the opposite of "affective neutrality," and "instrumentality." Soul is simply whatever is considered beautiful, honest, and virtuous in men.

Most definitions tied soul directly to Negro experience. As one hustler put it, "It is the ability to survive. We've made it with so much less. Soul is the Negro who has the spirit to sing in slavery to overcome the monotony." With very few exceptions, the men interviewed argued that soul was what Negroes had and whites did not. Negroes were "soul brothers," warm and emotional—whites cold as ice. Like other oppressed minorities these street Negroes believed they had nothing except their soul and their humanity,

and that this made them better than their oppressors.

THE PERSONAL DREAM

Soul is anchored in a past and present of exploitation and deprivation, but are there any street values and activities which relate to the future? The regular in the street set has no providential mission; he lives personally and instrumentally in the present, yet he dreams about the day when he will get himself together and move ahead to the rewards of a good job, money, and a family. Moreover, the personal dream coexists with a nascent political nationalism, the belief that Negroes can and will make it as Negroes. His present-future time is a combination of contradictions and developing possibilities. Here I will be content to document without weighing two aspects of his orientation: *fantasy personal future* and *fantasy collective future*. I use the word fantasy because street people have not yet the knowledge and means and perhaps the will to fulfill their dreams. It is hard enough to survive by the day.

When the members of the set were asked, "What do you really want out of life?" their responses were conventional, concrete, seemingly realistic, and—given their skills—rather hopeless. Two-thirds of the sample mentioned material aspirations—the finer things in life, a home, security, a family. For example, one said, in honest street language, "I want to get things for my kids and to make sure they have a father." Another said, jokingly, "a good future, a home, two or three girls living with me." Only one person didn't know, and the others deviated a little from the material response. They said such things as "for everyone to be on friendly terms—a better world . . . then I could get all I wish," "to be free," "to help people."

But if most of the set wanted money and security, they wanted it on their own terms. As one put it, "I don't want to be in a middle class bag, but I would like a nice car, home, and food in the icebox." He wanted the things and the comforts of middle class life, but not the hypocrisy, the venality, the coldness, the being forced to do what one does not want to do. All that was in the middle class bag. Thus the home and the money may be ends in themselves, but also fronts, security for carrying on the usual street values. Street people believed that they already had something that was valuable and looked down upon the person who made it and moved away into the middle class world. For the observer, the myths are difficult to separate from the truths—here where the truths are so bitter. One can only say safely that street people dream of a high status, and they really do not know how to get it.

THE COLLECTIVE FUTURE

The Negro dudes are political outsiders by the usual poll questions. They do not vote. They do not seek out civil rights demonstrations. They have very rudimentary knowledge of political organization. However, about the age of 18, when fighting and being tough are less important than before, street people begin to discuss their position in society. Verbally they care very much about the politics of race and the future of the Negro. The topic is always a ready catalyst for a soul session.

The political consciousness of the street can be summarized by noting those interview questions which attracted at least a 75 percent rate of agreement. The typical respondent was angry. He approves of the Watts incident, although from his isolated corner of the city he did not actively participate. He knows something about the history of discrimination and believes that if something isn't done soon America can expect violence: "What this country needs is a revolutionary change." He is more likely to praise the leadership of Malcolm X than Lyndon Johnson, and he is definitely opposed to the Vietnam war. The reason for his opposition is clear: Why fight for a country which is not mine, when the fight is here?

Thus his racial consciousness looks to the future and a world where he will not have to stand in the shadow of the white man. But his consciousness has neither clear plan nor political commitment. He has listened to the Muslims, and he is not a black nationalist. True, the Negro generally has more soul than the white. He thinks differently, his women may be different, yet integration is preferable to separatism. Or, more accurately, he doesn't quite understand what all these terms mean. His nationalism is real as a folk nationalism based on experience with other Negroes and isolation from whites.

The significance of a racial future in the day to day consciousness of street people cannot be assessed. It is a developing possibility dependent on unforeseen conditions beyond the scope of their skill and imagination. But bring up the topic of race and tomorrow, and the dreams come rushing in—dreams of superiority, dreams of destruction, dreams of human equality. These dreams of the future are salient. They are not the imagination of authoritarian personalities, except from the viewpoint of those who see spite lurking behind every demand for social change. They are certainly not the fantasies of the hipster living philosophically in the present without hope and ambition. One hustler summarized the Negro street concept of ambition and future time when he said:

The Negro has more ambition than the whites. He's got farther to go. "The man" is already there. But we're on your trail, daddy. You still have smoke in our eyes, but we're catching up.

FURTHER READING

CLAUDE BROWN, *Manchild in the Promised Land* (New York: The New American Library, 1966). An autobiographical account of street life in Harlem.

WILLIAM FOOTE WHYTE, *Street Corner Society* (Chicago: University of Chicago Press, 1943). A sociological account of street life among Italian-Americans in Boston.

J. T. FRASER, ed. *The Voices of Time* (New York: George Braziller, 1965). Essays on man's views of time as expressed by the sciences and the humanities.

EDWARD T. HALL, *The Silent Language* (Greenwich, Conn.: Fawcett Publications, 1963). An anthropologist describes how time and other cultural concepts are communicated without the use of words.

the standardization of sex temperament

MARGARET MEAD

We have now considered in detail the approved personalities of each sex among three primitive peoples. We found the Arapesh—both men

From Margaret Mead, "The Standardization of Sex Temperament," SEX AND TEMPERAMENT IN THREE PRIMITIVE SOCIETIES. Reprinted by permission of William Morrow and Company, Inc. and Routledge & Kegan Paul Ltd. Copyright © 1935 © 1963.

and women—displaying a personality that, out of our historically limited preoccupations, we would call maternal in its parental aspects, and feminine in its sexual aspects. We found men, as well as women, trained to be co-operative, unaggressive, responsive to the needs and demands of others. We found no idea that sex was a powerful driving force either for men or for women. In marked contrast to these attitudes, we found among the Mundugumor that both men and women developed as ruthless, aggressive, positively sexed individuals, with the maternal cherishing aspects of personality at a minimum. Both men and women approximated to a personality type that we in our culture would find only in an undisciplined and very violent male. Neither the Arapesh nor the Mundugumor profit by a contrast between the sexes; the Arapesh ideal is the mild, responsive man married to the mild, responsive woman; the Mundugumor ideal is the violent aggressive man married to the violent aggressive woman. In the third tribe, the Tchambuli, we found a genuine reversal of the sex-attitudes of our own culture, with the woman the dominant, impersonal, managing partner, the man the less responsible and the emotionally dependent person. These three situations suggest, then, a very definite conclusion. If those temperamental attitudes which we have traditionally regarded as feminine—such as passivity, responsiveness, and a willingness to cherish children—can so easily be set up as the masculine pattern in one tribe, and in another be outlawed for the majority of women as well as for the majority of men, we no longer have any basis for regarding such aspects of behaviour as sex-linked. And this conclusion becomes even stronger when we consider the actual reversal in Tchambuli of the position of dominance of the two sexes, in spite of the existence of formal patrilineal institutions.

The material suggests that we may say that many, if not all, of the personality traits which we have called masculine or feminine are as lightly linked to sex as are the clothing, the manners, and the form of head-dress that a society at a given period assigns to either sex. When we consider the behaviour of the typical Arapesh man or woman as contrasted with the behaviour of the typical Mundugumor man or woman, the evidence is overwhelmingly in favour of the strength of social conditioning. In no other way can we account for the almost complete uniformity with which Arapesh children develop into contented, passive, secure persons, while Mundugumor children develop as characteristically into violent, aggressive, insecure persons. Only to the impact of the whole of the integrated culture upon the growing child can we lay the formation of the contrasting types. There is no other explanation of race, or diet, or selection that can be adduced to explain them. We are forced to conclude that human nature is almost unbelievably malleable, responding accurately and contrastingly to contrasting cultural conditions. The differences between individuals who are members of different cultures, like the differences between individuals within a culture, are almost entirely to be laid to differences in conditioning, especially during early childhood, and the form of this conditioning is culturally determined. Standardized personality differences between the sexes are of this order, cultural creations to which each generation, male and female, is trained to conform. There remains, however, the problem of the origin of these socially standardized differences.

While the basic importance of social conditioning is still imperfectly recognized—not only in lay thought, but even by the scientist specifically concerned with such matters—to go beyond it and consider the possible influence of variations in hereditary equipment is a hazardous matter. The following pages will read very differently to one who has made a part of his thinking a recognition of the whole amazing mechanism of cultural conditioning—who has really accepted the fact that the same infant could be developed into a full participant in any one of these three cultures—than they will read to one who still believes that the minutiae of cultural behaviour are carried in the individual germ-plasm. If it is said, therefore, that when we have grasped the full significance of the malleability of the human organism and the preponderant importance of cultural conditioning, there are still further problems to solve, it must be remembered that these problems come *after* such a comprehension of the force of conditioning; they cannot precede it. The forces that make children born among the Arapesh grow up into typical Arapesh personalities are entirely social, and any discussion of the variations which do occur must be looked at against this social background.

With this warning firmly in mind, we can ask a further question. Granting the malleability of human nature, whence arise the differences between the standardized personalities that different cultures decree for all of their members, or which one culture decrees for the members of one sex as contrasted with the members of the opposite sex? If such differences are culturally created, as this material would most strongly suggest that they are, if the new-born child can be shaped with equal ease into an unaggressive Arapesh or an aggressive Mundugumor, why do these striking contrasts occur at all?

If the clues to the different personalities decreed for men and women in Tchambuli do not lie in the physical constitution of the two sexes—an assumption that we must reject both for the Tchambuli and for our own society—where can we find the clues upon which the Tchambuli, the Arapesh, the Mundugumor, have built? Cultures are man-made, they are built of human materials; they are diverse but comparable structures within which human beings can attain full human stature. Upon what have they built their diversities?

We recognize that a homogeneous culture committed in all of its gravest institutions and slightest usages to a co-operative, unaggressive course can bend every child to that emphasis, some to a perfect accord with it, the majority to an easy acceptance, while only a few deviants fail to receive the cultural imprint. To consider such traits as aggressiveness or passivity to be sex-linked is not possible in the light of the facts. Have such traits, then, as aggressiveness or passivity, pride or humility, objectivity or a preoccupation with person relationships, an easy response to the needs of the young and the weak or a hostility to the young and the weak, a tendency to initiate sex-relations or merely to respond to the dictates of a situation or another person's advances—have these traits any basis in temperament at all? Are they potentialities of all human temperaments that can be developed by different kinds of social conditioning and which will not appear if the necessary conditioning is absent?

When we ask this question we shift our emphasis. If we ask why an Arapesh man or an Arapesh woman shows the kind of personality that we have considered in the first section of this book, the answer is: Because of the Arapesh culture, because of the intricate, elaborate, and unfailing fashion in which a culture is able to shape each new-born child to the cultural image. And if we ask the same question about a Mundugumor man or woman, or about a Tchambuli man as compared with a Tchambuli woman, the answer is of the same kind. They display the personalities that are peculiar to the cultures in which they were born and educated. Our attention has been on the differences between Arapesh men and women as a group and Mundugumor men and women as a group. It is as if we had represented the Arapesh personality by a soft yellow, the Mundugumor by a deep red, while the Tchambuli female personality was deep orange, and that of the Tchambuli male, pale green. But if we now ask whence came the original direction in each culture, so that one now shows yellow, another red, the third orange and green by sex, then we must peer more closely. And leaning closer to the picture, it is as if behind the bright consistent yellow of the Arapesh, and the deep equally consistent red of the Mundugumor, behind the orange and green that are Tchambuli, we found in each case the delicate, just discernible outlines of the whole spectrum, differently overlaid in each case by the monotone which covers it. This spectrum is the range of individual differences which lie back of the so much more conspicuous cultural emphases, and it is to this that we must turn to find the explanation of cultural inspiration, of the source from which each culture has drawn.

There appears to be about the same range of basic temperamental variation among the Arapesh and among the Mundugumor, although the violent man is a misfit in the first society and a leader in the second. If human nature were completely homogeneous raw material, lacking specific drives and characterized by no important constitutional differences between individuals, then individuals who display personality traits so antithetical to the social pressure should not reappear in societies of such differing emphases. If the variations between individuals were to be set down to accidents in the genetic process, the same accidents should not be repeated with similar frequency in strikingly different cultures, with strongly contrasting methods of education.

But because this same relative distribution of individual differences does appear in culture after culture, in spite of the divergence between the cultures, it seems pertinent to offer a hypothesis to explain upon what basis the personalities of men and women have been differently standardized so often in the history of the human race. This hypothesis is an extension of that advanced by Ruth Benedict in her *Patterns of Culture*. Let us assume that there are definite temperamental differences between human beings which if not entirely hereditary at least are established on a hereditary base very soon after birth. (Further than this we cannot at present narrow the matter.) These differences finally embodied in the character structure of adults, then, are the clues from which culture works, selecting one temperament, or a combination of related and congruent types, as desirable, and embodying this choice in every thread of the social fabric—in the care of the young child, the games the children play, the songs the people sing, the structure of political organization, the religious observance, the art and the philosophy.

Some primitive societies have had the time and the robustness to revamp all of their institutions to fit one extreme type, and to develop educational techniques which will ensure that the majority of each generation will show a personality congruent with this extreme emphasis. Other societies have pursued a less definitive course, selecting their models not from the most extreme, most highly differentiated individuals, but from the less marked types. In such societies the approved personality is less pronounced, and the culture often contains the types of inconsistencies that many human beings display also; one institution may be adjusted to the uses of pride, another to a casual humility that is congruent neither with pride nor with inverted pride. Such societies, which have taken the more usual and less sharply defined types as models, often show also a less definitely patterned social structure. The culture of such societies may be likened to a house the decoration of which has been informed by no definite and precise taste, no exclusive emphasis upon dignity or comfort or pretentiousness or beauty, but in which a little of each effect has been included.

Alternatively, a culture may take its clues not from one temperament, but from several temperaments. But instead of mixing together into an inconsistent hotchpotch the choices and emphases of different temperaments, or blending them together into a smooth but not particularly distinguished whole, it may isolate each type by making it the basis for the approved social personality for an age-group, a sex-group, a caste-group, or an occupational group. In this way society becomes not a monotone with a few discrepant patches of an intrusive colour, but a mosaic, with different groups displaying different personality traits. Such specializations as these may be based upon any facet of human endowment —different intellectual abilities, different artistic abilities, different emotional traits. So the Samoans decree that all young people must show the personality trait of unaggressiveness and punish with opprobrium the aggressive child who displays traits regarded as appropriate only in titled middle-aged men. In societies based upon elaborate ideas of rank, members of the aristocracy will be permitted, even compelled, to display a pride, a sensitivity to insult, that would be deprecated as inappropriate in members of the plebeian class. So also in professional groups or in religious sects some temperamental traits are selected and institutionalized, and taught to each new member who enters the profession or sect. Thus the physician learns the bedside manner, which is the natural behaviour of some temperaments and the standard behaviour of the general practitioner in the medical profession; the Quaker learns at least the outward behaviour and the rudiments of meditation, the capacity for which is not necessarily an innate characteristic of many of the members of the Society of Friends.

So it is with the social personalities of the two sexes. The traits that occur in some members of each sex are specially assigned to one sex, and disallowed in the other. The history of the social definition of sex-differences is filled with such arbitrary arrangements in the intellectual and artistic field, but because of the assumed congruence between physiological sex and emotional endowment we have been less able to recognize that a similar arbitary selection is being made among emotional traits also. We have assumed that because it is convenient for a mother to wish to care for her child, this is a trait with which women have been more generously endowed by a carefully teleological process of evolution. We have assumed that because men have hunted, an activity requiring enterprise, bravery, and initiative, they have been endowed with these useful attitudes as part of their sex-temperament.

Societies have made these assumptions both overtly and implicitly. If a society insists that warfare is the major occupation for the male sex, it is therefore insisting that all male children display bravery and pugnacity. Even if the insistence upon the differential bravery of men and women is not made articulate, the difference in occupation makes this point implicitly. When, however, a society goes further and defines men as brave and women as timorous, when men are forbidden to show fear and women are indulged in the most flagrant display of fear, a more explicit element enters in. Bravery, hatred of any weakness, of flinching before pain or danger—this attitude which is so strong a component of *some human* temperaments has been selected as the key to masculine behaviour. The easy unashamed display of fear or suffering that is congenial to a different temperament has been made the key to feminine behaviour.

Originally two variations of human temperament, a hatred of fear or willingness to display fear, they

have been socially translated into inalienable aspects of the personalities of the two sexes. And to that defined sex-personality every child will be educated, if a boy, to suppress fear, if a girl, to show it. If there has been no social selection in regard to this trait, the proud temperament that is repelled by any betrayal of feeling will display itself, regardless of sex, by keeping a stiff upper lip. Without an express prohibition of such behaviour the expressive unashamed man or woman will weep, or comment upon fear or suffering. Such attitudes, strongly marked in certain temperaments, may by social selection be standardized for everyone, or outlawed for everyone, or ignored by society, or made the exclusive and approved behaviour of one sex only.

Neither the Arapesh nor the Mundugumor have made any attitude specific for one sex. All of the energies of the culture have gone towards the creation of a single human type, regardless of class, age, or sex. There is no division into age-classes for which different motives or different moral attitudes are regarded as suitable. There is no class of seers or mediums who stand apart drawing inspiration from psychological sources not available to the majority of the people. The Mundugumor have, it is true, made one arbitrary selection, in that they recognize artistic ability only among individuals born with the cord about their necks, and firmly deny the happy exercise of artistic ability to those less unusually born. The Arapesh boy with a tinea infection has been socially selected to be a disgruntled, antisocial individual, and the society forces upon sunny co-operative children cursed with this affliction a final approximation to the behaviour appropriate to a pariah. With these two exceptions no emotional rôle is forced upon an individual because of birth or accident. As there is no idea of rank which declares that some are of high estate and some of low, so there is no idea of sex-difference which declares that one sex must feel differently from the other. One possible imaginative social construct, the attribution of different personalities to different members of the community classified into sex-, age-, or caste-groups, is lacking.

When we turn however to the Tchambuli, we find a situation that while bizarre in one respect, seems nevertheless more intelligible in another. The Tchambuli have at least made the point of sex-difference; they have used the obvious fact of sex as an organizing point for the formation of social personality, even though they seem to us to have reversed the normal picture. While there is reason to believe that not every Tchambuli woman is born with a dominating, organizing, administrative temperament, actively sexed and willing to initiate sex-relations, possessive, definite, robust, practical and impersonal in outlook, still most Tchambuli girls grow up

to display these traits. And while there is definite evidence to show that all Tchambuli men are not, by native endowment, the delicate responsive actors of a play staged for the women's benefit, still most Tchambuli boys manifest this coquettish play-acting personality most of the time. Becuse the Tchambuli formulation of sex-attitudes contradicts our usual premises, we can see clearly that Tchambuli culture has arbitrarily permitted certain human traits to women, and allotted others, equally arbitrarily, to men.

If we then accept this evidence drawn from these simple societies which through centuries of isolation from the main stream of human history have been able to develop more extreme, more striking cultures than is possible under historical conditions of great intercommunication between peoples and the resulting heterogeneity, what are the implications of these results? What conclusions can we draw from a study of the way in which a culture can select a few traits from the wide gamut of human endowment and specialize these traits, either for one sex or for the entire community? What relevance have these results to social thinking?

Socialization

2

In recent years, the study of socialization has changed from an inquiry into the biology of a newborn organism to an inquiry into the sociology of family, peer group, and school and to an inquiry into the political economy of advanced industrial society. The change from biology to sociology came when social scientists began to discount the idea of internal "genetic destiny"; that is, the idea that buried in the inner-cellular spaces of a newly born bundle of biology was a genetic code that governed its future. The change led to intensive investigation of those external institutions and social relationships most proximal to the child—the family, the peer group, and the school. Early childhood experiences were thought to be decisive for future behavior and the general theory was that "as the twig is bent, so grows the tree." Eventually, the focus on early childhood gave way to a broader view, and socialization was understood to be a life-long process in which people were simply plugged into, and processed through, a system of interlocking roles and institutions from which they internalized a set of rules which prescribed how they ought to think, feel, and behave. Most investigators simply wanted to know what kind of imprint each subsequent institutional exposure left. The implicit assumption was that the institutions were legitimate and it was only natural for them to leave an imprint. No one wanted to know if the imprint *ought* to be left.

The issue of socialization changed from a question of sociology to a question of political economy when the young, the Blacks, and the women of our society challenged this tacit assumption and refused to concede the legitimacy and credibility of these institutions. For, to them, most institutions that fulfilled the socialization function, at whatever point in the life cycle, were simply conduits of prejudice, discrimination, repression, and, consequently, subjugation.

Lower-class black children who attended elementary schools run by middle-class whites underwent a negative educational experience—they did not learn, their measured intelligence declined, and their self-esteem decreased. White children from upper middle-class families were taught to compete for material rewards, to defer their gratification, and to seek security—in response, many went down the road to the counterculture. Females in all sectors of society were taught to be coquettish, submissive, and dependent. Eventually, their sense of desperation gave them the courage to transform their personal problems into a public issue and, through discussion and consciousness raising, to plant the seeds for a potentially revolutionary political and economic force. Thus, within the last two or three years the socialization question has become "who has the political power and economic resources to socialize whom, for what, and why?" Should parents socialize children, should middle-class whites socialize lower-class blacks, should men socialize women, and so on.

This new perspective turns the benign area of socialization into a political battleground and places the socialization process in the context of the total social and cultural structure. It seeks to uncover the impact of the distribution of wealth, property, and taxes on an individual's life chances. It raises questions about the constraints that prevailing moral codes, religious convictions, laws, and ideologies place on the realization of personal identities. It discloses the extent to which equal access to science, technology, and industry is denied. It recognizes that out of the complex interaction of the material and ideational forces of society comes an opportunity structure for "being" and "doing," for identity and activity, which establishes the existential circumstances within which lives are played out. It realizes that this opportunity structure must be made to be just.

Although we cannot but scratch the surface here, the articles that follow *begin* to explore some of these questions, especially that of socialization into sexual identity. For example, Sherri Cavan shows how human beings become rule-following actors who learn to show deference, respect, and civility toward others while remaining trustworthy and responsible themselves. William Simon and John Gagnon explore the ways in which responsible and trustworthy rule-following humans learn to take on sexual identity. And, finally, Sandra L. and Daryl J. Bem despair over how easily the acquisition of sexual identity, especially female sexual identity, leads responsible and trustworthy people into such patterns of respect, deference, and civility as to make them subordinate.

the etiquette of youth

SHERRI CAVAN

In general, the basic problem addressed by the process of socialization is what the participants in a particular social world must both know and do if they are not only to be accorded *bona fide* membership in that social world, but also become active participants in its maintenance.[1] The distinction between childhood socialization and adult socialization has, however, been a distinction which has dealt more with the age differences of those participants who are being socialized than with any differences in problems of socialization as it takes place with respect to children and adults.[2] Thus, for example, Brimm, in writing on personality development as role learning, states that the aim of socialization is that of: [3]

. . . producing individuals equipped to meet the variety of demands placed upon them by life in a society. Socialization is successful to the extent that it prepares individuals to perform adequately the many roles that will be expected of them in the normal course of their careers throughout society.

Within this formulation, the process of childhood socialization is the introduction of the child to those roles which he will be expected to perform as an adult. The basis of the socialization career of the child, as it is thus presented by Brimm, is the learning of the specific complexes of activity which constitutes social roles.

While it is undeniable that the child, as a child, does learn at least the fragments of many adult roles, it is questionable whether this in fact

[1] See, for example, P. Berger and T. Luckman, *The Social Construction of Reality*, Garden City, N.Y.: Doubleday and Co., 1966, pp. 119–135; and T. Shibutani, *Society and Personality*, Englewood Cliffs, N.J.: Prentice-Hall, 1961, pp. 472–475.

[2] Although the terms "primary" and "secondary" socialization are sometimes employed in the literature, by and large, the referents of these terms are no different than the referent of "childhood" and "adult" socialization.

[3] O. Brimm, "Personality Development as Role Learning," in I. Iscoe and H. W. Stevenson (eds.), *Personality Development in Children*, University of Texas Press, 1960, p. 138. This seems to be G. H. Mead's general position as well, when he speaks (albeit loosely) of the child learning "to take the role of the other." (Cf. *Mind, Self and Society*, University of Chicago Press, 1959, pp. 135–222.) However, at times it is unclear whether Mead is employing "role" as it is more customarily employed in contemporary American sociology—as a complex of behavior associated with some specifiable position in social life—or whether he is employing it in a much more general sense—as a diffuse attitude or orientation to the situation on the part of the actor.

is the *primary* product of childhood socialization. Brimm's statement of the process of socialization is analogous to Byzantium-like portrayal of children; children are miniature versions of adults, equipped with that array of socially sanctioned behavioral regularities which are taken for granted in adults.

But it would seem that childhood socialization, as distinct from adult socialization, addresses a problem prior to that of teaching specific role complexes—the problem of 'transforming newly born organisms into what will be accepted in the society as the basic model of a human being.

In terms of socialization as role learning, the advantage the army recruit and the medical student have over the child is that they are already more or less adequately programmed human beings; the army and the medical school need only worry about turning them into soldiers and doctors. While this role transformation may necessitate altering certain characteristics of their humanness, it is only an alteration and not a creation.

In effect, the problem faced by parents and other agents of childhood socialization is somewhat different than the problem faced by the army and the medical school. The raw material which the former has to work with is, although more pliable, less refined: in its original state it indiscriminately makes noise, demands, and waste matter and has no deference whatsoever for any ongoing social world. Thus the problem of childhood socialization is basically the problem of channelizing the newly born infants' gross activities into modes of conduct which are, at a minimum, harmonious with the social world into which they have

been born. But, beyond this, if that social world itself is to remain a viable world, it is not enough that those who populate it are merely inoffensive. They must somehow become responsible members. That is, they must also be trusted to take an active part in the maintenance of the normal features of the social order.

Both of these general problems of childhood socialization are evidenced in the following excerpt from a turn of the century etiquette book: [4]

> Nothing is more unkind than to allow a child to do as he pleases, for, as surely as he lives, he must learn sooner or later to yield to authority and to exercise self-control. The earlier the training begins, the earlier it will be. The child creeping about the room soon knows that the gentle, but firm "NO!" when spoken by the mother means that he must not touch the bit of bric-a-brac within reach. And even this lesson will stand him in good stead later on.
>
> The basic principle of home government must be love enforced by firmness. A punishment should seldom be threatened, but if promised, must be given. The time for threat and punishment is not in public. In the parlor, on the train, or boat, it is the height of ill-breeding to make a scene and to threaten a whipping, or a punishment of any kind. Were the child properly trained in private, parents and beholders would be spared the humiliating spectacle that too often confronts them in visiting and traveling.

To be trustworthy and responsible is not merely a matter of having

4 Marion Harland and Virginia Van De Water, *Everyday Etiquette*, Indianapolis, Ind.: The Bobbs-Merrill Co., 1905, pp. 262–263.

learned specified social roles that are to be enacted at particular times and in certain social situations. It may ultimately include such role learning. But by and large, to be accorded the status of a trustworthy and responsible member of a social world is contingent upon having learned much more general modes of conduct which are expected along with any role-specific courses of action, crosscut a great number of social situations, and are mostly without temporal limitations. Thus, while there are specific behavioral expectations associated with the positions of mother, janitor, customer, or physician, there are also more general expectations, such as civility, deference, and respect, which are independent of any specific social position, are applicable to all participants of the social occasion, and provide the basic guidelines within which more specific interactions can be carried on.

A major problem of childhood socialization would appear to be the teaching of these general norms of social behavior that are taken for granted in the variety of social situations in which specific roles are enacted.

In middle-class American society, short of crises such as emergencies and disasters, there are few situations where the general rules of etiquette are not treated as applicable criteria for the evaluation of behavior in general. Such rules of etiquette in essence incorporate many of the general expectations of social conduct which crosscut the situational norms of the society and the particular roles that are enacted in those situations.

In effect, the justification of the codification of rules of etiquette is characteristically made on the basis of the ubiquitous effects of proper general conduct in social life. Thus, in the introductory remarks in books of etiquette, statements such as the following are typical:

The world has fully recognized the fact that life's jostle and jar must of necessity be lessened if daily living is to be easy and pleasant. Upon this fact social regulations have founded and fashioned themselves. The rudeness which jostles, the selfishness which jars, whether against people or principles or opinions, are the first things ruled out and labeled "bad manners" when society formulates a code.

There are other offenses which receive the same label, although the offenders are neither selfish nor rude. They simply are ignorant of small social requirements, and all unwittingly, their words and acts cause friction with the smooth running system of society.[5]

To be loved is the instinctive desire of every human heart. To be respected, to be honored, to be successful, is the universal ambition. The ever constant desire of all is to be happy. This never varying instinct lies at the foundation of every action; it is the constantly propelling force in our every effort.

To be happy, we strive for the acquisition of wealth, for position and place, for social and political distinction. And when all is obtained, the real enjoyment in its possession comes from the thousand little courtesies that are exchanged between individuals—pleasant words and kindly acts, which the poor may enjoy as well as the rich.[6]

It is hard to say why the word "eti-

[5] The New York Society of Self-Culture, *Correct Social Usage*, 5th revised edition, New York: 1906, p. 9.

[6] T. Hill, *Never Give a Lady a Restive Horse: A 19th Century Handbook of Etiquette*, Berkeley: Diablo Press, 1967, p. 9.

quette" is so inevitably considered merely a synonym of the word "correct," as though it were no more than the fixed answer to a sum in arithmetic. In fact, it might be well to pull the word "correct" out by the roots and substitute "common sense." In short, I wish that those whose minds are focused on precise obedience to every precept would instead ask themselves, "What is the purpose of this rule? Does it help to make life pleasanter? Does it make the social machinery run more smoothly? Does it add to beauty? Is it essential to the code of good taste or to ethics?" If it serves any of these purposes, it is a rule to be cherished; but if it serves no helpful purpose, it is certainly not worth taking seriously.[7]

While etiquette books rarely cover all of the general expectations of sanctioned conduct, such as the proper distance or the proper spacial location for conversants,[8] and while all appropriate rules of etiquette are not actualized in all situations at all times, these books can serve at least as a partial codification of the precepts of befitting modes of general conduct.

Examining contemporary American etiquette books written specifically for young children, pre-adolescents, and adolescents, my concern with reference to the general problem of childhood socialization focuses on two questions:

1. What is the implicit world view or *Weltanschauung* which characterizes the social world inhabited by each

age group, and what are the implications of the *Weltanschauung* for the modes of behavior which are legitimately expected of each age group?

2. Given the rules for proper and fitting conduct for each age group, what can be said about the nature of trust and responsibility each cohort has for the ongoing interactional system?

The nine manners and etiquette books used in the following analysis represent about a third of the manners and etiquette books in the Children's Section of the San Francisco Public Library. Rather than being representative, they are merely indicative of the collection. The specific selections were made with the help of the Librarian of the Children's Section on the basis of the frequency of their circulation.[9]

Of the total collection of such books available to the children of San Francisco, by far the greatest proportion is addressed specifically to teen-age girls,[10] although there are some addressed to adolescents of both sexes. Of the total of 32 books in the collection, there were only two which were addressed to young chil-

---

[7] Emily Post, *Etiquette: The Blue Book of Social Usage*, New York: Funk & Wagnalls Co., 1955, p. 1.

[8] Cf. E. T. Hall, *The Silent Language*, Primer Books, 1961, and Robert Sommer, "Studies in Personal Space," *Sociometry*, 22 (1959), pp. 247–261.

[9] The distribution of books employed in the following analysis is as follows:
Young children (ages 4–8), two books addressed to both males and females.
Pre-adolescents (ages 8–12), one book addressed to males and females; one to females.
Adolescents (ages 13–18), two books addressed to males and females; three addressed to females.

[10] This is not surprising in view of the definition of woman as the expressive leader in American society. Cf. T. Parsons and R. F. Bales, *Family Socialization and Interaction Process*, Glencoe, Ill.: The Free Press, 1960, pp. 39–131, and J. Sirjamaki, "Cultural Configurations in the American Family," in N. W. Bell and E. F. Vogel (eds.), *The Family*, Glencoe, Ill.: The Free Press, 1960, pp. 295–304.

dren between the ages of four and eight. According to the librarian, while mothers mediate between the etiquette books and both young children (ages 4–8) and pre-adolescents (ages 8–12), adolescents (those 13–18) almost always obtain the books themselves.

THE WELTANSCHAUUNG OF CHILDHOOD AND ADOLESCENCE

The social world presented to the young child is a basically good world, which is in fact as it appears to be. Gradually, as the child approaches adolescence, not only do the number of social evils in the world increase, but the relationship between what the world appears to be and what it is in fact alters. Thus, while the young child is assured that behind every good act is a good person with a good intention, the adolescent is cautioned not to accept the world at its face value. For the young child, *persona* and person are identical; for the adolescent this may or may not be the case.

The world view presented to the young child is virtually a utopia, wherein nothing exists but goodness and truth. To fit into this world, the child need be only honest, fair, strong, and wise.[11] And, if he is honest, fair, strong, and wise, the implication is that the world will be his.[12]

If you are honest and promise to do something, others will trust you. They will share things with you, tell you secrets, lend you money and help

you to do many of the things you want to do.

Evil is at most a transitory phenomenon, which may be eradicated if one learns the proper behavior. Thus the young child is told: [13]

Look out for the person who pretends to be your friend but doesn't want you to like anyone else. That isn't a friend—it's a selfish person who is trying to own you and hasn't *learned* to share to be happy.

The pre-adolescent is also warned of jealousy. For him, "Jealousy is public enemy no. 1. Beware!" [14] The implication is that there are other evils. One must beware also of strange people on the streets who may be dangerous [15] as well as acquaintances who may be mean.[16] At the same time, by pre-adolescence one must be cautious of signs of evil in himself. But even though it is hard to be a good sport, and one is naturally disappointed when someone else wins,[17] one can still *learn* to be virtuous.[18]

By adolescence, the transitory character of evil has disappeared. To the social sin of selfishness is added hostility, while the goal is no longer the practice and learning of virtue, but the masking of vice.

[13] M. Leaf, *Manners Can Be Fun*, Philadelphia: J. B. Lippincott, 1958, p. 32 (emphasis added).
[14] B. Bryant, *Future Perfect*, Indianapolis: Bobbs-Merrill, 1957, p. 147.
[15] T. Lee, *Manners to Grow On*, Garden City, N.Y.: Doubleday & Co., 1955, p. 62.
[16] *Future Perfect*, op. cit., p. 142.
[17] *Manners to Grow On*, op. cit., pp. 15–16.
[18] *Ibid.*, p. 16; *Future Perfect*, op. cit., p. 151.

[11] M. Leaf, *How to Behave and Why*, Philadelphia: J. B. Lippincott Co., 1946, p. 10.
[12] *Ibid.*, p. 12.

Everybody is basically selfish and hostile to some degree; everybody is covering up something. What's more, *pretend* that you like someone, and strangely enough, often you will.[19] Don't show your scorn of dominoes, even if you would rather play rummy. It will not hurt you to *look as if* you were having a good time when you are not, and it will make things jollier for you and everybody else.[20]

Where the sanctioned world of the young child and pre-adolescent is populated by loving parents and friends,[21] the world of the adolescent is populated by *personae,* masks behind which one may or may not find an exact duplicate of the presented front.

The adolescent is admonished:

At a class or school dance, try to regard your partners as outside acquaintances, not just fellow students. Be aware of their different personalities. You may find that some of them have sides they have not shown in the classroom.[22]

The first thing people judge you by is your appearance. If what they see gives them a favorable impression, they are more interested in knowing the *you* behind it.[23]

When a boy takes the girl he loves home for the weekend to meet his parents . . . she should not take it for granted that his parents will understand what a fine girl she is. She must show them.[24]

Furthermore, the adolescent listens to his parents' opinion, not because of filial devotion, but because, "They have inside information on what lies at the other end of the stretch." [25]

The proper mode of behavior outlined for each age group varies according to the way in which the world has been defined for them.[26] In the world of the young child and the pre-adolescent, where everything is as it appears, good sportsmanship is the only mode of behavior necessary. In such a world, merit can be rewarded because it can be recognized. But by adolescence, the key words become "impression management"—the expression, during interaction, of what the actor wishes to convey to those in his presence.[27] Irrespective of how deserving the adolescent is, the world does not grant an automatic pay-off; he must engage in active work to be assured of his just rewards.

19 J. Jackson (H. L. Crounse), *Guide to Dating*, Englewood Cliffs, N. J.: Prentice-Hall, 1955, p. 16 (emphasis added).

20 E. Boykin, *This Way, Please*, New York: Macmillan, 1958, pp. 190–191 (emphasis added).

21 Cf. *How to Behave and Why*, op. cit.; *Manners Can Be Fun*, op. cit.; *Future Perfect*, op. cit.

22 *This Way, Please*, op. cit., p. 167.

23 *Ibid.*, p. 15 (emphasis in the original).

24 *Guide to Dating*, op. cit., p. 117.

25 *Ibid.*, p. 109.

26 "The fact of belonging to the same class, and that of belonging to the same generation or age group, have this in common, that both endow the individuals sharing in them with a common location in the social and historical process, and thereby limit them to a specific range of potential experience, predisposing them for certain characteristic modes of thought and experience and a characteristic type of historically relevant action. Any given location, then, excludes a large number of possible modes of thought, experience, feeling, and action, and restricts the range of self-expression open to the individual to certain circumscribed possibilities." K. Mannheim, "The Sociological Problems of Generations," in *Essays in the Sociology of Knowledge*, P. Kecskemeti (ed.), Routledge and Kegan Paul, Ltd., 1959, p. 291. See also Y. Cohen, *Social Structure and Personality*, Holt, Rinehart and Winston, 1961, pp. 310–311.

27 Cf. E. Goffman, *The Presentation of Self in Everyday Life*, University of Edinburgh, Monograph No. 2, 1958.

Thus, while the young child and pre-adolescent need only be pleasant and considerate for people to appreciate them, the adolescent must engage in "an earnest effort to portray one's real self. . . ." [28] While the pre-adolescent need only be attentive to the ongoing interaction to join in successfully,[29] the adolescent is counseled to prepare in advance.

> Make a mental note every time you hear a good gag or punch line and spike them into your conversation.[30] A girl who is weak in carrying on good conversation might plan comments in advance, taking care to slip them in at opportune moments.[31]

The theme of impression management is part of a larger theme which is presented to the adolescent: that of "working the system." [32] The adolescent is expected to be able to utilize, for his own personal gains, the legitimate activities of social life.

For the young child and the pre-adolescent, friends, games, activities, school, are presented as having intrinsic value. They are good in and of themselves. For the adolescent, to this intrinsic value is added another dimension: things may be good in and of themselves, but they may also be good because they can be used. For the young child and the pre-adolescent, it is simply fun to be a host; [33] for the adolescent, hosting can be useful: [34]

> Entertaining in the home offers a good opportunity for one to show her qualities . . . as hostess, a girl is very much the center of attention. . . . By organizing games and stunts, she has every opportunity of showing qualities of leadership and finesse. Boys are attracted to girls who are fine hostesses.
> And, last but not least in the ways to attract a boy is the party method. It's simple and *appears to be so undesigning*.[35]

For the young child and pre-adolescent, introductions merely occur as a natural part of the ever-widening social world; for the adolescent, the structure of the introduction can be used to make oneself available to the opposite sex.

> If you are anxious to meet a certain person of the opposite sex, never be bashful about asking a mutual friend to make the introduction. It may be a boy or girl you pass every day on the way to school, but a proper introduction is the accepted way of breaking the ice.[36]

> Even though the boy may be in one of your classes at school, you might well arrange to have a mutual friend introduce you. The motive behind the introduction does not have to be obvious. . . . The friend could stop the boy on some pretense or other . . . and then very casually turn and introduce you.[37]

Similarly the pre-adolescent is recommended to join the activities and organizations around him so that he may become acquainted with

---

28 *Guide to Dating*, op. cit., p. 21.

29 *Future Perfect*, op. cit., p. 18.

30 B. Betz, *Your Manners Are Showing*, New York: Grosset & Dunlap, 1946, p. 81.

31 *Guide to Dating*, op. cit., p. 29.

32 Cf. E. Goffman, "The Underlife of a Public Institution," in *Asylums*, Anchor Books, 1961, pp. 210–214.

33 Cf. *Manners Can Be Fun; Manners to Grow On*.

34 *Guide to Dating*, op. cit., p. 25.

35 B. Bryant, *Miss Behavior*, Indianapolis: Bobbs-Merrill, 1960, p. 43 (emphasis added).

36 *Your Manners Are Showing*, op. cit., p. 9.

37 *Guide to Dating*, op. cit., p. 5.

the world around him and come to appreciate that world.

> Know how the members of the Junior Civic League elect their officers, and you will know how the people of the United States elect their president. Join the choral club . . . "Serenade" becomes more real to a girl when she knows how Schubert came to compose it.[38]

But the adolescent is told to take part in the activities and organizations around him because, "In these groups she can plan things to say and do which will win the respect of other members." [39]

In one sense, then, the process of childhood socialization may be characterized as a gradual initiation into both the overt and the covert social world, where, by adolescence, the American youth is presented with most of the ordinarily unspoken secrets of the world and with many of the methods by which the overt world can be covertly used to his own advantage.

The main difference between the *Weltanschauung* and its concomitant modes of behavior in early childhood and adolescence appears to be not so much a contradiction as an addition of a further dimension of social life—that of the self-interest of the actor.[40]

At least in middle class American society, the young child, and, to a great extent, the pre-adolescent, appear to be defined more as objects than as acting subjects, while the change between childhood and adolescence appears to rest upon the legitimation of the child's possession of a self,[41] and its corresponding range of self-interests.

THE NATURE OF NON-ADULT TRUST AND RESPONSIBILITY

Since social life is not a random, fortuitous sequence of actions and events, the child, who eventually is to become a fully accountable person, must learn the general rules which account for and generate social order. As Hebb has written:

> The effects of moral education, and training in the rules of courtesy, and the compulsion to dress, talk, and act as others do, adds up to ensuring that the individual member of society will not act in a way that is a provocation to others—will not, that is, be a source of strong emotional disturbance, except in highly ritualized circumstances approved by society. . . . The problem of moral education, from this point of view, is not simply to produce a stable individual, but to produce an individual that will (1) be stable in the existing environment and (2) contribute to its protective uniformity.[42]

38 *Future Perfect,* op. cit., p. 140.

39 *Guide to Dating,* op. cit., p. 196.

40 The concern with self-interest would appear to be one important implication of what Hsu has called the American core value: self-reliance. "Under this ideal every individual is his own master, in control of his own destiny, and will advance and regress in society only according to his own effort." F. L. K. Hsu, *Psychological Anthropology,* Homewood, Ill.: Dorsey Press, 1961, p. 218.

41 I. H. Josselyn also notes a change in conception of self and world between childhood and adolescence, but the implication in her statement is that the change is a direct result of the psychological and physiological changes of puberty rather than any change of expectations applicable to childhood and adolescence. Cf. her "The Older Adolescent," in E. Ginzberg (ed.), *Values and Ideals of American Youth,* Columbia University Press, 1961, pp. 27–36.

42 D. O. Hebb, "The Mammal and His Environment," in T. Newcomb and E. Hartley (eds.), *Readings in Social Psychology,* 3rd edition, Holt, 1958, p. 341.

While the infant, the non-person, the organism without powers of self-control, may be expected only to be relatively unobtrusive within the system, by the time he is four or five years old, the social world gradually begins to grant the child *bona fide* membership, and from then on he is gradually held responsible for the general rules of proper social behavior.[43]

As the child begins to enter into the ongoing society as a participating member rather than as merely an object, these rules of social organization have the character of what he can be held accountable for: what kinds of social rights he is expected to respect and what kinds of social obligations he must meet. These are the responsibilities he has for the ongoing interactional system —the features that must be taken into account by each individual participant if successful social interaction is to ensue.

By the time the child enters adolescence, he is accountable for both knowing and respecting the ecological boundaries of other participants in the system, as well as his own. The characterization of "childish" behavior, as opposed to adult or mature behavior, revolves primarily around the notion that the child does not have a complete sense of other people's privacy, or of the limits of his own individual area.

Children are pictured as intruding and protruding at will.

Actually, by the time the young child is four or five years old, he is expected to learn at least that the boundaries of others' physical space exist and that they are something to be respected. He is admonished that,

> SNOOPERS walk right into rooms where other people are when the doors are closed. If they knocked first and asked if they might come in, people would not call them SNOOPERS.[44]
> This is a TOUCHER. Wherever he goes he touches. He never thinks whether he should or not—Maybe it's because he hasn't any head—he is all hands.[45]

So the young child is yet to learn that each person, himself included, has besides a delimited physical space, a personal space which is also to be respected.

By the time the child is 10 or 12 years old, he is expected to be fully responsible for the maintenance of both the physical and personal space of himself and others. To the specific injunctions against intruding into others' physical area and possessions[46] are added injunctions against intruding into others' activities and biographies as well.

From pre-adolescence on, the child is told that he must not "dip into" others' conversations,[47] look

[43] On the extent to which children and adolescents actively participate in the ongoing social order in America, see R. Barker and H. Wright, *Midwest and Its Children*, Evanston, Ill.: Row, Peterson and Co., 1955, pp. 99–122; and R. Barker and L. Barker, "Behavior Units for the Comparative Study of Culture," in B. Kaplan (eds.), *Studying Personality Cross-Culturally*, Evanston, Ill.: Row, Peterson and Co., 1961, pp. 457–478.

[44] *Manners Can Be Fun*, op. cit., p. 40.
[45] *Ibid.*
[46] Cf. O. R. Landers, *Modern Etiquette for Young People*, New York: Greenberg, 1936, pp. 84–85.
[47] *Manners to Grow On*, op. cit., p. 36; *This Way, Please*, op. cit., p. 83; *Modern Etiquette for Young People*, op. cit., p. 51.

over their shoulders,[48] nor stare directly at them.[49]

He is cautioned that, while he should show interest in his friends, he must not trespass into specified regions of their biographies.[50]

Be careful not to overdo the interest to the point of asking such questions as "How much money does you father make?" or "Are your parents divorced?" Be understanding and interested in any personal details which friends may tell you, but always let such information come from them.[51] Asking people questions is one way of getting them to talk about things that interest them. But unless you want to be avoided, don't ask prying questions that others may not want to answer—questions that are too curious or too personal.[52]

Although the pre-adolescent is warned only of the requirement of respecting the physical and personal space of others, the adolescent has the right to expect others to respect his own personal space: "If others pry, meet it with a pleasant, smiling gaze, and calmly change the subject." [53]

Besides being held accountable for not intruding into the territories of others, by pre-adolescence, the child is expected not to protrude from his own personal space. The pre-adolescent is told not to engage publicly in the "little repulsive habits of children" such as "picking your nose or ears, yawning, scratching your head or body, putting your fingers in your mouth, using a toothpick in public" [54] and the adolescent is presented with the rule: [55]

Do nothing in company that calls attention to the body or its functions. . . . If and when you must blow your nose, get out your handkerchief inconspicuously and do it as quietly as possible without making the act more noticeable by apologizing for it, unless you have had to stop in the midst of speaking. Follow the same practice when you are forced to sneeze or cough.

In addition, both pre-adolescent and adolescent are expected to contain their psychological space in public situations. The categorical rule is not to protrude one's moods or problems.[56]

Moods, both good and blue, are something we all have, but don't let your blue ones spoil your fun or your friendships. Never sulk when in a mood. It is better to stay to yourself if you think you might be unpleasant. . . . A blue mood soon passes, and

48 *This Way, Please,* op. cit., p. 20.
49 *Ibid.,* p. 83.
50 Cf. G. Simmels' statement on discretion in *The Sociology of Georg Simmel,* K. Wolfe (ed.), The Free Press, 1950, pp. 320–321: "Discretion consists by no means only in the respect for the secret of others, for his specific will to conceal this or that from us, but in staying away from the knowledge of all that the other does not expressly reveal to us. It does not refer to anything particular which we are not permitted to know, but to a quite natural general reserve in regard to the total personality."
51 *Manners to Grow On,* op. cit., pp. 11–12.
52 *This Way, Please,* op. cit., pp. 86–87.
53 *Modern Etiquette for Young People,* op. cit., p. 54.

54 *Future Perfect,* op. cit., pp. 75–76.
55 *This Way, Please,* op. cit., p. 20.
56 This may be contrasted with D. Matza's characterization of the Bohemia of youth, where the expression of moods forms an integral part of the culture. Cf. "Subterranean Traditions of Youth," *The Annals,* v. 338 (1961), pp. 101–118, especially p. 113.

then you can emerge your cheerful self again, ready to enjoy your friends and have them enjoy you.[57]

In the same way that you refrain from using nail file and toothpick in the presence of others, be able to keep your personal difficulties, troubles, and complaints to yourself as far as you possibly can.[58]

Learning the territorial rights of others and his own personal boundaries, the child is also expected gradually to learn the rules which govern social relationships. He is expected to learn the rules of proper social involvement.

Just as the very young child is only minimally introduced to the rules of territoriality, so is he minimally introduced to the rules of social relationships. In fact, the young child's encounters with the ongoing social system are defined merely in terms of the acknowledgement of the presence of others. He is expected to say, "How do you do" when being introduced to others and "Good day" if he already has been introduced.[59] Beyond this he has no other social obligations.

By pre-adolescence the child's responsibility for interaction is greatly increased. While the young child is expected to know only the proper response to an introduction, the pre-adolescent is expected to know the proper procedures for effecting introductions. The pre-adolescent is held accountable for knowing the general form of social presentations and the differential hierarchy they are to embody, as well as knowing

under what circumstances introductions must occur. The pre-adolescent is told,

Never let a person wait around while you chat on and on to someone he doesn't know. Don't introduce people who (sic) you meet very briefly, such as the person who stops just long enough to say a cheery hello. . . .[60]

For the pre-adolescent there are no restrictions on who may be introduced to whom, but the adolescent is warned that, since an introduction has implications for future involvements between the parties, care must be exercised not to bring together people who would be incompatible. The adolescent is cautioned,

You have a certain responsibility when you introduce people. Do not go out of your way to introduce two who are not likely to care about knowing each other.[61]

In a similar manner, while the pre-adolescent's inclusion into interaction must be mediated by a third person, by adolescence one may properly include oneself, providing that (1) the setting is one where the presence of the participants imply a mutual knowledge of some third person or institution, such as wedding receptions, houseparties, or school playgrounds; and (2) one is certain that the other will be receptive to the proffered sociability.[62]

The general topic of social involvement and obligation, which is absent from the expectations for the behavior of the young child, is only

[57] *Manners to Grow On*, op. cit., p. 14.
[58] *Modern Etiquette for Young People*, op. cit., p. 63.
[59] *Manners Can Be Fun*, op. cit., pp. 8–12.

[60] *Manners to Grow On*, op. cit., p. 9.
[61] *This Way, Please*, op. cit., p. 67.
[62] Cf. *ibid.*, pp. 68, 234; *Miss Behavior*, op. cit., p. 148.

touched upon in pre-adolescence.[63] The pre-adolescent is merely cautioned not to become overinvolved with others to the point of mutual utilization of private property [64] and to be careful about becoming committed to a negative position by stating that position in writing.[65]

In adolescence, social involvement and commitment become a major theme.[66] Not only is the adolescent told that the loaning and borrowing of physical objects leads to social obligations which may be undesirable, but that gifts and favors as well may result in such undesirable obligations.[67]

At the same time, the adolescent is admonished not to invest too much of himself in any particular relationship, and, primarily, in relationships with the other sex. The girl is advised not to show her eagerness when asked for a date,[68] and that:

It is better for a girl to make the mistake of seeming to have too little rather than too much affection, unless she is sure that the boy has at least as much as she.[69]

In contrast to the problem of becoming overly involved in a relationship is the problem of handling someone else's overinvolvement. The adolescent is cautioned that one cannot simply tell the other that he or she is investing too much in a relationship, but instead must engage in a series of tactical social maneuvers which signify to the other that he is exhibiting an improper degree of involvement, yet provide the other the opportunity to save face in the situation.

The adolescent girl is told that she must take particular care in turning down a date so that she does not hurt the boy's feelings,[70] and the boy is informed that,[71]

If she is already booked, don't take it as an insult, try again in a few days. If you don't succeed in landing some sort of a date after trying three or four times, then I suggest finding a new phone number. Chances are she's only brushing you off the nice way.

Boys are expected to offer the same face-saving opportunity to the girls. The boy is expected to "naturally have sense and consideration to break off a serious romance with a girl, if need be, in a manner which will be the least damaging to her." [72] He is expected to "avoid giving a girl the feeling of being 'dropped.' " [73]

Thus the granting of a self to the

63 Cf. E. Goffman, *Encounters*, The Bobbs-Merrill Co., 1961, pp. 39–40: "It is not only possible for participants to become involved in the encounter in progress, but it is also defined as obligatory that they sustain this involvement in given measure; too much is one kind of delict; too little, another." The exuberance of youth would appear to make only the former problematic.

64 *Manners to Grow On*, op. cit., pp. 14, 35.

65 *Ibid.*, p. 26; *Future Perfect*, op. cit., p. 180.

66 Simmel, in his essay "The Metropolis and Mental Life," treats the problem of social involvement and commitment under the concept of "reserve." Cf. Simmel, op. cit., pp. 414–418.

67 *Guide to Dating*, op. cit., pp. 72–73.

68 *Miss Behavior*, op. cit., p. 169.

69 *Modern Etiquette for Young People*, op. cit., p. 94.

70 *Guide to Dating*, op. cit., p. 10.

71 *Your Manners Are Showing*, op. cit., p. 92.

72 *Guide to Dating*, op. cit., p. 172.

73 *This Way, Please*, op. cit., p. 104.

child in adolescence certifies him as someone who can be expected to be a trustworthy and responsible member of the everyday social world.[74] All those who have been given the right to lay claim to a self are obligated both to keep that self in a proper state of social repair and to show the proper social care for the selves of other participants in the system.[75] The duty of social responsibility becomes, in effect, a concomitant duty to one's self as well as to others.

CONCLUSION

The focus of the present paper has been the content of childhood socialization in contemporary middle-class American society. Addressing the expectations about behavior contained in children's etiquette books for various ages, I have attempted to trace out the changing conception of the nature of the child as he moves through childhood, pre-adolescence, and adolescence. The specific concern has been the way the child and the world he is presented is socially

[74] For a general discussion of the problem of social responsibility and the identifiability of group members, see Simmel, op. cit., p. 374.

[75] Cf. E. Goffman, "On Face Work," *Psychiatry*, 18 (1955), pp. 213–231: "The combination of the rule of self-respect and the rule of considerateness is that the person tends to conduct himself during an encounter so as to maintain both his own face and the face of other participants." (See p. 215.)

For a further discussion of this general problem, see also Edward Gross and Gregory P. Stone, "Embarrassment and the Analysis of Role Requirements," *American Journal of Sociology,* 70 (1964), pp. 1–15.

defined for each age group, and the kinds of trust and responsibility demanded of each age group.

The basis of the present paper has been the assumption that the problem of childhood socialization is essentially different from the problem of adult socialization in that, in the process of childhood socialization, some form of a basic, efficacious self must be established in the new recruit, whereas in adult socialization, the concern is the development of some particular variety of that basic form.

To speak of the participants of social life as having a "formal self" as a prerequisite to having a particular variety of social self is essentially to speak of the social certification that members' general capacity for trust and responsibility can henceforth be taken for granted. At least as it is evidenced in middle-class American society, once a child has come to understand that both good and evil are normal features of the everyday world; that appearances may be deceiving; that merit is not always automatically rewarded; and that the arrangements of the social system merely set the conditions for individual action, rather than specifying what individual action must necessarily be, he has in effect been introduced into the world as it is known to the adult members. Concomitant with his entrance into the adult world of everyday life are the obligations for maintaining the sanctioned features of that world—its spacial allocations, its social relationships, and the variety of social selves that can be created and sustained therein.

psychosexual development

WILLIAM SIMON
JOHN H. GAGNON

Erik Erikson has observed that, prior to Sigmund Freud, "sexologists" tended to believe that sexual capacities appeared suddenly with the onset of adolescence. Sexuality followed those external evidences of physiological change that occurred concurrent with or just after puberty. Psychoanalysis changed all that. In Freud's view, libido—the generation of psychosexual energies—should be viewed as a fundamental element of human experience at least beginning with birth, and possibly before that. Libido, therefore, is essential, a biological constant to be coped with at all levels of individual, social, and cultural development. The truth of this received wisdom, that is, that sexual development is a continuous contest between biological drive and cultural restraint should be seriously questioned. Obviously sexuality has roots in biological processes, but so do many other capacities including many that involve physical and mental competence and vigor. There is, however, abundant evidence that the final states which these capacities attain escape the rigid impress of biology. This independence of biological constraint is rarely claimed for the area of sexuality, but we would like to argue that the sexual is precisely that realm where the sociocultural forms most completely dominate biological influences.

It is difficult to get data that might shed much light on the earliest aspects of these questions: Adults are hardly equipped with total recall and the pre-verbal or primitively verbal child does not have ability to report accurately on his own internal state. But it seems obvious—and it is a basic assumption of this paper—that with the beginnings of adolescence many new factors come into play, and to emphasize a straight-line developmental continuity with infant and childhood experiences may be seriously misleading. In particular, it is dangerous to assume that because some childhood behavior appears sexual to adults, it must be sexual. An infant, or a child engaged in genital play (even if orgasm is observed) can in no sense be seen as experiencing the complex set of feelings that accompanies adult or even adolescent masturbation.

Therefore, the authors reject the unproven assumption that "powerful" psychosexual drives are fixed biological attributes. More importantly, we reject the even more dubious assumption that sexual capacities or experiences tend to translate immediately into a kind of universal "knowing" or innate wisdom—that sexuality has a magical ability, possessed by no other capacity, that al-

From William Simon and John H. Gagnon, "On Psychosexual Development," in David A. Goslin (Ed.), HANDBOOK OF SOCIALIZATION THEORY AND RESEARCH, © *1969 by Rand McNally and Company, Chicago, pp. 733–752. Reprinted by permission.*

lows biological drives to be expressed directly in psychosocial and social behaviors.

The prevailing image of sexuality —particularly that of the Freudian tradition—is that of an intense, high-pressure drive that forces a person to seek physical sexual gratification, a drive that expresses itself indirectly if it cannot be expressed directly. The available data suggest to us a different picture—one that shows either lower levels of intensity, or, at least, greater variability. We find that there are many social situations or life-roles in which reduced sex activity or even deliberate celibacy is undertaken with little evidence that the libido has shifted in compensation to some other sphere.

A part of the legacy of Freud is that we have all become remarkably adept at discovering "sexual" elements in nonsexual behavior and symbolism. What we suggest instead (following Kenneth Burke's three-decade-old insight) is the reverse— that sexual behavior can often express and serve nonsexual motives.

NO PLAY WITHOUT A SCRIPT

We see sexual behavior therefore as *scripted* behavior, not the masked expression of a primordial drive. The individual can learn sexual behavior as he or she learns other behavior—through scripts that in this case give the self, other persons, and situations erotic abilities or content. Desire, privacy, opportunity, and propinquity with an attractive member of the opposite sex are not, in themselves, enough; in ordinary circumstances, nothing sexual will occur unless one or both actors organize these elements into an appropriate script. The very con-

cern with foreplay in sex suggests this. From one point of view, foreplay may be defined as merely progressive physical excitement generated by touching naturally erogenous zones. The authors have referred to this conception elsewhere as the "rubbing of two sticks together to make a fire" model. It would seem to be more valuable to see this activity as symbolically invested behavior through which the body is eroticized and through which mute, inarticulate motions and gestures are translated into a sociosexual drama.

A belief in the sociocultural dominance of sexual behavior finds support in cross-cultural research as well as in data restricted to the United States. Psychosexual development is universal—but it takes many forms and tempos. People in different cultures construct their scripts differently; and in our own society, different segments of the population act out different psychosexual dramas —something much less likely to occur if they were all reacting more or less blindly to the same superordinate urge. The most marked differences occur, of course, between male and female patterns of sexual behavior. Obviously, some of this is due to biological differences, including differences in hormonal functions at different ages. But the significance of social scripts predominate; the recent work of Masters and Johnson, for example, clearly points to far greater orgasmic capacities on the part of females than our culture would lead us to suspect. And within each sex—especially among men—different social and economic groups have different patterns.

Let us examine some of these variations, and see if we can decipher the scripts.

CHILDHOOD

Whether one agrees with Freud or not, it is obvious that we do not become sexual all at once. There is continuity with the past. Even infant experiences can strongly influence later sexual development.

But continuity is not causality. Childhood experiences (even those that appear sexual) will in all likelihood be influential not because they are intrinsically sexual, but because they can affect a number of developmental trends, *including* the sexual. What situations in infancy—or even early childhood—can be called psychosexual in any sense other than that of creating potentials?

The key term, therefore, must remain potentiation. In infancy, we can locate some of the experiences (or sensations) that will bring about a sense of the body and its capacities for pleasure and discomfort and those that will influence the child's ability to relate to others. It is possible, of course, that through these primitive experiences, ranges are being established—but they are very broad and overlapping. Moreover, if these are profound experiences to the child—and they may well be that —they are not expressions of biological necessity, but of the earliest forms of social learning.

In childhood, after infancy there is what appears to be some real sex play. About half of all adults report that they did engage in some form of sex play as children; and the total who actually did may be half again as many. But, however the adult interprets it later, what did it mean to the child at the time? One suspects that, as in much of childhood role-playing, their sense of the adult meanings attributed to the behavior is fragmentary and ill-formed. Many of the adults recall that, at the time, they were concerned with being found out. But here, too, were they concerned because of the real content of sex play, or because of the mystery and the lure of the forbidden that so often enchant the child? The child may be assimilating outside information about sex for which, at the time, he has no real internal correlate or understanding.

A small number of persons do have sociosexual activity during preadolescence—most of it initiated by adults. But for the majority of these, little apparently follows from it. Without appropriate sexual scripts, the experience remains unassimilated —at least in adult terms. For some, it is clear, a severe reaction may follow from falling "victim" to the sexuality of an adult—but, again, does this reaction come from the sexual act itself or from the social response, the strong reactions of others? (There is some evidence that early sexual activity of this sort is associated with deviant adjustments in later life. But this, too, may not be the result of sexual experiences in themselves so much as the consequence of having fallen out of the social main stream and, therefore, of running greater risks of isolation and alienation.)

In short, relatively few become truly active sexually before adolescence. And when they do (for girls more often than boys), it is seldom immediately related to sexual feelings or gratifications but is a use of sex for nonsexual goals and purposes. The "seductive" Lolita is rare; but she is significant: She illustrates a more general pattern of psychosexual development—a commitment to the social relationships linked to sex before one can really grasp the social meaning of the physical relationships.

Of great importance are the values (or feelings, or images) that children pick up as being related to sex. Although we talk a lot about sexuality, as though trying to exorcise the demon of shame, learning about sex in our society is in large part learning about guilt; and learning how to manage sexuality commonly involves learning how to manage guilt. An important source of guilt in children comes from the imputation to them by adults of sexual appetites or abilities that they may not have but that they learn, however imperfectly, to pretend they have. The gestural concomitants of sexual modesty are learned early. For instance, when do girls learn to sit or pick up objects with their knees together? When do they learn that the bust must be covered? However, since this behavior is learned unlinked to later adult sexual performances, what children must make of all this is very mysterious.

The learning of sex roles, or sex identities, involves many things that are remote from actual sexual experience, or that become involved with sexuality only after puberty. Masculinity or femininity, their meaning and postures, are rehearsed before adolescence in many nonsexual ways.

A number of scholars have pointed, for instance, to the importance of aggressive, deference, dependency, and dominance behavior in childhood. Jerome Kagan and Howard Moss have found that aggressive behavior in males and dependency in females are relatively stable aspects of development. But what is social role, and what is bi-

ology? They found that when aggressive behavior occurred among girls, it tended to appear most often among those from well-educated families that were more tolerant of deviation. Curiously, they also reported that "it was impossible to predict the character of adult sexuality in women from their preadolescent and early adolescent behavior," and that "erotic activity is more anxiety-arousing for females than for males," because "the traditional ego ideal for women dictates inhibition of sexual impulses."

The belief in the importance of early sex-role learning for boys can be viewed in two ways. First, it may directly indicate an early sexual capacity in male children. Or, second, early masculine identification may merely be an appropriate framework within which the sexual impulse (salient with puberty) and the socially available sexual scripts (or accepted patterns of sexual behavior) can most conveniently find expression. Our bias, of course, is toward the second.

But, as Kagan and Moss also noted, the sex role learned by the child does not reliably predict how he will act sexually as an adult. This finding also can be interpreted in the same two alternative ways. Where sexuality is viewed as a biological constant which struggles to express itself, the female sex role learning can be interpreted as the successful repression of sexual impulses. The other interpretation suggests that the difference lies not in learning how to handle a preexistent sexuality, but in learning how to *be* sexual. Differences between men and women, therefore, will have consequences both for *what* is done sexually, as well as *when*.

Once again, we prefer the latter interpretation, and some recent work that we have done with lesbians supports it. We observed that many of the major elements of their sex lives —the start of actual genital sexual behavior, the onset and frequency of masturbation, the time of entry in sociosexual patterns, the number of partners, and the reports of feelings of sexual deprivation—were for these homosexual women almost identical with those of ordinary women. Since sexuality would seem to be more important for lesbians—after all, they sacrifice much in order to follow their own sexual pathways—this is surprising. We concluded that the primary factor was something both categories of women share—the sex-role learning that occurs before sexuality itself becomes significant.

Social class also appears significant, more for boys than girls. Sex-role learning may vary by class; lower-class boys are supposed to be more aggressive and put much greater emphasis on early heterosexuality. The middle and upper classes tend to tolerate more deviance from traditional attitudes regarding appropriate male sex-role performances.

Given all these circumstances, it seems rather naive to think of sexuality as a constant pressure, with a peculiar necessity all its own. For us, the crucial period of childhood has significance not because of sexual occurrences, but because of nonsexual developments that will provide the names and judgments for later encounters with sexuality.

ADOLESCENCE

The actual beginnings and endings of adolescence are vague. Generally, the beginning marks the first time society, as such, acknowledges that the individual has sexual capacity. Training in the postures and rhetoric of the sexual experience is now accelerated. Most important, the adolescent begins to regard those about him (particularly his peers, but also adults) as sexual actors and finds confirmation from others for this view.

For some, as noted, adolescent sexual experience begins before they are considered adolescents. Kinsey reports that a tenth of his female sample and a fifth of his male sample had experienced orgasm through masturbation by age 12. But still, for the vast majority, despite some casual play and exploration that post-Freudians might view as masked sexuality, sexual experience begins with adolescence. Even those who have had prior experience find that it acquires new meanings with adolescence. They now relate such meanings to both larger spheres of social life and greater senses of self. For example, it is not uncommon during the transition between childhood and adolescence for boys and, more rarely girls to report arousal and orgasm while doing things not manifestly sexual—climbing trees, sliding down bannisters, or other activities that involve genital contact— without defining them as sexual. Often they do not even take it seriously enough to try to explore or repeat what was, in all likelihood, a pleasurable experience.

Adolescent sexual development, therefore, really represents the beginning of adult sexuality. It marks a definite break with what went on before. Not only will future experiences occur in new and more complex contexts, but they will be conceived of as explicitly sexual and thereby begin to complicate social relationships. The need to manage sexuality will rise not only from physical needs and desires, but also from the new implications of personal relationships. Playing, or associating, with members of the opposite sex now acquires different meanings.

At adolescence, changes in the developments of boys and girls diverge and must be considered separately. The one thing both share at this point is a reinforcement of their new status by a dramatic biological event —for girls, menstruation, and for boys, the discovery of the ability to ejaculate. But here they part. For boys, the beginning of a commitment to sexuality is primarily genital; within two years of puberty all but a relatively few have had the experience of orgasm, almost universally brought about by masturbation. The corresponding organizing event for girls is not genitally sexual but social: they have arrived at an age where they will learn role performances linked with proximity to marriage. In contrast to boys, only two-thirds of girls will report ever having masturbated (and, characteristically, the frequency is much less). For women, it is not until the late twenties that the incidence of orgasm from any source reaches that of boys at age 16. In fact, significantly, about half of the females who masturbate do so only after having experienced orgasm in some situation involving others. This contrast points to a basic distinction between the developmental processes for males and females: males move from privatized personal sexuality to sociosexuality; females do the reverse and at a later stage in the life cycle.

THE TURNED-ON BOYS

We have worked hard to demonstrate the dominance of social, psychological, and cultural influences over the biological; now, dealing with adolescent boys, we must briefly reverse course. There is much evidence that the early male sexual impulses— again, initially through masturbation—are linked to physiological changes, to high hormonal inputs during puberty. This produces an organism that, to put it simply, is more easily turned on. Male adolescents report frequent erections, often without apparent stimulation of any kind. Even so, though there is greater biological sensitization and hence masturbation is more likely, the meaning, organization, and continuance of this activity still tends to be subordinate to social and psychological factors.

Masturbation provokes guilt and anxiety among most adolescent boys. This is not likely to change in spite of more "enlightened" rhetoric and discourse on the subject (generally, we have shifted from stark warnings of mental, moral, and physical damage to vague counsels against nonsocial or "inappropriate" behavior). However, it may be that this very guilt and anxiety gives the sexual experience an intensity of feeling that is often attributed to sex itself.

Such guilt and anxiety do not follow simply from social disapproval. Rather, they seem to come from several sources, including the difficulty the boy has in presenting himself as a sexual being to his immediate family, particularly his parents. Another source is the fantasies or plans associated with masturbation—fantasies about doing sexual "things" to others or having others do sexual "things" to oneself; or having to learn and rehearse available but proscribed sexual scripts or patterns of behavior. And, of course, some guilt and anxiety center around the general disapproval of masturbation. After the early period of adolescence, in fact, most youths will not admit to their peers that they did or do it.

Nevertheless, masturbation is for most adolescent boys the major sexual activity, and they engage in it fairly frequently. It is an extremely positive and gratifying experience to them. Such an introduction to sexuality can lead to a capacity for detached sex activity—activity whose only sustaining motive is sexual. This may be the hallmark of male sexuality in our society.

Of the three sources of guilt and anxiety mentioned, the first—how to manage both sexuality and an attachment to family members—probably cuts across class lines. But the others should show remarkable class differences. The second one, how to manage a fairly elaborate and exotic fantasy life during masturbation, should be confined most typically to the higher classes, who are more experienced and adept at dealing with symbols. (It is possible, in fact, that this behavior, which girls rarely engage in, plays a role in the processes by which middle-class boys catch up with girls in measures of achievement and creativity and, by the end of adolescence, move out in front. However, this is only a hypothesis.)

The ability to fantasize during masturbation implies certain broad consequences. One is a tendency to see large parts of the environment in an erotic light, as well as the ability to respond, sexually and perhaps poetically, to many visual and auditory stimuli. We might also expect both a capacity and need for fairly elaborate forms of sexual activity. Further, since masturbatory fantasies generally deal with relationships and acts leading to coitus, they should also reinforce a developing capacity for heterosociality.

The third source of guilt and anxiety—the alleged "unmanliness" of masturbation—should more directly concern the lower-class male adolescent. ("Manliness" has always been an important value for lower-class males.) In these groups, social life is more often segregated by sex, and there are, generally, fewer rewarding social experiences from other sources. The adolescent therefore moves into heterosexual—if not heterosocial—relationships sooner than his middle-class counterparts. Sexual segregation makes it easier for him than for the middle-class boy to learn that he does not have to love everything he desires, and therefore to come more naturally to casual, if not exploitative, relationships. The second condition—fewer social rewards that his fellows would respect—should lead to an exaggerated concern for proving masculinity by direct displays of physical prowess, aggression, and visible sexual success. And these three, of course, may be mutually reinforcing.

In a sense, the lower-class male is the first to reach "sexual maturity" as defined by the Freudians. That is, he is generally the first to become aggressively heterosexual and exclusively genital. This characteristic, in fact, is a distinguishing difference between lower-class males and those above them socially.

But one consequence is that although their sex lives are almost exclusively heterosexual, they remain homosocial. They have intercourse with females, but the standards and the audience they refer to are those of their male fellows. Middle-class boys shift predominantely to coitus at a significantly later time. They, too, need and tend to have homosocial elements in their sexual lives. But their fantasies, their ability to symbolize, and their social training in a world in which distinctions between masculinity and feminity are less sharply drawn, allow them to withdraw more easily from an all male world. This difference between social classes obviously has important consequences for stable adult relationships.

One thing common in male experience during adolescence is that while it provides much opportunity for sexual commitment, in one form or another, there is little training in how to handle emotional relations with girls. The imagery and rhetoric of romantic love is all around us: we are immersed in it. But whereas much is undoubtedly absorbed by the adolescent, he is not likely to tie it closely to his sexuality. In fact, such a connection might be inhibiting, as indicated by the survival of the "bad-girl-who-does" and "good-girl-who-doesn't" distinction. This is important to keep in mind as we turn to the female side of the story.

WITH THE GIRLS

In contrast to males, female sexual development during adolescence is so similar in all classes that it is easy to suspect that it is solely determined by biology. But, while girls do not have the same level of hormonal sensitization to sexuality at puberty as adolescent boys, there is little evidence of a biological or social inhibitor either. The "equipment" for sexual pleasure is clearly present by puberty, but tends not to be used by many females of any class. Masturbation rates are fairly low, and among those who do masturbate, fairly infrequent. Arousal from "sexual" materials or situations happens seldom, and exceedingly few girls report feeling sexually deprived during adolescence.

Basically, girls in our society are not encouraged to be sexual—and may be strongly discouraged from being so. Most of us accept the fact that while "bad boy" can mean many things, "bad girl" almost exclusively implies sexual delinquency. It is both difficult and dangerous for an adolescent girl to become too active sexually. As Joseph Rheingold puts it, where men need only fear sexual failure, women must fear both success and failure.

Does this long period of relative sexual inactivity among girls come from repression of an elemental drive, or merely from a failure to learn how to be sexual? The answers have important implications for their later sexual development. If it is repression, the path to a fuller sexuality must pass through processes of loss of inhibitions, during which the girl unlearns, in varying degrees, attitudes and values that block the expression of natural internal feelings. It also implies that the quest for ways to express directly sexual behavior and feelings that had been expressed nonsexually is secondary and of considerably less significance.

On the other hand, the "learning" answer suggests that women create or invent a capacity for sexual behavior, learning how and when to be aroused and how and when to respond. This approach implies greater flexibilty; unlike the repression view, it makes sexuality both more and less than a basic force that may break loose at any time in strange or costly ways. The learning approach also lessens the power of sexuality altogether, all at once, particular kinds of sex activities need no longer be defined as either "healthy" or "sick." Lastly, subjectively, this approach appeals to the authors because it describes female sexuality in terms that seem less like a mere projection of male sexuality.

If sexual activity by adolescent girls assumes less specific forms than with boys, that does not mean that sexual learning and training do not occur. Curiously, though girls are, as a group, far less active sexually than boys, they receive far more training in self-consciously viewing themselves—and in viewing boys— as desirable mates. This is particularly true in recent years. Females begin early in adolescence to define attractiveness, at least partially, in sexual terms. We suspect that the use of sexual attractiveness for nonsexual purposes that marked our preadolescent "seductress" now begins to characterize many girls. Talcott Parsons' description of how the wife "uses" sex to bind the husband to the family, although harsh, may be quite accurate. More generally, in keeping with the childbearing and child-raising function of women, the development of a sexual role seems to involve a need to include in that role more than pleasure.

To round out the picture of the difference between the sexes, girls appear to be well-trained precisely in that area in which boys are poorly trained—that is, a belief in and a capacity for intense, emotionally-charged relationships and the language of romantic love. When girls during this period describe having been aroused sexually, they more often report it as a response to romantic, rather than erotic, words and actions.

In later adolescence, as dates, parties, and other sociosexual activities increase, boys—committed to sexuality and relatively untrained in the language and actions of romantic love—interact with girls, committed to romantic love and relatively untrained in sexuality. Dating and courtship may well be considered processes in which each sex trains the other in what each wants and expects. What data is available suggests that this exchange system does not always work very smoothly. Thus, ironically, it is not uncommon to find that the boy becomes emotionally involved with his partner and therefore lets up on trying to seduce her, at the same time that the girl comes to feel that the boy's affection is genuine and therefore that sexual intimacy is more permissible.

In our recent study of college students, we found that boys typically had intercourse with their first coital partners one to three times, while with girls it was ten or more. Clearly, for the majority of females first intercourse becomes possible only in stable relationships or in those with strong bonds.

"WOMAN, WHAT DOES SHE WANT?"

The male experience does conform to the general Freudian expectation that there is a developmental movement from a predominantly genital sexual commitment to a loving relationship with another person. But this movement is, in effect, reversed for females, with love or affection often a necessary precondition for intercourse. No wonder, therefore, that Freud had great difficulty understanding female sexuality—recall the concluding line in his great essay on women: "Woman, what does she want?" This "error"—the assumption that female sexuality is similar to or a mirror image of that of the male—may come from the fact that so many of those who constructed the theory were men. With Freud, in addition, we must remember the very concept of sexuality essential to most of nineteenth century Europe —it was an elemental beast that had to be curbed.

It has been noted that there are very few class differences in sexuality among females, far fewer than among males. One difference, however, is very relevant to this discussion—the age of first intercourse. This varies inversely with social class —that is, the higher the class, the later the age of first intercourse—a relationship that is also true of first marriage. The correlation between these two ages suggest the necessary social and emotional linkage between courtship and the entrance into sexual activity on the part of women. A second difference, perhaps only indirectly related to social class, has to do with educational achievement: here, a sharp border line seems to separate from all other women those who have or have had graduate or professional work. If sexual success may be measured by the percentage of sex acts that culminate in orgasm, graduate and professional women are the most sexually successful women in the nation.

Why? One possible interpretation derives from the work of Abraham Maslow: Women who get so far in higher education are more likely to be more aggressive, perhaps to have strong needs to dominate; both these characteristics are associated with heightened sexuality. Another, more general interpretation would be that in a society in which girls are expected primarily to become wives and mothers, going on to graduate school represents a kind of deviancy—a failure of, or alienation from, normal female social adjustment. In effect, then, it would be this flawed socialization—not biology—that produced both commitment toward advanced training and toward heightened sexuality.

For both males and females, increasingly greater involvement in the social aspects of sexuality—"socializing" with the opposite sex—may be one factor that marks the end of adolescence. We know little about this transition, especially among noncollege boys and girls, but our present feeling is that sexuality plays an important role in it. First, sociosexuality is important in family formation and also in learning the roles and obligations involved in being an adult. Second, and more fundamental, late adolescence is when a youth is seeking, and experimenting toward finding, his identity—who and what he is and will be; and sociosexual activity is the one aspect of this exploration that we associate particularly with late adolescence.

Young people are particularly vulnerable at this time. This may be partly due to the fact that society has difficulty protecting the adolescent from the consequences of sexual behavior that it pretends he is not engaged in. But, more importantly, it may be because, at all ages, we all have great problems in discussing our sexual feelings and experiences in personal terms. These, in turn, make it extremely difficult to get support from others for an adolescent's experiments toward trying to invent his sexual self. We suspect that success or failure in the discovery or management of sexual identity may have consequences in personal development far beyond merely the sexual sphere—perhaps in confidence and feelings of self-worth, belonging, competence, guilt, force of personality, and so on.

ADULTHOOD

In our society, all but a few ultimately marry. Handling sexual commitments inside marriage makes up the larger part of adult experience. Again, we have too little data for firm findings. The data we do have come largely from studies of broken and troubled marriages, and we do not know to what extent sexual problems in such marriages exceed those of intact marriages. It is possible that, because we have assumed that sex is important in most people's lives, we have exaggerated its importance in holding marriages together. Also, it is quite possible that, once people are married, sexuality declines relatively, becoming less important than other gratifications (such as domesticity or

parenthood); or it may be that these other gratifications can minimize the effect of sexual dissatisfaction. Further, it may be possible that individuals learn to get sexual gratification, or an equivalent, from activities that are nonsexual, or only partially sexual.

The sexual desires and commitments of males are the main determinants of the rate of sexual activity in our society. Men are most interested in intercourse in the early years of marriage—woman's interest peaks much later; nonetheless, coital rates decline steadily throughout marriage. This decline derives from many things, only one of which is decline in biological capacity. With many men, it is more difficult to relate sexually to a wife who is pregnant or a mother. Lower-class adult men receive less support and plaudits from their male friends for married sexual performance than they did as single adolescents; and we might also add the lower-class disadvantage of less training in the use of auxiliary or symbolic sexually stimulating materials. For middle-class men, the decline is not as steep, owing perhaps to their greater ability to find stimulation from auxiliary sources, such as literature, movies, music, and romantic or erotic conversation. It should be further noted that for about 30 percent of college-educated men, masturbation continues regularly during marriage, even when the wife is available. An additional (if unknown) proportion do not physically masturbate, but derive additional excitement from the fantasies that accompany intercourse.

But even middle-class sexual activity declines more rapidly than bodily changes can account for. Perhaps the ways males learn to be sexual in our society make it very difficult to keep it up at a high level with the same woman for a long time. However, this may not be vital in maintaining the family, or even in the man's personal sense of well-being, because, as previously suggested, sexual dissatisfaction may become less important as other satisfactions increase. Therefore, it need seldom result in crisis.

About half of all married men and a quarter of all married women will have intercourse outside of marriage at one time or another. For women, infidelity seems to have been on the increase since the turn of the century—at the same time that their rates of orgasm have been increasing. It is possible that the very nature of female sexuality is changing. Work being done now may give us new light on this. For men, there are strong social-class differences—the lower class accounts for most extramarital activity, especially during the early years of marriage. We have observed that it is difficult for a lower-class man to acquire the appreciation of his fellows for married intercourse; extramarital sex, of course, is another matter.

In general, we feel that far from sexual needs affecting other adult concerns, the reverse may be true: adult sexual activity may become that aspect of a person's life most often used to act out other needs.

There are some data that suggest this. Men who have trouble handling authority relationships at work more often have dreams about homosexuality; some others, under heavy stress on the job, have been shown to have more frequent episodic homosexual experiences. Such phenomena as the rise of sadomasochistic practices and experiments in group sex may also be tied to nonsexual tensions, the use of sex for nonsexual purposes.

It is only fairly recently in the history of man that he has been able to begin to understand that his own time and place do not embody some eternal principle or necessity, but are only dots on a continuum. It is difficult for many to believe that man can change, and is changing, in important ways. This conservative view is evident even in contemporary behavioral science; and a conception of man as having relatively constant sexual needs has become part of it. In an ever-changing world, it is perhaps comforting to think that man's sexuality does not change very much, and therefore is relatively easily explained. We cannot accept this. Instead, we have attempted to offer a description of sexual development as a variable social invention—an invention that in itself explains little, and requires much continuing explanation.

training the woman to know her place: the power of a nonconscious ideology

SANDRA L. BEM
DARYL J. BEM *

In the beginning God created the heaven and the earth. . . . And God said, Let us make man in our image, after our likeness; and let them have dominion over the fish of the sea, and over the fowl of the air, and over the cattle, and over all the earth. . . . And the rib, which the Lord God had taken from man, made he a woman and brought her unto the man. . . . And the Lord God said unto the woman, What is this that thou has done? And the woman said, The serpent beguiled me, and I did eat. . . . Unto the woman He said, I will greatly multiply thy sorrow and thy conception; in sorrow thou shalt bring forth children; and thy desire shall be to thy husband, and he shall rule over thee. (Gen. 1, 2, 3)

And lest anyone fail to grasp the moral of this story, Saint Paul provides further clarification:

For a man . . . is the image and glory of God; but the woman is the

* Order of authorship determined by the flip of a coin.

Sandra L. Bem and Daryl J. Bem, "Training the Woman to Know Her Place: The Power of a Nonconscious Ideology," from Daryl J. Bem, BELIEFS, ATTITUDES, AND HUMAN AFFAIRS, copyright © 1970, Wadsworth Publishing Company, Inc. Reprinted by permission of the publisher, Brooks/ Cole Publishing Company, Monterey, California, and the authors.

glory of the man. For the man is not of the woman, but the woman of the man. Neither was the man created for the woman, but the woman for the man. (1 Cor. 11)
Let the woman learn in silence with all subjection. But I suffer not a woman to teach, nor to usurp authority over the man, but to be in silence. For Adam was first formed, then Eve. And Adam was not deceived, but the woman, being deceived was in the transgression. Notwithstanding, she shall be saved in childbearing, if they continue in faith and charity and holiness with sobriety. (1 Tim. 2)

And lest it be thought that only Christians have this rich heritage of ideology about women, consider the morning prayer of the Orthodox Jew:

Blessed art Thou, oh Lord our God, King of the Universe, that I was not born a gentile.
Blessed art Thou, oh Lord our God, King of the Universe, that I was not born a slave.
Blessed art Thou, oh Lord our God, King of the Universe, that I was not born a woman.

Or the Koran, the sacred text of Islam:

Men are superior to women on account of the qualities in which God has given them pre-eminence.

Because they think they sense a decline in feminine "faith, charity, and holiness with sobriety," many people today jump to the conclusion that the ideology expressed in these passages is a relic of the past. Not so. It has simply been obscured by an equalitarian veneer, and the ideology has now become nonconscious. That is, we remain unaware of it because alternative beliefs and attitudes about women go unimagined. We are like the fish who is unaware that his environment is wet. After all, what else could it be? Such is the nature of all nonconscious ideologies. Such is the nature of America's ideology about women. For even those Americans who agree that a black skin should not uniquely qualify its owner for janitorial or domestic service continue to act as if the possession of a uterus uniquely qualifies *its* owner for precisely that.

Consider, for example, the 1968 student rebellion at Columbia University. Students from the radical left took over some administration buildings in the name of equalitarian principles which they accused the university of flouting. Here were the most militant spokesmen one could hope to find in the cause of equalitarian ideals. But no sooner had they occupied the buildings than the male militants blandly turned to their sisters-in-arms and assigned them the task of preparing the food, while they—the menfolk—would presumably plan further strategy. The reply these males received was the reply they deserved, and the fact that domestic tasks behind the barricades were desegregated across the sex line that day is an everlasting tribute to the class consciousness of the ladies of the left.

But these conscious coeds are not typical, for the nonconscious assumptions about a woman's "natural" talents (or lack of them) are at least as prevalent among women as they are among men. A psychologist named Philip Goldberg (1968) demonstrated this by asking female college students to rate a number of professional articles from each of six fields. The articles were collated into two equal sets of booklets, and the names of the authors were changed so that the identical article was attributed to a male author (e.g., John T. McKay) in one set of booklets and to a female author (e.g., Joan T. McKay) in the other set. Each student was asked to read the articles in her booklet and to rate them for value, competence, persuasiveness, writing style, and so forth.

As he had anticipated, Goldberg found that the identical article received significantly lower ratings when it was attributed to a female author than when it was attributed to a male author. He had predicted this result for articles from professional fields generally considered the province of men, like law and city planning, but to his surprise, these coeds also downgraded articles from the fields of dietetics and elementary school education when they were attributed to female authors. In other words, these students rated the male authors as better at everything, agreeing with Aristotle that "we should regard the female nature as afflicted with a natural defectiveness." We repeated this experiment informally in our own classrooms and discovered that male students show the same implicit prejudice against female authors that Goldberg's female students showed. Such is the nature of a nonconscious ideology!

It is significant that examples like these can be drawn from the college world, for today's students have challenged the established ways of looking at almost every other issue, and they have been quick to reject those practices of our society which conflict explicitly with their major values. But as the above examples suggest, they will find it far more difficult to shed the more subtle aspects of a sex-role ideology which—as we shall now attempt to demonstrate—conflicts just as surely with their existential values as any of the other societal practices to which they have so effectively raised objection. And as we shall see, there is no better way to appreciate the power of a society's nonconscious ideology than to examine it within the framework of values held by that society's avant-garde.

INDIVIDUALITY AND SELF-FULFILLMENT

The dominant values of today's students concern personal growth on the one hand, and interpersonal relationships on the other. The first of these emphasizes individuality and self-fulfillment; the second stresses openness, honesty, and equality in all human relationships.

The values of individuality and self-fulfillment imply that each human being, male or female, is to be encouraged to "do his own thing." Men and women are no longer to be stereotyped by society's definitions. If sensitivity, emotionality, and warmth are desirable human characteristics, then they are desirable for men as well as for women. (John

Wayne is no longer an idol of the young, but their pop-art satire.) If independence, assertiveness, and serious intellectual commitment are desirable human characteristics, then they are desirable for women as well as for men. The major prescription of this college generation is that each individual should be encouraged to discover and fulfill his own unique potential and identity, unfettered by society's presumptions.

But society's presumptions enter the scene much earlier than most people suspect, for parents begin to raise their children in accord with the popular stereotypes from the very first. Boys are encouraged to be aggressive, competitive, and independent, whereas girls are rewarded for being passive and dependent (Barry, Bacon, & Child, 1957; Sears, Maccoby, & Levin, 1957). In one study, six-month-old infant girls were already being touched and spoken to more by their mothers while they were playing than were infant boys. When they were thirteen months old, these same girls were more reluctant than the boys to leave their mothers; they returned more quickly and more frequently to them; and they remained closer to them throughout the entire play period. When a physical barrier was placed between mother and child, the girls tended to cry and motion for help; the boys made more active attempts to get around the barrier (Goldberg & Lewis, 1969). No one knows to what extent these sex differences at the age of thirteen months can be attributed to the mothers' behavior at the age of six months, but it is hard to believe that the two are unconnected.

As children grow older, more explicit sex-role training is introduced. Boys are encouraged to take more of an interest in mathematics and science. Boys, not girls, are given chemistry sets and microscopes for Christmas. Moreover, all children quickly learn that mommy is proud to be a moron when it comes to mathematics and science, whereas daddy knows all about these things. When a young boy returns from school all excited about biology, he is almost certain to be encouraged to think of becoming a physician. A girl with similar enthusiasm is told that she might want to consider nurse's training later so she can have "an interesting job to fall back upon in case—God forbid—she ever needs to support herself." A very different kind of encouragement. And any girl who doggedly persists in her enthusiasm for science is likely to find her parents as horrified by the prospect of a permanent love affair with physics as they would be by the prospect of an interracial marriage.

These socialization practices quickly take their toll. By nursery school age, for example, boys are already asking more questions about how and why things work (Smith, 1933). In first and second grade, when asked to suggest ways of improving various toys, boys do better on the fire truck and girls do better on the nurse's kit, but by the third grade, boys do better regardless of the toy presented (Torrance, 1962). By the ninth grade, 25 percent of the boys, but only 3 percent of the girls, are considering careers in science or engineering (Flanagan, unpublished; cited by Kagan, 1964). When they apply for college, boys and girls are about equal on verbal aptitude tests, but boys score significantly higher on mathematical aptitude tests—

about 60 points higher on the College Board examinations, for example (Brown, 1965, p. 162). Moreover, girls improve their mathematical performance if problems are reworded so that they deal with cooking and gardening, even though the abstract reasoning required for their solutions remains the same (Milton, 1958). Clearly, not just ability, but motivation too, has been affected.

But these effects in mathematics and science are only part of the story. A girl's long training in passivity and dependence appears to exact an even higher toll from her overall motivation to achieve, to search for new and independent ways of doing things, and to welcome the challenge of new and unsolved problems. In one study, for example, elementary school girls were more likely to try solving a puzzle by imitating an adult, whereas the boys were more likely to search for a novel solution not provided by the adult (McDavid, 1959). In another puzzle-solving study, young girls asked for help and approval from adults more frequently than the boys; and, when given the opportunity to return to the puzzles a second time, the girls were more likely to rework those they had already solved, whereas the boys were more likely to try puzzles they had been unable to solve previously (Crandall & Rabson, 1960). A girl's sigh of relief is almost audible when she marries and retires from the outside world of novel and unsolved problems. This, of course, is the most conspicuous outcome of all: the majority of American women become full-time homemakers. Such are the consequences of a nonconscious ideology.

But why does this process violate

the values of individuality and self-fulfillment? It is *not* because some people may regard the role of homemaker as inferior to other roles. That is not the point. Rather, the point is that our society is managing to consign a large segment of its population to the role of homemaker solely on the basis of sex just as inexorably as it has in the past consigned the individual with a black skin to the role of janitor or domestic. It is not the quality of the role itself which is at issue here, but the fact that in spite of their unique identities, the majority of America's women end up in the *same* role.

Even so, however, several arguments are typically advanced to counter the claim that America's homogenization of its women subverts individuality and self-fulfillment. The three most common arguments invoke, respectively, (1) free will, (2) biology, and (3) complementarity.

1. The free will argument proposes that a 21-year-old woman is perfectly free to choose some other role if she cares to do so; no one is standing in her way. But this argument conveniently overlooks the fact that the society which has spent twenty years carefully marking the woman's ballot for her has nothing to lose in that twenty-first year by pretending to let her cast it for the alternative of her choice. Society has controlled not her alternatives, but her motivation to choose any but one of those alternatives. The so-called freedom to choose is illusory and cannot be invoked to justify the society which controls the motivation to choose.

2. The biological argument suggests that there may really be inborn differences between men and women in, say independence or mathematical ability. Or that there may be biological factors beyond the fact that women can become pregnant and nurse children which uniquely dictate that they, but not men, should stay home all day and shun serious outside commitment. Maybe female hormones really are responsible somehow. One difficulty with this argument, of course, is that female hormones would have to be different in the Soviet Union, where one-third of the engineers and 75 percent of the physicians are women. In America, women constitute less than 1 percent of the engineers and only 7 percent of the physicians (Dodge, 1966). Female physiology *is* different, and it may account for some of the psychological differences between the sexes, but America's sex-role ideology still seems primarily responsible for the fact that so few women emerge from childhood with the motivation to seek out any role beyond the one that our society dictates.

But even if there really were biological differences between the sexes along these lines, the biological argument would still be irrelevant. The reason can best be illustrated with an analogy.

Suppose that every black American boy were to be socialized to become a jazz musician on the assumption that he has a "natural" talent in that direction, or suppose that his parents should subtly discourage him from other pursuits because it is considered "inappropriate" for black men to become physicians or physicists. Most liberal Americans, we submit, would disapprove. But suppose that it *could* be demonstrated that black Americans, *on the average,* did possess an inborn better sense of rhythm than white Americans. Would *that* justify ignoring the unique characteristics of a *particular* black youngster from the very beginning and specifically socializing him to become a musician? We don't think so. Similarly, as long as a woman's socialization does not nurture her uniqueness, but treats her only as a member of a group on the basis of some assumed *average* characteristic, she will not be prepared to realize her own potential in the way that the values of individuality and self-fulfillment imply she should.

The irony of the biological argument is that it does not take biological differences seriously enough. That is, it fails to recognize the range of biological differences between individuals within the same sex. Thus, recent research has revealed that biological factors help determine many personality traits. Dominance and submissiveness, for example, have been found to have large inheritable components; in other words, biological factors *do* have the potential for partially determining how dominant or submissive an individual, male or female, will turn out to be. But the effects of this biological potential could be detected only in males (Gottesman, 1963). This implies that only the males in our culture are raised with sufficient flexibility, with sufficient latitude given to their biological differences, for their "natural" or biologically determined potential to shine through. Females, on the other hand, are subjected to a socialization which so ignores their unique attributes that even the effects of biology seem to be swamped. In sum, the biological argument for continuing America's homogenization of its women gets hoist with its own petard.

3. Many people recognize that most women do end up as full-time homemakers because of their socialization and that these women do exemplify the failure of our society to raise girls as unique individuals. But, they point out, the role of the homemaker is not inferior to the role of the professional man: it is complementary but equal.

This argument is usually bolstered by pointing to the joys and importance of taking care of small children. Indeed, mothers *and* fathers find child-rearing rewarding, and it is certainly important. But this argument becomes insufficient when one considers that the average American woman now lives to age 74 and has her *last* child at about age 26; thus, by the time the woman is 33 or so, her children all have more important things to do with their daytime hours than to spend them entertaining an adult woman who has nothing to do during the second half of her life span. As for the other "joys" of homemaking, many writers (e.g., Friedan, 1963) have persuasively argued that the role of the homemaker has been glamorized far beyond its intrinsic worth. This charge becomes plausible when one considers that the average American homemaker spends the equivalent of a man's working day, 7.1 hours, in preparing meals, cleaning house, laundering, mending, shopping, and doing other household tasks. In other words, 43 percent of her waking time is spent in activity that would command an hourly wage on the open market well below the federally-set minimum for menial industrial work.

The point is not how little she would earn if she did these things in someone else's home, but that this use of time is virtually the same for homemakers with college degrees and for those with less than a grade school education, for women married to professional men and for women married to blue-collar workers. Talent, education, ability, interests, motivations: all are irrelevant. In our society, being female uniquely qualifies an individual for domestic work.

It is true, of course, that the American homemaker has, on the average, 5.1 hours of leisure time per day, and it is here, we are told, that each woman can express her unique identity. Thus, politically interested women can join the League of Women Voters; women with humane interests can become part-time Gray Ladies; women who love music can raise money for the symphony. Protestant women play Canasta; Jewish women play Mah-Jongg; brighter women of all denominations and faculty wives play bridge; and so forth.

But politically interested *men* serve in legislatures; *men* with humane interests become physicians or clinical psychologists; *men* who love music play in the symphony; and so forth. In other words, why should a woman's unique identity determine only the periphery of her life rather than its central core?

Again, the important point is not that the role of homemaker is necessarily inferior, but that the woman's unique identity has been rendered irrelevant. Consider the following "predictability test." When a boy is born, it is difficult to predict what he will be doing 25 years later. We cannot say whether he will be an artist, a doctor, or a college professor, because he will be permitted to develop and to fulfill his own unique potential, particularly if he is white and middle-class. But if the newborn child is a girl, we can usually predict with confidence how she will be spending her time 25 years later. Her individuality doesn't have to be considered; it is irrelevant.

The socialization of the American male has closed off certain options for him too. Men are discouraged from developing certain desirable traits such as tenderness and sensitivity just as surely as women are discouraged from being assertive and, alas, "too bright." Young boys are encouraged to be incompetent at cooking and child care just as surely as young girls are urged to be incompetent at mathematics and science.

Indeed, one of the errors of the early feminist movement in this country was that it assumed that men had all the goodies and that women could attain self-fulfillment merely by being like men. But that is hardly the utopia implied by the values of individuality and self-fulfillment. Rather, these values would require society to raise its children so flexibly and with sufficient respect for the integrity of individual uniqueness that some men might emerge with the motivation, the ability, and the opportunity to stay home and raise children without bearing the stigma of being peculiar. If homemaking is as glamorous as the women's magazines and television commercials portray it, then men, too, should have that option. Even if homemaking isn't all that glamorous, it would probably still be more fulfilling for some men than the jobs in which they now find themselves.

And if biological differences really do exist between men and women in "nurturance," in their inborn motivations to care for children, then this will show up automatically in the final distribution of men and women across the various roles: relatively fewer men will choose to stay at home. The values of individuality and self-fulfillment do not imply that there must be equality of outcome, an equal number of men and women in each role, but that there should be the widest possible variation in outcome consistent with the range of individual differences among people, regardless of sex. At the very least, these values imply that society should raise its males so that they could freely engage in activities that might pay less than those being pursued by their wives without feeling that they were "living off their wives." One rarely hears it said of a woman that she is "living off her husband."

Thus, it is true that a man's options are limited by our society's sex-role ideology, but as the "predictability test" reveals, it is still the woman in our society whose identity is rendered irrelevant by America's socialization practices. In 1954, the United States Supreme Court declared that a fraud and hoax lay behind the slogan "separate but equal." It is unlikely that any court will ever do the same for the more subtle motto that successfully keeps the woman in her place: "complementary but equal."

INTERPERSONAL EQUALITY

Wives, submit yourselves unto your own husbands, as unto the Lord. For the husband is the head of the wife, even as Christ is the head of the church; and he is the savior of the body. Therefore, as the church is subject unto Christ, so let the wives be to their own husbands in everything. (Eph. 5)

As this passage reveals, the ideological rationalization that men and women hold complementary but equal positions is a recent invention of our modern "liberal" society, part of the equalitarian veneer which helps to keep today's version of the ideology nonconscious. Certainly those Americans who value open, honest, and equalitarian relationships generally are quick to reject this traditional view of the male-female relationship; and, an increasing number of young people even plan to enter "utopian" marriages very much like the following hypothetical example:

Both my wife and I earned Ph.D. degrees in our respective disciplines. I turned down a superior academic post in Oregon and accepted a slightly less desirable position in New York where my wife could obtain a part-time teaching job and do research at one of the several other colleges in the area. Although I would have preferred to live in a suburb, we purchased a home near my wife's college so that she could have an office at home where she would be when the children returned from school. Because my wife earns a good salary, she can easily afford to pay a maid to do her major household chores. My wife and I share all other tasks around the house equally. For example, she cooks the meals, but I do the laundry for her and help her with many of her other household tasks.

Without questioning the basic happiness of such a marriage or its appropriateness for many couples, we can legitimately ask if such a marriage is, in fact, an instance of interpersonal equality. Have all the hidden assumptions about the woman's "natural" role really been eliminated? Has the traditional ideology really been exorcised? There is a very simple test. If the marriage is truly equalitarian, then its description should retain the same flavor and tone even if the roles of the husband and wife were to be reversed:

Both my husband and I earned Ph.D. degrees in our respective disciplines. I turned down a superior academic post in Oregon and accepted a slightly less desirable position in New York where my husband could obtain a part-time teaching job and do research at one of the several other colleges in the area. Although I would have preferred to live in a suburb, we purchased a home near my husband's college so that he could have an office at home where he would be when the children returned from school. Because my husband earns a good salary, he can easily afford to pay a maid to do his major household chores. My husband and I share all other tasks around the house equally. For example, he cooks the meals, but I do the laundry for him and help him with many of his other household tasks.

It seems unlikely that many men or women in our society would mistake the marriage *just* described as either equalitarian or desirable, and thus it becomes apparent that the ideology about the woman's "natural" role nonconsciously permeates the entire fabric of such "utopian" marriages. It is true that the wife gains some measure of equality when her career can influence the final place of residence, but why is it the unquestioned assumption that the husband's career solely determines the initial set of alternatives that are to be considered? Why is it the wife who automatically seeks the part-time position? Why is it *her* maid instead of *their* maid? Why *her* laundry? Why *her* household tasks? And so forth throughout the entire relationship.

The important point here is not that such marriages are bad or that their basic assumptions of inequality produce unhappy, frustrated women. Quite the contrary. It is the very happiness of the wives in such marriages that reveals society's smashing success in socializing its women. It is a measure of the distance our society must yet traverse toward the goals of self-fulfillment and interpersonal equality that such marriages are widely characterized as utopian and fully equalitarian. It is a mark of how well the woman has been kept in her place that the husband in such a marriage is often idolized by women, including his wife, for "permitting" her to squeeze a career into the interstices of their marriage as long as his own career is not unduly inconvenienced. Thus is the white man blessed for exercising his power benignly while his "natural" right to that power forever remains unquestioned.

Such is the subtlety of a nonconscious ideology!

A truly equalitarian marriage would permit both partners to pursue careers or outside commitments which carry equal weight when all important decisions are to be made. It is here, of course, that the "problem" of children arises. People often assume that the woman who seeks a role beyond home and family would not care to have children. They assume that if she wants a career or serious outside commitment, then children must be unimportant to her. But of course no one makes this assumption about her husband. No one assumes that a father's interest in his career necessarily precludes a deep and abiding affection for his children or a vital interest in their development. Once again America applies a double standard of judgment. Suppose that a father of small children suddenly lost his wife. No matter how much he loved his children, no one would expect him to sacrifice his career in order to stay home with them on a full-time basis—*even if he had an independent source of income.* No one would charge him with selfishness or lack of parental feeling if he sought professional care for his children during the day. An equalitarian marriage simply abolishes this double standard and extends the same freedom to the mother, while also providing the framework for the father to enter more fully into the pleasures and responsibilities of child rearing. In fact, it is the equalitarian marriage which has the most potential for giving children the love and concern of two parents rather than one.

But few women are prepared to make use of this freedom. Even those women who have managed to finesse society's attempt to rob them of their career motivations are likely to find themselves blocked by society's trump card: the feeling that the raising of the children is their unique responsibility and—in time of crisis—ultimately theirs alone. Such is the emotional power of a nonconscious ideology.

In addition to providing this potential for equalized child care, a truly equalitarain marriage embraces a more general division of labor which satisfies what might be called "the roommate test." That is, the labor is divided just as it is when two men or two women room together in college or set up a bachelor apartment together. Errands and domestic chores are assigned by preference, agreement, flipping a coin, given to hired help, or—as is sometimes the case—left undone.

It is significant that today's young people, many of whom live this way prior to marriage, find this kind of arrangement within marriage so foreign to their thinking. Consider an analogy. Suppose that a white male college student decided to room or set up a bachelor apartment with a black male friend. Surely the typical white student would not blithely assume his black roommate was to handle all the domestic chores. Nor would his conscience allow him to do so even in the unlikely event that his roommate would say: "No, that's okay. I like doing housework. I'd be happy to do it." We suspect that the typical white student would still not be comfortable if he took advantage of this offer, if he took advantage of the fact that his roommate had been socialized to be "happy" with such an arrangement. But change this hypothetical black roommate to a female marriage partner, and somehow the student's conscience goes to sleep. At most it is quickly tranquilized by the thought that "she is happiest when she is ironing for her loved one." Such is the power of a nonconscious ideology.

Of course, it may well be that she *is* happiest when she is ironing for her loved one.

Such, indeed, is the power of a nonconscious ideology!

REFERENCES

BARRY, H., III, BACON, M. K., and CHILD, I. L. A cross-cultural survey of some sex differences in socialization. *Journal of Abnormal and Social Psychology 55* (1957), 327–332.

BROWN, R. *Social Psychology.* New York: Free Press, 1965.

CRANDALL, V. J., and RABSON, A. Children's repetition choices in an intellectual achievement situation following success and failure. *Journal of Genetic Psychology 97* (1960), 161–168.

DODGE, N. D. *Women in the Soviet Economy.* Baltimore: The Johns Hopkins Press, 1966.

FLANAGAN, J. C. Project talent. Unpublished manuscript.

FRIEDAN, B. *The Feminine Mystique.* New York: Norton, 1963.

GOLDBERG, P. Are women prejudiced against women? *Transaction 5* (April 1968), 28–30.

GOLDBERG, S. and LEWIS, M. Play behavior in the year-old infant: early sex differences. *Child Development 40* (1969), 21–31.

GOTTESMAN, I. I. Heritability of personality: a demonstration. *Psychological Monographs 77* (1963), whole no. 572.

KAGAN, J. Acquisition and significance of sex typing and sex role identity. In M. L. Hoffman & L. W. Hoffman, eds. *Review of child development research, Vol. 1,* pp. 137–167. New York: Russell Sage Foundation, 1964.

McDAVID, J. W. Imitative behavior in preschool children. *Psychological Monographs 73* (1959), whole no. 486.

MILTON, G. A. Five studies of the relation between sex role identification and achievement in problem solving. Technical Report No. 3, Department of Industrial Administration, Department of Psychology, Yale University, December, 1958.

SEARS, R. R., MACCOBY, E. E., and LEVIN, H. *Patterns of child rearing.* Evanston, Ill.: Row, Peterson, 1957.

SMITH, M. E. The influence of age, sex, and situation on the frequency of form and functions of questions asked by preschool children. *Child Development 3* (1933), 201–213.

TORRANCE, E. P. *Guiding creative talent.* Englewood Cliffs, N.J.: Prentice-hall, 1962.

Interaction

3

Our approach to interaction hinges on the fact that reality construction occurs within it; in the process of interaction people *hammer out* a shared view of reality, by establishing who they are, what resources they have, what they want, and what they will give up. Although this approach to interaction is a fairly recent development, the seminal ideas which broke ground for it are of classical vintage. Max Weber, for example, always insisted that human action must be understood from the point of view of the actor. George Herbert Mead contended that individuals pick out, indicate, and select for themselves the reality to which they respond. W. I. Thomas stated that what men define as real is real in its consequences. And Emile Durkheim claimed that people continually revise, renew, and rebuild their normative order in the process of collective action.

Implicit in these statements are several radical notions. First, that reality is plural; second, that a shared reality is something to be constructed; third, that it is subject to revision; and fourth, that it has an imputed rather than an inherent meaning and value. In effect, reality is a taken, not a given, all of which lays to rest the Platonic notion of an immutable, eternal, out-there, given reality. Reality is fabricated and durable, but at its roots precarious, as is any other human product.

This approach has been used to great advantage especially within the area of deviant behavior. For example, to the degree that drug use is a marginal, if not illegal, activity, it usually is stigmatized as symptomatic of criminality or pathology. This stigma makes drug use more of a problem than it might otherwise be. The naive user of marijuana or LSD who experiences alterations in the perception of time, place, and objects may well interpret this alteration much as a nonuser would, that is, as an indication he is losing his mind, is out of control, or is going crazy. This *interpretation* of his unfamiliar subjective state can induce a massive attack of anxiety and cause him to panic. Investigators have observed, however, that if a naive user is in the company of regalar users they may help him interpret his unusual feelings so that he experiences them as pleasurable. The point is that through interaction *even* a *subjective* state that has typically been defined as abnormal and uncomfortable can be reinterpreted as normal and pleasurable. The difference, then, between panic and pleasure rests on prior interpretation.

The articles which follow depict the reality construction process as it occurs in *different* interaction contexts—in marriage, in a professional-client relationship, and between racial groups. The marital context exemplifies reality construction among status equals who cooperate in the construction of a micro-reality. In contrast, the professional-client and racial group contexts exemplify reality construction among status unequals who must struggle with each other. Running through all the cases is the theme of the relative power of the actors and the difference this makes in the final version of reality.

In the lead article Berger and Kellner suggest that marriage, especially in an advanced industrial society, is the interaction nexus in which reality construction occurs par excelence. A large mass, highly differentiated and regulated society compels its members to escape into the private sphere of life to gain some measure of human scale and personal autonomy. Marriage enables people to crystallize a shared and consistent world in which they merge their identities, interests, and ideas to such a degree that they eventually become an undifferentiated unit. Marriage allows for the construction of a little micro-reality, a small modular unit, which can detach from, transfer to, and plug into again—all of which is quite functional for—a high-mobility society.

The relative power of the participants to impose or secure their versions of reality becomes clear in Scheff's discussion of interrogation procedures, in which the aim is to establish whether or not something has happened and who, in fact, is responsible for it. The key idea is that the definition of what has taken place and the assignment of responsibility for it occurs through a negotiation process. One of Scheff's illustrations of the negotiation process occurs within a medical context. A patient comes to a psychiatrist and proposes reasons for requiring treatment. These reasons are rejected by the doctor who then makes counterproposals until an "illness" is agreed upon, with the clear understanding that the patient is responsible for having brought on her own illness and that only if she acknowledges this can she get better. Since the patient and physician have unequal power in the situation, it is always the doctor's definition of illness and assessment of responsibility that prevails. Throughout, the doctor, in very subtle ways, leaves no doubt that he is in control.

Just the reverse is true in the materials presented by Braroe. Here those in power go out of their way to disguise the fact that they have power and thereby pre-empt any challenge of it. Braroe presents the intergroup relations of reservation Indians and white town dwellers. The white image of the Indian is that he is stupid, irresponsible, and childish. The Indians do nothing to upset this image. Whites, for example, buy wooden posts from the reservation which the Indians illegally cut down from a nearby forest and soak in a "bluestone" preservative. Often, however, instead of soaking the wood, the Indians merely paint it over with laundry blueing and thus "con" the whites. The whites know they are being conned, but keep coming back for more. They never call the Indians to account, and the Indians gain great esteem among their fellows for having duped the whites again. It is apparently to the advantage of the whites to allow the Indians to believe the "con" has worked. In this way, the Indians, although they live under oppressive conditions, gain some satisfaction by conning the whites, and are not prone to challenge the white-dominated system. In effect, a "double-con" definition of reality turns out to be a mutually agreed upon and normal mode of interaction. One side remains oppressed but maintains in-group esteem; the other side remains "duped," but maintains overall control.

marriage and the construction of reality: an exercise in the microsociology of knowledge

PETER L. BERGER

HANSFRIED KELLNER

Ever since Durkheim it has been a commonplace of family sociology

Reprinted from Peter L. Berger and Hansfried Kellner, "Marriage and the Construction of Reality," DIOGENES, no. 46 (Summer 1964), 1–23, by permission of the author and publisher.

that marriage serves as a protection against anomie for the individual. Interesting and pragmatically useful though this insight is, it is but the negative side of a phenomenon of much broader significance. If one speaks of *anomic* states, then one ought properly to investigate also the *nomic* processes that, by their absence, lead to the aforementioned states. If, consequently, one finds a negative correlation between marriage and anomie, then one should be led to inquire into the character of marriage as a *nomos*-building instrumentality, that is, of marriage as a social arrangement that creates for the individual the sort of order in which he can experience his life as making sense. It is our intention here to discuss marriage in these terms. While this could evidently be done in a macrosociological perspective, dealing with marriage as a major social institution related to other broad structures of society, our focus will be microsociological, dealing primarily with the social processes affecting the individuals in any specific marriage, although, of course, the larger framework of these processes will have to be understood. In what sense this discussion can be described as microsociology of knowledge will hopefully become clearer in the course of it.[1]

Marriage is obviously only *one* social relationship in which this process of *nomos*-building takes place. It is, therefore, necessary to first look in more general terms at the character of this process. In doing so, we are influenced by three theoretical perspectives—the Weberian perspective on society as a network of meanings, the Meadian perspective on indentity as a social phenomenon, and the phenomeno-

logical analysis of the social structuring of reality especially as given in the work of Schutz and Merleau-Ponty.[2] Not being convinced, however, that theoretical lucidity is necessarily enhanced by terminological ponderosity, we shall avoid as much as possible the use of the sort of jargon for which both sociologists and phenomenologists have acquired dubious notoriety.

The process that interests us here is the one that constructs, maintains and modifies a consistent reality that can be meaningfully experienced by individuals. In its essential forms this process is determined by the society in which it occurs. Every society has its specific way of defining and perceiving reality—its world, its universe, its overarching organization of symbols. This is already given in the language that forms the symbolic base of the society. Erected over this base, and by means of it, is a system of ready-made typifications, through which the innumerable experiences of reality come to be ordered.[3] These typifications and their order are held in common by the members of society, thus acquiring not only the character of objectivity, but being taken for granted as *the* world *tout court*, the only world

---

[1] The present article has come out of a larger project on which the authors have been engaged in collaboration with three colleagues in sociology and philosophy. The project is to produce a systematic treatise that will integrate a number of now separate theoretical strands in the sociology of knowledge.

[2] Cf. especially Max Weber, *Wirtschaft und Gesellschaft* (Tuebingen: Mohr 1956), and *Gesammelte Aufsaetze zur Wissenschaftslehre* (Tuebingen: Mohr 1951); George H. Mead, *Mind, Self and Society* (University of Chicago Press 1934); Alfred Schutz, *Der sinnhafte Aufbau der sozialen Welt* (Vienna: Springer, 2nd ed. 1960) and *Collected Papers*, I (The Hague: Nijhoff 1962); Maurice Merleau-Ponty, *Phénoménologie de la perception* (Paris: Gallimard 1945) and *La structure du comportement* (Paris: Presses universitaires de France 1953).

[3] Cf. Schutz, *Aufbau*, 202–20 and *Collected Papers*, I, 3–27, 283–6.

that normal men can conceive of.[4] The seemingly objective and taken-for-granted character of the social definitions of reality can be seen most clearly in the case of language itself, but it is important to keep in mind that the latter forms the base and instrumentality of a much larger world-erecting process.

The socially constructed world must be continually mediated to and actualized by the individual, so that it can become and remain indeed *his* world as well. The individual is given by his society certain decisive cornerstones for his everyday experience and conduct. Most importantly, the individual is supplied with specific sets of typifications and criteria of relevance, predefined for him by the society and made available to him for the ordering of his everyday life. This ordering or (in line with our opening considerations) nomic apparatus is biographically cumulative. It begins to be formed in the individual from the earliest stages of socialization on, then keeps on being enlarged and modified by himself throughout his biography.[5] While there are individual biographical differences making for differences in the constitution of this apparatus in specific individuals, there exists in the society an overall consensus on the range of differences deemed to be tolerable. Without such consensus, indeed, society would be impossible as a going concern, since it would then lack the ordering principles by which alone experience can be shared and conduct can be mutually intelligible.

This order, by which the individual comes to perceive and define his world, is thus not chosen by him, except perhaps for very small modifications. Rather, it is discovered by him as an external datum, a ready-made world that simply is *there* for him to go ahead and live in, though he modifies it continually in the process of living in it. Nevertheless, this world is in need of validation, perhaps precisely because of an ever-present glimmer of suspicion as to its social manufacture and relativity. This validation, while it must be undertaken by the individual himself, requires ongoing interaction with others who co-inhabit this same socially constructed world. In a broad sense, *all* the other co-inhabitants of this world serve a validating function. Every morning the newspaper boy validates the widest co-ordinates of my world and the mailman bears tangible validation of my own location within these co-ordinates. However, some validations are more significant than others. Every individual requires the ongoing validation of his world, including crucially the validation of his identity and place in this world, by those few who are his truly significant others.[6] Just as the individual's deprivation of relationship with his significant others will plunge him into anomie, so their continued presence will sustain for him that *nomos* by which he can feel at home in the world at least most of the time. Again in a broad sense, all the actions of the significant others and even their simple presence serve this sustaining function. In everyday life, however, the principal method employed is speech. In this sense,

---

[4] Cf. Schutz, *Collected Papers*, I, 207–28.
[5] Cf. especially Jean Piaget, *The Child's Construction of Reality* (Routledge & Kegan Paul 1955).

[6] Cf. Mead, op. cit., 135–226.

it is proper to view the individual's relationship with his significant others as an ongoing conversation. As the latter occurs, it validates over and over again the fundamental definitions of reality once entered into, not, of course, so much by explicit articulation, but precisely by taking the definitions silently for granted and conversing about all conceivable matters on this taken-for-granted basis. Through the same conversation the individual is also made capable of adjusting to changing and new social contexts in his biography. In a very fundamental sense it can be said that one converses one's way through life.

If one concedes these points, one can now state a general sociological proposition: the plausibility and stability of the world, as socially defined, is dependent upon the strength and continuity of significant relationships in which conversation about this world can be continually carried on. Or, to put it a little differently: the reality of the world is sustained through conversation with significant others. This reality, of course, includes not only the imagery by which fellowmen are viewed, but also includes the way in which one views oneself. The reality-bestowing force of social relationships depends on the degree of their nearness,[7] that is, on the degree to which social relationships occur in face-to-face situations and to which they are credited with primary significance by the individual. In any empirical situation, there now emerge obvious sociological questions out of these considerations, namely, questions about the patterns of the world-building relationships, the social

forms taken by the conversation with significant others. Sociologically, one must ask how these relationships are *objectively* structured and distributed, and one will also want to understand how they are *subjectively* perceived and experienced.

With these preliminary assumptions stated we can now arrive at our main thesis here. Namely, we would contend that marriage occupies a privileged status among the significant validating relationships for adults in our society. Put slightly differently: marriage is a crucial nomic instrumentality in our society. We would further argue that the essential social functionality of this institution cannot be fully understood if this fact is not perceived.

We can now proceed with an ideal-typical analysis of marriage, that is, seek to abstract the essential features involved. Marriage in our society is a *dramatic* act in which two strangers come together and redefine themselves. The drama of the act is internally anticipated and socially legitimated long before it takes place in the individual's biography, and amplified by means of a pervasive ideology, the dominant themes of which (romantic love, sexual fulfilment, self-discovery and self-realization through love and sexuality, the nuclear family as the social site for these processes) can be found distributed through all strata of the society. The actualization of these ideologically pre-defined expectations in the life of the individual occurs to the accompaniment of one of the few traditional rites of passage that are still meaningful to almost all members of the society. It should be added that, in using the term "strangers," we do not mean, of course, that the candidates for the

7 Cf. Schutz, *Aufbau,* 181–95.

marriage come from widely discrepant social backgrounds—indeed, the data indicate that the contrary is the case. The strangeness rather lies in the fact that, unlike marriage candidates in many previous societies, those in ours typically come from different face-to-face contexts —in the terms used above, they come from different areas of conversation. They do not have a shared past, although their pasts have a similar structure. In other words, quite apart from prevailing patterns of ethnic, religious and class endogamy, our society is typically exogamous in terms of nomic relationships. Put concretely, in our mobile society the significant conversation of the two partners previous to the marriage took place in social circles that did not overlap. With the dramatic redefinition of the situation brought about by the marriage, however, all significant conversation for the two new partners is now centered in their relationship with each other—and, in fact, it was precisely with this intention that they entered upon their relationship.

It goes without saying that this character of marriage has its root in much broader structural configurations of our society. The most important of these, for our purposes, is the crystallization of a so-called private sphere of existence, more and more segregated from the immediate controls of the public institutions (especially the economic and political ones), and yet defined and utilized as the main social area for the individual's self-realization.[8] It can-

not be our purpose here to inquire into the historical forces that brought forth this phenomenon, beyond making the observation that these are closely connected with the industrial revolution and its institutional consequences. The public institutions now confront the individual as an immensely powerful and alien world, incomprehensible in its inner workings, anonymous in its human character. If only through his work in some nook of the economic machinery, the individual must find a way of living in this alien world, come to terms with its power over him, be satisfied with a few conceptual rules of thumb to guide him through a vast reality that otherwise remains opaque to his understanding, and modify its anonymity by whatever *human relations* he can work out in his involvement with it. It ought to be emphasized, against some critics of 'mass society,' that this does not inevitably leave the individual with a sense of profound unhappiness and lostness. It would rather seem that large numbers of people in our society are quite content with a situation in which their public involvements have little subjective importance, regarding work as a not too bad necessity and politics as at best a spectator sport. It is usually only intellectuals with ethical and political commitments who assume that such people must be terribly desperate. The point, however, is that the individual in this situation, no matter whether he is happy or not, will turn elsewhere for the experiences of self-realization that do have importance

8 Cf. Arnold Gehlen, *Die Seele im technischen Zeitalter* (Hamburg: Rowohlt 1957), 57–69 and *Anthropologische Forschung* (Hamburg: Rowohlt 1961), 69–77, 127–40; Helmut Schelsky, *Soziologie der Sexualitaet* (Hamburg: Rowohlt 1955), 102–33. Also cf. Thomas Luckmann, "On religion in modern society," *Journal for the Scientific Study of Religion* (Spring 1963), 147–62.

for him. The private sphere, this interstitial area created (we would think) more or less haphazardly as a by-product of the social metamorphosis of industrialism, is mainly where he will turn. It is here that the individual will seek power, intelligibility and, quite literally, a name—the apparent power to fashion a world, however Lilliputian, that will reflect his own being: a world that, seemingly having been shaped by himself and thus unlike those other worlds that insist on shaping him, is translucently intelligible to him (or so he thinks); a world in which, consequently, he is *somebody*—perhaps even, within its charmed circle, a lord and master. What is more, to a considerable extent these expectations are not unrealistic. The public institutions have no need to control the individual's adventures in the private sphere, as long as they really stay within the latter's circumscribed limits. The private sphere is perceived, not without justification, as an area of individual choice and even autonomy. This fact has important consequences for the shaping of identity in modern society that cannot be pursued here. All that ought to be clear here is the peculiar location of the private sphere within and between the other social structures. In sum, it is above all and, as a rule, only in the private sphere that the individual can take a slice of reality and fashion it into his world. If one is aware of the decisive significance of this capacity and even necessity of men to externalize themselves in reality and to produce for themselves a world in which they can feel at home, then one will hardly be surprised at the great importance which the private sphere

has come to have in modern society.[9]

The private sphere includes a variety of social relationships. Among these, however, the relationships of the family occupy a central position and, in fact, serve as a focus for most of the other relationships (such as those with friends, neighbors, fellow-members of religious and other voluntary associations). Since, as the ethnologists keep reminding us, the family in our society is of the conjugal type, the central relationship in this whole area is the marital one. It is on the basis of marriage that, for most adults in our society, existence in the private sphere is built up. It will be clear that this is not at all a universal or even cross culturally wide function of marriage. Rather has marriage in our society taken on a very peculiar character and functionality. It has been pointed out that marriage in contemporary society has lost some of its older functions and taken on new ones instead.[10] This is certainly correct, but we would prefer to state the matter a little differently. Marriage and the family used to be firmly embedded in a matrix of wider community relationships, serving as extensions and particularizations of the latter's social controls. There were few separating barriers between the world of the individual

[9] In these considerations we have been influenced by certain presuppositions of Marxian anthropology, as well as by the anthropological work of Max Scheler, Helmuth Plessner and Arnold Gehlen. We are indebted to Thomas Luckmann for the clarification of the social-psychological significance of the private sphere.

[10] Cf. Talcott Parsons and Robert Bales, *Family: Socialization and Interaction Process* (Routledge & Kegan Paul 1956), 3–34, 353–96.

family and the wider community, a fact even to be seen in the physical conditions under which the family lived before the industrial revolution.[11] The same social life pulsated through the house, the street and the community. In our terms, the family and within it the marital relationship were part and parcel of a considerably larger area of conversation. In our contemporary society, by contrast, each family constitutes its own segregated sub-world, with its own controls and its own closed conversation.

This fact requires a much greater effort on the part of the marriage partners. Unlike an earlier situation in which the establishment of the new marriage simply added to the differentiation and complexity of an already existing social world, the marriage partners now are embarked on the often difficult task of constructing for themselves the little world in which they will live. To be sure, the larger society provides them with certain standard instructions as to how they should go about this task, but this does not change the fact that considerable effort of their own is required for its realization. The monogamous character of marriage enforces both the dramatic and the precarious nature of this undertaking. Success or failure hinges on the present idiosyncrasies and the fairly unpredictable future development of these idiosyncrasies of only two individuals (who, moreover, do not have a shared past)— as Simmel has shown, the most unstable of all possible social relationships.[12] Not surprisingly, the decision to embark on this undertaking has a critical, even cataclysmic connotation in the popular imagination, which is underlined as well as psychologically assuaged by the ceremonialism that surrounds the event.

Every social relationship requires objectivation, that is, requires a process by which subjectively experienced meanings become objective to the individual and, in interaction with others, become common property and thereby massively objective.[13] The degree of objectivation will depend on the number and the intensity of the social relationships that are its carriers. A relationship that consists of only two individuals called upon to sustain, by their own efforts, an ongoing social world will have to make up in intensity for the numerical poverty of the arrangement. This, in turn, accentuates the drama and the precariousness. The later addition of children will add to the, as it were, density of objectivation taking place within the nuclear family, thus rendering the latter a good deal less precarious. It remains true that the establishment and maintenance of such a social world make extremely high demands on the principal participants.

The attempt can now be made to outline the ideal-typical process that takes place as marriage functions as an instrumentality for the social construction of reality. The chief protagonists of the drama are two individuals, each with a biographically accumulated and available stock of experience.[14] As members of a highly mobile society, these individuals have already internalized a degree of readiness to re-define them-

11 Cf. Philippe Ariès, *Centuries of Childhood* (New York: Knopf 1962), 339–410.

12 Cf. Georg Simmel (Kurt Wolff ed.), *The Sociology of Georg Simmel* (Collier-Macmillan 1950), 118–44.

13 Cf. Schutz, *Aufbau*, 29–36, 149–53.

14 Cf. Schutz, *Aufbau*, 186–92, 202–10.

selves and to modify their stock of experience, thus bringing with them considerable psychological capacity for entering new relationships with others.[15] Also, coming from broadly similar sectors of the larger society (in terms of region, class, ethnic and religious affiliations), the two individuals will have organized their stock of experience in similar fashion. In other words, the two individuals have internalized the same overall world, including the general definitions and expectations of the marriage relationship itself. Their society has provided them with a taken-for-granted image of marriage and has socialized them into an anticipation of stepping into the taken-for-granted roles of marriage. All the same, these relatively empty projections now have to be actualized, lived through and filled with experiential content by the protagonists. This will require a dramatic change in their definitions of reality and of themselves.

As of the marriage, most of each partner's actions must now be projected in conjunction with those of the other. Each partner's definitions of reality must be continually correlated with the definitions of the other. The other is present in nearly all horizons of everyday conduct. Furthermore, the identity of each now takes on a new character, having to be constantly matched with that of the other, indeed being typically perceived by people at large as being symbiotically conjoined with the identity of the other. In each partner's psychological economy of significant others, the marriage partner becomes the other *par*

15 David Riesman's well-known concept of 'other-direction' would also be applicable here.

excellence, the nearest and most decisive co-inhabitant of the world. Indeed, all other significant relationships have to be almost automatically re-perceived and re-grouped in accordance with this drastic shift.

In other words, from the beginning of the marriage each partner has new modes in his meaningful experience of the world in general, of other people and of himself. By definition, then, marriage constitutes a nomic rupture. In terms of each partner's biography, the event of marriage initiates a new nomic process. Now, the full implications of this fact are rarely apprehended by the protagonists with any degree of clarity. There rather is to be found the notion that one's world, one's other-relationships and, above all, oneself have remained what they were before—only, of course, that world, others and self will now be shared with the marriage partner. It should be clear by now that this notion is a grave misapprehension. Just because of this fact, marriage now propels the individual into an unintended and unarticulated development, in the course of which the nomic transformation takes place. What typically *is* apprehended are certain objective and concrete problems arising out of the marriage—such as tensions with in-laws, or with former friends, or religious differences between the partners, as well as immediate tensions between them. These are apprehended as external, situational and practical difficulties. What is *not* apprehended is the subjective side of these difficulties, namely, the transformation of *nomos* and identity that has occurred and that continues to go on, so that all problems and relationships are experienced in a quite new way, that is, experienced within a new and ever-changing reality.

Take a simple and frequent illustration—the male partner's relationships with male friends before and after the marriage. It is a common observation that such relationships, especially if the extra-marital partners are single, rarely survive the marriage, or, if they do, are drastically re-defined after it. This is typically the result of neither a deliberate decision by the husband nor deliberate sabotage by the wife. What rather happens, very simply, is a slow process in which the husband's image of his friend is transformed as he keeps talking about this friend with his wife. Even if no actual talking goes on, the mere presence of the wife forces him to see his friend differently. This need not mean that he adopts a negative image held by the wife. Regardless of what image she holds or is believed by him to hold, it will be different from that held by the husband. This difference will enter into the joint image that now must needs be fabricated in the course of the ongoing conversation between the marriage partners —and, in due course, must act powerfully on the image previously held by the husband. Again, typically, this process is rarely apprehended with any degree of lucidity. The old friend is more likely to fade out of the picture by slow degrees, as new kinds of friends take his place. The process, if commented upon at all within the marital conversation, can always be explained by socially available formulas about "people changing," "friends disappearing" or oneself "having become more mature." This process of conversational liquidation is especially powerful because it is onesided—the husband typically talks with his wife about his friend, but *not* with his friend about his wife. Thus the friend is deprived of the defense of, as it were, counter-defining the relationship. This dominance of the marital conversation over all others, is one of its most important characteristics. It may be mitigated by a certain amount of protective segregation of some non-marital relationships (say, "Tuesday night out with the boys," or "Saturday lunch with mother"), but even then there are powerful emotional barriers against the sort of conversation (conversation *about* the marital relationship, that is) that would serve by way of counter-definition.

Marriage thus posits a new reality. The individual's relationship with this new reality, however, is a dialectical one—he acts upon it, in collusion with the marriage partner, and it acts back upon both him and the partner, welding together their reality. Since, as we have argued before, the objectivation that constitutes this reality is precarious, the groups with which the couple associates are called upon to assist in co-defining the new reality. The couple is pushed towards groups that strengthen their new definition of themselves and the world, avoids those that weaken this definition. This in turn releases the commonly known pressures of group association, again acting upon the marriage partners to change their definitions of the world and of themselves. Thus the new reality is not posited once and for all, but goes on being re-defined not only in the marital interaction itself but also in the various maritally based group relationships into which the couple enters.

In the individual's biography marriage, then, brings about a decisive phase of socialization that can be compared with the phases of childhood and adolescence. This phase has a rather different structure from the earlier ones. There the individual was in the main socialized into already existing patterns. Here he actively collaborates rather than passively accommodates himself. Also, in the previous phases of socialization, there was an apprehension of entering into a new world and being changed in the course of this. In marriage there is little apprehension of such a process, but rather the notion that the world has remained the same, with only its emotional and pragmatic connotatons having changed. This notion, as we have tried to show, is illusionary.

The re-construction of the world in marriage occurs principally in the course of conversation, as we have suggested. The implicit problem of this conversation is how to match two individual definitions of reality. By the very logic of the relationship, a common overall definition must be arrived at otherwise the conversation will become impossible and, *ipso facto,* the relationship will be endangered. Now, this conversation may be understood as the working away of an ordering and typifying apparatus—if one prefers, an objectivating apparatus. Each partner ongoingly contributes his conceptions of reality, which are then "talked through," usually not once but many times, and in the process become objectivated by the conversational apparatus. The longer this conversation goes on, the more massively real do the objectivations become to the partners. In the marital conversation a world is not only built, but it is also kept in a state of repair and ongoingly refurnished. The subjective reality of this world for the two partners is sustained by the same conversation. The nomic instrumentality of marriage is concretized over and over again, from bed to breakfast table, as the partners carry on the endless conversation that feeds on nearly all they individually or jointly experience. Indeed, it may happen eventually that no experience is fully real unless and until it has been thus "talked through."

This process has a very important result—namely, a hardening or stabilization of the common objectivated reality. It should be easy to see now how this comes about. The objectivations ongoingly performed and internalized by the marriage partners become ever more massively real, as they are confirmed and reconfirmed in the marital conversation. The world that is made up of these objectivations at the same time gains in stability. For example, the images of other people, which before or in the earlier stages of the marital conversation may have been rather ambiguous and shifting in the minds of the two partners, now become hardened into definite and stable characterizations. A casual acquaintance, say, may sometimes have appeared as lots of fun and sometimes as quite a bore to the wife before her marriage. Under the influence of the marital conversation, in which this other person is frequently "discussed," she will now come down more firmly on one *or* the other of the two characterizations, or on a reasonable compromise between the two. In any of these three options, though, she will have concocted with her husband a much more stable image of the person in question than she is likely to have had before her marriage, when there may have been no conversational pressure to make a definite option at all. The same process of stabilization may be observed with regard to self-definitions as well. In this way, the wife in our example will not only be pressured to assign stable characterizations to others but also to herself. Previously uninterested politically, she now identifies herself as a liberal. Previously alternating between dimly articulated religious positions, she now declares herself an agnostic. Previously confused and uncertain about her sexual emotions, she now understands herself as an unabashed hedonist in this area. And so on and so forth, with the same reality—and identity—stabilizing process at work on the husband. Both world and self thus take on a firmer, more reliable character for both partners.

Furthermore, it is not only the ongoing experience of the two partners that is constantly shared and passed through the conversational apparatus. The same sharing extends into the past. The two distinct biographies, as subjectively apprehended by the two individuals who have lived through them, are overruled and re-interpreted in the course of their conversation. Sooner or later, they will "tell all"—or, more correctly, they will tell it in such a way that it fits into the self-definitions objectivated in the marital relationship. The couple thus construct not only present reality but reconstruct past reality as well, fabricating a common memory that integrates the recollections of the two individual pasts.[16] The comic fulfilment of this process may be seen in those cases when one partner "remembers" more clearly what happened in the other's past than the other does—and corrects him accordingly. Similarly, there occurs a sharing of future horizons, which leads not only to stabilization, but inevitably to a narrowing of the future projections of each partner. Before marriage the individual typically plays with quite discrepant daydreams in which his future self is projected.[17] Having now considerably stabilized his self-image, the married individual will have to project the future in accordance with this maritally defined identity. This narrowing of future horizons begins with the obvious external limitations that marriage entails, as, for example, with regard to vocational and career plans. However, it extends also to the more general possibilities of the individual's biography. To return to a previous illustration, the wife, having "found herself" as a liberal, an agnostic and a "sexually healthy" person, *ipso facto* liquidates the possibilities of becoming an anarchist, a Catholic or a Lesbian. At least until further notice she has decided upon who she is—and, by the same token, upon who she will be. The stabilization brought about by marriage thus affects the total reality in which the partners exist. In the most far-reaching sense of the word, the married individual "settles down"—and *must* do so, if the marriage is to be viable, in accordance with its contemporary institutional definition.

It cannot be sufficiently strongly

---

[16] Cf. Maurice Halbwachs, *Les Cadres sociaux de la mémoire* (Paris: Presses universitares de France 1952), especially 146–77; also cf. Peter Berger, *Invitation to Sociology—A Humanistic Perspective* (Garden City, N.Y.: Doubleday-Anchor 1963), 54–65 (available in Penguin).

[17] Cf. Schutz, *Collected Papers,* I, 72–3, 79–82.

emphasized that this process is typically unapprehended, almost automatic in character. The protagonists of the marriage drama do *not* set out deliberately to re-create their world. Each continues to live in a world that is taken for granted—and keeps its taken-for-granted character even as it is metamorphosed. The new world that the married partners, Prometheus-like, have called into being is perceived by them as the normal world in which they have lived before. Re-constructed present and re-interpreted past are perceived as a continuum, extending forwards into a commonly projected future. The dramatic change that has occurred remains, in bulk, unapprehended and unarticulated. And where it forces itself upon the individual's attention, it is retrojected into the past, explained as having always been there, though perhaps in a hidden way. Typically, the reality that has been "invented" within the marital conversation is subjectively perceived as a "discovery." Thus the partners "discover" themselves and the world, "who they really are," "what they really believe," "how they really feel, and always have felt, about so-and-so." This retrojection of the world being produced all the time by themselves serves to enhance the stability of this world and at the same time to assuage the "existential anxiety" that, probably inevitably, accompanies the perception that nothing but one's own narrow shoulders supports the universe in which one has chosen to live. If one may put it like this, it is psychologically more tolerable to be Columbus than to be Prometheus.

The use of the term "stabilization" should not detract from the insight into the difficulty and precariousness of this world-building enterprise. Often enough, the new universe collapses *in statu nascendi*. Many more times it continues over a period, swaying perilously back and forth as the two partners try to hold it up, finally to be abandoned as an impossible undertaking. If one conceives of the marital conversation as the principal drama and the two partners as the principal protagonists of the drama, then one can look upon the other individuals involved as the supporting chorus for the central dramatic action. Children, friends, relatives and casual acquaintances all have their part in reinforcing the tenuous structure of the new reality. It goes without saying that the children form the most important part of this supporting chorus. Their very existence is predicated on the maritally established world. The marital partners themselves are in charge of their socialization *into* this world, which to them has a pre-existent and self-evident character. They are taught from the beginning to speak precisely those lines that lend themselves to a supporting chorus, from their first invocations of "Daddy" and "Mummy" on to their adoption of the parents' ordering and typifying apparatus that now defines *their* world as well. The marital conversation is now in the process of becoming a family symposium, with the necessary consequence that its objectivations rapidly gain in density, plausibility and durability.

In sum: the process that we have been inquiring into is, ideal-typically, one in which reality is crystallized, narrowed and stabilized. Ambivalences are converted into certainties. Typifications of self and of others become settled. Most generally, possibilities become facticities. What is more, this process of transformation remains, most of the time, unapprehended by those who are both its authors and its objects.[18]

We have analyzed in some detail the process that, we contend, entitles us to describe marriage as a nomic instrumentality. It may now be well to turn back once more to the macrosocial context in which this process takes place—a process that, to repeat, is peculiar to our society as far as the institution of marriage is concerned, although it obviously expresses much more general human facts. The narrowing and stabilization of identity is functional in a society that, in its major public institutions, must insist on rigid controls over the individual's conduct. At the same time, the narrow enclave of the nuclear family serves as a macrosocially innocuous "play area," in which the individual can safely exercise his world-building proclivities without upsetting any of the important social, economic and political applecarts. Barred from expanding himself into the area occupied by these major institutions, he is given plenty of leeway to "discover himself" in his marriage and his family, and, in view of the difficulty of this undertaking, is provided with a number of auxiliary agencies that stand ready to assist him (such as counseling, psychotherapeutic and religious agencies).

[18] The phenomena here discussed could also be formulated effectively in terms of the Marxian categories of reification and false consciousness. Jean-Paul Sartre's recent work, especially *Critique de la raison dialectique*, seeks to integrate these categories within a phenomenological analysis of human conduct. Also cf. Henri Lefebvre, *Critique de la vie quotidienne* (Paris: l'Arche 1958–61).

The marital adventure can be relied upon to absorb a large amount of energy that might otherwise be expended more dangerously. The ideological themes of familism, romantic love, sexual expression, maturity and social adjustment, with the pervasive psychologistic anthropology that underlies them all, function to legitimate this enterprise. Also, the narrowing and stabilization of the individual's principal area of conversation within the nuclear family is functional in a society that requires high degrees of both geographical and social mobility. The segregated little world of the family can be easily detached from one milieu and transposed into another without appreciably interfering with the central processes going on in it. Needless to say, we are not suggesting that these functions are deliberately planned or even apprehended by some mythical ruling directorate of the society. Like most social phenomena, whether they be macro- or microscopic, these functions are typically unintended and unarticulated. What is more, the functionality would be impaired if it were too widely apprehended.

We believe that the above theoretical considerations serve to give a new perspective on various empirical facts studied by family sociologists. As we have emphasized a number of times, our considerations are ideal-typical in intention. We have been interested in marriage at a normal age in urban, middle-class, western societies. We cannot discuss here such special problems as marriages or remarriages at a more advanced age, marriage in the remaining rural subcultures, or in ethnic or lower-class minority groups. We feel quite justified in this limitation of scope, however, by the empirical findings that tend towards the view that a global marriage type is emerging in the central strata of modern industrial societies.[19] This type, commonly referred to as the nuclear family, has been analyzed in terms of a shift from the so-called family of orientation to the so-called family of procreation as the most important reference for the individual.[20] In addition to the well-known socioeconomic reasons for this shift, most of them rooted in the development of industrialism, we would argue that important macrosocial functions pertain to the nomic process within the nuclear family, as we have analyzed it. This functionality of the nuclear family must, furthermore, be seen in conjunction with the familistic ideology that both reflects and reinforces it. A few specific empirical points may suffice to indicate the applicability of our theoretical perspective. To make these we shall use selected American data.

The trend towards marriage at an earlier age has been noted.[21] This

has been correctly related to such factors as urban freedom, sexual emancipation and equalitarian values. We would add the important fact that a child raised in the circumscribed world of the nuclear family is stamped by it in terms of his psychological needs and social expectations. Having to live in the larger society from which the nuclear family is segregated, the adolescent soon feels the need for a "little world" of his own, having been socialized in such a way that only by having such a world to withdraw into can he successfully cope with the anonymous "big world" that confronts him as soon as he steps outside his parental home. In other words, to be "at home" in society entails, *per definitionem,* the construction of a maritally based sub-world. The parental home itself facilitates such an early jump into marriage precisely because its controls are very narrow in scope and leave the adolescent to his own nomic devices at an early age. As has been studied in considerable detail, the adolescent peer group functions as a transitional *nomos* between the two family worlds in the individual's biography.[22]

The equalization in the age of the marriage partners has also been noted.[23] This is certainly also to be related to equalitarian values and, concomitantly, to the decline in the "double standard" of sexual mo-

19 Cf. Renate Mayntz, *Die moderne Familie* (Stuttgart: Enke 1955); Helmut Schelsky, *Wandlungen der deutschen Familie in der Gegenwart* (Stuttgart: Enke 1955); Maximilien Sorre (ed.), *Sociologie comparée de la famille contemporaine* (Paris: Centre National de la Recherche Scientifique 1955); Ruth Anshen (ed.), *The Family—Its Function and Destiny* (New York: Harper 1959); Norman Bell and Ezra Vogel, *A Modern Introduction to the Family* (Routledge & Kegan Paul 1961).

20 Cf. Talcott Parsons, *Essays in Sociological Theory* (Collier-Macmillan 1949), 233–50.

21 In these as well as the following references to empirical studies we naturally make no attempt at comprehensiveness. References are given as representative of a much larger body of materials. Cf. Paul Glick, *American Families* (New York: Wiley 1957), 54. Also cf. his "The family cycle,"

American Sociological Review (April 1947), 164–74. Also cf. Bureau of the Census, *Statistical Abstracts of the United States* 1956 and 1958; *Current Population Reports,* Series P-20, no. 96 (Nov. 1959).

22 Cf. David Riesman, *The Lonely Crowd* (New Haven: Yale University Press 1953), 29–40; Frederick Elkin, *The Child and Society* (New York: Random House 1960), *passim.*

23 Cf. references given above note 21.

rality. Also, however, this fact is very conducive to the common reality-constructing enterprise that we have analyzed. One of the features of the latter, as we have pointed out, is the re-construction of the two biographies in terms of a cohesive and mutually correlated common memory. This task is evidently facilitated if the two partners are of roughly equal age. Another empirical finding to which our considerations are relevant is the choice of marriage partners within similar socio-economic backgrounds.[24] Apart from the obvious practical pressures towards such limitations of choice, the latter also ensure sufficient similarity in the biographically accumulated stocks of experience to facilitate the described reality-constructing process. This would also offer additional explanation to the observed tendency to narrow the limitations of marital choice even further, for example in terms of religious background.[25]

There now exists a considerable body of data on the adoption and mutual adjustment of marital roles.[26]

Nothing in our consideration detracts from the analyses made of these data by sociologists interested primarily in the processes of group interaction. We would only argue that something more fundamental is involved in this role-taking—namely, the individual's relationship to reality as such. Each role in the marital situation carries with it a universe of discourse, broadly given by cultural definition, but continually re-actualized in the ongoing conversation between the mariage partners. Put simply: marriage involves not only stepping into new roles, but, beyond this, stepping into a new world. The *mutuality* of adjustment may again be related to the rise of marital equalitarianism, in which comparable effort is demanded of both partners.

Most directly related to our considerations are data that pertain to the greater stability of married as against unmarried individuals.[27] Though frequently presented in misleading psychological terms (such as "greater emotional stability," "greater maturity," and so on), these data are sufficiently validated to be used not only by marriage counselors but in the risk calculations of insurance companies. We would contend that our theoretical perspective places these data into a much more intelligible sociological frame of reference, which also happens to be free of the particular value bias with which the psychological terms are loaded. It is, of course, quite true that married people are more stable

[24] Cf. W. Lloyd Warner and Paul Lunt, *The Social Life of a Modern Community* (New Haven: Yale University Press 1941), 436–40; August Hollingshead, "Cultural factors in the selection of marriage mates," *American Sociological Review* (October 1950), 619–27. Also cf. Ernest Burgess and Paul Wallin, "Homogamy in social characteristics," *American Journal of Sociology* (September 1943), 109–24.

[25] Cf. Gerhard Lenski, *The Religious Factor* (Garden City, N.Y.: Doubleday 1961), 48–50.

[26] Cf. Leonard Cottrell, "Roles in marital adjustment," *Publications of the American Sociological Society* (1933), 27, 107–15; Willard Waller and Reuben Hill, *The Family —A Dynamic Interpretation* (New York: Dryden 1951), 253–71; Morris Zelditch, "Role differentiation in the nuclear family," in Parsons and Bales, op. cit., 307–52. For a

general discussion of role interaction in small groups, cf. especially George Homans, *The Human Group* (Routledge & Kegan Paul 1951).

[27] Cf. Waller and Hill, op. cit., 253–71, for an excellent summation of such data.

emotionally (i.e. operating within a more controlled scope of emotional expression), more mature in their views (i.e. inhabiting a firmer and narrower world in conformity with the expectations of society), and more sure of themselves (i.e. having objectivated a more stable and fix-ated self-definition). *Therefore* they are more liable to be psychologically balanced (i.e. having sealed off much of their "anxiety," and reduced am-bivalence as well as openness towards new possibilities of self-definition) and socially predictable (i.e. keeping their conduct well within the so-cially esablished safety rules). All of these phenomena are concomi-tants of the overall fact of having "settled down"—cognitively, emo-tionally, in terms of self-identifica-tion. To speak of these phenomena as indicators of "mental health," let alone of "adjustment to reality," overlooks the decisive fact that real-ity is socially constructed and that psychological conditions of all sorts are grounded in a social matrix.

We would say, very simply, that the married individual comes to live in a more stable world, from which fact certain psychological conse-quences can be readily deduced. To bestow some sort of higher ontologi-cal status upon these psychological consequences is *ipso facto* a symptom of the mis-or non-apprehension of the social process that has produced them. Furthermore, the compulsion to legitimate the stabilized marital world, be it in psychologistic or in traditional religious terms, is an-other expression of the precarious-ness of its construction.[28] This is

not the place to pursue any further the ideological processes involved in this. Suffice it to say that contempo-rary psychology functions to sustain this precarious world by assigning to it the status of "normalcy," a legiti-mating operation that increasingly links up with the older religious as-signment of the status of "sacred-ness." Both legitimating agencies have established their own rites of passage, validating myths and rituals, and individualized repair services for crisis situations. Whether one legiti-mates one's maritally constructed reality in terms of "mental health" or of the "sacrament of marriage" is today largely left to free consumer preference, but it is indicative of the crystallization of a new overall uni-verse of discourse that it is increas-ingly possible to do both at the same time.

Finally, we would point here to the empirical data on divorce.[29] The prevalence and, indeed, increas-ing prevalence of divorce might at first appear as a counter-argument to our theoretical considerations. We would contend that the very opposite is the case, as the data themselves bear out. Typically, individuals in our society do not divorce because marriage has become unimportant to them, but because it has become so important that they have no toler-ance for the less than completely successful marital arrangement they have contracted with the particular individual in question. This is more fully understood when one has grasped the crucial need for the sort of world that only marriage can pro-duce in our society, a world without which the individual is powerfully threatened with anomie in the full-

28 Cf. Dennison Nash and Peter Berger, "The family, the child and the religious re-vival in suburbia," *Journal for the Scientific Study of Religion* (Fall 1962), 85–93.

29 Cf. Bureau of the Census, op. cit.

est sense of the word. Also, the frequency of divorce simply reflects the difficulty and demanding character of the whole undertaking. The empirical fact that the great majority of divorced individuals plan to remarry and a good majority of them actually do, at least in America, fully bears out this contention.[30]

The purpose of this article is not polemic, nor do we wish to advocate any particular values concerning marriage. We have sought to debunk the familistic ideology only in so far as it serves to obfuscate a sociological understanding of the phenomenon. Our purpose has rather been twofold. First, we wanted to show that it is possible to develop a sociological theory of marriage that is based on clearly sociological presuppositions, without operating with psychological or psychiatric categories that have dubious value with-

[30] Cf. Talcott Parsons, "Age and Sex in the Social Structure of the United States," *American Sociological Review* (December 1942), 604–16; Paul Glick, "First marriages and remarriages," *American Sociological Review* (December 1949), 726–34; William Goode, *After Divorce* (Chicago: Free Press 1956), 269–85.

in a sociological frame of reference. We believe that such a sociological theory of marriage is generally useful for a fully conscious awareness of existence in contemporary society, and not only for the sociologist. Secondly, we have used the case of marriage for an exercise in the sociology of knowledge, a discipline that we regard as most promising. Hitherto this discipline has been almost exclusively concerned with macrosociological questions, such as those dealing with the relationship of intellectual history to social processes. We believe that the microsociological focus is equally important for this discipline. The sociology of knowledge must not only be concerned with the great universes of meaning that history offers up for our inspection, but with the many little workshops in which living individuals keep hammering away at the construction and maintenance of these universes. In this way, the sociologist can make an important contribution to the illumination of that everyday world in which we all live and which we help fashion in the course of our biography.

negotiating reality: notes on power in the assessment of responsibility*

THOMAS J. SCHEFF

This paper illustrates the difference between absolute and social conceptions of responsibility, by employing the perspective of the sociology of knowledge. Comparing the degree of shared awareness and the organization of the format of the transaction in initial psychiatric and legal interviews, propositions showing the relationship between the power and authority of the interactants, and the resultant shared definition of the client's responsibility, are suggested. The implications of these points for psychiatric and legal policy, and for social science research are discussed in the conclusion.

The use of interrogation to reconstruct parts of an individual's past history is a common occurrence in human affairs. Reporters, jealous lovers, and policemen on the beat are often faced with the task of determining events in another person's life, and the extent to which he was responsible for those events. The most dramatic use of interrogation to determine responsibility is in criminal trials. As in everyday life, criminal trials are concerned with both act and intent. Courts, in most

Reprinted from Thomas J. Scheff, "Negotiating Reality: Notes on Power in the Assessment of Responsibility," SOCIAL PROBLEMS, 16 (Summer 1968), 3–17 by permission of the author and The Society for the Study of Social Problems.

* The author wishes to acknowledge the help of the following persons who criticized earlier drafts: Aaron Cicourel, Donald Cressey, Joan Emerson, Erving Goffman, Michael Katz, Lewis Kurke, Robert Levy, Sohan Lal Sharma, and Paul Weubben. The paper was written during a fellowship provided by the Social Science Research Institute, University of Hawaii.

cases, first determine whether the defendant performed a legally forbidden act. If it is found that he did so, the court then must decide whether he was "responsible" for the act. Reconstructive work of this type goes on less dramatically in a wide variety of other settings, as well. The social worker determining a client's eligibility for unemployment compensation, for example, seeks not only to establish that the client actually is unemployed, but that he has actively sought employment, i.e., that he himself is not responsible for being out of work.

This paper will contrast two perspectives on the process of reconstructing past events for the purpose of fixing responsibility. The first perspective stems from the common sense notion that interrogation, when it is sufficiently skillful, is essentially neutral. Responsibility for past actions can be fixed absolutely and independently of the method of reconstruction. This perspective is held by the typical member of society, engaged in his day-to-day tasks. It is also held, in varying degrees, by most professional interrogators. The basic working doctrine is one of *absolute* responsibility. This point of view actually entails the comparison of two different kinds of items: first, the fixing of actions and intentions, and secondly, comparing these actions and intentions to some pre-determined criteria of responsibility. The basic premise of the doctrine of absolute responsibility is that both actions and intentions, on the one hand, and the criteria of responsibility, on the other, are absolute, in that they can be assessed independently of social context.[1]

An alternative approach follows from the sociology of knowledge. From this point of view, the reality within which members of society conduct their lives is largely of their own construction.[2] Since much of reality is a construction, there may be multiple realities, existing side by side, in harmony or in competition. It follows, if one maintains this stance, that the assessment of responsibility involves the construction of reality by members; construction both of actions and intentions, on the one hand, and of criteria of responsibility, on the other. The former process, the continuous reconstruction of the normative order, has long been the focus of sociological concern.[3] The discussion in this paper will be limited, for the most part, to the former process, the way in which actions and intentions are constructed in the act of assessing responsibility.

My purpose is to argue that responsibility is at least partly a product of social structure. The alternative to the doctrine of absolute responsibility is that of relative responsibility: the assessment of responsibility always includes a process of negotiation. In this process, responsibility is in part constructed by the negotiating parties. To illustrate this thesis, excerpts from two dialogues of negotiation will be discussed: a real psychotherapeutic interview, and an interview between a defense attorney and his client, taken from a work of fiction. Before presenting these excerpts it will be useful to review some prior discussions of negotiation, the first in courts of law, the second in medical diagnosis.[4]

The negotiation of pleas in criminal courts, sometimes referred to as "bargain justice," has been frequently noted by observers of legal

---

[1] The doctrine of absolute responsibility is clearly illustrated in psychiatric and legal discussions of the issue of "criminal responsibility," i.e., the use of mental illness as an excuse from criminal conviction. An example of the assumption of absolute criteria of responsibility is found in the following quotation, "The finding that someone is criminally responsible means to the psychiatrist that the criminal must change his behavior before he can resume his position in society. *This injunction is dictated not by morality, but, so to speak, by reality.*" See Edward J. Sachar, "Behavioral Science and Criminal Law," *Scientific American*, 209 (1963), pp. 39–45, (emphasis added).

[2] *Cf.* Peter L. Berger and Thomas Luckmann, *The Social Construction of Reality: A Treatise in the Sociology of Knowledge*, New York: Doubleday, 1966.

[3] The classic treatment of this issue is found in E. Durkheim, *The Elementary Forms of the Religious Life.*

[4] A sociological application of the concept of negotiation, in a different context, is found in Anselm Strauss, *et al.*, "The Hospital and its Negotiated Order," in Eliot Freidson, editor, *The Hospital in Modern Society*, New York: Free Press, 1963, pp. 147–169.

processes.[5] The defense attorney, or (in many cases, apparently) the defendant himself, strikes a bargain with the prosecutor—a plea of guilty will be made, provided that the prosecutor will reduce the charge. For example, a defendant arrested on suspicion of armed robbery may arrange to plead guilty to the charge of unarmed robbery. The prosecutor obtains ease of conviction from the bargain, the defendant, leniency.

Although no explicit estimates are given, it appears from observers' reports that the great majority of criminal convictions are negotiated. Newman states:

> A major characteristic of criminal justice administration, particularly in jurisdictions characterized by legislatively fixed sentences, is charge reduction to elicit pleas of guilty. Not only does the efficient functioning of criminal justice rest upon a high proportion of guilty pleas, but plea bargaining is closely linked with attempts to individualize justice, to obtain certain desirable conviction consequences, and to avoid undesirable ones such as "undeserved" mandatory sentences.[6]

It would appear that the bargaining process is accepted as routine. In the three jurisdictions Newman studied, there were certain meeting places where the defendant, his client, and a representative of the prosecutor's office routinely met to negotiate the plea. It seems clear that

in virtually all but the most unusual cases, the interested parties expected to, and actually did, negotiate the plea.

From these comments on the routine acceptance of plea bargaining in the courts, one might expect that this process would be relatively open and unambiguous. Apparently, however, there is some tension between the fact of bargaining and moral expectations concerning justice. Newman refers to this tension by citing two contradictory statements: an actual judicial opinion, "Justice and liberty are not the subjects of bargaining and barter"; and an off-the-cuff statment by another judge, "All law is compromise." A clear example of this tension is provided by an excerpt from a trial and Newman's comments on it.

The following questions were asked of a defendant after he had pleaded guilty to unarmed robbery when the original charge was armed robbery. This reduction is common, and the judge was fully aware that the plea was negotiated:

Judge: You want to plead guilty to robbery unarmed?
Defendant: Yes, Sir.
Judge: Your plea of guilty is free and voluntary?
Defendant: Yes, Sir.
Judge: No one has promised you anything?
Defendant: No.
Judge: No one has induced you to plead guilty?
Defendant: No.
Judge: You're pleading guilty because you are guilty?
Defendant: Yes:
Judge: I'll accept your plea of guilty to robbery unarmed and refer it to the probation depart-

5 Newman reports a study in this area, together with a review of earlier work, in "The Negotiated Plea," Part III of Donald J. Newman, *Conviction: The Determination of Guilt or Innocence Without Trial*, Boston: Little, Brown, 1966, pp. 76–130.

6 *Ibid.*, p. 76.

ment for a report and for sentencing Dec. 28.[7]

The delicacy of the relationship between appearance and reality is apparently confusing, even for the sociologist-observer. Newman's comment on this exchange has an Alice-in-Wonderland quality:

This is a routine procedure designed to satisfy the statutory requirement and is not intended to disguise the process of charge reduction.[8]

If we put the tensions between the different realities aside for the moment, we can say that there is an explicit process of negotiation between the defendant and the prosecution which is a part of the legal determination of guilt or innocence, or in the terms used above, the assessment of responsibility.

In medical diagnosis, a similar process of negotiation occurs, but is much less self-conscious than plea bargaining. The English psychoanalyst Michael Balint refers to this process as one of "offers and responses":

Some of the people who, for some reason or other, find it difficult to cope with problems of their lives resort to becoming ill. If the doctor has the opportunity of seeing them in the first phases of their being ill, i.e. before they settle down to a definite "organized" illness, he may observe that the patients, so to speak, offer or propose various illnesses, and that they have to go on offering new illnesses until between doctor and patient an agreement can be reached resulting in the acceptance by both

[7] Ibid., p. 83.
[8] Idem.

of them of one of the illnesses as justified.[9]

Balint gives numerous examples indicating that patients propose reasons for their coming to the doctor which are rejected, one by one, by the physician, who makes counter-proposals until an "illness" acceptable to both parties is found. If "definition of the situation" is substituted for "illness," Balint's observations become relevant to a wide variety of transactions, including the kind of interrogation discussed above. The fixing of responsibility is a process in which the client offers definitions of the situation, to which the interrogator responds. After a series of offers and responses, a definition of the situation acceptable to both the client and the interrogator is reached.

Balint has observed that the negotiation process leads physicians to influence the outcome of medical examinations, independently of the patient's condition. He refers to this process as the "apostolic function" of the doctor, arguing that the physician induces patients to have the kind of illness that the physician thinks is proper:

Apostolic mission or function means in the first place that every doctor has a vague, but almost unshakably firm,

[9] Michael Balint, The Doctor, His Patient, and The Illness, New York: International Universities Press, 1957, p. 18. A description of the negotiations between patients in a tuberculosis sanitarium and their physicians is found in Julius A. Roth, Timetables: Structuring the Passage of Time in Hospital Treatment and Other Careers. Indianapolis: Bobbs-Merrill, 1963, pp. 48–59. Obviously, some cases are more susceptible to negotiation than others. Balint implies that the great majority of cases in medical practice are negotiated.

idea of how a patient ought to behave when ill. Although this idea is
anything but explicit and concrete,
it is immensely powerful, and influences, as we have found, practically
every detail of the doctor's work with
his patients. It was almost as if every
doctor had revealed knowledge of
what was right and what was wrong
for patients to expect and to endure,
and further, as if he had a sacred
duty to convert to his faith all the
ignorant and unbelieving among his
patients.[10]

Implicit in this statement is the notion that interrogator and client
have unequal power in determining
the resultant definition of the situation. The interrogator's definition
of the situation plays an important
part in the joint definition of the
situation which is finally negotiated.
Moreover, his definition is more important than the client's in determining the final outcome of the
negotiation, principally because he
is well trained, secure, and self-con-
fident in his role in the transaction,
whereas the client is untutored, anxious, and uncertain about his role.
Stated simply, the subject, because
of these conditions, is likely to be
susceptible to the influence of the
interrogator.

Note that plea bargaining and the
process of "offers and responses" in
diagnosis differ in the degree of self-
consciousness of the participants. In
plea bargaining the process is at
least partly visible to the participants
themselves. There appears to be
some ambiguity about the extent
to which the negotiation is morally
acceptable to some of the commentators, but the parties to the negotiations appear to be aware that bar-

[10] Balint, *op. cit.*, p. 216.

gaining is going on, and accept the
process as such. The bargaining
process in diagnosis, however, is
much more subterranean. Certainly
neither physicians nor patients recognize the offers and responses process as being bargaining. There is
no commonly accepted vocabulary
for describing diagnostic bargaining,
such as there is in the legal analogy,
e.g. "copping out" or "copping a
plea." It may be that in legal processes there is some appreciation of
the different kinds of reality, i.e. the
difference between the public (official, legal) reality and private reality, whereas in medicine this difference is not recognized.

The discussion so far has suggested that much of reality is arrived
at by negotiation. This thesis was
illustrated by materials presented on
legal processes by Newman, and
medical processes by Balint. These
processes are similar in that they
appear to represent clear instances
of the negotiation of reality. The
instances are different in that the
legal bargaining processes appear to
be more open and accepted than the
diagnostic process. In order to outline some of the dimensions of the
negotiation process, and to establish
some of the limitations of the analyses by Newman and Balint, two excerpts of cases of bargaining will be
discussed: the first taken from an
actual psychiatric "intake" interview, the second from a fictional account of a defense lawyer's first interview with his client.

THE PROCESS OF NEGOTIATION

The psychiatric interview to be discussed is from the first interview in
The Initial Interview in Psychiatric

Practice.[11] The patient is a thirty-four year old nurse, who feels, as she says, "irritable, tense, depressed." She appears to be saying from the very beginning of the interview that the external situation in which she lives is the cause of her troubles. She focuses particularly on her husband's behavior. She says he is an alcoholic, is verbally abusive, and won't let her work. She feels that she is cooped up in the house all day with her two small children, but that when he is home at night (on the nights when he *is* at home) he will have nothing to do with her and the children. She intimates, in several ways, that he does not serve as a sexual companion. She has thought of divorce, but has rejected it for various reasons (for example, she is afraid she couldn't take proper care of the children, finance the baby sitters, etc.). She feels trapped.[12]

In the concluding paragraph of their description of this interview, Gill, Newman, and Redlich give this summary:

> The patient, pushed by we know not what or why at the time (the children—somebody to talk to) comes for help apparently for what she thinks of as help with her external situation (her husband's behavior as she sees it). The therapist does not respond to this but seeks her role and how it is that she plays such a role. Listening to the recording it sounds as if the therapist is at first bored and disinterested and the patient defensive. He gets down to work and keeps asking, "What is it all about?" Then he becomes more interested and sympathetic and at the same time very active (participating) and demanding. *It sounds as if she keeps saying, "This is the trouble." He says, "No! Tell me the trouble." She says, "This is it!" He says, "No, tell me," until the patient finally says, "Well I'll tell you." Then the therapist says, "Good! I'll help you."* [13]

From this summary it is apparent that there is a close fit between Balint's idea of the negotiation of diagnosis through offers and responses, and what took place in this psychiatric interview. It is difficult, however, to document the details. Most of the psychiatrist's responses, rejecting the patient's offers, do not appear in the written transcript, but they are fairly obvious as one listens to the recording. Two particular features of the psychiatrist's responses especially stand out: (1) the flatness of intonation in his responses to the patient's complaints about her external circumstances; and (2) the rapidity with which he introduces new topics, through questioning, when she is talking about her husband.

Some features of the psychiatrist's coaching are verbal, however:

T. 95: Has anything happened recently that makes it . . . you feel that . . . ah . . . you're sort of coming to the end of your rope? I mean I wondered what led you . . .

P. 95: (Interrupting.) It's nothing special. It's just everything in general.

---

11 Merton Gill, Richard Newman, and Fredrick C. Redlich, *The Initial Interview in Psychiatric Practice,* New York: International Universities Press, 1954.

12 Since this interview is complex and subtle, the reader is invited to listen to it himself, and compare his conclusions with those discussed here. The recorded interview is available on the first L.P. record that accompanies Gill, Newman, and Redlich, *op. cit.*

13 *Ibid.,* p. 133. (Italics added.)

T. 96: What led you to come to a . . .

P. 96: (Interrupting.) It's just that I . . .

T. 97: . . . a psychiatrist just now? (1)

P. 97: Because I felt that the older girl was getting tense as a result of . . . of my being stewed up all the time.

T. 98: Mmmhnn.

P. 98: Not having much patience with her.

T. 99: Mmmhnn. (Short pause.) Mmm. And how had you imagined that a psychiatrist could help with this? (Short pause.) (2)

P. 99: Mmm . . . maybe I could sort of get straightened out . . . straighten things out in my mind. I'm confused. Sometimes I can't remember things that I've done, whether I've done 'em or not or whether they happened.

T. 100: What is it that you want to straighten out? (Pause.)

P. 100: I think I seem mixed up.

T. 101: Yeah? You see that, it seems to me, is something that we really should talk about because . . . ah . . . from a certain point of view somebody might say, "Well now, it's all very simple. She's unhappy and disturbed because her husband is behaving this way, and · unless something can be done about that how could she expect to feel any other way." But, instead of that, you come to the psychiatrist, and you say that you think there's something about you that needs straightening out. (3) I don't quite get it. Can you explain that to me? (Short pause.)

P. 101: I sometimes wonder if I'm emotionally grown up.

T. 102: By which you mean what?

P. 102: When you're married you should have one mate. You shouldn't go around and look at other men.

T. 103: You've been looking at other men?

P. 103: I look at them, but that's all.

T. 104: Mmmhnn. What you mean . . . you mean a grown-up person should accept the marital situation whatever it happens to be?

P. 104: That was the way I was brought up. Yes. (Sighs.)

T. 105: You think that would be a sign of emotional maturity?

P. 105: No.

T. 106: No. So?

P. 106: Well, if you rebel against the laws of society you have to take the consequences.

T. 107: Yes?

P. 107: And it's just that I . . . I'm not willing to take the consequences. I . . . I don't think it's worth it.

T. 108: Mmhnn. So in the meantime then while you're in this very difficult situation, you find yourself reacting in a way that you don't like and that you think is . . . ah . . . damaging to your children and yourself? Now what can be done about that?

P. 108: (Sniffs; sighs.) I dunno. That's why I came to see you.

T. 109: Yes. I was just wondering what you had in mind. Did you think a psychiatrist could . . . ah . . . help you face this kind of a situation calmly and easily and maturely? (4) Is that it?

P. 109: More or less. I need somebody to talk to who isn't emotionally involved with the family. I have a few friends, but I don't like to bore them. I don't think they should know . . . ah

. . . all the intimate details of what goes on.

T. 110: Yeah?

P. 110: It becomes food for gossip.

T. 111: Mmmhnn.

P. 111: Besides they're in . . . they're emotionally involved because they're my friends. They tell me not to stand for it, but they don't understand that if I put my foot down it'll only get stepped on.

T. 112: Yeah.

P. 112: That he can make it miserable for me in other ways. . . .

T. 113: Mmm.

P. 113: . . . which he does.

T. 114: Mmmhnn. In other words, you find yourself in a situation and don't know how to cope with it really.

P. 114: I don't.

T. 115: You'd like to be able to talk that through and come to understand it better and learn how to cope with it or deal with it in some way. Is that right?

P. 115: I'd like to know how to deal with it more effectively.

T. 116: Yeah. Does that mean you feel convinced that the way you're dealing with it now. . . .

P. 116: There's something wrong of course.

T. 117: . . . something wrong with that. Mmmhnn.

P. 117: There's something wrong with it.[14]

Note that the therapist reminds her *four times* in this short sequence that she has come to see a *psychiatrist*. Since the context of these reminders is one in which the patient it attributing her difficulties to an external situation, particularly her husband, it seems plausible to hear these reminders as subtle requests for analysis of her own contributions to her difficulties. This interpretation is supported by the therapist's subsequent remarks. When the patient once again describes external problems, the therapist tries the following tack:

T. 125: I notice that you've used a number of psychiatric terms here and there. Were you specially interested in that in your training, or what?

P. 125: Well, my great love is psychology.

T. 126: Psychology?

P. 126: Mmmhnn.

T. 127: How much have you studied?

P. 127: Oh (Sighs.) what you have in your nurse's training, and I've had general psych, child and adolescent psych, and the abnormal psych.

T. 128: Mmmhnn. Well, tell me . . . ah . . . what would you say if you had to explain yourself what is the problem?

P. 128: You don't diagnose yourself very well, at least I don't.

T. 129: Well you can make a stab at it. (Pause.)[15]

This therapeutic thrust is rewarded: the patient gives a long account of her early life which indicates a belief that she was not "adjusted" in the past. The interview continues:

T. 135: And what conclusions do you draw from all this about why you're not adjusting now the way you think you should?

P. 135: Well, I wasn't adjusted then. I feel that I've come a long

[14] *Ibid.,* pp. 176–182. (Numbers in parenthesis added.)

[15] *Ibid.,* pp. 186–187.

way, but I don't think I'm
still . . . I still don't feel
that I'm adjusted.

T. 136: And you don't regard your
husband as being the dif-
ficulty? You think it lies
within yourself?

P. 136: Oh he's a difficulty all right,
but I figure that even . . .
ah . . . had . . . if it had
been other things that . . .
this probably—this state—
would've come on me.

T. 137: Oh you do think so?

P. 137: (Sighs.) I don't think he's
the sole factor. No.

T. 138: And what are the factors
within. . . .

P. 138: I mean. . . .

T. 139: . . . yourself?

P. 139: Oh it's probably remorse for
the past, things I did.

T. 140: Like what? (Pause.) It's
sumping' hard to tell, hunh?
(Short pause.) [16]

After some parrying, the patient
tells the therapist what he wants to
hear. She feels guilty because she
was pregnant by another man when
her present husband proposed. She
cries. The therapist tells the patient
she needs, and will get psychiatric
help, and the interview ends, the patient still crying. The negotiational
aspects of the process are clear: After
the patient has spent most of the
interview blaming her current difficulties on external circumstances,
she tells the therapist a deep secret
about which she feels intensely
guilty. The patient, and not the
husband, is at fault. The therapist's
tone and manner change abruptly.
From being bored, distant, and rejecting, he becomes warm and solici-
tous. Through a process of offers
and responses, the therapist and pa-

tient have, by implication, negotiated a shared definition of the situation—the patient, not the husband,
is responsible.

A CONTRASTING CASE

The negotiation process can, of
course, proceed on the opposite premise, namely that the client is not
responsible. An ideal example
would be an interrogation of a client
by a skilled defense lawyer. Unfortunately, we have been unable to
locate a verbatim transcript of a defense lawyer's initial interview with
his client. There is available, however, a fictional portrayal of such an
interview, written by a man with
extensive experience as defense lawyer, prosecutor, and judge. The
excerpt to follow is taken from the
novel, *Anatomy of a Murder.*[17]

The defense lawyer, in his initial
contact with his client, briefly questions him regarding his actions on
the night of the killing. The client
states that he discovered that the
deceased, Barney Quill, had raped
his wife; he then goes on to state
that he then left his wife, found
Quill and shot him.

". . . How long did you remain with
your wife before you went to the
hotel bar?"
"I don't remember."
"I think it is important, and I sug-
gest you try."
After a pause. "Maybe an hour."
"Maybe more?"
"Maybe."
"Maybe less?"
"Maybe."

[16] *Ibid.,* pp. 192–194.

[17] Robert Traver, *Anatomy of a Murder,*
New York: Dell, 1959.

I paused and lit a cigar. I took my time. I had reached a point where a few wrong answers to a few right questions would leave me with a client—if I took his case—whose cause was legally defenseless. Either I stopped now and begged off and let some other lawyer worry over it or I asked him the few fatal questions and let him hang himself. Or else, like any smart lawyer, I went into the Lecture. I studied my man, who sat as inscrutable as an Arab, delicately fingering his Ming holder, daintily sipping his dark mustache. He apparently did not realize how close I had him to admitting that he was guilty of first degree murder, that is, that he "feloniously, wilfully and of his malice afore-thought did kill and murder one Barney Quill." The man was a sitting duck.[18]

The lawyer here realizes that his line of questioning has come close to fixing the responsibility for the killing on his client. He therefore shifts his ground by beginning "the lecture":

The Lecture is an ancient device that lawyers use to coach their clients so that the client won't quite know he has been coached and his lawyer can still preserve the face-saving illusion that he hasn't done any coaching. For coaching clients, like robbing them, is not only frowned upon, it is downright unethical and bad, very bad. Hence the Lecture, an artful device as old as the law itself, and one used constantly by some of the nicest and most ethical lawyers in the land. "Who, me? I didn't tell him what to say," the lawyer can later comfort himself. "I merely explained the law, see." It is a good practice to scowl and shrug here and add virtuously: "That's my duty, isn't it?"

18 *Ibid.*, p. 43.

. . . "We will now explore the absorbing subject of legal justification or excuse," I said.

. . . "Well, take self-defense," I began. "That's the classic example of justifiable homicide. On the basis of what I've so far heard and read about your case I do not think we need pause too long over that. Do you?"

"Perhaps not," Lieutenant Manion conceded, "we'll pass it for now."

"Let's," I said dryly, "Then there's the defense of habitation, defense of property, and the defense of relatives or friends. Now there are more ramifications to these defenses than a dog has fleas, but we won't explore them now. I've already told you at length why I don't think you can invoke the possible defense of your wife. When you shot Quill her need for defense had passed. It's as simple as that."

"Go on," Lieutenant Manion said, frowning.

"Then there's the defense of a homicide committed to prevent a felony—say you're being robbed—; to prevent the escape of the felon—suppose he's getting away with your wallet—; or to arrest a felon—you've caught up with him and he's either trying to get away or has actually escaped." . . .

. . . "Go on, then; what are some of the other legal justifications or excuses?"

"Then there's the tricky and dubious defense of intoxication. Personally I've never seen it succeed. But since you were not drunk when you shot Quill we shall mercifully not dwell on that. Or were you?"

"I was cold sober. Please go on."

"Then finally there's the defense of insanity." I paused and spoke abruptly, airily: "Well, that just about winds it up." I arose as though making ready to leave.

"Tell me more."

"There is no more." I slowly paced up and down the room.

"I mean about this insanity."

"Oh, insanity," I said, elaborately surprised. It was like luring a trained seal with a herring. "Well, insanity, where proven, is a complete defense to murder. It does not legally justify the killing, like self-defense, say, but rather excuses it." The lecturer was hitting his stride. He was also on the home stretch. "Our law requires that a punishable killing—in fact, any crime—must be committed by a sapient human being, one capable, as the law insists, of distinguishing between right and wrong. If a man is insane, legally insane, the act of homicide may still be murder but the law excuses the perpetrator."

Lieutenant Manion was sitting erect now, very still and erect. "I see—and this—this perpetrator, what happens to him if he should—should be excused?"

"Under Michigan law—like that of many other states—if he is acquitted of murder on the grounds of insanity it is provided that he must be sent to a hospital for the criminally insane until he is pronounced sane." . . .

. . . Then he looked at me. "Maybe," he said, "maybe I was insane."

. . . Thoughtfully: "Hm. . . . Why do you say that?"

"Well, I can't really say," he went on slowly. "I—I guess I blacked out. I can't remember a thing after I saw him standing behind the bar that night until I got back to my trailer."

"You mean—you mean you don't remember shooting him?" I shook my head in wonderment.

"Yes, that's what I mean."

"You don't even remember driving home?"

"No."

"You don't remember threatening Barney's bartender when he followed you outside after the shooting—as the newspaper says you did?" I paused and held my breath. "You don't remember telling him, 'Do you want some, too, Buster?' ?"

The smoldering dark eyes flickered ever so little. "No, not a thing."

"My, my," I said blinking my eyes, contemplating the wonder of it all. "Maybe you've got something there."

The Lecture was over; I had told my man the law; and now he had told me things that might possibly invoke the defense of insanity. . . .[19]

The negotiation is complete. The ostensibly shared definition of the situation established by the negotiation process is that the defendant was probably not responsible for his actions.

Let us now compare the two interviews. The major similarity between them is their negotiated character: they both take the form of a series of offers and responses that continue until an offer (a definition of the situation) is reached that is acceptable to both parties. The major difference between the transactions is that one, the psychotherapeutic interview, arrives at an assessment that the client is responsible; the other, the defense attorney's interview, reaches an assessment that the client was not at fault, i.e., not responsible. How can we account for this difference in outcome?

[19] *Ibid.*, pp. 46–47, 57, 58–59, and 60.

DISCUSSION

Obviously, given any two real cases of negotiation which have different outcomes, one might construct a reasonable argument that the difference is due to the differences between the cases—the finding of responsibility in one case and lack of responsibility in the other, the only outcomes which are reasonably consonant with the facts of the respective cases. Without rejecting this argument, for the sake of discussion only, and without claiming any kind of proof or demonstration, I wish to present an alternative argument; that the difference in outcome is largely due to the differences in technique used by the interrogators. This argument will allow us to suggest some crucial dimensions of negotiation processes.

The first dimension, consciousness of the bargaining aspects of the transaction, has already been mentioned. In the psychotherapeutic interview, the negotiational nature of the transaction seems not to be articulated by either party. In the legal interview, however, certainly the lawyer, and perhaps to some extent the client as well, is aware of, and accepts the situation as one of striking a bargain, rather than as a relentless pursuit of the absolute facts of the matter.

The dimension of shared awareness that the definition of the situation is negotiable seems particularly crucial for assessments of responsibility. In both interviews, there is an agenda hidden from the client. In the psychotherapeutic interview, it is probably the psychiatric criteria for acceptance into treatment, the criterion of "insight." The psycho-

therapist has probably been trained to view patients with "insight into their illness" as favorable candidates for psychotherapy, i.e., patients who accept, or can be led to accept, the problems as internal, as part of their personality, rather than seeing them as caused by external conditions.

In the legal interview, the agenda that is unknown to the client is the legal structure of defenses or justifications for killing. In both the legal and psychiatric cases, the hidden agenda is not a simple one. Both involve fitting abstract and ambiguous criteria (insight, on the one hand, legal justification, on the other) to a richly specific, concrete case. In the legal interview, the lawyer almost immediately broaches this hidden agenda; he states clearly and concisely the major legal justifications for killing. In the psychiatric interview, the hidden agenda is never revealed. The patient's offers during most of the interview are rejected or ignored. In the last part of the interview, her last offer is accepted and she is told that she will be given treatment. In no case are the reasons for these actions articulated by either party.

The degree of shared awareness is related to a second dimension which concerns the format of the conversation. The legal interview began as an interrogation, but was quickly shifted away from that format when the defense lawyer realized the direction in which the questioning was leading the client, i.e., toward a legally unambiguous admission of guilt. On the very brink of such an admission, the defense lawyer stopped asking questions and started, instead, to make statements. He listed the principle legal justifications for killing, and, in response to the *client's* questions, gave an explanation of each of the justifications. This shift in format put the client, rather than the lawyer, in control of the crucial aspects of the negotiation. It is the client, not the lawyer, who is allowed to pose the questions, assess the answers for their relevance to his case, and most crucially, to determine himself the most advantageous tack to take. Control of the definition of the situation, the evocation of the events and intentions relevant to the assessment of the client's responsibility for the killing, was given to the client by the lawyer. The resulting client-controlled format of negotiation gives the client a double advantage. It not only allows the client the benefit of formulating his account of actions and intentions in their most favorable light, it also allows him to select, out of a diverse and ambiguous set of normative criteria concerning killing, that criteria which is most favorable to his own case.

Contrast the format of negotiation used by the psychotherapist. The form is consistently that of interrogation. The psychotherapist poses the questions; the patient answers. The psychotherapist then has the answers at his disposal. He may approve or disapprove, accept or reject, or merely ignore them. Throughout the entire interview, the psychotherapist is in complete control of the situation. Within this framework, the tactic that the psychotherapist uses is to reject the patient's "offers" that her husband is at fault, first by ignoring them, later, and ever more insistently, by leading her to define the situation as one in which she is at fault. In effect,

what the therapist does is to reject her offers, and to make his own counteroffers.

These remarks concerning the relationship between technique of interrogation and outcome suggest an approach to assessment of responsibility somewhat different than that usually followed. The common sense approach to interrogation is to ask how accurate and fair is the outcome. Both Newman's and Balint's analyses of negotiation raise this question. Both presuppose that there is an objective state of affairs that is independent of the technique of assessment. This is quite clear in Newman's discussion, as he continually refers to defendants who are "really" or "actually" guilty or innocent.[20] The situation is less clear in Balint's discussion, although occasionally he implies that certain patients are really physically healthy, but psychologically distressed.

The type of analysis suggested by this paper seeks to avoid such presuppositions. It can be argued that *independently* of the facts of the case, the technique of assessment plays a part in determining the outcome. In particular, one can avoid making assumptions about actual responsibility by utilizing a technique of textual criticism of a transaction. The key dimension in such work

[20] In his Foreword the editor of the series, Frank J. Remington, comments on one of the slips that occurs frequently, the "acquittal of the guilty," noting that this phrase is contradictory from the legal point of view. He goes on to say that Newman is well aware of this, but uses the phrase as a convenience. Needless to say, both Remington's comments and mine can both be correct: the phrase is used as a convenience, but it also reveals the author's presuppositions.

would be the relative power and authority of the participants in the situation.[21]

As an introduction to the way in which power differences between interactants shape the outcome of negotiations, let us take as an example an attorney in a trial dealing with "friendly" and "unfriendly" witnesses. A friendly witness is a person whose testimony will support the definition of the situation the attorney seeks to convey to the jury. With such a witness the attorney does not employ power, but treats him as an equal. His questions to such a witness are open, and allow the witness considerable freedom. The attorney might frame a question such as "Could you tell us about your actions on the night of ———?"

The opposing attorney, however, interested in establishing his own version of the witness' behavior on the same night, would probably approach the task quite differently. He might say: "You felt angry and offended on the night of ———, didn't you?" The witness frequently will try to evade so direct a question with an answer like: "Actually, I had started to . . . ." The

attorney quickly interrupts, addressing the judge: "Will the court order the witness to respond to the question, yes or no?" That is to say, the question posed by the opposing attorney is abrupt and direct. When the witness attempts to answer indirectly, and at length, the attorney quickly invokes the power of the court to coerce the witness to answer as he wishes, directly. The witness and the attorney are not equals in power; the attorney used the coercive power of the court to force the witness to answer in the manner desired.

The attorney confronted by an "unfriendly" witness wishes to control the format of the interaction, so that he can retain control of the definition of the situation that is conveyed to the jury. It is much easier for him to neutralize an opposing definition of the situation if he retains control of the interrogation format in this manner. By allowing the unfriendly witness to respond only by yes or no to his own verbally conveyed account, he can suppress the ambient details of the opposing view that might sway the jury, and thus maintain an advantage for his definition over that of the witness.

In the psychiatric interview discussed above, the psychiatrist obviously does not invoke a third party to enforce his control of the interview. But he does use a device to impress the patient that she is not to be his equal in the interview, that is reminiscent of the attorney with an unfriendly witness. The device is to pose abrupt and direct questions to the patient's open-ended accounts, implying that the patient should answer briefly and directly;

---

[21] Berger and Luckman *op. cit.,* p. 100, also emphasize the role of power, but at the societal level. "The success of particular conceptual machineries is related to the power possessed by those who operate them. The confrontation of alternative symbolic universes implies a problem of power—which of the conflicting definitions of reality will be "made to stick" in the society." Haley's discussions of control in psychotherapy are also relevant. See Jay Haley, "Control in Psychoanalytic Psychotherapy," *Progress in Psychotherapy,* 4, New York: Grune and Stratton, 1959, pp. 48–65; see also by the same author, "The Power Tactics of Jesus Christ" (in press).

and, through that implication, the psychiatrist controls the whole transaction. Throughout most of the interview the patient seeks to give detailed accounts of her behavior and her husband's, but the psychiatrist almost invariably counters with a direct and, to the patient, seemingly unrelated question.

The first instance of this procedure occurs at T6, the psychiatrist asking the patient, "what do you do?" She replies "I'm a nurse, but my husband won't let me work." Rather than responding to the last part of her answer, which would be expected in conversation between equals, the psychiatrist asks another question, changing the subject: "How old are you?" This pattern continues throughout most of the interview. The psychiatrist appears to be trying to teach the patient to follow his lead. After some thirty or forty exchanges of this kind, the patient apparently learns her lesson; she cedes control of the transaction completely to the therapist, answering briefly and directly to direct questions, and elaborating only on cue from the therapist. The therapist thus implements his control of the interview not by direct coercion, but by subtle manipulation.

All of the discussion above, concerning shared awareness and the format of the negotiation, suggests several propositions concerning control over the definition of the situation. The professional interrogator, whether lawyer or psychotherapist, can maintain control if the client cedes control to him because of his authority as an expert, because of his manipulative skill in the transaction, or merely because the interrogator controls access to something the client wants, e.g., treatment, or a legal excuse. The propositions are:

1a. Shared awareness of the participants that the situation is one of negotiation. (The greater the shared awareness the more control the client gets over the resultant definition of the situation.)

b. Explicitness of the agenda. (The more explicit the agenda of the transaction, the more control the client gets over the resulting definition of the situation.)

2a. Organization of the format of the transaction, offers and responses. (The party to a negotiation who responds, rather than the party who makes the offers, has relatively more power in controlling the resultant shared definition of the situation.)

b. Counter-offers. (The responding party who makes counter-offers has relatively more power than the responding party who limits his response to merely accepting or rejecting the offers of the other party.)

c. Directness of questions and answers. (The more direct the questions of the interrogator, and the more direct the answers he demands and receives, the more control he has over the resultant definition of the situation.)

These concepts and hypotheses are only suggestive until such times as operational definitions can be developed. Although such terms as offers and responses seem to have an immediate applicability to most conversation, it is likely that a thorough and systematic analysis of any given conversation would show the need for clearly stated criteria of class inclusion and exclusion. Perhaps a good place for such research would be in the transactions for assessing responsibility discussed above. Since some 90 percent of all criminal convictions in the United States are based on guilty pleas, the extent to which techniques of interrogation subtly influence outcomes would have immediate policy implication. There is considerable evidence that interrogation techniques influence the outcome of psychotherapeutic interviews also.[22] Research in both of these areas would probably have implications for both the theory and practice of assessing responsibility.

CONCLUSION: NEGOTIATION IN SOCIAL SCIENCE RESEARCH

More broadly, the application of the sociology of knowledge to the negotiation of reality has ramifications which may apply to all of social science. The interviewer in a survey, or the experimenter in a social psychological experiment, is also involved in a transaction with a client —the respondent or subject. Recent studies by Rosenthal and others strongly suggest that the findings in such studies are negotiated, and influenced by the format of the study.[23] Rosenthal's review of bias in research suggests that such bias is produced by a pervasive and subtle process of interaction between the investigator

and his source of data. Those errors which arise because of the investigator's influence over the subject (the kind of influence discussed in this paper as arising out of power disparities in the process of negotiation), Rosenthal calls "expectancy effects." In order for these errors to occur, there must be direct contact between the investigator and the subject.

A second kind of bias Rosenthal refers to as "observer effects." These are errors of perception or reporting which do not require that the subject be influenced by investigation. Rosenthal's review leads one to surmise that even with techniques that are completely non-obtrusive, observer error could be quite large.[24]

The occurrence of these two kinds of bias poses an interesting dilemma for the lawyer, psychiatrist, and social scientist. The investigator of human phenomena is usually interested in more than a sequence of events, he wants to know why the events occurred. Usually this quest for an explanation leads him to deal with the motivation of the persons involved. The lawyer, clinician, social psychologist, or survey researcher try to elicit motives directly, by questioning the participants. But in the process of questioning, as suggested above, he himself becomes involved in a process of negotiation, perhaps subtly influencing the informants through expectancy effects. A historian, on the other hand, might try

22 Thomas J. Scheff, *Being Mentally Ill,* Chicago: Aldine, 1966.

23 Robert Rosenthal, *Experimenter Effects in Behavioral Research,* New York: Appleton-Century Crofts, 1966. Friedman, reporting a series of studies of expectancy effects, seeks to put the results within a broad sociological framework; Neil Friedman, *The Social Nature of Psychological Research: The Psychological Experiment as Social Interaction,* New York: Basic Books, 1967.

24 Critics of "reactive techniques" often disregard the problem of observer effects. See, for example, Eugene J. Webb, Donald T. Campbell, Richard D. Schwartz, and Lee Sechrest, *Unobtrusive Measures: Nonreactive Research in Social Science,* Chicago: Rand-McNally, 1966.

to use documents and records to determine motives. He would certainly avoid expectancy effects in this way, but since he would not elicit motives directly, he might find it necessary to collect and interpret various kinds of evidence which are only indirectly related, at best, to determine motives of the participants. Thus through his choice in the selection and interpretation of the indirect evidence, he may be as susceptible to error as the interrogator, survey researcher, or experimentalist—his error being due to observer effects, however, rather than expectancy effects.

The application of the ideas outlined here to social and psychological research need to be developed. The five propositions suggested above might be used, for example, to estimate the validity of surveys using varying degrees of open-endedness in their interview format. If some technique could be developed which would yield an independent assessment of validity, it might be possible to demonstrate, as Aaron Cicourel has suggested, the more reliable the technique, the less valid the results.

The influence of the assessment itself on the phenomena to be assessed appears to be an ubiquitous process in human affairs, whether in ordinary daily life, the determination of responsibility in legal or clinical interrogation, or in most types of social science research. The sociology of knowledge perspective, which suggests that people go through their lives constructing reality, offers a framework within which the negotiation of reality can be seriously and constructively studied. This paper has suggested some of the avenues of the problem that might require further study. The prevalence of the problem in most areas of human concern recommends it to our attention as a substantial field of study, rather than as an issue that can be ignored or, alternatively, be taken as the proof that rigorous knowledge of social affairs is impossible.

reciprocal exploitation in an indian-white community [1]

NIELS WINTHER BRAROE

In this paper I shall examine the manner in which conceptions of self and other held by Indians and whites contribute stability to a community structure of roles and values which is riddled with apparent inconsistency and contradiction. As a point of departure, I shall focus on a recurrent type of behavior: the practice by Indians and whites alike of "victimizing" on another, of misrepresenting the self and self-motivations in social and economic transactions. The insight gleaned from consideration of these performances will be offered in support of the hypothesis that these misrepresentations allow both Indians and whites to resolve value and role contradictions which might otherwise engender social conflict or personal disorganization.

Reprinted from Niels Winther Braroe, "Reciprocal Exploitation in an Indian-White Community," SOUTHWESTERN JOURNAL OF ANTHROPOLOGY, *21 (1965) by permission of the author and publisher.*

[1] The research upon which this paper is based was done in the summer of 1963, and was supported by the University of Illinois and in part by the Saskatchewan Cultural Ecology Research Program, NSF Grant G23815, administered by the Social Science Institute of Washington University, and directed by John W. Bennett. I am indebted to Edward M. Bruner, Joseph R. Gusfield and George L. Hicks for critical comments and suggestions.

I

The perspective adopted in this paper draws on the work of Rose, Goffman, Berreman and others relating to the nature of the self and human interaction. Human beings are categorized according to the major roles they enact in society, roles being a "cluster of related meanings and values that guide and direct an individual's behavior in a given social setting . . ." (Rose 1962:10). Roles and the self are seen as growing out of continuous social symbolic interaction in which individuals present and express themselves in ways intended to influence a shared definition of the situation. A large portion of this interaction is concerned with crediting or discrediting the selves thus presented: "this imputation—this self—is a *product* of the scene that comes off . . ." (Goffman 1952:252).

Two aspects of this perspective are prominent in the following pages. The first deals with the tendency of the participants in a community or a social setting to arrive at a working consensus, an agreement about how they will behave toward one another and upon the symbols and meanings which will guide this action. Secondly, people generally work to support consensus and devise means of avoiding its disintegration and the associated failure of self-validations.

A person is an individual who becomes involved in a value of some kind . . . and then makes a public claim that he is to be defined and treated as someone who possesses the value or property in question. The limits to his claims, and hence the limits to his self, are primarily determined by the objective facts of his social life and secondarily determined by the degree to which a sympathetic interpretation of these facts can bend them in his favor. Any event which demonstrates that someone has made a false claim, defining himself as something which he is not, tends to destroy him (Goffman 1962:500).

This paper explores self and other images of white and Indian persons vis-à-vis one another. Attention is directed to the ways in which each credits or validates the roles and self of the other in the context of a community "working consensus" that provides the framework of day-to-day interaction. One question is central to this discussion: how do Indians adapt to circumstances of economic and social deprivation? How do they adapt to membership in the lowest category of a rigidly hierarchical status system?

II

Jasper is a town of about 2400 persons on the western prairie of Saskatchewan.[2] Small-scale cattle ranching and mixed farming are the predominant economic activities of whites in this region; they come to Jasper for goods and services, and often move there after retirement. In Jasper there are two general stores, a movie theatre, two small

[2] The name Jasper, and the names of all informants mentioned in this paper, are pseudonyms.

hotels, a pub, three Chinese-owned restaurants, several auto and farm equipment stores and so on. The town, however, is no longer the isolated focus of patterns of leisure and consumption, as area residents now make frequent trips to a shopping center in a small city about sixty miles away.

Twenty miles from town is a small non-treaty Indian reserve which is the home of about a hundred and ten Plains Cree. The Indians make their living by the sale of poplar posts to ranchers and to the lumber yard in town, and by seasonal agricultural labor. All receive government relief, their most stable source of income. Jasper Indians do not identify with whites to the extent that white cultural goals and values are outwardly accepted and Indian ones entirely rejected. They revere generosity and sharing, for example, and ridicule white ideas about the dignity of work, the accumulation of material goods, punctuality and the like. The fact that so few of them are acculturated—that is, display their selves as white—is not difficult to understand given the nature of their relations with the dominant society; these relations impede the communication of white culture and limit the participation of Indians in white institutional activities. Until six years ago there was no school for Indian children; even now their school is segregated on the reserve. Since most parents do not value education, class attendance is poor. Children do not learn to speak English until they are six or seven years old. Jasper Indians uniformly profess belief in "Indian" religion and emphatically call attention to their participation in it. None of the Indians are even nominally Christian, and there is no record of any effort in the past generation to convert them. No one among them has ever served in the military.

While Indians go to town frequently, even in the worst weather, the reserve itself is isolated. Whites seldom visit it and never live there. A policeman said, "We don't really know what goes on up there, and don't really care as long as they don't make trouble in town." Lacking electricity, reserve Indians have no radios or television sets, and hence are further isolated by minimal exposure to mass media.[3] Occupational opportunities in town do not exist. None of the merchants or businessmen questioned said that they were willing to hire Indians, even for the most menial tasks.

Similarly, the legal status of Indians and their dependence on paternalistic government relief are important factors in their marginal involvement in the local economy. They do not have the capital resources to increase the income from communally-owned reserve holdings. They have not learned skills that would bring them regular employment in the Jasper community or allow them to emigrate to a more favorable urban location.[4]

Attitudes of whites toward Indians are obstacles to Indian assimilation. The common denominator of nearly all of these attitudes is that Indians are childish and irresponsible. For some, such as the man to whom Indians bring their dilapi-

dated cars for repair, this is mixed with pity. He knows that his work will likely go unpaid, but he says, "They can't help it, they're just kids with money. They got nothing, and whenever they do get a little money they can't wait to spend it." At the other extreme there are people who share this appraisal of Indian character as child-like, but who express a spare-the-rod-spoil-the-child opinion. They insist that Indians should be compelled to behave responsibly and that they ought to be given no social privileges or aid until they do so. Others, including many ranchers, think that the Indians should be allowed to rot. "I can make a living off this land," they say, "why can't they? It's because we help them so much that they're so lazy."

Jasper whites not only consider Indians to be irresponsible, but speak of them as worthless. Some see them circumstantially so, others consider Indians worthless as human beings. For the latter, Indians are innately without value, and no amount of "help" by white society will ever make Indians self-sufficient. They are regarded as parasites, a liability inherited from the past. Few whites, however, display active hostility toward Indians, not excluding those who consider them little more than superfluous appendages to white society. The absence of malice on the part of whites is one of the most remarkable aspects of Indian-white relations. Even those white men who have been involved in brawls with Indians do not bear animosity toward them. In fact, both Indians and whites describe these events with the greatest amusement.

The conception which whites have of Indians differs dramatically from

---

[3] Several families have quite recently acquired small transistor radios.

[4] One family of Jasper Indians does travel to Alberta each summer to work on the beet farms there. They return at the end of each season to spend the winter on the reserve.

whites' image of themselves. They extol responsibility, independence and self-sufficiency. The residents of Jasper and its surroundings feel themselves close to the western frontier era—indeed this part of North America was the scene of the closing days of the "Old West" (Stegner 1955:127–138). A sentiment commonly expressed by Jasper whites is one of confidence in the face of adversity, of dauntlessness in the confrontation of nature. Town-dwelling men speak with pride of the ability to "take care of myself." Only Indians go on relief. The image of the strong, silent cowboy is taken seriously in Jasper. With it go the attributes of unwavering integrity, fairness and helpfulness. Jasper is a particularistic community, where people applaud the man who is willing to help others without demanding repayment; but they believe that a man must not accept a hand unless he intends to reciprocate someday. These values pervade the complex, reticulate cooperative work groups among ranchers.

III

The whites' emphasis upon the values of integrity and charity are often not discernible in their day-to-day behavior toward Indians. Indians who have cut and cured poplar posts near the reserve, and who do not have trucks, persuade whites to haul the posts to town. For his small investment of time, the white charges as much as 25 percent of the load's value; customarily he goes into the lumber yard office to collect his money from the manager while the Indian unloads the posts in the yard. Whites say that one has to pocket one's money before the Indian "gets

his hands on it," or risk never being paid. Again, whites frequently take advantage of the restrictions placed upon Indians in disposing of reserve resources. The law forbids Indians to sell cattle or hay without permission from the Indian agent, and the money from such sales is supposed to go to a common reserve fund rather than to individual Indians. To circumvent this, Indians sell these things to whites, but for only a fraction of their value.[5] Similarly, a few ranchers take advantage of the Indians' desire for spending money, by arranging to place cattle on reserve pasture for much less than it would cost if legal channels were used. In this way a small "grazing fee" is collected by an Indian who needs money for a trip to a Sun Dance on another reserve, and the white is enabled to feed his cattle for a pittance. Indians are overcharged for merchandise and services in town, and they are paid less for their labor than a white man would be. Indian women are not infrequently objects of white sexual gratification.

White belief in the irresponsibility of Indians is demonstrated continuously. For example, at the suggestion of some Jasper residents, the Indian department no longer gives relief money directly to the Indians. Instead, a local general store receives these funds, which are credited to Indian families to whom supplies of food and clothing are doled out on a weekly basis.

While not all whites engage in

5 Six years ago, the Indian Affairs Branch supplied reserve families with a total of about seventy cows: today there are only about twenty-five. They have been sold (illegally), eaten and allowed to starve or freeze to death.

these practices, those who do are neither publicly nor privately censured by those who do not have such dealings with Indians. Neither do white members of the Jasper community comment upon the less direct deprivation of Indians. The legal and political status of Indians is, of course, a matter of national governmental policy. But whites make no effort to bring about policy changes which might lead to Indian self-sufficiency, nor do they take action at the local community level to provide Indians with occupational skills or agricultural training which would improve Indian standards of living.

In a particularistic community where standards of honesty and humaneness are prized, the exploitation and deprivation of a segment of that community stands out as a manifest anomaly. It is not out of place to ask how the conceptions of self which incorporate these values also incorporate behavior and attitudes which contradict them. One way to minimize this conflict is to insist upon maintaining social distance between whites and Indians. This amounts to ignoring that a conflict exists. To a certain extent, the white members of the Jasper community take this solution. For instance, an examination of back issues of the weekly Jasper newspaper for its sixty year history revealed that, apart from mentions of Indians in the "Police Court" column, there has been no recognition that an Indian reserve exists near Jasper. Not even editorial notice has been taken of the Indian members of the community.

It is impossible, nonetheless, for Jasper whites always to ignore the presence and condition of Indians. There are other features of white deportment toward Indians which lend understanding of how apparent value contradictions are resolved. To identify these, it is useful to consider some of the ways that Indians, in turn, "con" white men.

Jasper Indians find one source of income in the poplar posts which they cut from reserve lands and (illegally) from the nearby forest preserve. Ordinarily, these are soaked in a "bluestone" preservative for about a day. Sometimes an impatient Indian will paint the posts with laundry blueing instead and then sell them to an unsuspecting white man. Another quick way of getting money is to sell a quantity of posts sight unseen, telling the buyer that they are stacked at some spot on the reserve. When the white man returns later, having found no posts, the Indian innocently conjectures that "somebody musta stole 'em." Again, Indians are able to stack posts for white buyers in such a way that there appear to be more than there actually are.

The "con game" played by Indians against whites is often carried out in the context of enduring relationships. For example, one Indian, John Sweet Grass, receives a monthly disability check from the government for about seventy dollars. Each month, he takes part of it to the owner of an appliance store in Jasper to "hold" for him, with the understanding that he may request small amounts of it at any time. By the end of every month John has overdrawn his allowance, and the financial state of affairs between him and his "banker" is hopelessly confused, as it has been for years. In effect, John has a reliable, permanent source of spending money. The storekeeper laments, "I really don't know anymore *how* much he owes me, I probably never will. What can I do? If I don't take care of him, he'll probably starve."

At every turn, Indians act the part of con artists in their dealings with whites. An Indian will call at the home of an absent white man and tell his wife that her husband instructed him to get from her several dollars due him for some work done. When the husband returns, his wife discovers that the payment was for an imaginary task—*he* hasn't seen this Indian in weeks.

Incidents of Indians duping whites occur with persistent, almost monotonous regularity: an Indian persuades a white to transport him and his family home from town in sub-zero weather for some agreed-upon price. When they arrive at the reserve, the Indian proclaims that he "hasn't got the money now, but I'll pay you later," which means never. A common way for Indians to borrow money is to offer some useless, worthless item as security— a piece of clothing or household utensil—and then never return to claim it, nor to pay the debt.

One of the most celebrated recent coups concerned the illegal sale of a water pump and windmill by several Indians to a neighboring rancher. This man paid for the machinery and steel tower on which it was mounted without a permit from the Indian agent, whose office is more than a hundred miles from Jasper. The rancher and his son disassembled the purchase and took it home. That night, the same Indians collected the tower and pump, hauled it into town, and resold it the next day to a junk dealer. In these transactions, whites do not hold Indians guilty for their behavior. They

do not complain to the police when they suffer losses, even in cases where there is proof that Indians are the malefactors. A rancher, from whom Indians regularly poach chickens, says, "They know that all they have to do is ask me for 'em if they were really hungry, but they'd rather steal 'em."

Why, one may ask, does a white man, whom we should expect to know better, buy a pig-in-a-poke? Why, in their relations with Indians, do whites keep coming back for more? Why is an Indian lent money when all past experience must teach that it probably will never be returned? One outcome of the usual sequence of events in a con is that the "mark" learns his lesson; he is presumably a poorer but a more cautious man. We must look elsewhere for the source of white gullibility than in some sort of "mass stupidity" or failure to learn from experience. In fact, Jasper whites *expect* to be conned by Indians; storekeepers extend credit to Indians knowing that the accounts will never be settled.[6] It may be suggested that whites allow Indians to con them in order that Indian irresponsibility and childishness may be demonstrated and confirmed. A rancher pays an Indian in advance for his labor in stacking bales of hay. When the Indian does not show up to fulfill his part of the bargain, the rancher's image of the Indian as irresponsible

[6] White residents of Jasper, especially those who have fewest contacts with Indians, and who are the most literate members of the community, point to a novel as an accurate portrayal of Indian character. *Stay Away, Joe*, by Dan Cushman, describes the slapstick adventures of a young Indian in his con game with white society. "If you want to know what Indians are *really* like," they advise, "read that book, it's a scream."

is validated. His tolerance of the social deprivation of Indians can then be justified: "They *are* children and irresponsible. They are not really men, so they cannot be expected to participate in the adult world." Similarly, those whites who directly exploit Indians are provided a means of preserving a defensible image of self: "Sure, he takes advantage of me, but then, that is to be expected of children. I graze my cattle on the reserve, but then I'm the one who takes care of him, who gives him money, and sees that he does not starve." Not a few whites are persuaded that Indians have no desire to adopt white roles. A veterinarian claimed, "The last thing they want is to live like white men —they're no more than unemployed buffalo hunters, and happy just like they are."

IV

Looking at these transactions from an Indian point of view, an arresting feature is disclosed. Most Indians do not accept white judgments of their role, their self or their personal worth. Still, they seldom openly dispute white conceptions of Indian character—in fact, as we have seen, they behave in such a way to validate the white image of themselves.

Indians do not regard themselves as foolish children; on the contrary they consider themselves rather artful and successful exploiters of white men. What they do is to represent themselves to white audiences as the sort of persons whites take them to be, and represent themselves to other Indians as something different. In their performances before whites, Indians acknowledge irresponsibility, but they perform for a dual audi-

ence; to other Indians they are seen as turning to account (mistaken) white imputations of themselves.

Backstage, in Goffman's terminology, Indians, "drop the front." In this region, "the impression fostered by the performance is knowingly contradicted as a matter of course" (Goffman 1959:112). Jokes are made about the stupidity of whites and the ease with which they are taken in. Fine points of strategy are discussed. "The way to get off easy," according to one informant, "is to act like a dumb Indian in front of the magistrate." This way, the punishment for being drunk and disorderly will be lighter than a white man would receive, and "credit" can even be arranged—the magistrate will give the guilty Indian months to pay his fine.

Much of this backstage activity resembles that reported by Berreman for the Aleut. Aleuts, though they identify with whites as a *valuation group,* respond to the denial of entrance into white institutional activities by valuation group alienation. They have come to look more appreciatively at white society, but, deprived of acceptance by whites, they orient themselves negatively towards those people toward whose cultural values and goals they are drawn. "Role segregation" and "role-distance" are two of the means Aleuts employ to cope with their ambivalence (Berreman 1964:235).

Earlier, we observed that Jasper Indians are excluded from playing white roles, and that structural barriers prevent Indian participation in the larger society. It was noted that, to a greater or lesser extent, most Jasper Indians do not perform in the presence of a white audience in a fashion which suggests that they embrace white cultural goals. The impression of them was that they are relatively "unacculturated." Nevertheless, it is evident that Jasper Indians too have begun to identify positively with white culture. In spite of the barriers to acculturation, they show signs of having recognized the taking of white roles as desirable. Perhaps one of the facilitating circumstances of this process has been the similarity between some of the principal values of traditional Plains Indian culture and those of the Anglo-American Jasper community. Standards of masculinity, competitiveness, a dual standard of sex behavior, qualities of leadership and the like are features of value orientations among Jasper whites which are remarkably like value orientations of the formerly more autonomous Plains Cree. We may expect that a group of one cultural heritage will identify with a group of another with greater ease when their conceptions of the male role contain analogous properties.

Many aspects of the structural relations between whites and Indians have worked toward acceptance by Indians of white cultural goals and meanings. For one, the extermination of the buffalo and the demise of the traditional pattern of Plains subsistence forced Indians to search elsewhere for means of livelihood. Formerly, Indians were spatially less isolated from whites than today: in the last ten years all of the white families but one which lived in the hills near the reserve have moved away because of the cold, lonely winters. Today also, with modern mechanized agriculture, the demand for Indian labor has declined. In the early reserve period, after the turn of the century, it was common

for Indian families to live for long periods on the property of ranchers for whom they worked. Some Jasper adults, in fact, were born on ranches where their parents lived permanently, in familiar interaction with their white employers.

Indians have other opportunities for exposure to white culture. All Indian women now go to the hospital in Jasper to have their children; Indian men mix with whites in the pub; Indian children now have a white scholteacher; Jasper Indians maintain close relations with members of other reserves who are more acculturated than they.

Continuous face to face interaction over generations leads to some consensual definition of the situation, and it is reasonable to expect that the subordinate Indians should have incorporated into their conceptions of self some of the content of white roles. One piece of evidence indicating that Indians have come to regard whites as a positive reference group is that they frequently judge their own behavior by white standards. It is not uncommon for Indians to show remorse about excessive drinking, for example. Most Indians express a desire to be self-supporting, and to own land and cattle the same as their white neighbors. An excerpt from the author's field diary is illustrative:

Saturday nite: Charlie Running Calf, his wife and I strolled around town this evening. Charlie, who had been hauling bales on Newcomb's ranch for the past two days, had just come from the pub and was a little tight. We passed Roger McDougal. Charlie said, "Hiya Roger, how you been," in an expansive tone. Charlie's wife said, "*Charlie*, you can't talk to those people like that." He replied,

"Whatdya mean, I'm a *workin'* man, ain't I?"

However much Indians embrace white culture, they are refused the privilege of playing white roles. They cannot go into business for themselves, as has been indicated, because their legal status prohibits the accumulation of the capital necessary to engage in full-scale farming or ranching. Nor have they skills which would allow wage employment off the reserve. Consequently, Jasper Indians are alienated from their valuation group just as Berreman's Aleuts were. If they cannot be white, however, it is necessary for them to define the self ". . . along defensible lines" (Goffman 1962:493). This must furthermore be done in a way that permits validation of this self by whites. To the Indian, then, his "irresponsible" performances declare: "Because I can trick white men so easily, they are not as smart as they think they are. *I'm* the one who's taking advantage of them. I can make a living by my wits."

V

We have looked at some of the ways whites and Indians in a small community portray the self in the ordinary course of daily life. We have seen also how the actions of each group validate the claims of the other. Indians and whites successfully predict one another's behavior, in a manner which mutually credits images of Indian and white selves. Among the consequences of this exchange, two are selected here for discussion.

In his article, "On Cooling the Mark Out," Erving Goffman (1962: 482–505) addresses himself to the problem of adaptations which people make to failure, to the ways that individuals deal with repudiations of the self which are implied by the unsuccessful fulfillment of some role. It often becomes necessary that a person whose self has suffered failure be "consoled" by some other person. He is helped to adjust to his loss, he is "cooled out." This is particularly important when a person is deeply engaged in this self, and where its loss reflects upon him negatively. It sometimes occurs, Goffman adds, that the various participants in a network of interaction take measures to avoid altogether the troublesome procedure of cooling out; they attempt to cover up the fact that a person has failed or that his value as an individual is negligible.

Such processes may be recognized in transactions between Jasper whites and Indians. Indians do not have the liberty of playing white roles, but at the same time they increasingly identify with these roles and with white cultural values. They are accordingly in the plight of people whose worth is denied. Indians cannot salvage much of their value in the estimation of whites, but they do have means of saving face in the eyes of other Indians. This is accomplished, we have noted, when the Indian sub-community observes one of its members making a fool of a white man, bringing off some deception with impunity. In effect, the validation of this transaction by whites serves to "cool out" Indians. Now, few Jasper Indians show evidence of serious personal disorganization, a consequence, it is proposed, of whites and Indians having found a way of avoiding a confrontation. Whites, at the same time, are spared the malaise of recognising moral inconsistency in their own behavior.

Routines of self-presentation and identification in Jasper have consequences for stability at the structural as well as at the personal level.[7] The successful cooling out of a failure means that he will be less likely to protest or to threaten the established system of social relationships. The position of Indians in Jasper is one of subordination and deprivation. The social-psychological dynamics of role-playing and identification take place in a manner which contributes to the perpetuation of a caste-like status system. Indians are provided an "out," entailing adjustment to a place in their social environment which would otherwise be intolerable. The alternative to acquiescence, of course, would be for Indians to try to alter their environment, to challenge white superordination. Support for this assertion can be found in historical data, and in the examination of instances where the customary validations of Indian and white images of self fail.

Nearly a hundred years ago, not far from Jasper, a group of white traders "massacred" a small band of Indian horse-thieves (Cf. Sharp 1955:55–77). The expedition was organized by a white man whose horse had been stolen by an Indian, sold back to him, and then stolen again by the same Indian; the whites attacked a camp where they believed the culprit was hiding. The significant aspect of white ideas about Indians at that time was that they were held responsible for their behavior and punishable for their deceptions. In this and numerous other instances, whites were not indulgently disposed to treat Indians as irresponsible, and the outcome was frequently violent.

Today, when representations of Indian and white selves fail, persons are embarrassed, insulted or provoked. An Indian, for example, inopportunely asked a white man in town for several dollars. He was refused, and told that he was a worthless beggar, incapable of properly supporting his wife and children. The Indian was affronted, enraged, and the two men exchanged blows in the street. It was not so much the refusal that brought violence, as the white's rejection of the self presented by the Indian. The normal course of interaction was disrupted when the white man withheld agreement to a definition of the situation including an image of the Indian as uncommitted to white values and unobligated by white standards of responsibility.

In this paper, I have described something of the tenor of Indian-white interaction, employing the social-psychological perspective which stresses role-taking, performances and the self. It was suggested that a social structure including the superordination of whites over Indians is supported through a consensual

[7] Both Indians and whites are, of course, largely unaware of the social and personal consequences of their behavior. It is likely that this ignorance is requisite to the achievement of these results. See Schneider (1962:494–495) for a discussion of the *structural* necessity for keeping "failures" ignorant of their status.

definition of the situation embodying images of self which Indians and whites present to one another. The analysis was not exclusively concerned with the *results* of acculturation,· or the extent to which Indians overtly embrace white values, but considered as well the kinds of involvement of these values in selves identified with whites and Indians vis-à-vis one another. In other words, the emphasis has been on the *mechanisms* of acculturative processes rather than upon the conditions of culture contact or the larger, more abstract, results of contact. As much space has been devoted to the "how" of persistence of Indian segregation—the complimentary presentation of diverse self images—as to the "why."

A final comment is in order. Looking at the results of acculturation rather than at the daily interplay between whites and Indians, one might conclude that differences in cultural values expressed in the different presentations of self represent points of tension or potential conflict between whites and Indians. The evidence presented above suggests that such a view is not entirely accurate. The different sets of values embodied in Indian and white roles constitute an accommodation or a *solution* to certain conflicts and not merely a source of them. It is, in fact, because of the contrasting images of Indian and white man that interaction proceeds with as little conflict as actually occurs.

BIBLIOGRAPHY

BERREMAN, GERALD D.
(1964) "Aleut Reference Group Alienation, Mobility, and Acculturation." *American Anthropologist* 66:231–250.

CUSHMAN, DAN
(1953) *Stay Away, Joe*. New York: Viking Press.

GOFFMAN, ERVING
(1959) *The Presentation of Self in Everyday Life*. New York: Doubleday.
(1962) "On Cooling the Mark Out," in *Human Behavior and Social Processes* (ed. by A. M. Rose), pp. 482–505. Boston: Houghton Mifflin.

ROSE, ARNOLD M.
(1962) "A Systematic Summary of Symbolic Interaction Theory," in *Human Behavior and Social Processes* (ed. by A. M. Rose), pp. 3–19. Boston: Houghton Mifflin.

SCHNEIDER, LOUIS
(1962) "The Role of the Category of Ignorance in Sociological Theory: an Exploratory Statement." *American Sociological Review* 27:492–508.

SHARP, PAUL F.
(1955) *Whoop-Up Country*. Minneapolis: University of Minnesota Press.

STEGNER, WALLACE
(1955) *Wolf-Willow: A History, A Story, and A Memory of the Last Plains Frontier*. New York: Viking Press.

Formal
Organizations

4

When sociologists speak or write of organizations, they typically refer to *formal, complex, bureaucratic* organizations. Formal organizations nearly always have: (1) a fairly explicit goal, or objective, toward which its members, ideally, direct their activities; (2) explicit and specific rules designed to govern the activities of its members or participants; (3) a high degree of specialization in the activities or functions of its members; (4) an authority structure which is clear and hierarchical.

These characteristics form an ideal, a kind of model; they are not absolutes. The exceptions and qualifications are just as important as the generalizations. First, *formalization is a matter of degree.* At one end we have the "pure type" of a formal organization—such as General Electric, the Los Angeles Police Department, or Columbia University. At the other end, we have completely informal gatherings, such as a small circle of friends, a crowd listening to a political speech, or a few addicts who frequent a certain "shooting gallery"; clearly, none of these are formal organizations in any way. But there are many in-between types, which are to some degree formalized. Take, for example, the guerilla band: the authority structure is hierarchical, the goals are clear-cut, but a leader's authority is diffuse rather than specific, and based on his charisma, or personal magnetism, rather than on his formal office.

A second qualification to our ideal type is that goals are often *rhetorical.*

In any organization there are some members who do not necessarily want to achieve the stated objective of the organization. They may espouse it merely to gain support for the organization. Members of a bureaucracy may actually even frustrate the supposed goals of their organization. Sometimes achieving the stated goal would be disastrous for the organization. Actually, the most important function of any organization is to *survive*. And often, an outcome will profit one segment of an organization while ruining others.

A third qualification to our ideal type is that there is always an *informal* structure superimposed on the formal structure. Formal organizations generally have some form of "company chart." This, however, may bear no relation whatsoever to the way things actually run. The president of a company may be the son of the founder, an incompetent alcoholic; the company may be run, informally, by an underling. One foreman may have far more informal authority than another. Sergeants often know their men better, and command more respect, than the lieutenants above them. A company will usually set a productivity output level for its workers—but they will establish their own quotas. These examples underline the importance of the informal norms and networks. It would be a stupendous blunder to assume that the officially-sanctioned patterns of authority and duties tell us exactly what happens.

Of the many reasons why sociologists are particularly interested in bureaucracies, perhaps the most important is that they can *get things done* to a degree, and with an efficiency, that scattered individuals could not possibly achieve. Organizations such as the American Medical Association can prevent (and actually have prevented) men who disagree with their policies from reaching high government office. A high degree of organization permits the manufacture of stupendous quantities of material goods. The effective coordination of the bureaucracy can blanket and intimidate isolated and scattered individuals with its awesome might and legitimacy; it can convince the aspiring junior executive to organize his entire life around the demands of a single corporation; it can impress the religious novitiate with the majesty of the Catholic Church, and it can stun a populace into submission with the military might of a conquering army. An effective bureaucracy represents crystallized power and authority; the will of those making high-level decisions in any large complex organization is far more likely to be carried out than the will of many individuals who are outside an organizational structure. Organizations are a type of machinery for the implementation of the will of some men, or some groups or strata, in society.

When we look at formal organizations in this way, a number of questions immediately come to mind; some are: (1) What exactly is the process by which those in positions of authority in a bureaucracy wrest compliance from their subordinates? (2) What is the situation of the subordinate in a bureaucracy—and how does he experience it? (3) What is the nature of the process by which organizations manage to get things done? (4) Under what circumstances can the efforts of organizations be resisted? (5) What is the future of the bureaucracy?

The essays in this section will attempt to answer these and related questions. Our first selection, written by sociologist Amitai Etzioni, provides an excellent overview of complex organizations. It is primarily concerned with how those in power in bureaucracies make sure their subordinates comply with their dictates. "Compliance," Etzioni writes, "is a central element of organizational structure." There are three principal means of insuring compliance in organizations—coercive, remunerative, and normative; organizations have at their disposal mainly physical force, material rewards, or ideological inducements. Moreover, organizations tend to rely more on one *or* another inducement. Just as organizations differ in their reliance on different means of inducing subordinate compliance, subordinates differ as to their degree of involvement *with* the organization. Rank and file involvement ranges from alienative—or intense negative involvement—through calculative, meaning a low intensity involvement, to a moral involvement, or a positive involvement of high intensity. One thing that is so interesting about bureaucracies is that they tend to fall into a systematic pattern. Organizations like the army or a prison are characterized both by alienative involvement among lower participants *and* by the dominance of physical sanctions to insure compliance. Organizations like businesses rank low on intensity of involvement of their members, and they rely mainly on remuneration. And organizations such as religious groups tend to generate a higher and more positive level of involvement, and, in addition, to rely on moral suasion.

Formal organizations can be just as effective in blocking change and preventing things from getting done as in initiating it. A bureaucracy becomes an entity unto itself. It may be funded for certain specific purposes, but its participants may have entirely different purposes in mind. It is necessary to be aware of just who makes up the constituency of an organization. To say that an organization serves "the public" would be naive because the question that follows is, which segment of the public? To which constituency is one or another organization accountable? And which members of the organization are, in fact, actually accountable? The members of most organizations have become relatively isolated from, and indifferent to, an amorphous public, but they are very sensitive to the demands of specific segments of that public.

Today, most people think of good health care, adequate housing, quality education, fair employment, public transportation, and police protection as social rights rather than status privileges. Most people also look to government—federal, state, and local—to provide them. Why are government agencies or public bureaucracies so painfully slow in making good on these rights? We shall look at three contributing factors: (1) the difficulties elected officials and client populations have in making public bureaucracies accountable to them, (2) the *seemingly* apolitical posture of agency planners, and (3) the qualitative deficits of quantitative planning techniques.

James and Anne Hudson point out that bureaucratic agencies must acquire ever higher levels of professional competence to deliver services effectively and efficiently. Agencies that become highly professional, however, are then less subject to control by lay officials who, although they are the elected representatives of the people, simply do not have the expertise to evaluate and control the agencies. Agency personnel, moreover, generally form professional associations which act as political voting blocks and threaten the tenure of elected officials. Public officials, understandably, are prone to adopt a hands-off policy.

The second problem emerges when the client population served by these professionalized agencies demands a voice in determining the nature and scope of services. Much as elected officials are without the expertise to cope with professionals, so, to an even greater extent, are the client populations. As Rose suggests, even in those cases where client populations have been able to organize themselves and hire their own set of experts to counter the agency experts, nothing comes of it. For, despite the political aspiration of the client population, the plans which their own experts devise are nearly always identical with the plans devised by the agency experts. Upon reflection, this makes sense because all the experts, regardless of who they work for, went to the same professional schools, absorbed the same planning philosophies, and see the world much the same way. Thus, political differences seem to be neutralized in the planning process. Or, put another way, the implicit and shared political biases of the planners wash out the explicit political preferences of their employers.

The third problem arises with the realization that the planners, given their emphasis on methods and techniques, take as given the political, economic, and social goals of the very system which precipitates the crises they are hired to resolve. In other words, problem solution does not attack the global system but rather occurs within its bounds. All the latest planning tools, such as systems analysis, cost benefit analysis, and planned program budgeting are concerned only with locating structural faults and identifying inefficient investments. As such, all planning tools bypass, ignore, or take for granted the political process, the long range effects of programs, and the personal reactions of individuals. Furthermore, because efficient investment of resources requires some tangible returns, the only programs instituted are those in which the client population has some chance of helping itself. As a result, a perpetual under-class of people who cannot help themselves is not given help—at all. Finally, in some problem areas, government agencies have attempted to involve the resources of private industry—frequently, those very industries whose policies have created the problem in the first place. In consequence, those private industries whose quest for profit has produced the social ills are now being encouraged to pursue profits again by eliminating them. Thus, private industry makes money all the way around.

a basis for comparative analysis of complex organizations

AMITAI ETZIONI

A DEFINITION OF COMPLIANCE

Compliance is universal, existing in all social units. It is a major element of the relationship between those who have power and those over whom they exercise it.[1] Despite its universality, it has been chosen as a base for this comparative study because it is a central element of organizational structure. The emphasis on compliance within the organization differentiates the latter from other types of social units. Characteristics of organizations such as their specificity, size, complexity and effectiveness each enhances the need for compliance. An in turn, compliance is systematically related to many central organizational variables.

Compliance refers both to a relation in which an actor behaves in accordance with a directive supported by another actor's power, and to the orientation of the subordi-

nated actor to the power applied.[2]

By *supported* we mean that those who have power manipulate means which they command in such a manner that certain other actors find following the directive rewarding, while not following it incurs deprivations. In this sense, compliance relations are asymmetric (or "vertical"). But it is not assumed that the subordinates have no power, only that they have less.[3]

The power-*means,* manipulated to support the directives, include physical, material, and symbolic rewards and deprivations. Organizations tend to allocate these means systematically and strive to ensure that they will be used in conformity with the organizational norms.

The *orientation of the subordinated actor* can be characterized as positive (commitment) or negative (alienation). It is determined in part by the degree to which the power applied is considered legitimate by the subordinated actor, and in part by its congruence with the line of action he would desire. We

[1] G. Simmel, "Superiority and subordination as subject matter of sociology," *Amer. J. Sociol.,* 1896, **2,** 167–189, 392–415.

[2] For other usages of the term see R. Bendix, "Bureaucracy: The problem and its setting," *Amer. sociol. Rev.,* 1947, **12,** 502–507, and H. L. Zetterberg, "Complaint actions," *Acta Sociologica,* 1957, **2,** 179–201.

[3] T. Parsons, "The distribution of power in American society," *World Politics,* 1957, **10,** 139; cf. R. Dahrendorf, *Class and class conflict in industrial society* (Stanford, Calif.: Stanford University Press, 1959), p. 169.

refer to this orientation, whether positive or negative, as *involvement* in the organization. In sum, there are two parties to a compliance relationship: an actor who exercises power, and an actor, subject to this power, who responds to this subjection with either more or less alienation or more or less commitment.

The next task is to use compliance as here defined to develop an analytical base for the classification of organizations. This is done in three steps. First, three kinds of *power* are differentiated; then, three kinds of *involvement* are specified; and finally, the associations of kinds of power with kinds of involvement are indicated. These associations—which constitute *compliance relationships*—then serve as the basis of our classification of organizations.

THREE KINDS OF POWER: A COMPARATIVE DIMENSION

A Classification of Power

Power is an actor's ability to induce or influence another actor to carry out his directives or any other norms he supports.[4] Goldhamer and Shils state that "a person may be said to have power to the extent that he influences the behavior of others in accordance with his own intentions." [5] Of course, "his own intentions" might be to influence a person to follow others' "intentions" or those of a collectivity. In organizations, enforcing the collectivity norms is likely to be a condition de-

termining the power-holder's access to the means of power.

Power positions are positions whose incumbents regularly have access to means of power. Statements about power positions imply a particular group (or groups) who are subject to this power. For instance, to state that prison guards have a power position implies the subordination of inmates. In the following analysis we focus on power relations in organizations between those higher and those lower in rank. We refer to those in power positions, who are higher in rank, as *elites* or as organizational *representatives*. We refer to those in subject positions, who are lower in rank, as *lower participants*.

Power differs according to the *means* employed to make the subjects comply. These means may be physical, material, or symbolic.[6]

Coercive power rests on the application, or the threat of application, of physical sanctions such as infliction of pain, deformity, or death; generation of frustration through restriction of movement; or control-

---

[4] See T. Parsons, *The social system* (New York: Free Press, 1951), p. 121.

[5] H. Goldhamer and E. A. Shils, "Types of power and status," *Amer. J. Sociol.*, 1939, **45,** 171.

[6] We suggest that this typology is exhaustive, although the only way we can demonstrate this is by pointing out that every type of power we have encountered so far can be classified as belonging to one of the categories or to a combination of them.

Boulding, Neuman, and Commons have suggested similar typologies. Boulding has developed a typology of "willingness" of persons to serve organizational ends which includes identification, economic means, and coercion. He suggests, however, that identification should be seen as an "economic" way of inducing willingness, a position which we believe is unacceptable to most sociologists. See K. E. Boulding, *The organizational revolution,* New York: Harper & Row, 1953, p. xxxi; and R. Niebuhr, "Coercion, self-interest, and love," *ibid.,* pp. 228–244.

ling through force the satisfaction of needs such as those for food, sex, comfort, and the like.

Remunerative power is based on control over material resources and rewards through allocation of salaries and wages, commissions and contributions, "fringe benefits," services and commodities.

Normative power rests on the allocation and manipulation of symbolic rewards and deprivations through employment of leaders, manipulation of mass media, allocation of esteem and prestige symbols, administration of ritual, and influence over the distribution of "acceptance" and "positive response." (A more eloquent name for this power would be persuasive, or manipulative, or suggestive power. But all these terms have negative value connotations which we wish to avoid.)

There are two kinds of normative power. One is based on the manipulation of esteem, prestige, and ritualistic symbols (such as a flag or a benediction); the other, an allocation and manipulation of acceptance and positive response.[7] Although both powers are found both in vertical and in horizontal relationships, the first is more frequent in vertical relations, between actors who have different ranks, while the second is more common in horizontal relations, among actors equal in rank—in particular, in the power of an "informal" or primary group over its members. Lacking better terms, we refer to the first kind as *pure normative power,* and to the second as *social power.* Social power could be treated as a distinct kind of power. But since powers are here classed according to the means of control employed, and since both social and pure normative power rest on the same set of means—manipulation of symbolic rewards—we treat these two powers as belonging to the same category.

From the viewpoint of the organization, pure normative power is more useful, since it can be exercised directly down the hierarchy. Social power becomes organizational power only when the organization can influence the group's powers, as when a teacher uses the class climate to control a deviant child, or a union steward agitates the members to use their informal power to bring a deviant into line.

Organizations can be ordered according to their power structure, taking into account which power is predominant, how strongly it is stressed compared with other organizations in which the same power is predominant, and which power constitutes the secondary source of control.[8]

Neutralization of Power

Most organizations employ all three kinds of power, but the degree to which they rely on each differs from organization to organization. Most organizations tend to emphasize only one means of power, relying less on the other two. Eveidence to this effect is presented below in the analysis of the compliance structures of various organizations. The major reason for power specialization seems to be that when two kinds

[7] T. Parsons, *The social system, op. cit.,* p. 108.

[8] Two methodological problems raised by such an ordering are discussed in Chapter XII of Amitai Etzioni, *A comparative analysis of complex organizations* (New York: Free Press, 1961), pp. 297–298.

of power are emphasized at the same time, over the same subject group, they tend to neutralize each other.

Applying force, for instance, usually creates such a high degree of alienation that it becomes impossible to apply normative power successfully. This is one of the reasons why rehabilitation is rarely achieved in traditional prisons, why custodial measures are considered as blocking therapy in mental hospitals, and why teachers in progressive schools tend to oppose corporal punishment.

Similarly, the application of renumerative powers makes appeal to "idealistic" (pure normative) motives less fruitful. In a study of the motives which lead to purchase of war bonds, Merton pointed out that in one particularly effective drive (the campaign of Kate Smith), all "secular" topics were omitted and the appeal was centered on patriotic, "sacred" themes. Merton asked a sample of 978 people: "Do you think that it is a good idea to give things to people who buy bonds?"

> Fifty per cent were definitely opposed in principle to premiums, bonuses and other such inducements, and many of the remainder thought it a good idea only for "other people" who might not buy otherwise.[9]
> By omitting this [secular] argument, the authors of her scripts were able to avoid the strain and incompatibility between the two main lines of motivation: unselfish, sacrificing love of country and economic motives of sound investment.[10]

It is possble to make an argument for the opposite position. It might

be claimed that the larger the number of personal needs whose satisfaction the organization controls, the more power it has over the participants. For example, labor unions that cater to and have control over the social as well as the economic needs of their members have more power over those members than do unions that focus only on economic needs. There may be some tension between the two modes of control, some ambivalence and uneasy feeling among members about the combination, but undoubtedly the total control is larger. Similarly, it is obvious that the church has more power over the priest than over the average parishioner. The parishioner is exposed to normative power, whereas the priest is controlled by both normative and remunerative powers.

The issue is complicated by the fact that the *amount* of each kind of power applied must be taken into account. If a labor union with social powers has economic power which is much greater than that of another union, this fact may explain why the first union has greater power in sum, despite some "waste" due to neutralization. A further complication follows from the fact that neutralization may also occur through application of the "wrong" power in terms of the cultural definition of what is appropriate to the particular organization and activity. For example, application of economic power in religious organizations may be less effective than in industries, not because two kinds of power are mixed, but because it is considered illegitimate to use economic pressures to attain religious goals. Finally, some organizations manage to apply two kinds of power abun-

[9] R. K. Merton, *Mass persuasion: The social psychology of a war bond drive* (New York: Harper & Row, 1946), p. 47.
[10] *Ibid.*, p. 45.

dantly and without much waste through neutralization, because they segregate the application of one power from that of the other. The examination below of combat armies and labor unions supplies an illustration of this point.

We have discussed some of the factors related to the tendency of organizations to specialize their power application. In conclusion, it seems that although there can be little doubt that ˈsuch a tendency exists, its scope and a satisfactory explanation for it have yet to be established.

THREE KINDS OF INVOLVEMENT: A COMPARATIVE DIMENSION

Involvement, Commitment, and Alienation

Organizations must continually recruit means if they are to realize their goals. One of the most important of these means is the positive orientation of the participants to the organizational power. *Involvement* [11] refers to the cathectic-evaluative orientation of an actor to an object, characterized in terms of intensity and direction.

The intensity of involvement

ranges from high to low. The direction is either positive or negative. We refer to positive involvement as *commitment* [12] and to negative involvement *as alienation*.[13] (The advantage of having a third term, *involvement,* is that it enables us to refer to the continuum in a neutral way.) Actors can accordingly be placed on an involvement continuum which ranges from a highly intense negative zone through mild negative and mild positive zones to a highly positive zone.[14]

[12] Mishler defined *commitment* in a similar though more psychological way: "An individual is committed to an organization to the extent that central tensions are integrated through organizationally relevant instrumental acts." Cited by C. Argyris, *Personality and organization* (New York: Harper & Row, 1957), p. 202.

[13] We draw deliberately on the associations this term has acquired from its usage by Marx and others. For a good analysis of the idea of alienation in Marxism and of its more recent development, see D. Bell, "The 'rediscovery' of alienation," *J. Phil.,* 1959, **56**, 933–952, and his *The end of ideology* (New York: Free Press, 1960), pp. 335–368.

[14] Several sociologists have pointed out that the relationship between intensity and direction of involvement is a curvilinear one: the more positive or negative the orientation, the more intensely it is held. L. Guttman, "The Cornell technique for scale and intensity analysis," *Educ. & psychol. Measurement,* 1947, **7**, 247–279. By the same author see "The principal components of scale analysis" in S. A. Stouffer *et al., Measurement and prediction* (Princeton, N.J.: Princeton University Press, 1950), pp. 312–371, and "The principal components of scalable attitudes." In P. F. Lazarsfeld (ed.), *Mathematical thinking in the social sciences* (New York: Free Press, 1954), pp. 229–230. See also E. A. Suchman, "The intensity component in attitude and opinion research," in S. A. Stouffer *et al., Measurement and prediction, op. cit.,* pp. 213–276; and E. L. A. McDill, "A comparison of three measures of attitude intensity," *Social Forces,* 1959, **38**, 95–99.

[11] *Involvement* has been used in a similar manner by Nancy C. Morse, *Satisfactions in the white-collar job* (Ann Arbor, Mich.: Survey Research Center, University of Michigan, 1953), pp. 76–96. The term is used in a somewhat different way by students of voting, who refer by it to the psychological investment in the outcome of an election rather than in the party, which would be parallel to Morse's usage and ours. See, for example, A. Campbell, G. Gurin, and W. E. Miller, *The voter decides* (Evanston, Ill.: Row, Peterson & Company, 1954), pp. 33–40.

Three Kinds of Involvement

We have found it helpful to name three zones of the involvement continuum, as follows: *alienative,* for the high alienation zone; *moral,* for the high commitment zone; and *calculative,* for the two mild zones. This classification of involvement can be applied to the orientations of actors in all social units and to all kinds of objects. Hence the definitions and illustrations presented below are not limited to organizations, but are applicable to orientations in general.

Alienative Involvement. Alienative involvement designates an intense negative orientation; it is predominant in relations among hostile foreigners. Similar orientations exist among merchants in "adventure" capitalism, where trade is built on isolated acts of exchange, each side trying to maximize immediate profit.[15] Such an orientation seems to dominate the approach of prostitutes to transient clients.[16] Some slaves seem to have held similar attitudes to their masters and to their work. Inmates in prisons, prisoners of war, people in concentration camps, enlisted men in basic training, all tend to be alienated from their respective organizations.[17]

[15] H. H. Gerth and C. W. Mills, *From Max Weber: Essays in sociology* (New York: Oxford, 1946), p. 67.

[16] K. Davis, "The sociology of prostitution," *Amer. sociol. Rev.,* 1937, **2,** 748–749.

[17] For a description of this orientation see D. Clemmer, *The prison community* (New York: Holt, Rinehart, and Winston, 1958), pp. 152 ff. Attitudes toward the police, particularly on the part of members of the lower classes, are often strictly alienative. See, for example, E. Banfield, *The moral basis of a backward society* (New York: Free Press, 1958).

Calculative Involvement. Calculative involvement designates either a negative or a positive orientation of low intensity. Calculative orientations are predominant in relationships of merchants who have continuous business contracts. Attitudes of (and toward) permanent customers are often predominantly calculative, as are relationships among entrepreneurs in modern (rational) capitalism. Inmates in prisons who have established contact with prison authorities, such as "rats" and "peddlers," often have predominantly calculative attitudes toward those in power.[18]

Moral [19] *Involvement.* Moral involvement designates a positive orienation of high intensity. The involvement of the parishioner in his church, the devoted member in his party, and the loyal follower in his leader are all "moral."

There are two kinds of moral involvement, pure and social. They differ in the same way pure normative power differs from social power. Both are intensive modes of commitment, but they differ in their foci of orientation and in the structural conditions under which they develop. Pure moral commitments are based on internalization of norms and identification with authority (like Riesman's inner-directed "mode of conformity"); social commitment rests on sensitivity to pressures of primary groups and their members (Riesman's "other-directed"). Pure

[18] G. M. Sykes, *The society of captives* (Princeton, N.J.: Princeton University Press, 1958), pp. 87–95.

[19] The term "moral" is used here and in the rest of the article to refer to an orientation of the actor; it does not involve a value position of the observer. See T. Parsons, E. A. Shils *et al., Toward a general theory of action* (Cambridge, Mass.: Harvard University Press, 1952), pp. 170 ff.

moral involvement tends to develop in vertical relationships, such as those between teachers and students, priests and parishioners, leaders and followers. Social involvement tends to develop in horizontal relationships like those in various types of primary groups. Both pure moral and social orientations might be found in the same relationships, but, as a rule, one orientation predominates.

Actors are means to each other in alienative and in calculative relations; but they are ends to each other in "social" relationships. In pure moral relationships the means-orientation tends to predominate. Hence, for example, the willingness of devoted members of totalitarian parties or religious orders to use each other. But unlike the means-orientation of calculative relationships, the means-orientation here is expected to be geared to needs of the collectivity in serving its goals, and not to those of an individual.

As has been stated, the preceding classification of involvement can be applied to the orientations of actors in all social units and to all kinds of objects. The analysis in this book applies the scheme to orientations of lower participants in organizations to various organizational objects, in particular to the organizational power system. The latter includes (1) the directives the organization issues, (2) the sanctions by which it supports its directives, and (3) the persons who are in power positions. The choice of organizational power as the prime object of involvement to be examined here follows from a widely held conception of organization as an administrative system or control structure. To save breath, the orientation of lower participants to the organization as a power (or

control) system is referred to subsequently as *involvement in the organization*. When other involvements are discussed, the object of orientation—for example, organizational goals—is specified.

Organizations are placed on the involvement continuum according to the modal involvement pattern of their lower participants. The placing of organizations in which the participants exhibit more than one mode of involvement is discussed in a later chapter.

COMPLIANCE AS A COMPARATIVE BASE

A Typology of Compliance

Taken together, the two elements —that is, the power applied by the organization *to* lower participants, and the involvement in the organization developed *by* lower participants —constitute the compliance relationship. Combining three kinds of power with three kinds of involvement produces nine types of compliance, as shown in the accompanying table.[20]

The nine types are not equally likely to occur empirically. *Three —the diagonal cases, 1, 5, and 9— are found more frequently than the other six types.* This seems to be true because these three types constitute *congruent* relationships, whereas the other six do not.

The Congruent Types. The in-

[20] A formalization of the relationship between rewards allocation (which comes close to the concept of power as used here) and participation (which, as defined, is similar to the concept of involvement) has been suggested by R. Breton, "Reward structures and participation in an organization." Paper presented to the Eastern Sociological Society, April 1960.

TABLE 1

A Typology of Compliance Relations

Kinds of Power	Kinds of Involvement		
	Alienative	*Calculative*	*Moral*
Coercive	1	2	3
Remunerative	4	5	6
Normative	7	8	9

volvement of lower participants is determined by many factors, such as their personality structure, secondary socialization, memberships in other collectivities, and so on. At the same time, organizational powers differ in the kind of involvement they tend to generate. When the kind of involvement that lower participants have because of other factors [21] and the kind of involvement that tends to be generated by the predominant form of organizational power are the same, we refer to the relationship as *congruent*. For instance, inmates are highly alienated from prisons; coercive power tends to alienate; hence this is a case of a congruent compliance relationship.

Congruent cases are more frequent than noncongruent ones primarily because congruence is more effective, and organizations are social units under external and internal pressure to be effective. The effective application of normative powers, for example, requires that lower participants be highly committed. If lower participants are only mildly committed to the organization, and particularly if they are alienated from it, the application of normative power is likely to be ineffective. Hence the association of normative power with moral commitment.

[21] "Other factors" might include previous applications of the power.

Remuneration is at least partially wasted when actors are highly alienated, and therefore inclined to disobey despite material sanctions; it is also wasted when actors are highly committed, so that they would maintain an effective level of performance for symbolic, normative rewards only. Hence the association of remuneration with calculative involvement.

Coercive power is probably the only effective power when the organization is confronted with highly alienated lower participants. If, on the other hand, it is applied to committed or only mildly alienated lower participants, it is likely to affect adversely such matters as morale, recruitment, socialization, and communication, and thus to reduce effectiveness. (It is likely, though, to create high alienation, and in this way to create a congruent state.)

The Incongruent Types. Since organizations are under pressure to be effective, the suggestion that the six less effective incongruent types are not just theoretical possibilities but are found empirically calls for an explanation. The major reason for this occurrence is that organizations have only limited control over the powers they apply and the involvement of lower participants. The exercise of power depends on the resources the organization can recruit and the license it is allowed in utilizing them. Involvement depends in part on external factors, such as membership of the participants in other collectivities (e.g., membership in labor unions[22]); basic value commitments (e.g., Catholic versus Protestant religious commitments[23]); and the personality structure of the participants (e.g., authoritarian[24]). All these factors may reduce the expected congruence of power and involvement.

A Dynamic Hypothesis. Congruent types are more effective than incongruent types. Organizations are under pressure to be effective. Hence, to the degree that the environment of the organization allows, *organizations tend to shift their compliance structure from incongruent to congruent types* and *organizations which have congruent compliance structures tend to resist factors pushing them toward incongruent compliance structures.*

[22] On the effect of membership in labor unions on involvement in the corporation, see B. Willerman, "Overlapping group identification in an industrial setting." Paper presented to the American Psychological Association. Denver, September 1949, p. 4.

[23] See W. F. Whyte *et al., Money and motivation* (New York: Harper & Row, 1955), pp. 45–46. Protestants are reported to be more committed to the values of saving and productivity, whereas Catholics are more concerned with their social standing in the work group. This makes for differences in compliance: Protestants are reported to be more committed to the corporation's norms than Catholics.

[24] For instance, authoritarian personality structure is associated with a "custodial" orientation to mental patients. See Doris C. Gilbert, and D. J. Levinson, " 'Custodialism' and 'humanism' in staff ideology." In M. Greenblatt, D. J. Levinson, and R. H. Williams (eds.), *The patient and the mental hospital* (New York: Free Press, 1957), pp. 26–27.

Congruence is attained by a change in either the power applied by the organization or the involvement of lower participants. Change of power takes place when, for instance, a school shifts from the use of corporal punishment to stress on the "leadership" of the teachers. The involvement of lower participants may be changed through socialization, changes in recruitment criteria, and the like.

Because the large majority of cases falls into the three categories representing congruent compliance, these three types form the basis for subsequent analysis. We refer to the coercive-alienative type as *coercive compliance;* to the remunerative-calculative type as *utilitarian compliance;* and to the normative-moral type as *normative compliance.* Students of organizational change, conflict, strain, and similar topics may find the six incongruent types more relevant to their work.

Compliance and Authority

The typology of compliance relationships presented above highlights some differences between the present approach to the study of organizational control and that of studies conducted in the tradition of Weber. These studies tend to focus on authority, or legitimate power, as this concept is defined.[25] The significance of authority has been emphasized in modern sociology in the past,

[25] For various definitions and usages of the concept, see C. J. Friedrich (ed.), *Authority* (Cambridge, Mass.: Harvard University Press, 1958). For a formalization of the concept in relation to power and leadership, see A. H. Barton, "Legitimacy, power, and compromise within formal authority structures—a formal model" (Bureau of Applied Social Research, Columbia University, 1958). Mimeographed.

in order to overcome earlier biases that overemphasized force and economic power as the sources of social order. This emphasis, in turn, has led to an overemphasis on legitimate power. True, some authority can be found in the control structure of lower participants in most organizations. True, authority plays a role in maintaining the long-run operations of the organization. But so does nonlegitimated power. Since the significance of legitimate power has been fully recognized, it is time to lay the ghost of Marx and the old controversy, and to give full status to both legitimate and nonlegitimate sources of control.

Moreover, the concept of authority does not take into account differences among powers other than their legitimacy, in particular the nature of the sanctions (physical, material, or symbolic) on which power is based. All three types of power may be regarded as legitimate by lower participants: thus there is normative,[26] remunerative, and coercive authority (differentiated by the kind of power employed, for instance, by a leader, a contractor, and a policeman). But these powers differ in the likelihood that they will be considered legitimate by those subjected to them. Normative power is most likely to be considered legitimate; coercive, least likely; and remunerative is intermediate.

Finally, it is important to emphasize that involvement in the organization is affected both by the legitimacy of a directive and by the degree to which it frustrates the subordinate's need-dispositions. Alienation is produced not only by illegitimate exercise of power, but also by power which frustrates needs, wishes, desires. Commitment is generated not merely by directives which are considered legitimate but also by those which are in line with internalized needs of the subordinate. Involvement is positive if the line of action directed is conceived by the subordinate as both legitimate and gratifying. It is negative when the power is not granted legitimacy and when it frustrates the subordinate. Involvement is intermediate when either legitimation or gratification is lacking. Thus the study of involve-

---

[26] The concept of "normative authority" raises the question of the difference between this kind of authority and normative power. There is clearly a high *tendency* for normative power to be considered legitimate and thus to form an authority relationship. The reason for this tendency is that the motivational significance of rewards and deprivations depends not only on the objective nature of the power applied, but also on the meaning attached to it by the subject. Coercive and remunerative means of control are considerably less dependent on such interpretations than normative ones. Most actors in most situations will see a fine as a deprivation and confinement as a punishment. On the other hand, if the subject does not accept as legitimate the power of a teacher, a priest, or a party official, he is not likely to feel their condemnation or censure as depriving. Since normative power depends on manipulation of symbols, it is much more dependent on "meanings,"

and, in this sense, on the subordinate, than other powers. But it is by no means necessary that the application of normative power always be regarded as legitimate.

A person may, for example, be aware that another person has influenced his behavior by manipulation of symbolic rewards, but feel that he had no right to do so, that he ought not to have such power, or that a social structure in which normative powers are concentrated (e.g., partisan control over mass media; extensive advertising) is unjustified. A Catholic worker who feels that his priest has no right to condemn him because of his vote for the "wrong" candidate may still fear the priest's condemnation and be affected by it.

ment, and hence that of compliance, differs from the study of authority by taking into account the effects of the cathectic as well as the evaluative impact of directives on the orientation of lower participants.

LOWER PARTICIPANTS AND ORGANIZATIONAL BOUNDARIES

Before we can begin our comparisons, the following questions still remain to be answered. Why do we make compliance of lower participants the focus of the comparison? Who exactly are "lower participants"? What are the lower boundaries of an organization? In answering these questions, we employ part of the analytical scheme suggested above, and thus supply the first test of its fruitfulness.

Why Lower Participants?

Compliance of lower participants is made the focus of this analysis for several reasons. First, the control of lower participants is more problematic than that of higher participants because, as a rule, the lower an actor is in the organizational hierarchy, the fewer rewards he obtains. His position is more deprived; organizational activities are less meaningful to him because he is less "in the know," and because often, from his position, only segments of the organization and its activities are visible.[27] Second, since we are concerned with systematic differences

among organizations (the similarities having been more often explored), we focus on the ranks in which the largest differences in compliance can be found.   An interorganizational comparison of middle and higher ranks would show that their compliance structures differ much less than those of the lower ranks.

Who Are Lower Participants?

Organizational studies have used a large number of concrete terms to refer to lower participants: employees, rank-and-file, members, clients, customers, inmates.[28]   These terms are rarely defined.   They are customarily used to designate lower participants in more than one organization, but none can be used for all.

Actually, these terms can be seen as reflecting different positions on at least three analytical dimensions.[29] One is the *nature* (direction and intensity) of the actors' *involvement* in the organization.   Unless some qualifying adjectives such as "cooperative" or "good" are introduced, *inmates* implies alienative involvement.   *Clients* designates people with alienative or calculative involvement. *Customers* refers to people who have a relatively more alienative orientation than clients; one speaks of the clients of professionals

---

[27] The term "visible" is used here and throughout this article as defined by Merton: "the extent to which the norms and the role performances within a group are readily open to observation by others." *Social theory and social structure*, rev. ed. (New York: Free Press, 1957), pp. 319 ff.

[28] For one of the best discussions of the concept of participation, its definition and dimensions, see J. H. Fichter, *Social relations in the urban parish* (Chicago: University of Chicago Press, 1954), Part I, *passim*.

[29] The difference between concrete and analytic membership in corporations has been pointed out by A. S. Feldman, "The interpenetration of firm and society." Paper presented at the International Social Science Council Round Table on Social Implications of Technical Change, Paris, 1959.

but not ordinarily of their customers. *Member* is reserved for those who have at least some, usually quite strong, moral commitment to their organization. *Employee* is used for people with various degrees of calculative involvement.

A second dimension underlying these concrete terms is the degree to which lower participants are *subordinated* to organizational powers. Inmates, it seems, are more subordinated than employees, employees more than members, and members more than clients. A study in which subordination is a central variable would take into account that it includes at least two subvariables: the extent of control in each area (e.g., "tight" versus remote control); and the scope of control, measured by the number of areas in which the subject is subordinated. Such refinement is not required for our limited use of this dimension.

A third dimension is the amount of *performance* required from the participants by the organization: it is high for employees, low for inmates, and lowest for clients and customers.[30]

Using concrete terms to designate groups of participants without specifying the underlying dimensions creates several difficulties. First of all,

the terms cannot be systematically applied. Although "members" are in general positively involved, sometimes the term is used to designate lower participants with an alienative orientation. Archibald, for instance, uses this term to refer to members of labor unions who are members only *pro forma* and who see in the union simply another environmental constraint, to which they adjust by paying dues.

> Most workers entered the yards not merely ignorant of unions, but distrustful of them. . . . They nonetheless joined the unions, as they were compelled to do, with little protest. They paid the initiation fees, averaging not more than twenty dollars, much as they would have bought a ticket to the county fair: it cost money, but maybe the show would be worth the outlay. As for dues, they paid them with resignation to the principle that all joys of life are balanced by a measure of pain.[31]

The term *customers* suggests that the actors have no moral commitments to their sources of products and services. But sometimes it is used to refer to people who buy from cooperatives, frequent only unionized barbers, and remain loyal to one newspaper—that is, to people who are willing to suffer some economic loss because they see in these sources of service something which is "good in itself"—people who, in short, have some moral commitments.

Any moral commitment on the part of mental patients, designated as *inmates,* is viewed either with

---

[30] Participants of a social unit might also be defined as all those who share an institutionalized set of role-expectations. We shall not employ this criterion since it blurs a major distinction, that between the organization as such and its social environment. Members of most groups share such role-expectations with outsiders.

A criterion of participation which is significant for other purposes than ours is whether lower participants have formal or actual powers, such as those reflected in the right to vote, submit grievances, or strike.

[31] Katherine Archibald, *Wartime shipyards* (Berkeley and Los Angeles: University of California Press, 1947), pp. 131–132.

surprise or as a special achievement of the particular mental hospital; on the other hand, members of labor unions are "expected" to show moral commitment and are labeled "apathetic" if they do not. The fact that some mental patients view their hospital as their home, and thus are positively involved, whereas labor union members may see their organization as a secondary group only, is hidden by the terminology employed. The same point could be made for differences in performance and in subordination.

Although the use of such concrete terms leads to overgeneralization, by implying that all lower participants of an organization have the characteristics usually associated with the label, they can also impede generalization. An illustration is supplied by studies of parishioners. Many of these studies focus on problems of participation, such as "apathy," high turnover, and declining commitment. But rarely are comparisons drawn, or insights transferred, from the study of members of voluntary associations and political organizations. Actually, all these organizations are concerned with the moral commitment of lower participants who have few performance obligations and little subordination to the organization.

Another advantage of specifying the analytical dimensions underlying these concepts is that the number of dimensions is limited, whereas the number of concrete terms grows continuously with the number of organizations studied. Thus the study of hospitals introduces patients; the analysis of churches brings up parishioners; and the examination of armies adds soldiers. Following the present procedure, we can proceed to characterize the lower participants of additional organizations by the use of the same three dimensions.

Specifying the underlying dimensions enables us not only to formulate analytical profiles of a large variety of lower participants, but also to compare them systematically with each other on these three dimensions. For instance, "soldiers" (in combat) are high on all three dimensions, whereas inmates are high on subordination and alienation but low on performance; employees are medium in involvement and subordination, but high on performance obligations. The import of such comparisons will become evident later.

Finally, whereas concrete terms tend to limit analysis to participants at particular levels, analytical terms such as alienative, calculative, and moral can be applied equally well to participants at all levels of the organizational hierarchy.

Ideally, in a book such as this, we should refer to lower participants in analytical terms, those of various degrees of involvement, subordination, and performance obligations. Since this would make the discussion awkward, the concrete terms are used, but only to refer to *typical* analytical constellations. *Inmates* are lower participants with high alienation, low performance obligations, and high subordination. The term will not be used to refer to other combinations which are sometimes found among lower participants in prisons. *Members* is used to refer only to lower participants who are highly committed, medium on subordination, and low on performance obligations; it is not used to refer to

TABLE 2

Analytical Specifications of Some Concepts
Referring to Lower Participants *

Lower Participants	Nature of Involvement (Intensity and Direction)	Subordination	Performance Obligations
Inmates	High, negative	High	Low
Employees	Low, negative or positive	Medium	High
Customers	Low, negative or positive	None	Low
Parishioners	High, positive	Low	Low
Members	High, positive	Medium to Low	Low
Devoted Adherents	High, positive	High	High

* This table contains a set of definitions to be used. It is not exhaustive, either in concepts referring to lower participants or in possible combinations of "scores" on the various dimensions.

alienated lower participants in voluntary associations. Similarly, other terms are used as specified in Table 2.

Lower versus Higher Participants

Higher participants have a "permanent" power advantage over lower participants because of their organizational position. Thus, by definition, higher participants as a group are less *subordinated* than lower participants. Often, though not in all organizational types, they are also more *committed,* and have more *performance obligations* (if we see decision making and other mental activities as performances). Thus the three dimensions which serve to distinguish among various types of lower participants also mark the dividing line between lower and higher participants. These very dimensions also enable us to suggest a way to delineate the organizational boundaries—that is, to distinguish between participants and nonparticipants.

Organizational Boundaries

Students of organizations must often make decisions about the boundaries of the unit they are studying: who is a participant, who an outsider. March and Simon, for example, take a broad view of organizational boundaries: "When we describe the chief participants of most business organizations, we generally limit our attention to the following five major classes: employees, investors, suppliers, distributers, and consumers." [32]

We follow a narrower definition and see as participants all actors who are high on at least one of the three dimensions of participation: involvement, subordination, and performance. Thus, students, inmates, soldiers, workers, and many others are included. Customers and clients, on the other hand, who score low on

[32] J. G. March and H. Simon, *Organizations* (New York: Wiley, 1958), p. 89.

all three criteria, are considered "outsiders."

We should like to underscore the importance of this way of delineating the organizational boundaries. It draws the line much "lower" than most studies of bureaucracies, which tend to include only persons who are part of a formal hierarchy: priests, but not parishioners; stewards, but not union members; guards, but not inmates; nurses, but not patients. We treat organizations as collectivities of which the lower participants are an important segment. To exclude them from the analysis would be like studying colonial structures without the natives, stratification without the lower classes, or a political regime without the citizens or voters.

It seems to us especially misleading to include the lower participants in organizational charts when they have a formal role, as privates in armies or workers in factories, and to exclude them when they have no such status, as is true for parishioners or members. This practice leads to such misleading comparisons as seeing the priests as the privates of the church and teachers as the lowest-ranking participants of schools, in both cases ignoring the psychological import of having "subordinates." One should not let legal or administrative characteristics stand in the way of a sociological analysis. However, the main test of the decision to delineate the organization as we have chosen follows: it lies in the scope, interest, and validity of the propositions this approach yields. . . .[33]

[33] A preliminary review of research conducted since the first publication of these lines by a number of scholars. See Amitai Etzioni, "Organizational Dimensions and Their Interrelations: a Theory of Compliance," in Bernard Indik and S. Kenneth Berrien, eds., *People, Groups and Organizations* (New York: Teachers College Press, 1968; Columbia University Press, 1968), pp. 94–109.

public bureaucracies:
the issue of accountability*

JAMES R. HUDSON
ANNE MOONEY HUDSON

THE EXPANDED ROLE OF PUBLIC BUREAUCRACIES

As a result of social legislation passed in the forty years since the election of Franklin D. Roosevelt and the promulgation of the New Deal, government at every level, largely on impetus from the federal level, has expanded greatly its direct services to individual citizens. As circumstances changed, the definition of essential services, and hence that of desirable official programs and policies, changed (Miller and Rein, 1964; Reich, 1964; Reiss, 1965). Periodic expansion and redefinition of government's responsibilities followed from shifts in the economic situation, technology, composition and distribution of population, and ideas about what constitutes a decent standard of living (Titmuss, 1968).

One consequence of this governmental expansion has been a proliferation of rules and regulations stipulating eligibility and continuity of services; this increases greatly the

government's jurisdiction over the individual citizen (Carlin et al., 1966: 35–36). Reich (1964: 739), for example, demonstrates that the government is in a position to allocate various kinds of wealth in the form of "a profession, job, or right to receive income, [which] are the basis of . . . various statuses in society, and may therefore be the most meaningful and distinctive wealth" an individual can possess. For all practical purposes, the government, in fact, may be the only source of certain benefits and services for much of the population. If one needs low-rent housing, medical care, compensation for a disability, or income during periods of unemployment, the best and perhaps the only way to get them is to deal with an agency of government.

Many of the services provided by public bureaucracies were, until recently, defined not as rights, but as privileges that could be granted, sometimes at the cost of civil and political rights, or denied. The movement to recognize as social rights [1] as access to such services as

* The research upon which this paper is based was supported by the National Institute of Mental Health (#1 RO 1 MH 14997-01). Additional funds for clerical assistance were made available under a Grant-in-Aid from the Graduate School of the State University of New York at Stony Brook.

Prepared especially for this volume.

[1] Marshall (1963:65–122) distinguishes three categories of citizen rights—civil, political and social—each of which is associated with a particular institution of government. Civil rights permit ownership of property and insure individual freedom and justice. They are maintained and protected primarily through the courts. Political rights give the citizen access to political decision-making, either as a voter

housing, medical care, education, and police protection received great impetus from the civil rights movement. Excluded citizens and their representatives began to insist that services nominally provided for the whole citizenry, but, in fact, provided differentially for separate segments of the population, be available without discrimination everywhere. For example, ghetto residents, not just the outsiders with businesses there, demanded law enforcement in their areas on a par with the rest of the community. School boards were harassed to repair buildings, distribute qualified teachers fairly, and expend funds more evenly through their districts, rather than differentially according to the class and power of the area residents. Black citizens demanded to be addressed with the respectful titles accorded others and not to be harassed by police for actions that would draw no attention if the person were white. Equality of citizens was to be redefined to cover members of the population previously excluded.

The civil rights movement also challenged the traditional relationship between the public bureaucracy and its citizen-clients. Agency staffs, echoing an old ideology (Marshall, 1963:80–81), tended to regard their clients as supplicants rather than as

rights-bearing citizens. Or the clients were seen as patients, unable to fend for themselves and dependent upon the agency for direction (Carlin et al., 1966:34). If the client is regarded as a patient, then the services provided can be viewed as therapeutic; offering or withholding them is done in accordance with some theory of therapy. Since the client is in need of help, the diagnosis must be left in the hands of the professional staff and the client cannot be permitted to "prescribe" for himself. Other labels have similar consequences for client-agency interaction.

The critical role of public bureaucracies in insuring social rights would itself justify consideration of how they are held accountable. But a still more compelling reason exists. A growing literature on the operations of social welfare departments, public schools, and municipal police forces describes the policies and programs of these agencies as not simply less progressive than might be desired, but as actually more debilitating than constructive for their clientele (Briar, 1966; Chevigny, 1969; Garfinkel, 1955). The critics claim that public agencies contribute, to a substantial degree, to the very problems that they are called upon to alleviate (Cahn and Cahn, 1964; Marris and Rein, 1967).

Public agencies not only deny social rights, but violate civil and political rights as well. For example, political activities by residents of public housing have served as justification for eviction (Rosen, 1967: 195; Smith, 1969). Some agencies have disallowed benefits or services for questionable reasons (Smith, 1969; Aspelund, 1969–70). There has also been the more general criti-

---

or as an office-holder. The exercise of political rights is most closely associated with legislatures and executive offices at all levels of government. Social rights are less clearly defined and institutionalized. They include a minimum of economic security, the opportunity to share in the social heritage of the nation, and the capacity to exercise civil and political rights. Social rights are guaranteed to an important degree by educational institutions and social services.

cism that social welfare agencies foster "welfare colonialism" rather than creating independent clients.

The public school system, at least that part of it which serves minority groups, has been accused not only of failing to give the same level of services to all segments of the population, but also of providing negative education (Kozol, 1967). The pupil not only fails to learn, but, in fact, he declines in measured intelligence. He leaves the school relatively "poorer" than he entered it. The schools become a means of keeping minorities in subordinate positions rather than a route to liberation (Clark, 1967:111–163).

Finally, the burden of several studies and presidential commission reports has been that local police contribute to malaise in urban centers by discriminatory practices (Report to the National Advisory Commission on Civil Disorders, 1968; Skolnick, 1969:241–292). The police do not treat minority group members with the same deference they show to other citizens. In addition, police services are not the same in lower-class neighborhoods as they are in middle-class neighborhoods. There is evidence that crimes committed against blacks by other blacks are not taken as seriously as crimes by blacks against whites (Banton, 1964:172–176; Wilson, 1968:279–299).

This catalog of criticisms could be enlarged, but what has been presented is sufficient to document the centrality of public agencies in the lives of American citizens. If citizens are to enjoy their social as well as their civil and political rights, considerable change must be made in the quality of services, attitudes toward clients, and the administration of policies. Some means must be found to make public agencies more responsible to their clients and to the community of citizens.

THE AUTONOMY AND POWER OF PUBLIC BUREAUCRACIES

As public bureaucracies have gained an ever more central role in American society, *the degree to which they can be held accountable to the political process has decreased.* Reduction in direct political accountability of these bureaucracies has come about both through civil service reform and professionalization.

The civil service merit system was instituted to eliminate direct political pressure on public servants. That system has presumably contributed, as was intended, to at least minimum competence of public employees, on the one hand, and to job protection and promotion for merit, on the other. Thus, rational, efficient, fair, and apolitical operation of government bureaus is fostered. But reform has had the latent consequence that public servants were able, over the years, to enclose themselves in a protective mantle of administrative procedure (Rogers, 1968:266–323; Sayre and Kaufman, 1960:402–451).

Another development effectively separates government employees still further from any (even legitimate) outside supervision and control. This is the demand for recognition of professional status, with its implicit privilege of being judged for performance only, by peers. Social welfare workers, school teachers, and lately policemen have claimed professional status and have been variously successful in gaining recognition. Once professional status has been conferred on public employees, it is extremely hard to undermine their claims for (1) autonomy in their day-to-day work, (2) rejection of nonprofessional review of individual decisions, and (3) nearly complete authority to accept, modify, or reject innovations proposed by lay boards of supervisors, administrative heads, or elected officials.

Claims for professional status are not made in a void. As the mandate for services has become more complex, greater expertise has been required. Part of the power of the public bureaucrats rests upon their monopoly of such skills. For example, a modern police department with its centralized communication system, its sophisticated arsenal, and its broad mandate for law enforcement needs to recruit a better-trained cadre of officers. The rise of police science courses in community colleges and universities reflects that change in police training. It is small wonder, then, that the police ask for more autonomy.

Although legislative mandates vary in the amount of autonomy they grant to local public agencies, it is clear that many maintain a great deal of discretionary power. Even in programs that are highly structured, the interpretation of rules leads to differences in execution. Derthick (1968:258), in a comprehensive study of Aid to Families of Dependent Children programs in Massachusetts, found differences among 29 cities in (1) rates of eligibility, (2) amount of cash grant, and (3) attitudes toward clients. She attributed these differences to the rigidity with which the local welfare

director interpreted regulations. His ability to interpret rested with his monopoly of knowledge of the rules. "The local administrator becomes an unchallengeable authority on what the rules require, not because his mastery of them is perfect, but because it far exceeds that of anyone outside the agency" (Derthick, 1968: 258). And, given constant revision of the rules, this power is increased, making it difficult for the AFDC recipient or an elected official to determine what discretion the administrator has and how he is using it.

In a more loosely organized program, local housing authorities have been delegated a great deal of power by the federal government over the formulation of rules determining eligibility and continued occupancy of public housing. The outcome is that those who are applying for admission, and those who are being evicted, find it next to impossible to discover what criteria are being employed (Rosen, 1967:157). The ability to make and interpret rules gives the agency a tremendous advantage in dealing with clients and would-be clients.

Other organizational features give public agencies power in their relations with clients or with locally elected officials. Administrators at the local level can claim that they must follow guidelines established at state or national levels. In a centralized public school system, control over curriculum may not rest with individual schools, and administrators are reluctant to encourage innovations that jeopardize their position vis-à-vis the central administration. This same claim to lack of flexibility can be made in organizations that must maintain accreditation by a professional association or a federated watchdog agency. The outcome is the same; local administrators are able to hide behind other authority structures.

At the same time that these organizations have gained more hegemony over internal operations, the members of these agencies have banded into politically active partisan employee associations. And the focus of these associations includes not only struggles over scarce fiscal resources, but also job descriptions, promotion and tenure proceedings, working conditions in general, and physical mobility on the job.

More important, many major political issues are directly linked to these agencies; public safety, education, sanitation, housing, and social welfare all have been politicized. Sometimes the issue is financial, as in the annual or biannual bargaining over contracts, where the bargaining agents for public employees are willing to use job actions, strikes, and confrontations to gain their collective goals. At other times, the issue involves the quality, quantity, and availability of service; clients and potential clients mobilize to challenge the distribution of these services and the hegemony of the public bureaucracies over their administration.

Where the work of municipal agencies is a political issue, the success of any mayor is bound up with his ability to gain their confidence and cooperation. It is important to remember that the mayor's life expectancy in office is much shorter than that of a public bureaucrat. Given the security that comes with tenure and civil service protection, the latter can take a longer view

than a mayor, who must produce dramatic results quickly to stay in office. The advantage is with the public employee, who can be less demanding in any given situation but who never loses sight of his long-term goals.

ACCOUNTABILITY STRATEGIES

These developments have generated concern among clients, client groups, social planners, and those who are responsible for policies that regulate public bureaucracies. They have proposed and implemented a number of strategies that would make these agencies more responsive and responsible. One can distinguish among these strategies three broad categories: (1) direct actions taken by the clients themselves, such as picketing, sit-ins, and other forms of confrontation; (2) government programs or policies directed at encouraging client participation, such as Community Action Programs under OEO and community control of services; and (3) procedures for review and redress of agency actions as exemplified by fair hearing procedures, civilian review boards for police, and legal services.

The tactics of confrontation center in mobilizing clients and potential clients to challenge directly actions taken or not taken by public agencies. Although the main target is the agency itself, another objective is to generate support from third parties who might be able to bring pressure (Lipsky, 1970). Confrontations seek both immediate alterations in official practices and permanent policy changes. Although the style of confrontation is non-bureaucratic, if long-term effects are to occur, the demands must be translated into routines and, therefore, bureaucratized.

Intervention to give clients more say in the operations of public agencies has taken several forms. For example, Community Action Programs were created under OEO to stimulate the involvement of the poor. In some cases, direct participation in policy making was fostered under the maximum feasible participation provision in the original act. Some programs recruited the poor to fill slots in newly created agencies, with the aim of developing organizational skills among the client population. Alternatively, some of these programs were to build a constituency capable of social action among the poor (Kramer, 1970:260–273). The diagnosis of poverty that stimulated these programs and policies emphasized the alienation of the poor from the agencies that ostensibly served their needs and the apathy that seemed to pervade poor communities. These programs sought to alter the social organization of poor people.

The final strategy for making public bureaucracies more accountable to their clienteles lies in citizen-initiated complaint procedures, e.g., fair hearings in social welfare departments and public housing authorities, civilian-controlled police review boards, and legal assistance. The client can challenge a specific action taken by the agency either by appealing to a hearing board or by initiating legal proceedings. The question addressed by citizen-initiated complaint procedures is whether the client is getting fair, equitable, or just treatment from a public bureaucracy.

LIMITATIONS OF ACCOUNTABILITY STRATEGIES

Characteristics of the Clients

If one stands back and looks at each of these strategies, certain common elements emerge that raise serious questions about their effectiveness for insuring social rights. These elements can be distinguished analytically as characteristics of individuals and of organizations, although this separation cannot always be made empirically.

Social rights, as understood by Marshall (1968) include the ability of a citizen to use his civil and political rights. Enjoyment of these rights rests upon an important condition, namely, the knowledge of what they are, vis-à-vis the government and its agents. Almond and Verba (1963:169) formulate this problem of client knowledge in terms of subject competence: "The competence of the subject is more a matter of being aware of his rights under the rules than in participation in the making of the rules." Carlin and others (1966:70), in a more narrow vein, discuss legal competence and assert that the legally competent citizen "will know how to use this machinery and when to use it." Thus, at the individual level, these strategies depend upon a knowledgeable citizen. The question then becomes, to ascertain just how knowledgeable the target population is about these strategies.

The evidence about such knowledge is rather definite with regard to fair hearing procedures and legal assistance. Many who might employ such channels of redress do not know of their existence. Handler (1968), for example, studied the use of fair hearing procedures among AFDC recipients in Wisconsin. He found that "despite apparent efforts of the state department [Wisconsin Department of Health and Social Services] to provide a simple method of appeal that would bypass the county administration and place the client in the guiding hands of the district supervisor, only 6 percent of the entire sample knew of their rights and knew enough to use the department procedural route" (1968:28). In another study of low income individuals in Wisconsin, Levine and Preston (1970:105) found that 60 percent of their sample had never heard of Legal Aid and 40 percent had no knowledge of legal services under OEO, although there had been "considerable publicity about the program after OEO started funding."

These studies confirm that many clients of public bureaucracies are either unaware of avenues of redress or uninformed about what their rights are, and hence unsure about taking action. But even if citizens know about redress procedures, they may be unwilling to use them. The decision to employ these strategies has several related dimensions. One is the citizen's evaluation of the possible effectiveness of pursuing a given course. If it is perceived to offer very little chance of success, the citizen will refuse to activate the procedure. His willingness to use redress strategies may be influenced also by his relationship with the agency. He must decide whether initiating action against an agency is going to cost him more than he gains. For example, to challenge a caseworker on a given decision can jeopardize future decisions. If the

worker has a certain degree of discretion in dealing with a welfare client, the client may consider it a wiser choice not to complain in order to stay in the good graces of the worker. Handler (1966:170) used the example of a mother who has been advised to obtain a job. While privately objecting to the decision, she concludes that "in the 'long run' it would be 'better' if she agreed with the caseworker and went to work." On the other hand, a client may be more willing to initiate a complaint when an agency decision would completely deprive him of benefits. Thus, threats of eviction from public housing or denial of an application may prod the citizen to action. The point, however, remains: to initiate action depends upon the agency-client relationship, and the power in a continuous relationship rests with the agency.

Finally, the client's motivation to challenge an agency's decision depends upon his conception of the legal status of the benefits he has applied to receive. Has he a right to certain grants or services, or is he the recipient of charities that obligate him not to complain about or interfere with agency procedures and decisions? Brian (1966:53) found that, among welfare applicants in a California city, the approach toward the agency "is not that of a rights-bearing citizen claiming benefits to which he is entitled by law but that of suppliant." Interview questions about the right of welfare department workers to ask questions, visit the recipient's home at night, or advise budget counseling elicited responses supporting the agency's right to invade a client's privacy. Indeed, the powers that applicants say should be granted to the agency by recipients indicate a clear lack of self-esteem. If this study is representative of clients' attitudes toward themselves and toward the welfare bureaucracy, the motivation to challenge or question public agencies must be exceedingly low.

On the individual level, then, the two major variables affecting client and would-be client use of strategies to modify the behavior of public bureaucracies are (1) knowledge of the procedures and (2) willingness to employ them. To build a system of accountability of public agencies that assumes these features to be present in the target population is open to serious question, since this population has been found to be politically uninformed, socially isolated, and more generally unaware and unwilling to act.

Organizational Impact

The most serious organizational weakness of the change strategies stems from the imbalance of power between the two groups involved, clients and bureaucrats. Most of these strategies are designed for individual complaintants or appellants from a rather amorphous mass of potential users. Dissatisfied citizens who use these avenues of redress to challenge public agencies usually do so on a one-time basis. For the citizens, then, maintaining channels of redress is not always a central concern.

The imbalance between citizens and bureaucracies remains even if citizens organize to carry out systematic confrontations. Lipsky's (1970) study of the New York City rent strikes details the problems that citizens faced in trying to bring about not only policy changes on the

part of landlords, but reforms in agencies that administer housing regulations. In building an organizational base, the protest leaders had to solve a number of confounding problems. First, to mobilize a constituency they needed to provide inducements or rewards for involvement. While symbolic rewards are useful in the short run, e.g., promises of action, newspaper publicity, etc., these must be supplemented by more substantial rewards sooner or later. Protest politics uses resources; one of the paradoxes of protest is: "the greater the resource expended in protest, the greater the public attention; but the more expensive the protest, the more difficult to initiate or repeat" (Lipsky, 1970:167).

The needs of a protest organization pull leaders in two directions: they must attend to the day-to-day demands of the organization, but must also participate in the public side of protests, like picketing, marching, and speaking. The protest organization also needs a battery of counter-experts to challenge the established bureaucrats, such as lawyers, architects, city planners, and grantsmen to negotiate with the government and foundations. Finally, if the protest organization gains enough legitimacy to enter into policy-making discussion, it needs consultants and staff "with expertise and experience in the policy area" (Lipsky, 1970:175). Few protest groups are able to put together that kind of organization.

By contrast, the bureaucracies and the bureaucrats form much more tightly woven bodies, distrustful of those outside the organization. Rank-and-file police hostility toward the civilian review board in Philadelphia was based on its non-bureaucratic character. Policemen could not anticipate the possible outcomes of a hearing, nor could they evaluate the consequences of hearings for their careers (Hudson, forthcoming). Because of their organization, it is relatively easy for public bureaucrats to challenge reforms, and, if necessary, to mobilize a constituency—as was the case in New York City with the civilian complaint review board.

Agencies against which attacks are launched can mobilize a number of tactics to blunt the impact of protest. These tactics include dispensing such symbolic satisfactions as on-the-spot inspections, calls for new studies, or a shift in official rhetoric. They can take immediate action on the most extreme cases, thereby robbing the protest group of its most visible and dramatic instances of official neglect. Public agencies can claim lack of jurisdiction, mandate, and resources, and in the end, may use the protest to justify a request for more resources. Finally, these agencies can postpone actions for a given time while the protest group's resources are depleted. If confrontations are to be effective, action must be swift. In a long, drawn-out match, the protesters are in a much more vulnerable position than public agencies.

Lipsky concludes that the New York City rent strikes were of limited success. Although some changes were achieved, the public agencies remained well entrenched. "Rent strike organizations played little part in determining the nature of solutions to housing maintenance problems" (Lipsky, 1970:192). The protest groups did not have the staff, the expertise, nor the style to penetrate decision-making.

The most interesting feature of legal action is that it seeks to redefine the client as a rights-bearing citizen rather than a supplicant. The services agencies provide are regarded as property to which eligible clients are entitled. The effectiveness of legal assistance is greatest where a class action is feasible. Unlike confrontations, it can rely upon a single individual or a few clients to carry the case to completion, eliminating the necessity to keep a constituency constantly mobilized. But legal action based upon a single case has one drawback. As Rosen (1967: 249) points out in reference to public housing, the "attorney who challenges a local housing authority will frequently have to sell his precedent making case if he is offered the price which he cannot refuse: an apartment for his client." The willingness of a public agency to settle an individual case out of court also reduces the chances for publicity and thus lessens the impact of a favorable settlement on potential plaintiffs.

Another characteristic of all these strategies is the level of the organization at which complaints are made and resolved. Fair hearing procedures, civilian complaint review boards, and some legal actions deal solely with the delivery level. Each resolution is a settlement between one citizen and the agency. The serial settlement of complaints does not open the agency to general review of policies. The issue, as seen from the point of view of the urgency, is that in a specific case some mismanagement, miscalculation, or oversight may have occurred. Operating at the delivery level of the organization, these accountability strategies do not penetrate beyond the periphery. The core of the organization can be successfully protected.

It has been argued to the contrary (Minter, 1964) that fair hearings in social welfare agencies can have a more permanent effect. "What one appeal reveals about the effectiveness of the agency policy and administrative practice *should* [emphasis added] serve to strengthen both policy and practice" (Minter, 1964:2). But a careful reading of this argument reveals that any general review of policy and practice is the burden of the agency. There is no evidence that accumulated complaints alter agency practice, but only that the *potential* is there. The more important observation is that power to formulate policy rests with the agency and not with the client population or its representatives. The agency stance is not to be accountable for its policy, but only for whether actions taken by its representatives are in line with its policy. Investigation of the Philadelphia Police Advisory Board, a civilian-controlled review agency, also revealed serial settlement of complaints. The Board, from time to time, did make more general recommendations about recurring problems, and while some were incorporated into police policies, the Board had no authority to insist on their adoption nor any means to ascertain what action had been taken. Thus, the autonomy of the police department was preserved.

Finally, to return to an earlier theme, the organizational base of public bureaucracies gives them a tremendous amount of political power. Several examples demonstrate this power. The civilian complaint review boards in both Philadelphia and New York City were targets of concentrated and continuous opposition by the associations of police officers in those cities. In the case of Philadelphia, the review board was subject to a number of lawsuits that curtailed operations during its ten-year history. Although the Supreme Court of Pennsylvania ruled in its favor, the mayor of Philadelphia disbanded the Board over the strong protests of civil rights and civil liberties organizations. In New York City, the Patrolman's Benevolent Association was able to put the civilian review board issue on the ballots as a referendum. The PBA backed its campaign with tremendous financial resources and mobilized a powerful anti-review board coalition. The supporters of civilian review, who included most of the major political leaders and a phalanx of liberal groups, were simply no match.

The history of OEO programs also reveals the political imbalance between the client population and the bureaucratic power structure. Both the legal aid program and the community action program became political issues in a number of communities. As Kramer (1969:262) notes, the debate over whether CAPs were to be the core of a social movement or, rather, a social service agency, generated strains "around the *control* and *purpose* of the CAP, in which it became increasingly obvious that CAP could not represent the interests of the poor *and* the establishment, nor successfully promote the development of social service programs *and* at the same time organize the poor effectively." In the struggle, it became clear that the poor could not organize as an effective constituency to challenge the organizational power of established agencies of local government.

The weaknesses of strategies to make public agencies more accountable to their clients or potential clients, as viewed from the organizational level, can be summarized as follows: the poor lack resources (1) to mobilize for continuous political action and (2) to develop organizations that can successfully challenge the existing power structure. Where strategies exist that the client population can employ, the bureaucracies have a number of tactics to soften the impact of citizen complaints by making limited concessions. Finally, where complaint procedures operate, the agency can hold the line at the periphery of the organization so that policy formation remains in their control.

MAXIMIZING EFFECTIVENESS

As we pointed out in the beginning, increased concern for the provision of social rights to all citizens has made public bureaucracies more central to the lives of large segments of the population than was previously the case. These public agencies have become the means for delivering a wide range of services to many citizens, services like financial aid, housing, medical care, and education. At the same time, the agencies have become the focus of criticism— over both the adequacy of services and the manner in which they are delivered. It was argued, in part, that in providing social rights the civil and political rights of recipients were jeopardized.

To reduce the autonomy of public bureaucracies and to make them more responsive, responsible, and accountable, a number of strategies have been developed. The effectiveness of these strategies, however, proved to be problematic for reasons that stemmed from the individual characteristics of the target population, the organizational potential of that population, and the organizational strength of the public bureaucracies. Taken as a whole, the public agencies have been able to neutralize these strategies by bureaucratic delays, political action, and control of vital information.

Nevertheless, it would not be a fair conclusion that these strategies have failed in all instances. Confrontations, government-sponsored programs, and review and redress procedures have operated in many communities for the benefit of client populations. Lipsky (1970), for example, concluded that some alterations in the behavior of certain government agencies were achieved through confrontation. The CAPs did stimulate citizens to become more active on their own behalf and did bring about some reforms in public agency practices. During its history, the Philadelphia Police Advisory Board settled a number of grievances between citizens and police and produced some reforms in police practices. The Legal Service program under OEO certainly gave some citizens relief in their dealings with public agencies (Piven and Cloward, 1971:306–320). On balance, then, one may state that public agencies can be made more aware of the rights of clients, more accountable for their actions, and more receptive to policy changes.

The political and bureaucratic structures, however, have been able to challenge some of these strategies.

The dismantling of civilian review boards in Philadelphia and New York City attests to the success that public bureaucrats and their employee associations have had in guarding their autonomy. In the same way, the revision in OEO policy in the 1967 amendments reveals the weaknesses of the target population in keeping such channels viable (Moynihan, 1969:158).

What we are witnessing is probably a protracted struggle between public agencies and their client populations. The pendulum now appears to be swinging back toward public agencies; they seem to be in a commanding position. The services public agencies provide are not going to decrease in importance. Most of the signs suggest that they are going to play an increasingly important role in the lives of many of us. It will not be long before new services—government-sponsored health services, for example—become the responsibility of public bureaucracies. As the client population of these services expands to include more middle-class citizens, the problem of mobilizing or creating greater political pressure will also increase. What this portends for the balance of power between client and agency can only be a matter of speculation. It seems clear, however, that some strategies will receive new support and will be institutionalized and legitimated.

REFERENCES

ALMOND, GABRIEL A., and SIDNEY VERBA
1965 *The Civic Culture.* Boston: Little, Brown and Company.

ASPELUND, CARL L.
1969–70 "Constitutional Law—Search and Seizure in Welfare Cases." *Loyola Law Review* 16, 495–506.

BANTON, MICHAEL
1964 *The Policeman in the Community.* London: Tavestock.

BRIAR, SCOTT
1966 "Welfare From Below: Recipients' Views of the Public Welfare System," in Jacobus ten-Broek and California Law Review (eds.). *The Law of the Poor,* pp. 46–61. San Francisco, California: Chandler Publishing Company.

CAHN, E. S., and J. C. CAHN
1964 "The War on Poverty: A Civilian Perspective." *Yale Law Journal* 73 (July), 1317–1345.

CARLIN, JEROME E., JAN HOWARD and SHELDON L. MESSINGER
1966 "Civil Justice and the Poor." *Law and Society Review* 1 (November), 9–89.

CHEVIGNY, PAUL
1969 *Police Power: Police Abuses in New York City.* New York: Torchbooks.

CLARK, KENNETH B.
1967 *Dark Ghetto: Dilemmas of Social Power.* New York: Harper Torchbooks.

DERTHICK, MARTHA
1968 "Intercity Differences in Administration of the Public Assistance Program: The Case of Massachusetts," in James Q. Wilson (ed.). *City Politics and Public Policy,* pp. 243–266. New York: John Wiley & Sons.

GARFINKEL, HAROLD
1955 "Conditions of Successful Degradation Ceremonies." *American Journal of Sociology* 61 (March), 420–424.

HANDLER, JOEL F.
1966 "Controlling Official Behavior in Welfare Administration,"

in Jacobus tenBroek and California Law Review (eds.). *The Law of the Poor*, pp. 155–186. San Francisco, California: Chandler Publishing Company.

HANDLER, JOEL F.
1969 "Justice for the Welfare Recipient: Fair Hearings in AFDC —The Wisconsin Experience." *Social Service Review* 43 (March), 12–34.

HUDSON, JAMES R.
1972 "Organizational Aspects of Internal and External Review." *The Journal of Criminal Law, Criminology, and Police Science* 63 (June).

KOZOL, JONATHAN
1967 *Death at an Early Age.* New York: Bantam Books.

KRAMER, RALPH M.
1969 *Participation of the Poor: Comparative Community Case Studies in the War on Poverty.* Englewood Cliffs: Prentice-Hall, Inc.

LEVINE, FELICE J. and ELIZABETH PRESTON
1970 "Community Resource Orientation Among Low Income Groups." *Wisconsin Law Review* (1970), 80–113.

LIPSKY, MICHAEL
1970 *Protest in City Politics: Rent Strikes, Housing and the Power of the Poor.* Chicago: Rand McNally & Company.

MARRIS, PETER and MARTIN REIN
1967 *Dilemmas of Social Reform.* New York: Atherton Press.

MARSHALL, T. H.
1964 *Class, Citizenship, and Social Development.* New York: Doubleday & Co.

MILLER, S. M., and MARTIN REIN
1964 "Poverty and Social Change." *The American Child* (March). New York: National Committee on Employment of Youth.

MINTER, ELLOUISE MITCHELL
1964 "The Fair Hearing: A Core Strength." *The Social Service Review* 38 (March), 1–16.

MOYNIHAN, DANIEL P.
1969 *Maximum Feasible Misunderstanding: Community Action in the War on Poverty.* New York: Free Press.

REICH, C. A.
1963 "Midnight Welfare Searches and the Social Security Act." *Yale Law Journal* 72 (June), 1347–1360.

REICH, C. A.
1964 "The New Property." *Yale Law Journal* 73 (April), 733–787.

REISS, ALBERT J., JR. (ed.)
1965 *Schools in a Changing Society.* New York: The Free Press.

REPORT OF THE NATIONAL ADVISORY COMMISSION ON CIVIL DISORDERS.
1968 New York: Bantam Books.

ROGERS, DAVID
1968 *110 Livingston Street: Politics and Bureaucracy in the New York City School System.* New York: Random House.

ROSEN, MICHAEL B.
1967 "Government Housing Programs," in Norman Dorsen and Stanley Zimmerman (eds.). *Housing for the Poor: Rights and Remedies,* pp. 154–261. New York: New York University School of Law.

SAYRE, WALLACE S., and HERBERT KAUFMAN
1960 *Governing New York City.* New York: Russell Sage Foundation.

SKOLNICK, JEROME H.
1969 *The Politics of Protest.* New York: Simon and Schuster.

SMITH, J. CLAY, JR.
1969 "Due Process and the Poor in Public Housing." *Howard Law Journal* 15 (Spring), 422–438.

TITMUSS, RICHARD M.
  1968 Commitment to Welfare. New York: Pantheon Books.

WILSON, JAMES Q.
  1968 *Varieties of Police Behavior.*

Cambridge, Massachusetts: Harvard University Press.

ZEITZ, LEONARD
  1965 "Survey of Negro Attitudes Toward Law." *Rutgers Law Review* 19, 288–316.

ideology and urban planning: the muddle of model cities

STEPHEN M. ROSE

This paper will examine the social planning process which served as the context for citizen participation in the guidance and management of social change as planned in the Model Cities program and its forerunners, the Community Action Program, the President's Committee on Juvenile Delinquency and Youth Crime, and the Gray Areas program of the Ford Foundation.

We will begin at the present and look back from the Model Cities program to the Ford Foundation Gray Areas projects, in order to examine (1) the nature and type of planned change intended, (2) the programmatic outcomes of the "new generation" of urban-related programs developed in the 1960s, and (3) the explanatory framework that served as a legitimizing rationale for each program.

The so-called "new generation" programs actually began with the Ford Foundation Gray Areas proj-

ects and were continued in the form of the President's Committee on Juvenile Delinquency and Youth Crime (hereafter, JD, the Community Action Program of OEO (CAP), and the Model Cities Program of the Department of Housing and Urban Development (HUD). In each of these projects, and in the aggregate, two themes have emerged: the role of citizenry in planning the programs purportedly operating in their behalf, and the emphasis upon coordinated, scientific, carefully planned objectives. While the role of the residents to be served by the program and the weight placed upon the rational-technical considerations in planning varied from one of the new generation programs to another, these two themes were salient features. These themes will be discussed first as they appear in the Model Cities Program, and then each of the previously mentioned programs will be reviewed in an attempt to define the rationale for each and for the aggregate.

Prepared especially for this volume.

As with the new programs which preceded it, the Model Cities Program published a guide to communities, a set of detailed instructions on how to compile an application or proposal for funds to plan a comprehensive attack on urban misery. *Improving the Quality of Urban Life,* the HUD guidebook, set forth the following standards among others:

1. The program should be comprehensive. While urging localities to develop program components relative to their own local needs, the guide sets forth some suggestions as to what a comprehensive program includes: a physical improvement section, a housing component, a transportation component, and other sections on education, manpower and economic development, recreation and culture, crime reduction, health, social services, and public assistance.

2. The program should provide for administrative machinery at the local level to carry out the program on a consolidated and coordinated basis. This machinery, in the form of a City Demonstration Agency (CDA), also had high standards which it was supposed to meet:

   —It had to be closely related to governmental decision-making in a way that permits the exercise of leadership by responsible elected officials.

   —It should have sufficient powers, authority, and stature to achieve the coordinated administration of all aspects of the program.

   —It should have skill and objectivity to reconcile conflicting plans, establish priorities, eliminate overlap, and evaluate the ongoing programs against stated goals.

   —It should provide a meaningful role in policy-making to area residents and to the major agencies expected to contribute projects and activities to the program.

3. The program should provide for widespread citizen participation.

4. The program should be consistent with comprehensive planning in the entire urban or metropolitan area.

5. The program should make maximum use of new and improved technology and design, including cost-reduction technique.

6. The program should include analysis of the costs and benefits of alternative courses of action to meet urban needs and the establishment of programming systems.

As with other earlier programs, with perhaps less complicated guidelines, HUD received numerous applications for planning grants which corresponded to the guidelines set forth in the booklet, assuring the Model Cities Administration that indeed all the standards had been met. Yet, as Roland Warren pointed out,[1] the planning process in the local communities frequently did not follow the rational course set forth either in its own application for a planning grant or in the projected time phasing of the Model Cities Administration. Despite the technical compilation of a comprehensive plan, many cities experienced severe political conflict between the City Demonstration Agency and the model neighborhood residents.

The projected process of Model Cities planning as represented by the guidelines revealed a distinct lack of awareness by the planners of the social movements underway in our

[1] Roland L. Warren, "Model Cities First Round: Politics, Planning, and Participation," *Journal of the American Institute of Planners,* XXXV (July 1969).

cities, but no lack of sensitivity to the interests of those holding official positions. The "maximum feasible participation" clause in the earlier Community Action Program had aroused controversy and provoke re-action from city officials and agency personnel. The Model Cities legis-lation attempted to construct a par-ticipatory form which retreated from the stance taken in the CAP, by de-moting citizens to advisory status. In backing away from the stance adopted by the CAP and removing neighborhood residents from official policy-making roles, the planners of the Model Cities legislation pro-vided the basis for local community conflict which was to emerge in many cities. The contest was over power and the form of participation that would involve neighborhood resi-dents in the Model Cities planning process. Preliminary evidence indi-cates that negotiations between residents of the projected model neighborhoods and the City Demon-stration Agencies dominated the early phases of the planning period and that actual work on the Model Cities plan itself frequently did not begin until these conflicts were resolved. Thus, rather than devel-oping in a rational, coordinated fashion, the pattern of CDA devel-opment frequently included severe conflict, readjustments in decision-making processes, and continual postponement of the creation of "effective administrative machinery" pending the outcome of political bargaining.

Initial data from a study of nine cities engaged in Model Cities plan-ning indicates that two distinct styles of relationship between model neigh-borhood residents and the CDA emerged. In three of the cities, a coalition or cooperative form of re-lationship developed in which the residents usually served in an ad-visory capacity to various planning bodies consisting of CDA staff and local agency personnel. A contrast-ing style, here called the "adversary relationship," became apparent in the remaining cities: its general form grew out of an organization of model neighborhood residents which chal-lenged the legitimacy of the CDA to plan *for* them, and competed with the CDA for decision-making power in developing the comprehensive Model Cities plan. In several cities manifesting this latter style, the resi-dents' group incorporated and was able to attract funds of its own for planning purposes. In each case, it became clear that the adversary-style groups were able to gain veto power vis-à-vis the CDA over all Model Cities program components, which indicates a degree of community con-trol (modified by final program au-thorization powers vested in the City Council and the funding agencies). The differentiation between the coalition and adversary relationships at first glance appears to be of great substance—power is held by resi-dents in one situation, by City Hall in the other. Given the widely pub-licized hostility of residents towards municipal government and other established institutions, differences in the programs generated by cities manifesting the different styles of citizen participation could be antici-pated.

Whatever the form of citizen participation negotiated in each community, one fact appears clear— power has been interpreted by neigh-borhood residents to mean decision-making capacity in relation to the allocation of resources for neighborhood programs. Thus, in those cities where the residents have agitated for a more substantial part in the Model Cities planning process, and where they have won that role by virtue of programmatic control through veto power, the power which was sought and obtained was the administrative control over decisions determining which program components would be included in the comprehensive Model Cities plan. Some investigation into the process of program planning in cities with an adversary style of citizen participation is required before it can be conclusively stated or assumed that the power which has accrued to the model neighborhood residents is in fact substantive.

Generally, the planning process took similar form in all cities, no matter what style of citizen participation evolved. In most instances, a task force or component review committee was mandated to develop programs in a substantive area such as education, health, housing, or employment. Most often, these committees or task forces were composed of varying proportions of neighborhood residents, officials of the CDA, and staff members from community agencies and municipal service departments. In the fury and controversy over citizen participation which reigned during the early phases of the planning stage the role of these agencies was submerged. It is helpful to recall that several such agencies were marginally involved during the preplanning phase, supplying documentation data for presentation of the local community problems and supplying strategy suggestions, but their role became less clear in

the confusion over citizen participation. In the *Journal of The American Institute of Planners*,[2] Warren noted the superficial excitement over citizen participation, but reminded the reader to beware the staying power of the traditional agencies. This cautionary note appears to have been an accurate forecast about the working sessions which produced the various components of the Model Cities plan. The detailed technical work required in the preparation of proposals, along with the inevitability of delegating or subcontracting the programs out to organizations during the implementation stage, brought the local agency structure back into the planning process even in those cities where neighborhood people had won veto power.

The systematic inclusion of the professionals, some of whom were salaried by the residents' organizations, provided technical assistance in the formulation of most programs. Their functional responsibility in structural terms varied from full membership on the task forces, to non-voting membership, to consultant. But whatever their formal role vis-à-vis the neighborhood representatives, their influence was great: they controlled the language process requisite to receiving funds, and often they spoke in behalf of the organizations which would be charged with responsibility for operating the programs designed by the task forces. In practice, once the substantive areas were delineated in accord with problem foci suggested in HUD guidelines—and usually the residents had no role in this process—the professionals in the various fields were able to offer program options

2 *Ibid.*

among which were those later to be selected by the separate task force groups. This planning process was not coordinated since the different Task Forces had little idea about the programs developed by other groups with a different area of concern. Thus, with the problem defined in the form of administrative decisions regarding the substantive program areas and with the funding process requiring participation by the professionals, the decision-making power of the residents of even the strongest neighborhood organization was substantially compromised. Veto power, as such, extended only to the capacity to determine which among competing proposals, *as opposed to competing problem definitions,* would be selected for inclusion in the Model Cities plan. Although it appeared to have substantial political influence, this process was in fact an administrative matter extending the legitimation of the CDA and other community agencies: the definition of the problems to be addressed was left with the CDA (there were no task forces on political organization of the poor, or revolutionary education), and the operational conversion of ideas into programs was left to the professionals who wrote the proposals consistent with their demonstrated control over the language. As might have been anticipated from this complex of variables, the programs developed across the nine cities of the study appear similar in content and not unlike programs developed earlier: neither coordination nor innovation was achieved.

The entire process of planning, from administration rhetoric to program implementation was not unlike the Community Action Program,

which—in turn—was not unlike the program of the President's Committee, and so on through to the Ford Foundation. Marris and Rein, in the *Dilemmas of Social Reform,*[3] examined the last two programs on this list, finding in them illustrations of the difficulties involved in precipitating planned social reform in America. This paper will expand on their notions to address not only the political complexities involved, but also the conceptual ones which must be confronted by prospective agents of social change.

The Department of Housing and Urban Development issued the guideline document which sets forth the rationale and procedures for the Model Cities program. Two assertions are prominent in the guidelines: first, that it is possible to identify the local community's interest in a rational fashion (through an effective "administrative machinery"), and second, that, as defined, the community interest can be operationalized in the form of coordinated program components. The rational-technical approach to planning is pervasive in the guidelines, appearing in various forms, such as the causal analysis of problems, statistical description of problem areas, programs of comprehensive scope, cost-benefit comparisons of programs, and commitments to utilization of the latest technology. The emphatic commitment to the more technical aspects of planning, and the aforementioned neglect of the neighborhood political situation in many cities, is based on the assumption that community consensus can be reached around a plan which

3 Peter Marris and Martin Rein, *The Dilemmas of Social Reform* (Chicago: Atherton, 1967).

will accommodate the interests and needs of all "relevant" factions. That our nation's urban reality significantly differs from these assumptions—as manifest by the data accumulating in various Commission Reports documenting urban violence and decay—seems not to matter. It is as if the planners, obedient to their plans, accuse either those charged with program administration or those charged with financial appropriations for the destruction of the urban utopia.

The assumed value of the planning process and its ability to produce desired outcomes also pervaded the CAP and JD programs, but in slightly different fashion. The scientific orientation of the JD staff, with its entrenched commitment to research, controlled experimentation, and rational-technical planning is noted emphatically by Marris and Rein,[4] Thernstrom,[5] and Levitan.[6] In discussing the differences between the Committee (JD) and the Ford Projects, Marris and Rein note:

They differed most in their provision for planning. The Committee tried to guard the integrity of its aims against political pressures by insisting that each community work out a conceptual framework, from which the goals and method of action would derive. Every proposal was to be justified by reference to this rational analysis of the nature of the problems.[7]

4 Ibid.
5 Stephen Thernstrom, Poverty, Planning and Politics in the New Boston: The Origins of ABCD (New York: Basic Books, 1969).
6 Sar Levitan, The Great Society's Poor Law: A New Approach to Poverty (Baltimore: Johns Hopkins University Press, 1969).
7 Marris and Rein, p. 23.

The primary outcome for the JD Committee would be a logically comprehensive program to combat juvenile delinquency, based upon causal analysis of the problem from which would derive related and coordinated programs.

The coordination of program effort was a value shared with the Ford Foundation, which emphasized this attribute in a fashion parallel to the JD endorsement of rational planning: "Reform, they both believed, must grow out of a much more coherent integration of relevant institutions."[8] This theme also influenced the Community Action Program, which called for the mobilization of resources in an attack on poverty:

Where several (community) agencies are working in the same functional area, they relate to each other in a 'service system.' The mobilization of resources for a community action program should bring these various service systems together in a concerted attack on poverty.[9]

As already indicated, the value placed on coordination reached its height—explicitly—in the Model Cities program: the local community was to develop an effective administrative machinery.

Such machinery should be capable of carrying out the planning of a comprehensive program, resolving conflicting goals and plans of participating agencies designing effective projects and activities to carry out program goals, and perfecting the

8 Ibid, p. 24.
9 Community Action Program, Office of Economic Opportunity, Guide to Applicants—Volume I (Washington: U.S. Government Printing Office, 1966), p. 15.

administrative machinery for carrying out a consolidated and coordinated programs.[10]

This statement is not too far afield from that issued by the President's Committee in a *Report to the President* which noted that JD policy ". . . requires close coordination of (those) activities with the planning, program and training efforts of local communities whenever they are ready to mobilize a comprehensive redevelopment of youth services." [11]

The operational programs mounted by these efforts have had minimal impact upon the lives of those living in poverty or urban squalor. That such is the case appears not to be accounted for in either the rhetoric or anticipated outcomes of the "new generation" programs. According to the conceptual base, as noted in the program guides, each avenue to upward mobility and improved urban life would be covered and coordinated, each attributed cause attacked, no stone unturned, all in scientific manner. Only a fool, blinded by distortions of perception or technology, would argue that the promises made by the new generation of programs, whether implicit or explicit, have been realized. With this assertion as a salient issue, perhaps it is time to explore potential defects in the conceptualization of the problems and method of attack manifest in the new generation of problem-solving programs.

If we begin by looking at the operational determinants explicit in the program guidelines, we note several recurring technical prescriptions which seem to form the premises for the planning required to receive funds from any one of the programs under examination; these technical guides include avoidance of duplication (of services), elimination of overlap (in services), optimized resource allocation, coordination of effort, comprehensive effort, systematic, scientific management, action taken in the public or the community's interest, service delivery systems, systems analysis, and evaluation research. These factors are named as prerequisite to adequate conceptualization, independent of the outcome of the planning process: that is, they are to be procedural guides which, by nature of their being free of political or parochial interests, will assist local communities in reaching their own rationally determined goals. This assumption has generally gone unchallenged by the planning boards or national task forces, by the Congress, and by the client groups.

The paradox of increasing technological approaches to our social problems coupled with the intractability of the same problems can be addressed by looking at the problem-solving approach in the context of a pervasive ideological system, the scope of which is determined by existing power arrangements in the society. For purposes of this discussion, the term or concept "Ideology" will be understood as defined by Mannheim:

The concept 'ideology' reflects the one discovery which emerged from political conflict, namely that ruling

[10] Department of Housing and Urban Development, *Improving the Quality of Urban Life* (Washington: U.S. Government Printing Office, 1966), p. 4.

[11] President's Committee on Juvenile Delinquency and Youth Crime, *Report to the President,* May 31, 1962, unpublished manuscript, p. 2.

groups can in their thinking become so intensively interest-bound to a situation that they are simply no longer able to see certain facts which would undermine their sense of domination. There is implicit in the word 'ideology' the insight that in certain situations the collective unconscious of certain groups obscures the real condition of society both to itself and to others and thereby stabilizes it.[12]

An ideology serves to justify or rationalize existing power arrangements in the society—some might call it the "Establishment"—as they are expressed in terms of control over the institutions of the society. Horowitz notes the influence of ideology in society:

> By expanding our definition of the function of ideology to make room not only for justification (Marx) and rationalization (Weber), but also for the role of ideology in organizing and institutionalizing social drives, one can more readily understand the binding force of an ideological complex upon a social structure.[13]

As ideologically determined communications saturate the society, filtered through socialization processes managed by institutions created and legitimated by the power holders, what comes to be "known" or "knowable" is ideologically conditioned or socially constructed in accordance with the interests of those possessing power. In short, power becomes defined anew to mean the capacity to define knowledge and, in so doing, to construct an official reality. Deviation from this reality, when activated by an individual [14] or by a social movement,[15] is necessarily responded to by various forms of social control.

Having argued the existence of ideological determinants of knowledge and of official definitions of reality, the task remains to relate this ideology to the earlier discussion of "new generation" urban programs.

The distinguishing feature of these new programs was their claim to innovative problem definitions, to the establishment of new paradigms explaining the existence of poverty, delinquency, urban blight in an otherwise affluent society. The focus of the new paradigm, supposedly, was the social structure of the society cast as destructive or dysfunctional. This was opposed to historically compelling problem approaches based on varying analyses of individual inadequacy or deviance. The Community Action Program of OEO, perhaps more than the other programs, manifests the rhetoric of the new paradigm.[16] With its emphasis on citizen participation and its language ablaze with attacks on "the Establishment," an expectation of institutional change-oriented programming arose. For some, this rhetoric was a sign of hope, for others an ominous threat. When the rhetoric gave way to pro-

12 Karl Mannheim, *Ideology and Utopia* (New York: Harcourt, Brace, Jovanovich, 1936), p. 40.

13 Irving Louis Horowitz, *Professing Sociology: Studies in the Life Cycle of a Social Science* (Chicago: Aldine Publishing Co., 1968), p. 73.

14 Thomas Szasz, *Ideology and Insanity* (Garden City, N.Y.: Doubleday and Co., 1970).

15 Stephen M. Rose, "Schools and Social Reality" (Paper presented at the annual meeting of The Society for the Study of Social Problems, San Francisco, 1969).

16 John C. Donovan, *The Politics of Poverty* (Racine, Wis.: Western Publishing Co., 1967).

grams in communities across the nation, the initially threatened agency structure reigned supreme: institutions challenged by CAP language expanded their hegemony over the poor with CAP funds. Problems were defined in accord with the traditional perspective, insuring the institutional order against further attack. The transformation of community action programs is documented in a study by this author: [17] more than 97 percent of CAP funds spent over a two-year period in a sample of twenty cities went into programs premised on the defectiveness of low-income people and the presumed effectiveness of established institutions (the social structure, if you will) to aid the poor in their return to normalcy.

Acknowledging the perpetuation of the same problems which gave rise to the antipoverty program, along with three continuous summers of urban ghetto disorder, the government planners went back to the drawing boards. When they came up with the Model Cities program, designed to concentrate all previously uncoordinated efforts in an area containing approximately 10 percent of the city's population, the target of the new effort was as clear as the assumed cause for their unrest. Ghetto blacks were to have their needs met by coordination of programs and agencies previously assumed to be operating in their interests but in a fragmented, unscientific manner. The same agencies which were to be coordinated into a comprehensive attack on poverty, which were to be reformed through

their participation in the CAP, which were to redefine problems in a way that acknowledged their own complicity, were to be involved again in settling the unrest of the period.

At some point the validity of this process of system maintenance and its legitimation must be challenged. This can be accomplished by examining the premises on which the new generation programs were based and by extending the analysis beyond the ontological myths to the epistemological system which conveyed them. Nieuwenhuijze, a Dutch social scientist, has claimed that, "Faith makes the rational system watertight." [18] What tenets do we have to accept on faith in order to comprehend the position of the planners? Beyond that, what epistemology allows for the movement from the articles of faith to the operational conclusions reached in the plans?

A starting point in this type of analysis may be found in the comparison of the administrative regulations issued by the new generation programs instructing applicants in construction of the correct proposal, its premises and ingredients. These guidelines, as they have come to be called, are the operational determinants of the programs planned, yardsticks against which proposals are measured. The several recurring technical indicators found throughout include avoidance of duplication of services, elimination of overlap, optimized resource allocation, coordination of effort, comprehensive programming, management systems,

[17] Stephen M. Rose, *The Betrayal of the Poor* (Cambridge, Mass.: Schenkman Publishing Co., 1972).

[18] C. A. O. vanNieuwenhuijze, *Society as Process* (The Hague: Mouton & Co., 1962), p. 114.

service delivery systems, systems analysis, evaluation research, and the "community interest." These premises seem to form the prerequisites to adequate conceptualization of programs; it is of immediate interest to note their irrelevance to the analysis or definition of the problems which those programs were supposed to address. This irony holds consistent throughout the series of guidelines, indicating that in the mind of the planner the manner is the message. Rhetoric aside, problem analysis is reduced to management manipulation. The more "scientific" or systematic the management, the greater the likelihood that the problems to be addressed, whatever they may be, will be resolved.

Another indicator of the planner's notion of change is seen in the fact that the procedural guides to program formulation, again quite apart from problem construction, are seen as existing in isolation from political or parochial interests. These guiding concepts, presumably, will assist local communities in reaching their own rationally determined goals. It is in the statement of these goals that there exists the belief in a community interest which overrides the fragmented interests of various contending groups in the community. Again, the manner is the message— the pursuit of funds through the required specifications established in the operational concepts metaphysically manages the political conflicts into administrative matters, eliminating by definition any substantive or ideological differences which may exist. The administrative management of problem definition through program foci independent of the problem also works to the advantage

of administratively organized potential beneficiaries: that is, the organizations best able to relate their operations to the demands set forth in the guidelines clearly have the edge in the competition for control over a new agency (such as the community action agency) or for new funds. Surprisingly, little challenge to this process has been raised even at the neighborhood level.

The paradox of increasing the technological approaches to our social problems and decreasing interest in the analysis of those problems can be seen in terms of the historical development of an ideologically generated explanatory paradigm. Thomas Kuhn, in *The Structure of Scientific Revolutions,* discusses the development and function of a paradigm: when anomalies occur in a given setting, a theoretical explanation is generated which defines the problem in a way which guarantees the existence of a stable set of solutions.[19] The anomalies referred to in Kuhn's scientific examples can be extended in the realm of politics to correspond to the documentation of racism in a nation premised on equality, of poverty in a nation of affluence, of urban decay, crime, mental illness, hunger in a nation whose legitimated civics textbooks could never lead their readers to conclude that such phenomena existed. Faced with the agitation of the Civil Rights movement in the early 1960s, the manifestation of these "paradoxical" social problems had to be recognized. To recognize the problem is to define it—a definition of reality had to be constructed which both

19 Thomas S. Kuhn, *The Structure of Scientific Revolutions* (Chicago: University of Chicago Press, 1962), p. 28.

accounted for the political conflicts expressed by the people and simultaneously maintained the existing economic and political structure. The paradigm which emerged was historically consistent; the pejorative view of the "undeserving poor" as morally and spiritually defective was updated and transformed into concepts of psychopathology and individual or subcultural deviance.

The impact of this paradigm on perception is one of reality definition. Having established the theorectical explanation of a phenomenon, the professionals operating within the confines of the paradigm generally attempt to expand its utility in three ways: by increasing the accuracy and scope of the knowledge of the facts legitimated by the paradigm, by comparing the facts with predictions from the paradigm, or by articulating the paradigm theory by resolving some of its ambiguities. Inevitably in the course of these functions, there appear inventions generated to measure paradigm-related facts. These inventions are in the form of instrumentation designed to verify the theory and often contain within them aspects of the theory itself. Thus, in the social sciences, research on recipe-based premises is conducted and popularized (see Oscar Lewis' works on the culture of poverty), quantitative attitudinal research is done comparing imputed values of the lower class vis-à-vis middle class, and instrumentation is developed to carry the paradigm into operational programs. Legitimated knowledge is reduced to what can be explained by the paradigm and ordered for the transmission to future professional practitioners. In Kuhn's words, the socialization process is as follows:

The study of paradigms . . . is what mainly prepares the student for membership in the particular scientific community with which he will later practice. Because he there joins men who learned the bases of their field from the same concrete models, his subsequent practice will seldom evoke overt disagreement over fundamentals.[20]

At this point, given some understanding of the construction of reality and its system-maintaining function in relation to poverty, the question must be raised as to the relationship of this construction to the planned efforts at change. By this time, it should be clear that the commonly accepted knowledge based in the paradigm serves the purpose of bypassing the need for problem definition. The work which goes into defining the problem is primarily a matter of applying a specific institutional language to the problem in order to legitimate that institution to receive funds for applying its prestructured technology to the phenomena. The remaining task is to analyze the leap of faith which covers the ground from the theoretical formulation of the problem in the paradigm to the operational criteria for establishing paradigm-based programs. This leap of faith first encounters the chasm of epistemology. We have to begin to analyze the processes of knowing which characterize the planner's position.

To begin this exploration, the premises for knowing must be located in some epistemology. Mannheim points out that epistemologies have social contextual roots based on the model of normal science preva-

20 *Ibid.,* pp. 10–11.

lent in any socio-historical period: "every theory of knowledge is itself influenced by the form which science takes at the time and from which it alone can obtain its conception of the nature of knowledge."[21] The transfer of normal science models of investigation to the social sciences has carried with it the assumed conditions for scientific investigation: objectification of the observed unit, controlled environments in which the observed units act, universal constants which regulate the conditions of the environment, and the potential for resolution of the problem studied by application of a set of rules of procedure and logic internally consistent and outside of both the guiding theory and the observed social unit.

These procedural assumptions condition what can be considered truth, yet they carry with them the paradigm of truth itself in that the procedures for knowing are a priori based on assumptions about what one wants to know. In Mannheim's words,

> The exact physiognomy of the concept of truth at a given time is not a chance phenomenon. Rather there is a clue to the construction of the conception of truth of that time, in the representative modes of thought and their structure, from which a conception is built up as to the nature of truth in general. We see therefore, not merely that the notion of knowledge in general is dependent upon the concretely prevailing form of knowledge and the modes of knowing expressed therein and accepted as ideal, but also that the concept of truth itself is dependent upon the already existing types of knowledge.[22]

[21] Mannheim, p. 287.
[22] *Ibid,* pp. 291–92.

We can conclude that both "legitimated knowledge" and legitimated ways of knowing any "truth" are contextually determined and based upon the existence of explanatory paradigms. The future development of knowledge within a paradigm contains aspects of the paradigm in its content and in its epistemology, guaranteeing the continuity of the theoretical stance. This form of internally closed system or circularity is perpetuated through the growth of instrumentation which measures the predictable phenomenon in forms guaranteed to be validating. The technician then applies this "knowledge" to social phenomena using instrumentation which perpetuates the definition of the phenomena. Since the paradigm excludes alternative explanations of the phenomena from its definition, neither the methodologist nor the technician can be expected to generate findings or programs which transcend measures of efficiency— how well the paradigm is being applied. Such is the premise of technological program development by the professional planner and quantitative program evaluation by the professional resarcher.

The inextricability of ideology from the substance of knowledge and epistemology employed by the planner can now be summarized: based on the system-maintaining paradigm of individual defect causation, the anomaly of program management vis-à-vis problem analysis becomes clarified. Once the paradigm is accepted, further work on problem definition is contained within it, hence the work to be done is absorbed by fitting organizational subspecialties to the paradigm. The established institutions do this through the application of their language apparatus to the paradigm-conditioned problem definition. Once the matter of reconciliation of language ambiguity is worked out, the technology of the specialty is applicable to the problem *by definition*. The relationship is accomplished through an approximation of logic and "scientific method"— the "knowledge" savored by the various professions has been gathered within the theoretical parameters of the paradigm by procedures based in the paradigm and is extended to operational or program areas according to criteria founded in the paradigm. The evaluations conducted on the program also have their theoretical and procedural bases within the paradigm, completing the circle.

If we return for a moment to the administrative guidelines and their proposal criteria, we can see the link most clearly: the emphasis on systems approaches (comprehensiveness, scientific management, service delivery, systems analysis) derives from notions about control over the environment; the emphasis on management through coordination (avoidance of duplication, elimination of overlap) represents the belief in objectification of observed units; a combination of these two characteristics explains the reliance on the possibility of optimizing the allocation of resources; and the construction of programs articulated as representing the "community interest" or the "public interest" manifests the assumption of universal constants which are derivable through rational procedures. Those procedures obviously determine what can and cannot be considered "rational."

Thus the new generation programs, from the administrative guidelines at the beginning to the evaluation research at the end, consist of a circuitous ideologically constrained closed system whose primary function is to sustain the paradigm which serves as its premise. The paradigm functions to extend the control of institutions over the lives of their victims by legitimating the participation of these institutions in the "solutions" to problems defined to exclude the role of the economic and political structures. The existing system of power and resource distribution is maintained and protected from intrusion or challenge by the capacity of its institutions to maintain the dominance of its paradigm through cooptation or coercion. Little question is raised about the process, at any level, because the populace and the professions are socialized into acceptance of the explanation offered by the paradigm.

Yet the paradigm contains its own contradiction. It will not solve the problems, since it never addresses them. Poverty, racism, and squalor monotonously progress and produce increasing alienation both from the institutions which dominate the social structure and from their mythology. It is in this alienation that the seeds of change exist. It is in the interests of the victims that a new paradigm must be created premised on the corruption of an economic system which exploits its workers and impoverishes the majority of its population and which denies to the tremendous percentage of its population the right to engage in making decisions which control their lives.

Stratification
and Social Class

5

The members of all societies, everywhere and at all times, *rank* one another—they assign different quantities of honor and prestige to others, to what others do, and to what others represent. Social stratification refers simply to the process of *differential evaluation*—to the universal invidious ranking of one's fellow man and woman—as well as to the process of the *differential distribution of society's rewards.* Because stratification is universal it does not necessarily follow that it is inevitable; we should never presume that stratification is "necessary" for the functioning and survival of a society or societies in general. But wherever something is valued, it will always be the case that some people will have more of it, or do better at it, than others. Rewards have never been equally distributed; one may speculate as to whether or not they ever will be. The sociologist finds the ubiquity of social stratification an interesting and curious phenomenon, something worthy of his systematic attention. *Why* stratification?

Social class is one form of these broader stratificational processes; theoretically, while *any* attribute could serve as a basis for ranking one another (size of feet, strength of grip, speed of reading, body odor, etc.), in industrial societies, these hierarchies have been based on occupation and occupation-related criteria—most notably: (1) the prestige of one's occupation; (2) one's income; (3) education; (4) power. Social classes usually refer to aggregates of individuals with roughly the same occupational ranking in a society or a community.

Stratification is one of the absolutely central facts of any individual's existence, as well as of the workings of the society. If you or I were to be magically dropped down into the midst of an unknown civilization, past, present or future, one of the first things we would notice about the ways of the people we are among would be their ranking system, what consequences it has, and on what it is based. Although all societies possess some forms of ranking, some kind of hierarchy, they differ substantially on: (1) *what rank is based on*—piety, skill in hunting, courage in battle, ancestry, beauty, wealth, etc.; (2) *how much difference* there is between the privileged and the underprivileged; (3) the *accessibility* of privilege, prestige, and power—whether it is automatically ascribed, or it is achieved; (4) what *consequences* invidious ranking has for the society and its members—whether ranked equals form communities and friendships, whether social "classes" exist or not, what the relationship is between the various dimensions of stratification, and so on.

Anthropologists and sociologists have found that probably the main source of variation in the four issues raised above is the *technology* of the society in question. Societies whose members have not developed the techniques of growing food, and who rely on foraging from nature are called "hunting and gathering societies." They tend to be the most primitive and inefficient technologically, which means that nearly everyone in the society must work hard and long to keep himself alive and fairly comfortable. There is very little economic *surplus* in hunting and gathering societies; there is almost nothing left over after everyone's needs are met. Such subsistence econo- mies generally do not generate great differences in prestige, power, or wealth. Everyone is not precisely equal, but the differences in rank that do exist are small.

As a society's technology becomes increasingly efficient through the in- vention and utilization of tools for exploiting nature, particularly agricultural advances, comes greater wealth and a larger and larger surplus. And the larger a society's surplus, the greater the differences in stratification between rich and poor, powerful and powerless, honored and dishonored. Learning how to grow greater quantities of food efficiently means that there is more to go around, less need for everyone to work at basic necessities, and the increased possibility of allowing some in the society the right of not working at basic essential pursuits. This seemingly simple development has momentous consequences, especially with regard to social stratification. It would seem that a greater efficiency would men a higher standard of living for everyone. But greater wealth has never meant a higher standard for everyone equally; it has always meant—at least until well past the indus- trial revolution—a much higher standard of living for a few, and basically the same for everyone else. The greater the economic surplus over and above subsistence that a society's technology generates, the lower the percentage of the population that must grow food, and the greater the number of people who do not have to work at all. A large surplus means that the following things are possible: (1) cities; (2) armies; (3) kingdoms; (4) empires; (5) class-based subcultures; (6) courts; (7) writing; (8) money; (9) hereditary offices and positions; (10) a leisure class. Wealthy societies can support various means of control and repression that are monopolized by a small number of individuals to their own advantage.

Inequality probably reaches its peak in what anthropologists call "agrarian" societies, that is, those which have developed and used the plow, an extremely efficient means of growing food—generating an enormous surplus, and consequently great wealth. Ancient Rome was an agrarian society, as were Ancient China, Babylonia, Assyria, Egypt, Europe in the Middle Ages, and the Turkish Ottoman Empire, as well as most of the societies today which have not yet fully industrialized. Obviously, huge differences exist among these many diverse societies, but they all had or have one thing in common: comparatively efficient techniques for growing food, and, consequently, a great surplus left over above and beyond subsistence. Which, in turn, means a well-defined system of stratification, with very large differences between rich and poor. Throughout human history—and especially so the more efficient a society's technology became—the powerful have managed to convince the powerless, through techniques ranging from brute armed force to moral exhortation, that most of what they, the masses, produced, actually "belonged" to them, the rulers. The peasants in all agrarian societies have had to relinquish much, or even most, of what they grew and manufactured to those in power. Concomitant with advances in agriculture came advances in military technology—making the task of confiscation easier and less risky.

Historians, sociologists, and anthropologists have estimated that in agrarian societies, roughly one-quarter of all of the goods and services produced each year (what economists call the "gross national product") was in the hands of the royal family. Another quarter was successfully acquired by the nobility, which comprised less than one percent of the population. And a third quarter found its way to what could be regarded as the "middle class"—the tax collectors, country squires, merchants, skilled artisans, retainers, petty bureaucrats, priests, and so on, who made up about ten percent of the population in agrarian societies. The wealthiest and most privileged members of agrarian societies possessed millions of times more goods and services than the poorest. And parallel with these economic differences were immeasurable differences in honor, esteem, and prestige. The lowliest members of agrarian societies—slaves and peasants—had little more respect from others than animals; royalty, in contrast, was placed slightly below the gods—and at times and in some places, equal to them. Elaborate codes of deference developed—humility and homage flowing upward, arrogance and disdain flowing downward. Kings, czars, sultans, and emperors had life and death powers over their subjects, and could imprison them, murder them, confiscate their property, almost at will. (Some subjects, obviously, had a bit more power to resist than others.) Prior to the industrial revolution, it had been true that the wealthier the society, the greater the power, prestige, and privilege differences between the upper and the lower classes in that society.

It would seem that industrialization would merely accentuate and accelerate this tendency—that more wealth and a greater surplus above and beyond subsistence would produce even greater inequality, greater disparities in stratification. For a variety of reasons, this seems not to have occurred in industrialized societies. The rulers and elites in technologically advanced societies do not monopolize as much relative wealth and income, nor as much power or deference, as rulers in agrarian societies did. Disparities are still monstrous—but less so than in the past. No single family controls a quarter of any industrialized nation's economy, as was true in agrarian societies of the royal family. And the bulk of the working and "lower" classes lives considerably above subsistence level. The middle levels of industrialized societies have managed to wrest a larger slice of the economic pie away from the most privileged segments of society. Sources of prestige are not centralized, as in ancient societies, but are markedly varied and dispersed. In the U. S. in the late 1960s, according to the *Statistical Abstracts of the United States,* the wealthiest 10 percent of the population earned only slightly more than a quarter of the total money income. This proportion has not changed markedly since the beginning of this century (demonstrating the failure of supposedly progressive taxes to redistribute income). Thus, inequality is the rule in industrialized societies— but its magnitude is less than in nonindustrialized societies.[1]

Why stratification?

During the 1940s and 1950s, the dominant theory within sociology concerning social class and stratification was called "functional" theory. Its principal tenet was (and is) that stratification is a nonconsciously devised and employed mechanism to insure that the "most important" positions are filled by the "most qualified" individuals—who must also be motivated to perform the demands of these positions competently. Looking back at this theory from today's vantage point, it is remarkable that it was taken seriously at one time. There are too many profound flaws with the functional theory of stratification to be able to accept its conclusions as valid. To begin with, what is "functionally important" (a key concept in the theory) would be almost impossible to measure. If what is meant by "functional importance" is what the members of a society *believe* to be important, then the theory is a tautology—true by definition—because a society's rewards is one measure of the imputed importance of an occupation. On the other hand, if an occupation's contribution to the society's sheer *survival* is taken to mean "importance," then the function proposition is quite simply false; certainly college professors, lawyers, and clergymen contribute far less to a society's survival than do farmers, plumbers, and garbage collectors—and yet, on an individual basis, the first three of these occupations receive more of society's rewards (prestige, income, privileges) than the second three. Moreover, large segments of society with only normal intelligence (that is, at least half of the population or more) could be trained to perform competently at almost any high-prestige occupation. The relationship between native ability and achievement is questionable to begin with. In fact, for many

[1] The material on the next two pages is essentially based on Gerhard Lenski's monograph, *Power and Privilege: A Theory of Social Stratification* (New York: McGraw-Hill, 1966).

high-prestige, highly paid occupations, an extremely high IQ may actually produce less competent performance. And lastly, as has been pointed out many times previously, stratification systems do more to stifle initiative and block able people of humble origins from achieving status and recognition in high-prestige positions—as well as untalented people from being weeded out of prestigious positions—than they do to reward ability and encourage competent performance in "functionally important" roles in society.

The functional theory, both in the area of stratification specifically as well as in sociology as a whole, has often been accused of assuming a kind of "natural harmony of interests" in society, of conceiving of societies as being more cohesive and unified than they actually are. Some critics have replaced this "consensus" perspective of the functionalists with a "conflict" model. Rather than looking at stratification as fulfilling specific functions for the entire society, "conflict" sociologists conceive of it as being in the interests of *certain segments* of society—often at the expense of others. This view holds that the most prestigious and well-paid occupations do not receive these rewards because they contribute most to a society; rather, they receive rewards because they have been successful in managing to convince the rest of the population of their great contributions. Thus, the focus must be shifted away from abstract reward and merit processes, to the wielding of power, and domination of the channels of communication. Certain occupations have been granted an aura of *mystification*—prestige and legitimacy having relatively little to do with their actual characteristics.

However, far more important than the causes of stratification are its consequences. In spite of America's extraordinarily high average per capita income (second only to that of Kuwait, a tiny oil-rich sheikdom on the Arabian peninsula), the fact is, this income is not *distributed* very equitably. Blacks receive only between 50 and 60 percent of the income of whites, and this percentage has not changed very much in the past 25 years or so. Some observers might object that this inequity is only because of inequalities in the amount and the quality of education by race, but income gaps *increase* as education increases; it is among college graduates that income inequalities are greatest, indicating that the answer to inequality in income lies not simply in increasing the average level of education among Blacks. It is in the area of discrimination where the solution must first be sought. Consider the fact that Blacks die about seven years younger than whites do in America —64 versus 71—indicating the inability of this society to deliver adequate medical care to all who need it.

Inequality between the sexes is every bit as great and powerful—and as pervasive—as between the races. At every level, women receive substantially fewer rewards for the same contribution, even at the very same job level, and even when education and experience are held constant. And the picture does not appear to be improving very much—the same kind of "tokenism" occurs with both women and Blacks. Women's pay is approximately 55 percent of that of men's. (The male-female income gap is almost identical to the Black-white income gap.) And this has remained more or less constant, with minor fluctuations, during the past 75 years. The percentage of professionals—physicians, lawyers, dentists, professors, engineers—who are women has remained stable (and even declined somewhat in some fields) since approximately the turn of the century. And yet this exclusion of women from prestigious, powerful, and higher-paying occupations is not universal. In Czechoslovakia, over two-thirds of all district judges are women. In the Soviet Union, a majority of all physicians, and nearly half of all engineers, are women. And, as Margaret Mead points out in a selection in this volume, in some societies, the women perform the principal economic work, and control the significant power. The assignment of certain roles on the basis of sex or race—or social class—is arbitrary, and not at all a function of either potential or actual performance of the groups in question. Basically (and perhaps a bit too crudely) the issue boils down to who has the power and credibility to define reality for the rest of society. Societies, particularly large, complex and heterogeneous ones, attempt to clothe these arbitrary role assignments (women should raise children, Blacks should be given occupations with an inferior status, workers should receive less prestige than professionals) with the mantle of rationality and reason. Attempts are made to convince us all that it is women's "destiny" to carry out certain activities, that Blacks "achieve" what they "deserve," that certain occupations receive more pay and prestige because they are more "functionally important." These rationalizations have provided justificatory underpinnings to stratification systems for thousands of years.

Our selections on class and stratification explore the subject from a variety of angles. It is difficult to confront and assimilate the brutal fact that abject starvation-level poverty is common in the world's wealthiest nation. Robert Perrucci and Marc Pilisuk document its existence. Hunger is ugly, and a society in which millions cannot feed themselves is a society with a gross imbalance in the distribution of its wealth and income. Moreover, the very conditions which breed this problem also block its solution. The interpenetration of poverty, stratification, race, and power, explored briefly in the first selection, is dealt with in greater detail in the article by Robert Blauner. It is common to regard Blacks in America as equivalent to European immigrant nationality groups, most of whom entered into the class system at the bottom and became assimilated into the country's vast middle class. The analogy appears to be particularly weak with Blacks, because (1) their "immigration" was involuntary; (2) because the hostility and discrimination directed at them by the dominant society has been qualitatively greater than for any other ethnic group; and (3) because while European immigrant groups have entered at the bottom and rise, Blacks have tended to stay at the bottom. Blauner argues convincingly that the colonial parallel is far stronger for Blacks in America than is the immigrant analogy. True, there are some differences—the absence of a land base being one of them. But the "internal colonialism" of Afro-Americans is persuasive by virtue of the fact that (1) the slave trade was part of an imperialist colonizing effort; (2) Blacks continue to live, for the most part, in semi-permanent ghettos which are politically administered and economically exploited by whites; (3) the agents of social control—the army in the case of the colony, the police in the case of the ghetto—largely protect the interests of the dominant whites rather than those of the Blacks and the colonized people; (4) one key element in the colonizing effort is cultural imperialism—an attempt to de-legitimate the original civilization and to impose European culture in its place. If any theme can be said to be dominant in both internal and external colonialism, it is an overwhelming sense of powerlessness on the part of the subject groups—and a consequent sense of Black rage.

Harvey Molotch uses the Santa Barbara oil spills in January and February, 1969, as a means of illuminating generalizations concerning the distribution of power in American society. Santa Barbara is an affluent, comfortable upper-middle class community on the Pacific coast. The residents of this small city, irate over the desecration of their natural environment, and enraged at their impotence in the face of the power of oil interests, began to be radicalized, to see each federal agency as "the captive of the industry that it is to regulate," to become acutely aware of the disjunction between "strategic profitability" and "social utility." The oil episode was also instructive from the point of view of how power is densely interwoven with credibility and the control of information and communications. Powerful organizations can hire and support supposed experts to attempt to smooth ruffled feathers during the debate and to present a view of the situation favorable to oil interests—and can, moreover, exert pressure on the media to prevent views unfavorable to their own from being aired and widely disseminated.

Our last selection, by Philip Stearn, documents how tax laws are a direct reflection of the demands of the wealthy and the powerful; the federal tax system, in fact, amounts to a "welfare program—for the rich."

racism, poverty, and inequality

ROBERT PERRUCCI

MARC PILISUK

Estimates of the number of poor in the United States range from a low

From Robert Perrucci and Marc Pilisuk, THE TRIPLE REVOLUTION EMERGING: SOCIAL PROBLEMS IN DEPTH, *pp. 319–329. Reprinted by permission of the publisher, © 1971 by Little, Brown, and Company.*

of 20 million to a high of 40 million persons. The great variation in these estimates is due almost entirely to the definitions used to classify an individual or family above or below the poverty line. This reflects the relative nature of poverty (or luxury for that matter) and illustrates an important point: persons are classified as poor in relation to other persons and to a standard of living that is currently accepted as statistically normal. Failure to understand this basic fact often leads to efforts to show how America's "poor" earn more than the vast majority of persons in the rest of the world, or that the "poor" have television sets, cars, and other "luxuries." Such comparisons do not make use of some basic understandings concerning the *social* definitions of poverty.

In 1963 the Department of Health, Education and Welfare found that there were some 34½ million persons in the United States with incomes below a minimum budget; the budget is based on a minimum level of living for families and persons living alone (Miller, 1966). About 5 million of the poor lived alone, and 30 million, one-half of these being children, lived in families. Many of those families below the poverty line are not there because of unemployment. About one-half of the families are headed by males who had full-time employment at some point throughout the year. This indicates that many of the poverty families are working families with poor incomes and with little chance to improve their incomes because of limited skills and education.

In the last few years the number of families *defined* as poor (i.e., with income below the official poverty line) has decreased. This decrease is probably due to the effect of the poverty program in getting money and programs into low-income areas. Despite these gains, however, the rapidly rising cost of living in the last decade has virtually wiped out any of the apparent gains reflected

in the declining number of poor families. In 1959, poverty was defined as income for a family of four below $3100, while the Bureau of Labor estimated that $7000 was needed for a "modest but adequate" living. In 1969, the poverty level for a family of four was $3335, and the "modest but adequate" living increased to $9200 (Reissmann, 1969). In short, the gap between the poverty level and what is needed for an adequate living has increased quite sharply.

A substantial number of the poor are the older persons in our society. There are approximately 8 million Americans over 65 with incomes below the poverty line, with about 1.5 million of these who live alone on an income of less than $500 a year. The plight of the aged poor is described in the following account of a man on a pension.

> Mr. MacIntosh depended on hard-boiled eggs because his hotel room has no refrigerator and he can't afford to eat out. He is trying to live on his $50-a-month Social Security check. Room rent is $38.50 a month, which provides a room with clean linen every two weeks and clean towels every day. The remainder goes for food and chewing tobacco. Every week friends on the same floor buy him two dozen eggs, seven small cans of V-8 juice, two cans of Spam, a carton of dry cereal (because the box says, "Minimum daily requirement of vitamins") and his tobacco. He boils his eggs at once and eats them morning and evening. He stretches a can of Spam for three days or so. It has cost him violent nausea to discover that hard-boiled eggs and opened Spam need refrigeration in warm weather. (Bagdikian, 1966.)

The effects of poverty are also revealed in the facts of hunger and malnutrition facing millions of Americans. The extent of hunger might still be secret but for the take-over of an abandoned Air Force base in Mississippi in 1965 by 35 Negroes whose leaflets said, "We are here because we are hungry and cold and we have no jobs or land." They were promptly evicted but a furor of federal food-stamp programs, replacing direct surplus-food distribution centers, were claiming success in eliminating hunger in Mississippi. Further investigation, however, showed the new food-stamp programs to be working to the detriment of people too poor to purchase the stamps. The wheels of the Department of Agriculture and the Congress grind slowly. Direct payments to assist people in purchase of food stamps was tried after some delays. Even with this, a team of doctors investigating the health of Mississippi children in 1967 made a report which stated:

> In child after child we saw: evidence of vitamin and mineral deficiencies; serious untreated skin infestation and ulcerations; eye and ear diseases, also unattended bone diseases secondary to poor food intake; the prevalence of bacterial and parasitic disease as well as severe anemia, with resulting loss of energy and ability to live a normally active life; diseases of the heart and lungs—requiring surgery —which have gone undiagnosed and untreated; epileptic and other neurological disorders; severe kidney ailments, that in other children would warrant immediate hospitalization; and finally, in boys and girls in every county we visited, obvious evidence of severe malnutrition with injury to the body's tissues—its muscles, bones, and skin as well as an associated psychological state of fatigue, listlessness, and exhaustion.

> We saw children afflicted with chronic diarrhea, chronic sores, chronic leg and arm (untreated) injuries and deformities. We saw homes without running water and live with germ-bearing mosquitoes and flies everywhere around. We saw homes with children who are lucky to eat one meal a day—and that one inadequate so far as vitamins, minerals, or protein is concerned. We saw children who don't get to drink milk, don't get to eat fruit, green vegetables, or meat. They live on starches—grits, bread, Kool Aid. Their parents may be declared ineligible for commodities, ineligible for the food stamp program, even though they have literally nothing. We saw children fed communally— that is, by neighbors who give scraps of food to children whose own parents have nothing to give them. (Quoted in Citizens' Board of Inquiry into Hunger and Malnutrition in the U.S., 1968.)

How the federal government operates in the face of such destitute conditions teaches us an important lesson about the workings of American government at all levels. At the county level, local control over food-assistance programs left local governments to request, pay for, and run the programs, thus putting those areas least responsive to their own poor in a position to deny those poor federally offered food. Control by local government is not the same as local democratic control by a community of program participants, and the latter rarely exists in this country.

The politics of the national failure to respond during the Johnson Administration are described in Elizabeth Drew's account of "Going Hungry in America." She summarizes:

Yet so little was accomplished not because of mechanical or industrial failures, but because of what can happen to men in policy-making positions in Washington. When they stay in a difficult job too long, they can be overwhelmed by the complexity of it all, and they become overly defensive. Man's pride, particularly the pride of a man who can tell himself he has done some good, can overtake his intellectual honesty. Thus, not Southern politicians, not Orville Freeman, not Lyndon Johnson could face the fact when it was pointed out that many people were hungry, that they weren't wearing clothes. In this they reflected a national trait: it has been easier to stir sustained national concern over hunger in Bihar or Biafra than places at home for which we are more directly responsible. The problems are looked at in terms of the workings of Washington, not in terms of the problems. Decent men could sit and discuss statistical reliability and administrative neatness and the importance of good precedents while people went hungry. (Drew, 1968, p. 61.)

An even more callous administrative response is found in President Nixon's administration as revealed by Nick Kotz's recent book so aptly titled *Let Them Eat Promises.* The contrast between bureaucratic political process and the reality of human need cannot be exaggerated. This gap is a measure of governmental failure. In the wealthiest nation in history there are babies who die in infancy because they cannot get milk; there are anemic children, and those with stunted growth stemming from protein deficiency; there are scurvy and rickets through lack of milk and citrus juice; there are the hookworms, roundworms, and other parasitic infections; and there are the thousands who go to school with-

out breakfast and have no money for lunch. The shocking facts of starving children, adults, and old people are contained in *Hunger USA,* a report on the more than 14 million Americans without enough food to maintain health.

The impact of poverty upon the poor has been well documented. The sense of despair, alienation, and hopelessness combine to produce limited aspirations and a sense of powerlessness among the young. It is in the *adaptations* to poverty that these conditions are maintained and transmitted intergenerationally. Poverty does breed poverty! Other adaptations to poverty which have become part of the life style of the poor are often responded to as if they were the causes of the problems of the poor. Claude Brown (1965), in his personal account of growing up in Harlem, illustrates how the role of the "hustler" is simply one of many deviant occupations providing the outward symbols of success that are available to ghetto youth. Similarly, Gertrude Samuels' (1959) description of New York youth gangs reveals how gangs function to provide that sense of security and personal worth that their members cannot obtain in socially acceptable ways.

Yet we must be careful not to place too great an emphasis on the psychological impact of poverty which leads to self-defeating personal and cultural patterns. For to do so would turn our attention away from the more basic causes of poverty which are to be found in existing social institutions in American society. Moreover, an overemphasis on the pathological aspects of poverty leads us to neglect the stable patterns of social organization that are to be found in ghettos and low-income areas. In seeking out such existing strengths we may come to understand that there are many viable patterns of social life in American society in addition to the dominant middle-class patterns. In other words, the poor should not have to be required to be totally transformed in order to enjoy a decent standard of living and equal access to the rights guaranteed to all citizens.

Many of the issues raised here have been brought into very sharp focus within the context of the civil-rights movement. Black men have been given legal equality as many of the unequal-treatment laws have been declared unconstitutional and new legislation has provided guarantees of equality in education and voting. Yet while there have been great strides toward legal equality, the Negro has been denied the economic and political power necessary for social equality. It is hardly likely that Negroes derive any great satisfaction from knowing that racist explanations for his inferiority have been replaced by economic and political ones.

. . . The South has been the traditional setting in which the Negroes' quest for equality has taken place. The civil-rights movement as an organizational weapon had its greatest impact with the early boycotts and sit-ins. The nationally televised accounts of beating, police dogs, gas, and cattle prods as the Southern communities' response to the awakened Negro were sufficient to raise a national clamor for much of the civil-rights legislation currently in effect. The experience of the early years of the civil-rights movement has been vividly described by Peter Weiss (1964) in his account of a voter-registration project in Mississippi. He reveals the difficulties in voter registration of poor Negroes and whites after years of subordination and intimidation have left them apathetic or fearful, with little knowledge of their rights as citizens. It took great courage for civil-rights workers to enter Mississippi where the authorities were themselves lawless. Weiss recounts an incident in which a highway patrolman stopped a car with five SNCC workers inside, enroute to a meeting. The patrolman said, "You goddamn niggers want to change our way of life"; (hardly a traffic problem). Four of the occupants were delivered handcuffed to the sheriff at the Lowndes County Jail. The fifth, seventeen-year-old James Black, was taken to a spot a mile away by the patrolman. His affidavit dated June 8, 1964, reads:

He told me to get out of the car; I refused to get out. So he pulled me out. He started hitting me with his fists, and after about twenty blows he got out his blackjack and hit me one time with it and knocked me down. Then he told me to get back in the car. While he was beating me, he asked if any white folks had ever treated me bad; I told him yes, and he hit me again. He asked me again had any white folks in Mississippi treated me bad, and I told him no. At that point he helped me back into the car.

Then he took me to the county jail (Lowndes) where I was questioned by the sheriff. The sheriff asked for my driver's license and to take everything out of my pockets. . . . I had a friend's I.D. card in my pocket and he asked me if my friend was a Negro or a nigger. I told him a Negro. The same highway patrolman was there, and took out his blackjack and again asked if my friend was a Negro or a nigger. He started to hit me with the blackjack, and I told him my friend was a nigger.

The white Northerner's support of the civil-rights movement *in the South* was often accompanied by a smug complacency that the North was civilized and aware of human decency and the law of the land. The response of the white Northerners to the civil-rights movement was seen in Cicero, Illinois, and Milwaukee, Wisconsin, as Negroes sought to move into white workingclass neighborhoods; it was seen in the support received by George Wallace in Democratic primaries in Wisconsin and Indiana; it was seen in the repeal of an open-housing law by the voters of California. As the civil-rights movement attempted to deal with problems in the North, the moral superiority of the white Northerner over the white Southerner vanished. The comforting belief that racist America was only found in the South was shattered.

The response of the middle-class white Northerner to the growing consciousness and militancy of the Negro can only be understood in terms of the more general problem of poverty, inequality, and insecurity in American society. Poverty has to do with the inability of persons to achieve a level of income needed to live according to prevailing standards of living. As indicated earlier, the gap between the official poverty line and what is needed for a modest but adequate living has been increasing rather than shrinking. In contrast to poverty, inequality refers to the distribution of wealth or income among the general population. It is concerned with the relative share of total economic output that goes to different segments of the population. Thus, in 1960, the upper 20 percent of the population received 45 percent of total income, while the lower 20 percent received 5 percent of total income (Miller, 1964).

Unsure of his own economic and social status, the lower-middle class American feels his own chances for middle-class status restricted by technological change and a tightening opportunity structure. One consequence of this is that the working-class white becomes both envious and resentful of the attention being given to the Negro at a time when no one seems concerned with his own plight. The combination of economic insecurity, resentment toward upper-middle-class whites, and envy over the growing consciousness of Negroes is revealed in the following statement by a mother from a working-class family that is barely able to make ends meet.

They may be poorer than a lot of white people, but not by very much. Anyway, what they don't get in money they more than gain in popularity these days. The papers have suddenly decided that the Negro is teacher's pet. Whatever he does good is wonderful, and we should clap. But if he does anything bad, it's our fault. I can't read the papers anymore when they talk about the race thing. I'm sick of their editorials. All of a sudden they start giving us a lecture every day on how bad we are. They never used to care about anything, the Negro or anything else. Now they're so worried. And the same goes with the Church. I'm as devout a Catholic as you'll find around. My brother is a priest, and I do more than go to Church once a week. But I just can't take what some of our priests are saying these days. They're talking as if we did something wrong for being white. I don't understand it at all. Priests never used to talk about the Negro when I was a child. Now they talk to my kids about them all the time. I thought the Church is supposed to stand for religion, and eternal things. They shouldn't get themselves into every little fight that comes along. The same goes with the schools. I went to school here in Boston, and nobody was talking about Negroes and busing us around. The Negroes were there in Roxbury and we were here. Everybody can't live with you, can they? Everybody likes his own. But now even the school people tell us we have to have our kids with this kind and that kind of person, or else they will be hurt, or something. Now how am I supposed to believe everything all these people say? They weren't talking that way a few years ago. The governor wasn't either. Nor the mayor. They're all just like cattle stampeding to sound like one another. The same with those people out in the suburbs. Suddenly they're interested in the Negro. They worked and worked to get away from him, of course, and get away from us, too. That's why they moved so far, instead of staying here, where they can do something, if they mean so well. But no. They moved and now they're all ready to come back— but only to drive a few Negro kids out for a Sunday picnic. Who has to live with all this, and pay for it in taxes and everything? Whose kids are pushed around? And who gets called 'prejudiced' and all the other sneery words? I've had enough of it. It's hypocrisy, right down the line. And we're the ones who get it; the final buck gets passed to us. (Quoted in Coles, 1956, p. 56.)

A detailed account of the facts of poverty and inequality is presented by Parker in the article "The Myth of Middle America." Parker examines the contemporary versions of the Horatio Alger myth that have dominated America's beliefs about its progress and prosperity: we are the middle-class society, wallowing in the abundance of a technological miracle and distributing our material benefits to all regardless of status, class, or ethnic origin. Contrary to the myths, however, there are the tens of millions of Americans who, although above the official poverty line, are nonetheless "deprived." The myth of America as the middle-class affluent society is shattered in the face of its 30 million poor, its 70 million deprived, its inadequate health and welfare system, and its literacy and infant-mortality rates.

As the rich in America keep getting richer, even the liberal solutions of a guaranteed annual wage or negative income tax will not deal with the stubborn facts of poverty, deprivation, and inequality. Such solutions will only serve to institutionalize poverty and detract from the large-scale changes necessary for a more just distribution of the benefits of our economy. The particular relation between poverty and inequality in wealthy Western societies was captured in Paul Jacobs' study of business techniques designed to remove any money from the hands of the poor before it can be used for their betterment. His conclusion reflects the strain of being kept poor amidst apparent wealth.

All of us are born into a state of anxiety, and many, or even most, of us must cope, throughout our lives, with deep-rooted feelings of personal inadequacy. For the poor, these feelings are continuously reinforced by the economic circumstances in which they live and by their relationships with the rest of society. In an egalitarian society where everyone is living in poverty, being poor generates neither much anxiety nor strong feelings of inadequacy. But in a society such as ours, which measures achievement primarily by financial and material standards, to be poor is to be scorned by others, and even worse, by one's own self. It is for this reason that in America the taste and smell of poverty are so sour. (Jacobs, 1966, p. 27.)

Much of the difficulty in dealing with poverty among various subgroups in American society resides in the inability of existing social institutions to adapt to the patterns of life in the disadvantaged groups. Residents of urban ghettos are limited in their contacts with legal and welfare institutions to the policeman and social worker who come into their area but are not from their area. There is often little opportunity for the ghetto resident to make legal and welfare services more adaptable to his needs. The low-status client without power has great difficulty in influencing the professionals who come into the ghetto to serve him. Migratory poor have even less power. Truman Moore deals with the plight of the 2 million migrants who move about the country harvesting crops. For not only are the migrants without the power needed to influence state and federal agencies, but they are also transients who do not remain in an area long enough to be eligible to use existing services or to make agencies feel obligated to provide such services.

Moore indicates the failure of existing agencies at the state and national levels in providing minimum-wage protection, decent housing, health services, and schooling for children. The economic interests of the corporate farms that employ migrants are clearly of greater importance to those who make legislation than are the interests of the migrant. The vulnerability of an unprotected, economically disadvantaged group is probably found in more extreme form among migrants than among urban poor who at least have the *potential* for group power through their more stable residence patterns.

The question raised earlier in this essay—regarding whether one chooses to emphasize the barriers to full equality that reside within the disadvantaged group, or to emphasize the barriers that exist in the institutional structure which fails to adapt to the needs of the poor—remains as one of the persistent issues surrounding the causes of, and solutions to, poverty. The issue became a matter of public debate in 1965, with the appearance of a Department of Labor report entitled *The Negro Family: The Case for National Action,* written by Daniel P. Moynihan with the assistance of Paul Barton and Ellen Broderich. The essential argument of the Moynihan report was that the government efforts to lift the legal barriers in the area of discrimination would not lead to full equality for the Negro. Moynihan reasoned that the history of slavery and subordination had such a marked impact upon the Negro social structure (particularly the family) that many Negroes would be unable to take advantage of the new opportunities that were made available to them. As stated in the report: "at the heart of the deterioration of the fabric of Negro society is the deterioration of the Negro family." Moynihan used this argument to urge the establishment of a national family policy designed to enhance "the stability and resources of the Negro American family."

Controversy in government circles, the civil-rights movement, the press, and among academic social scientists followed this report. Many of the reactions to the report have been collected in a single volume by Rainwater and Yancey (1967). The controversy over the objectives of the report is less pronounced than the disagreement over its emphasis on the pathology of the ghetto and the breakdown of the Negro family. Such emphases can often serve to turn attention away from the defective features of American society that have failed to provide full equality for the Negro. There is no doubt that black Americans bear some scars from a brutal history inflicted upon them. But the Moynihan report ignored three vital points. First, that female dominance of households in Ireland, Poland, and in Western society generally, has always followed (rather than caused) economic destitution (Carper, 1968). Second, who resides with whom, supports whom, marries whom, or has children with whom is none of the government's business. Diverse cultural life styles remain the right of the individual and the community. Third, Black people no less than women or other disadvantaged minority groups are not currently being victimized by the damage that was done to their ancestors 150 years earlier (about which nothing can be done). They are being damaged by the current racism and current inequitable distribution of wealth and power in American society (about

which something must be done).

Despite the fact that the large majority of poor Americans are white, poverty is a condition that has come to be identified with black Americans, Mexican-Americans, and American Indians. It is this identification that is partly responsible for the way Americans continue to ignore the existence of the poor. The nonwhite poor can be ignored more easily when there are also justifying beliefs of the sort that sees nonwhite people as less worthy, less motivated, more immoral, or any other stereotype that goes into the construction of racist beliefs.

REFERENCES

BAGDIKIAN, BEN H., "Ed MacIntosh: Man on a Pension," in H. P. Miller (ed.), *Poverty, American Style* (Belmont, Calif.: Wadsworth, 1966).

BROWN, CLAUDE, *Manchild in the Promised Land* (New York: Macmillan, 1965).

CARPER, LAURA, "The Negro Family and the Moynihan Report," *Dissent* (March–April 1966), pp. 133–140; reproduced in R. Perrucci and M. Pilisuk (eds.), *The Triple Revolution: Social Problems in Depth* (Boston: Little, Brown, 1968), pp. 461–468.

CASAVANTES, EDWARD, "Pride and Prejudice: A Mexican American Dilemma," *Civil Rights Digest,* 3 (Winter 1970), pp. 22–27.

CLOWARD, RICHARD A., and FRANCES F. PIVAN, "Birth of a Movement," *Nation* (May 8, 1967).

COLES, ROBERT, "The White Northerner: Pride and Prejudice," *Atlantic* (June 1966), pp. 53–57; reproduced in R. Perrucci and M. Pilisuk (eds.), *The Triple Revolution: Social Problems in Depth* (Boston: Little, Brown, 1968), pp. 398–406.

COSER, LEWIS A., "The Sociology of Poverty," *Social Problems,* 13 (1965), pp. 140–145.

DREW, ELIZABETH, "Going Hungry in America," *Atlantic* (December 1968), pp. 53–61.

ELMAN, RICHARD M., *The Poorhouse State: The American Way of Life on Public Assistance* (New York: Pantheon, 1966).

FERMAN, LOUIS A., JOYCE L. KORNBLUH, and ALAN HABER (eds.), *Poverty in America* (Ann Arbor: Univ. of Michigan Press, 1965).

HARRINGTON, MICHAEL, *The Other America* (Baltimore: Penguin, 1962).

HAYDEN, TOM, "Colonialism and Liberation in America," *Viet-Report* (Summer 1968), pp. 32–39.

JACOBS, PAUL, "Keeping the Poor Poor," *New Politics,* 5 (1966), pp. 3–16, 19–20, 25–27.

KOPKIND, ANDREW, "Of, by, and for the Poor," *New Republic* (June 19, 1965), pp. 15–19; reproduced in R. Perrucci and M. Pilisuk (eds.), *The Triple Revolution: Social Problems in Depth* (Boston: Little, Brown, 1968), pp. 515–523.

KOTZ, NICK, *Let Them Eat Promises: The Politics of Hunger in America* (Englewood Cliffs, N.J.: Prentice-Hall, 1969).

MILLER, HERMAN, P., "Facts about Poverty, Revised," in H. P. Miller (ed.), *Poverty, American Style* (Belmont, Calif.: Wadsworth, 1966).

MILLER, HERMAN P., *Rich Man, Poor Man* (New York: Crowell, 1964).

MILLER, S. M., "Poverty and Inequality in America: Implications for the Social Services," *Child Welfare,* 42:9 (November 1963), pp. 442–445; reproduced in R. Perrucci and M. Pilisuk (eds.), *The Triple Revolution: Social Problems in Depth* (Boston: Little, Brown, 1968), pp. 488–493.

MILLER, S. M., and PAMELA ROBY, *The Future of Inequality* (New York: Basic Books, 1970).

MONTEZ, PHILIP, "Will the Real Mexican American Please Stand Up," *Civil Rights Digest,* 3 (Winter 1970), pp. 28–31.

MOYNIHAN, DANIEL P., "The President and the Negro: The Moment Lost," *Commentary* (February 1967), pp. 3–17; reproduced in R. Perrucci and M. Pilisuk (eds.), *The Triple Revolution: Social Problems in Depth* (Boston: Little, Brown, 1968), pp. 431–460.

Negro Family, The: The Case for National Action (Moynihan Report) (Washington D.C.: U.S. Government Printing Office, March 1965).

Newsweek, "Tio Taco Is Dead" (June 29, 1970), pp. 22–28.

RAINWATER, LEE, and WILLIAM L. YANCEY, *The Moynihan Report and the Politics of Controversy* (Cambridge, Mass.: M. I. T. Press, 1967).

REISSMAN, LEONARD, *Urban Affairs Quarterly* (March 1969).

RUSTIN, BAYARD, "The 'Watts Manifesto' and the McCone Report," *Commentary* (March 1966), pp. 29–35; reproduced in R. Perrucci and M. Pilisuk (eds.), *The Triple Revolution: Social Problems in Depth* (Boston: Little, Brown, 1968), pp. 469–481.

SAMUELS, GERTRUDE, "Why 'The Assassins' Can't Be 'Punks,'" *New York Times Magazine* (August 16, 1959), p. 13ff.

SUTHERLAND, ELIZABETH (ed.), *Letters from Mississippi* (New York: McGraw-Hill, 1965).

U.S. Commission on Civil Rights, *The Mexican American* (Washington, D.C.: U.S. Government Printing Office, 1968).

WEISS, PETER, "Nightmare in Mississippi," *The Progressive* (September 1964), pp. 19–22; reproduced in R. Perrucci and M. Pilisuk (eds.), *The Triple Revolution: Social Problems in Depth* (Boston: Little, Brown, 1968), pp. 391–397.

internal colonialism and ghetto revolt [1]

ROBERT BLAUNER

It is becoming almost fashionable to analyze American racial conflict today in terms of the colonial analogy. I shall argue in this paper that the utility of this perspective depends upon a distinction between colonization as a process and colonialism as a social, economic, and political system. It is the experience of colonization that Afro-Americans share with many of the non-white people of the world. But this subjugation has taken place in a societal context that differs in important respects from the situation of "classical co-

Reprinted from Robert Blauner, "Internal Colonialism and Ghetto Revolt," SOCIAL PROBLEMS *16 (1969) by permission of the author and The Society for the Study of Social Problems.*

[1] This is a revised version of a paper delivered at the University of California Centennial Program, "Studies in Violence," Los Angeles, June 1, 1968. For criticisms and ideas that have improved an earlier draft, I am indebted to Robert Wood, Lincoln Bergman, and Gary Marx. As a good colonialist I have probably restated (read: stolen) more ideas from the writings of Kenneth Clark, Stokely Carmichael, Frantz Fanon, and especially such contributors to the Black Panther Party (Oakland) newspaper as Huey Newton, Bobby Seale, Eldridge Cleaver, and Kathleen Cleaver than I have appropriately credited or generated myself. In self-defense I should state that I began working somewhat independently on a colonial analysis of American race relations in the fall of 1965; see my "Whitewash Over Watts: The Failure of the McCone Report," *Trans-action*, 3 (March–April, 1966), pp. 3–9, 54.

lonialism." In the body of this essay I shall look at some major developments in Black protest—the urban riots, cultural nationalism, and the movement for ghetto control—as collective responses to colonized status. Viewing our domestic situation as a special form of colonization outside a context of a colonial system will help explain some of the dilemmas and ambiguities within these movements.

The present crisis in American life has brought about changes in social perspectives and the questioning of long accepted frameworks. Intellectuals and social scientists have been forced by the pressure of events to look at old definitions of the character of our society, the role of racism, and the workings of basic institutions. The depth and volatility of contemporary racial conflict challenge sociologists in particular to question the adequacy of theoretical models by which we have explained American race relations in the past.

For a long time the distinctiveness of the Negro situation among the ethnic minorities was placed in terms of color, and the systematic discrimination that follows from our deep-seated racial prejudices. This was sometimes called the caste theory, and while provocative, it missed essential and dynamic features of American race relations. In the past ten years there has been a tendency to view Afro-Americans as another ethnic group not basically different in experience from previous ethnics and whose "immigration" condition in the North would in time follow their upward course. The inadequacy of this model is now clear— even the Kerner Report devotes a chapter to criticizing this analogy. A more recent (though hardly new) approach views the essence of racial subordination in economic class terms: Black people as an underclass are to a degree specially exploited and to a degree economically dispensable in an automating society. Important as are economic factors, the power of race and racism in America cannot be sufficiently explained through class analysis. Into this theory vacuum steps the model of internal colonialism. Problematic and imprecise as it is, it gives hope of becoming a framework that can integrate the insights of caste and racism, ethnicity, culture, and economic exploitation into an overall conceptual scheme. At the same time, the danger of the colonial model is the imposition of an artificial analogy which might keep us from facing up to the fact (to quote Harold Cruse) that "the American black and white social phenomenon is a uniquely new world thing." [2]

During the late 1950's, identification with African nations and other colonial or formerly colonized peoples grew in importance among Black militants.[3] As a result the U.S. was increasingly seen as a colonial power and the concept of domestic colonialism was introduced into the political analysis and rhetoric of militant nationalists. During the same period Black social theorists began developing this frame of reference for explaining American realities. As early as 1962, Cruse characterized race relations in this country as "domestic colonialism." [4] Three years later in Dark Ghetto, Kenneth Clark demonstrated how the political, economic, and social structure of Harlem was essentially that of a colony.[5] Finally in 1967, a full-blown elaboration of "internal colonialism" provided the theoretical framework for Carmichael and Hamilton's widely read Black Power.[6] The following year the colonial analogy gained currency and new "respectability" when Senator McCarthy habitually referred to Black Americans as a colonized people during his campaign. While the rhetoric of internal colonialism was catching on, other social scientists began to raise questions about its appropriateness as a scheme of analysis.

The colonial analysis has been rejected as obscurantist and misleading by scholars who point to the significant differences in history and social-political conditions between our domestic patterns and what took place in Africa and India. Colonialism traditionally refers to the estab-

2 Harold Cruse, Rebellion or Revolution, New York: 1968, p. 214.

3 Nationalism, including an orientation toward Africa, is no new development. It has been a constant tendency within Afro-American politics. See Cruse, ibid., esp. chaps. 5–7.

4 This was six years before the publication of The Crisis of the Negro Intellectual, New York: Morrow, 1968, which brought Cruse into prominence. Thus the 1962 article was not widely read until its reprinting in Cruse's essays, Rebellion or Revolution, op. cit.

5 Kenneth Clark, Dark Ghetto, New York: Harper and Row, 1965. Clark's analysis first appeared a year earlier in Youth in the Ghetto, New York: Haryou Associates, 1964.

6 Stokely Carmichael and Charles Hamilton, Black Power, New York: Random, 1967.

lishment of domination over a geographically external political unit, most often inhabited by people of a different race and culture, where this domination is political and economic, and the colony exists subordinated to and dependent upon the mother country. Typically the colonizers exploit the land, the raw materials, the labor, and other resources of the colonized nation; in addition a formal recognition is given to the difference in power, autonomy, and political status, and various agencies are set up to maintain this subordination. Seemingly the analogy must be stretched beyond usefulness if the American version is to be forced into this model. For here we are talking about group relations within a society; the mother country—colony separation in geography is absent. Though whites certainly colonized the territory of the original Americans, internal colonization of Afro-Americans did not involve the settlement of whites in any land that was unequivocably Black. And unlike the colonial situation, there has been no formal recognition of differing power since slavery was abolished outside the South. Classic colonialism involved the control and exploitation of the majority of a nation by a minority of outsiders. Whereas in America the people who are oppressed were themselves originally outsiders and are a numerical minority.

This conventional critique of "internal colonialism" is useful in pointing to the differences between our domestic patterns and the overseas situation. But in its bold attack it tends to lose sight of common experiences that have been historically shared by the most subjugated racial minorities in America and non-white peoples in some other parts of the world. For understanding the most dramatic recent developments on the race scene, this common core element—which I shall call colonization—may be more important than the undeniable divergences between the two contexts.

The common features ultimately relate to the fact that the classical colonialism of the imperialist era and American racism developed out of the same historical situation and reflected a common, world economic and power stratification. The slave trade for the most part preceded the imperialist partition and economic exploitation of Africa, and in fact may have been a necessary prerequisite for colonial conquest—since it helped deplete and pacify Africa, undermining the resistance to direct occupation. Slavery contributed one of the basic raw materials for the textile industry which provided much of the capital for the West's industrial development and need for economic expansionism. The essential condition for both American slavery and European colonialism was the power domination and the technological superiority of the Western world in its relation to peoples of non-Western and non-white origins. This objective supremacy in technology and military power buttressed the West's sense of cultural superiority, laying the basis for racist ideologies that were elaborated to justify control and exploitation of non-white people. Thus because classical colonialism and America's internal version developed out of a similar balance of technological, cultural, and power relations, a common *process* of social oppression characterized the racial patterns in the two contexts—despite the variation in political and social structure.

There apepar to be four basic components of the colonization complex. The first refers to how the racial group enters into the dominant society (whether colonial power or not). Colonization begins with a forced, involuntary entry. Second, there is an impact on the culture and social organization of the colonized people which is more than just a result of such "natural" processes as contact and acculturation. The colonizing power carries out a policy which constrains, transforms, or destroys indigenous values, orientations, and ways of life. Third, colonization involves a relationship by which members of the colonized group tend to be administered by representatives of the dominant power. There is an experience of being managed and manipulated by outsiders in terms of ethnic status.

A final fundament of colonization is racism. Racism is a principle of social domination by which a group seen as inferior or different in terms of alleged biological characteristics is exploited, controlled, and oppressed socially and psychically by a superordinate group. Except for the marginal case of Japanese imperialism, the major examples of colonialism have involved the subjugation of non-white Asian, African, and Latin American peoples by white European powers. Thus racism has generally accompanied colonialism. Race prejudice can exist without colonization—the experience of Asian-American minorities is a case in point—but racism as a system of domination is part of the complex of colonization.

The concept of colonization stresses the enormous fatefulness of the historical factor, namely the manner in which a minority group becomes a part of the dominant society.[7] The crucial difference between the colonized Americans and the ethnic immigrant minorities is that the latter have always been able to operate fairly competitively within that relatively open section of the social and economic order because these groups came voluntarily in search of a better life, because their movements in society were not administratively controlled, and because they transformed their culture at their own pace—giving up ethnic values and institutions when it was seen as a desirable exchange for improvements in social position.

In present-day America, a major device of Black colonization is the powerless ghetto. As Kenneth Clark describes the situation:

> Ghettoes are the consequence of the imposition of external power and the institutionalization of powerlessness. In this respect, they are in fact social, political, educational, and above all —economic colonies. Those confined within the ghetto walls are subject peoples. They are victims of the greed, cruelty, insensitivity, guilt and fear of their masters. . . .
> The community can best be described in terms of the analogy of a powerless colony. Its political leadership is divided, and all but one or two of its political leaders are shortsighted and dependent upon the larger political power structure. Its social agencies are financially precarious and dependent upon sources of support outside the community. Its churches are iso-

[7] As Eldridge Cleaver reminds us, "Black people are a stolen people held in a colonial status on stolen land, and any analysis which does not acknowledge the colonial status of black people cannot hope to deal with the real problem." "The Land Question," *Ramparts*, 6 (May, 1968), p. 51.

lated or dependent. Its economy is dominated by small businesses which are largely owned by absentee owners, and its tenements and other real property are also owned by absentee landlords.

Under a system of centralization, Harlem's schools are controlled by forces outside of the community. Programs and policies are supervised and determined by individuals who do not live in the community. . . .[8]

Of course many ethnic groups in America have lived in ghettoes. What make the Black ghettoes an expression of colonized status are three special features. First, the ethnic ghettoes arose more from voluntary choice, both in the sense of the choice to immigrate to America and the decision to live among one's fellow ethnics. Second, the immigrant ghettoes tended to be a one and two generation phenomenon; they were actually way-stations in the process of acculturation and assimilation. When they continue to persist as in the case of San Francisco's Chinatown, it is because they are big business for the ethnics themselves and there is a new stream of immigrants. The Black ghetto on the other hand has been a more permanent phenomenon, although some individuals do escape it. But most relevant is the third point. European ethnic groups like the Poles, Italians, and Jews generally only experienced a brief period, often less than a generation, during which their residential buildings, commercial stores, and other enterprises were owned by outsiders. The Chinese and Japanese faced handicaps of color prejudice that were almost as strong as the Blacks faced, but very soon gained control of their internal communities, because their traditional ethnic culture and social organization had not been destroyed by slavery and internal colonization. But Afro-Americans are distinct in the extent to which their segregated communities have remained controlled economically, politically, and administratively from the outside. One indicator of this difference is the estimate that the "income of Chinese-Americans from Chinese-owned businesses is in proportion to their numbers 45 times as great as the income of Negroes from Negro owned businesses."[9] But what is true of business is also true for the other social institutions that operate within the ghetto. The educators, policemen, social workers, politicians, and others who administer the affairs of ghetto residents are typically whites who live outside the Black community. Thus the ghetto plays a strategic role as the focus for the administration by outsiders which is also essential to the structure of overseas colonialism.[10]

8 *Youth in the Ghetto, op. cit.,* pp. 10–11, 79–80.

9 N. Glazer and D. P. Moynihan, *Beyond the Melting Pot,* Cambridge, Mass.: M.I.T., 1963, p. 37.

10 "When we speak of Negro social disabilities under capitalism, . . . we refer to the fact that he does not own anything— *even what is ownable in his own community.* Thus to fight for black liberation *is to fight for his right to own.* The Negro is politically compromised today because he owns nothing. He has little voice in the affairs of state because he owns nothing. The fundamental reason why the Negro bourgeois-democratic revolution has been aborted is because American capitalism has prevented the development of a black class of capitalist owners of institutions and economic tools. To take one crucial example, Negro radicals today are severely hampered in their tasks of educating the black masses on political issues because Negroes do not

The colonial status of the Negro community goes beyond the issue of ownership and decision-making within Black neighborhoods. The Afro-American population in most cities has very little influence on the power structure and institutions of the larger metropolis, despite the fact that in numerical terms, Blacks tend to be the most sizeable of the various interest groups. A recent analysis of policy-making in Chicago estimates that "Negroes really hold less than 1 percent of the effective power in the Chicago metropolitan area. [Negroes are 20 percent of Cook County's population.] Realistically the power structure of Chicago is hardly less white than that of Mississippi."[11]

Colonization outside of a traditional colonial structure has its own special conditions. The group culture and social structure of the colonized in America is less developed; it is also less autonomous. In addition, the colonized are a numerical minority, and furthermore they are ghettoized more totally and are more dispersed than people under classic colonialism. Though these

realities affect the magnitude and direction of response, it is my basic thesis that the most important expressions of protest in the Black community during the recent years reflect the colonized status of Afro-America. Riots, programs of separation, politics and community control, the Black revolutionary movements, and cultural nationalism each represent a different strategy of attack on domestic colonialism in America. Let us now examine some of these movements.

RIOT OR REVOLT?

The so-called riots are being increasingly recognized as a preliminary if primitive form of mass rebellion against a colonial status. There is still a tendency to absorb their meaning within the conventional scope of assimilation-integration politics: some commentators stress the material motives involved in looting as a sign that the rioters want to join America's middle-class affluence just like everyone else. That motives are mixed and often unconscious, that Black people want good furniture and television sets like whites is beside the point. The guiding impulse in most major outbreaks has not been integration with American society, but an attempt to stake out a sphere of control by moving against that society and destroying the symbols of its oppression.

In my critique of the McCone report I observed that the rioters were asserting a claim to territoriality, an unorganized and rather inchoate attempt to gain control over their community or "turf."[12] In succeed-

own any of the necessary means of propaganda and communication. The Negro owns no printing presses, he has no stake in the networks of the means of communication. Inside his own communities he does not own the house he lives in, the property he lives on, nor the wholesale and retail sources from which he buys his commodities. He does not own the edifices in which he enjoys culture and entertainment or in which he socializes. In capitalist society, an individual or group that does not own anything is powerless." H. Cruse, "Behind the Black Power Slogan," in Cruse, *Rebellion or Revolution, op. cit.,* pp. 238–239.

[11] Harold M. Baron, "Black Powerlessness in Chicago," *Trans-action,* 6 (Nov., 1968), pp. 27–33.

[12] R. Blauner, "Whitewash Over Watts," *op. cit.*

ing disorders also the thrust of the action has been the attempt to clear out an alien presence, white men and officials, rather than a drive to kill whites as in a conventional race riot. The main attacks have been directed at the property of white business men and at the police who operate in the Black community "like an army of occupation" protecting the interests of outside exploiters and maintaining the domination over the ghetto by the central metropolitan power structure.[13] The Kerner Report misleads when it attempts to explain riots in terms of integration: "What the rioters appear to be seeking was fuller participation in the social order and the material benefits enjoyed by the majority of American citizens. Rather than rejecting the American system, they were anxious to obtain a place for themselves in it."[14] More accurately, the revolts pointed to alienation from this system on the part of many poor and also not-so-poor Blacks. The sacredness of private property, that unconsciously accepted bulwark of our social arrangements, was rejected; people who looted apparently without guilt generally remarked that they were taking things that "really belonged" to them anyway.[15] Obviously the

society's bases of legitimacy and authority have been attacked. Law and order has long been viewed as the white man's law and order by Afro-Americans; but now this perspective characteristic of a colonized people is out in the open. And the Kerner Report's own data question how well ghetto rebels are buying the system: In Newark only 33 percent of self-reported rioters said they thought this country was worth fighting for in the event of a major war; in the Detroit sample the figure was 55 percent.[16]

One of the most significant consequences of the process of colonization is a weakening of the colonized's individual and collective will to resist his oppression. It has been easier to contain and control Black ghettoes because communal bonds and group solidarity have been weakened through divisions among leadership, failures of organization, and a general disspiritment that accompanies social oppression. The riots are a signal that the will to resist has broken the mold of accommodation. In some cities as in Watts they also represented nascent movements toward community identity. In several riot-torn ghettoes the outbursts have stimulated new organizations and movements. If it is true that the riot phenomenon of 1964–68 has passed its peak, its historical import may be more for the "internal" organizing momentum generated than

---

[13] "The police function to support and enforce the interests of the dominant political, social, and economic interests of the town" is a statement made by a former police scholar and official, according to A. Neiderhoffer, *Behind the Shield*, New York: Doubleday, 1967 as cited by Gary T. Marx, "Civil Disorder and the Agents of Control," *Journal of Social Issues,* forthcoming.

[14] Report of the National Advisory Commission on Civil Disorders, N.Y.: Bantam, March, 1968, p. 7.

[15] This kind of attitude has a long history among American Negroes. During slavery, Blacks used the same rationalization

to justify stealing from their masters. Appropriating things from the master was viewed as *"taking* part of his property for the benefit of another part; whereas *stealing* referred to appropriating something from another slave, an offense that was not condoned." Kenneth Stampp, *The Peculiar Institution,* Vintage, 1956, p. 127.

[16] Report of the National Advisory Commission on Civil Disorders, *op. cit.,* p. 178.

for any profound "external" response of the larger society facing up to underlying causes.

Despite the appeal of Frantz Fanon to young Black revolutionaries, America is not Algeria. It is difficult to foresee how riots in our cities can play a role equivalent to rioting in the colonial situation as an integral phase in a movement for national liberation. In 1968 some militant groups (for example, the Black Panther Party in Oakland) had concluded that ghetto riots were self-defeating of the lives and interests of Black people in the present balance of organization and gunpower, though they had served a role to stimulate both Black consciousness and white awareness of the depths of racial crisis. Such militants have been influential in "cooling" their communities during periods of high riot potential. Theoretically oriented Black radicals see riots as spontaneous mass behavior which must be replaced by a revolutionary organization and consciousness. But despite the differences in objective conditions, the violence of the 1960's seems to serve the same psychic function, assertions of dignity and manhood for young Blacks in urban ghettoes, as it did for the colonized of North Africa described by Fanon and Memmi.[17]

CULTURAL NATIONALISM

Cultural conflict is generic to the colonial relation because colonization involves the domination of Western technological values over the more communal cultures of non-Western peoples. Colonialism played havoc with the national integrity of the peoples it brought under its sway. Of course, all traditional cultures are threatened by industrialism, the city, and modernization in communication, transportation, health, and education. What is special are the political and administrative decisions of colonizers in managing and controlling colonized peoples. The boundaries of African colonies, for example, were drawn to suit the political conveniences of the European nations without regard to the social organization and cultures of African tribes and kingdoms. Thus Nigeria as blocked out by the British included the Yorubas and the Ibos, whose civil war today is a residuum of the colonialist's disrespect for the integrity of indigenous cultures.

The most total destruction of culture in the colonization process took place not in traditional colonialism but in America. As Frazier stressed, the integral cultures of the diverse African peoples who furnished the slave trade were destroyed because slaves from different tribes, kingdoms, and linguistic groups were purposely separated to maximize domination and control. Thus language, religion, and national loyalties were lost in North America much more completely than in the Caribbean and Brazil where slavery developed somewhat differently. Thus on this key point America's internal colonization has been more total and extreme than situations of classic colonialism. For the British in India and the European powers in Africa were not able—as outnumbered minorities—to destroy the national and tribal cultures of the colo-

17 Frantz Fanon, *Wretched of the Earth*, New York: Grove, 1963; Albert Memmi, *The Colonizer and the Colonized*, Boston: Beacon, 1967.

nized. Recall that American slavery lasted 250 years and its racist aftermath another 100. Colonial dependency in the case of British Kenya and French Algeria lasted only 77 and 125 years respectively. In the wake of this more drastic uprooting and destruction of culture and social organization, much more powerful agencies of social, political, and psychological domination developed in the American case.

> Colonial control of many peoples inhabiting the colonies was more a goal than a fact, and at Independence there were undoubtedly fairly large numbers of Africans who had never seen a colonial administrator. The gradual process of extension of control from the administrative center on the African coast contrasts sharply with the total uprooting involved in the slave trade and the totalitarian aspects of slavery in the United States. Whether or not Elkins is correct in treating slavery as a total institution, it undoubtedly had a far more radical and pervasive impact on American slaves than did colonialism on the vast majority of Africans.[18]

Yet a similar cultural process unfolds in both contexts of colonialism. To the extent that they are involved in the larger society and economy, the colonized are caught up in a conflict between two cultures. Fanon has described how the assimilation-oriented schools of Martinique taught him to reject his own culture and Blackness in favor of Westernized, French, and white values.[19] Both the colonized elites under traditional colonialism and perhaps the majority of Afro-Americans today experience a parallel split in identity, cultural loyalty, and political orientation.[20]

The colonizers use their culture to socialize the colonized elites (intellectuals, politicians, and middle class) into an identification with the colonial system. Because Western culture has the prestige, the power, and the key to open the limited opportunity that a minority of the colonized may achieve, the first reaction seems to be an acceptance of the dominant values. Call it brainwashing as the Black Muslims put it; call it identifying with the aggressor if you prefer Freudian terminology; call it a natural response to the hope and belief that integration and democratization can really take place if you favor a more commonsense explanation, this initial acceptance in time crumbles on the realities of racism and colonialism. The colonized, seeing that his success within colonialism is at the expense of his group and his own inner identity, moves radically toward a rejection of the Western culture and develops a nationalist outlook that celebrates his people and their traditions. As Memmi describes it:

> Assimilation being abandoned, the colonized's liberation must be carried out through a recovery of self and of autonomous dignity. Attempts at imitating the colonizer required self-denial; the colonizer's rejection is the indispensable prelude to self-discovery. That accusing and annihilat-

[18] Robert Wood, "Colonialism in Africa and America: Some Conceptual Considerations," December, 1967, unpublished paper.

[19] F. Fanon, *Black Skins, White Masks,* New York: Grove, 1967.

[20] Harold Cruse has described how these two themes of integration with the larger society and identification with ethnic nationality have struggled within the political and cultural movements of Negro Americans. *The Crisis of the Negro Intellectual, op. cit.*

ing image must be shaken off; oppression must be attacked boldly since it is impossible to go around it. After having been rejected for so long by the colonizer, the day has come when it is the colonized who must refuse the colonizer.[21]

Memmi's book, *The Colonizer and the Colonized,* is based on his experience as a Tunisian Jew in a marginal position between the French and the colonized Arab majority. The uncanny parallels between the North African situation he describes and the course of Black-white relations in our society is the best impressionist argument I know for the thesis that we have a colonized group and a colonizing system in America. His discussion of why even the most radical French anti-colonialist cannot participate in the struggle of the colonized is directly applicable to the situation of the white liberal and radical vis-à-vis the Black movement. His portrait of the colonized is as good an analysis of the psychology behind Black Power and Black nationalism as anything that has been written in the U.S. Consider for example:

Considered *en bloc* as *them, they,* or *those,* different from every point of view, homogeneous in a radical heterogeneity, the colonized reacts by rejecting all the colonizers *en bloc.* The distinction between deed and intent has no great significance in the colonial situation. In the eyes of the colonized, all Europeans in the colonies are de facto colonizers, and whether they want to be or not, they are colonizers in some ways. By their privileged economic position, by belonging to the political system of oppression, or by participating in an

effectively negative complex toward the colonized, they are colonizers. . . . They are supporters or at least unconscious accomplices of that great collective aggression of Europe.[22]

The same passion which made him admire and absorb Europe shall make him assert his differences; since those differences, after all, are within him and correctly constitute his true self.[23] The important thing now is to rebuild his people, whatever be their authentic nature; to reforge their unity, communicate with it, and to feel that they belong.[24]

Cultural revitalization movements play a key role in anti-colonial movements. They follow an inner necessity and logic of their own that comes from the consequences of colonialism on groups and personal identities; they are also essential to provide the solidarity which the political or military phase of the anti-colonial revolution requires. In the U.S. an Afro-American culture has been developing since slavery out of the ingredients of African world-views, the experience of bondage, Southern values and customs, migration and the Northern lower-class ghettoes, and most importantly, the political history of the Black population in its struggle against racism.[25] That Afro-Americans are moving to-

21 Memmi, *op. cit.,* p. 128.

22 *Ibid.,* p. 130.
23 *Ibid.,* p. 132.
24 *Ibid.,* p. 134.
25 In another essay, I argue against the standard sociological position that denies the existence of an ethnic Afro-American culture and I expand on the above themes. The concept of "Soul" is astonishingly parallel in content to the mystique of "Negritude" in Africa; the Pan-African culture movement has its parallel in the burgeoning Black culture mood in Afro-American communities. See "Black Culture: Myth or Reality" in Peter Rose, editor, *Americans From Africa,* Atherton, 1969.

ward cultural nationalism in a period when ethnic loyalties tend to be weak (and perhaps on the decline) in this country is another confirmation of the unique colonized position of the Black group. (A similar nationalism seems to be growing among American Indians and Mexican-Americans.)

THE MOVEMENT FOR GHETTO CONTROL

The call for Black Power unites a number of varied movements and tendencies.[26] Though no clear-cut program has yet emerged, the most important emphasis seems to be the movement for control of the ghetto. Black leaders and organizations are increasingly concerned with owning and controlling those institutions that exist within or impinge upon their community. The colonial model provides a key to the understanding of this movement, and indeed ghetto control advocates have increasingly invoked the language of colonialism in pressing for local home rule. The framework of anticolonialism explains why the struggle for poor people's or community control of poverty programs has been more central in many cities than the

26 Scholars and social commentators, Black and white alike, disagree in interpreting the contemporary Black Power movement. The issues concern whether this is a new development in Black protest or an old tendency revised; whether the movement is radical, revolutionary, reformist, or conservative; and whether this orientation is unique to Afro-Americans or essentially a Black parallel to other ethnic group strategies for collective mobility. For an interesting discussion of Black Power as a modernized version of Booker T. Washington's separatism and economism, see Harold Cruse, *Rebellion or Revolution, op. cit.,* pp. 193–258.

content of these programs and why it has been crucial to exclude whites from leadership positions in Black organizations.

The key institutions that anticolonists want to take over or control are business, social services, schools, and the police. Though many spokesmen have advocated the exclusion of white landlords and small businessmen from the ghetto, this program has evidently not struck fire with the Black population and little concrete movement toward economic expropriation has yet developed. Welfare recipients have organized in many cities to protect their rights and gain a greater voice in the decisions that affect them, but whole communities have not yet been able to mount direct action against welfare colonialism. Thus schools and the police seem now to be the burning issues of ghetto control politics.

During the past few years there has been a dramatic shift from educational integration as the primary goal to that of community control of the schools. Afro-Americans are demanding their own school boards, with the power to hire and fire principals and teachers and to construct a curriculum which would be relevant to the special needs and culture style of ghetto youth. Especially active in high schools and colleges have been Black students, whose protests have centered on the incorporation of Black Power and Black culture into the educational system. Consider how similar is the spirit behind these developments to the attitude of the colonized North African toward European education:

He will prefer a long period of educational mistakes to the continuance of the colonizer's school organization. He will choose institutional disorder in order to destroy the institutions built by the colonizer as soon as possible. There we will see, indeed a reactive drive of profound protest. He will no longer owe anything to the colonizer and will have definitely broken with him.[27]

Protest and institutional disorder over the issue of school control came to a head in 1968 in New York City. The procrastination in the Albany State legislature, the several crippling strikes called by the teachers union, and the almost frenzied response of Jewish organizations makes it clear that decolonization of education faces the resistance of powerful vested interests.[28] The situation is too dynamic at present to assess probable future results. However, it can be safely predicted that some form of school decentralization will be institutionalized in New York, and the movement for community control of education will spread to more cities.

This movement reflects some of the problems and ambiguities that stem from the situation of colonization outside an immediate colonial context. The Afro-American community is not parallel in structure to the communities of colonized nations under traditional colonialism. The significant difference here is the lack of fully developed indigenous institutions besides the church. Outside of some areas of the South there is really no Black economy, and

most Afro-Americans are inevitably caught up in the larger society's structure of occupations, education, and mass communication. Thus the ethnic nationalist orientation which reflects the reality of colonization exists alongside an integrationist orientation which corresponds to the reality that the institutions of the larger society are much more developed than those of the incipient nation.[29] As would be expected the movement for school control reflects both tendencies. The militant leaders who spearheaded such local movements may be primarily motivated by the desire to gain control over the community's institutions— they are anti-colonialists first and foremost. Many parents who support them may share this goal also, but the majority are probably more concerned about creating a new education that will enable their children to "make it" in the society and the economy as a whole—they know that the present school system fails ghetto children and does not prepare them for participation in American life.

There is a growing recognition that the police are the most crucial institution maintaining the colonized status of Black Americans. And of all establishment institutions, police departments probably include the highest proportion of individual racists. This is no accident since central to the workings of racism (an essential component of colonization) are attacks on the hu-

[27] Memmi, *op. cit.*, pp. 137–138.
[28] For the New York school conflict see Jason Epstein, "The Politics of School Decentralization," *New York Review of Books*, June 6, 1968, pp. 26–32; and "The New York City School Revolt," *ibid.*, 11, no. 6, pp. 37–41.

[29] This dual split in the politics and psyche of the Black American was poetically described by Du Bois in his *Souls of Black Folk*, and more recently has been insightfully analyzed by Harold Cruse in *The Crisis of the Negro Intellectual*, *op. cit.* Cruse has also characterized the problem of the Black community as that of underdevelopment.

manity and dignity of the subject group. Through their normal routines the police constrict Afro-Americans to Black neighborhoods by harassing and questioning them when found outside the ghetto; they break up groups of youth congregating on corners or in cars without any provocation; and they continue to use offensive and racist language no matter how many inter-group understanding seminars have been built into the police academy. They also shoot to kill ghetto residents for alleged crimes such as car thefts and running from police officers.[30]

Police are key agents in the power equation as well as the drama of dehumanization. In the final analysis they do the dirty work for the larger system by restricting the striking back of Black rebels to skirmishes inside the ghetto, thus deflecting energies and attacks from the communities and institutions of the larger power structure. In a his-

torical review, Gary Marx notes that since the French revolution, police and other authorities have killed large numbers of demonstrators and rioters; the rebellious "rabble" rarely destroys human life. The same pattern has been repeated in America's recent revolts.[31] Journalistic accounts appearing in the press recently suggest that police see themselves as defending the interests of white people against a tide of Black insurgence; furthermore the majority of whites appear to view "blue power" in this light. There is probably no other opinion on which the races are as far apart today as they are on the question of attitudes toward the police.

In many cases set off by a confrontation between a policeman and a Black citizen, the ghetto uprisings have dramatized the role of law enforcement and the issue of police brutality. In their aftermath, movements have arisen to contain police activity. One of the first was the Community Alert Patrol in Los Angeles, a method of policing the police in order to keep them honest and constrain their violations of personal dignity. This was the first

---

[30] A recent survey of police finds "that in the predominantly Negro areas of several large cities, many of the police perceive the residents as basically hostile, especially the youth and adolescents. A lack of public support—from citizens, from courts, and from laws—is the policeman's major complaint. But some of the public criticism can be traced to the activities in which he engages day by day, and perhaps to the tone in which he enforces the 'law' in the Negro neighborhoods. Most frequently he is 'called upon' to intervene in domestic quarrels and break up loitering groups. He stops and frisks two or three times as many people as are carrying dangerous weapons or are actual criminals, and almost half of these don't wish to cooperate with the policeman's efforts." Peter Rossi *et al.,* "Between Black and White—The Faces of American Institutions and the Ghetto," in Supplemental Studies for The National Advisory Commission on Civil Disorders, July 1968, p. 114.

[31] "In the Gordon Riots of 1780 demonstrators destroyed property and freed prisoners, but did not seem to kill anyone, while authorities killed several hundred rioters and hung an additional 25. In the Rebellion Riots of the French Revolution, though several hundred rioters were killed, they killed no one. Up to the end of the Summer of 1967, this pattern had clearly been repeated, as police, not rioters, were responsible for most of the more than 100 deaths that have occurred. Similarly, in a related context, the more than 100 civil rights murders of recent years have been matched by almost no murders of racist whites." G. Marx, "Civil Disorders and the Agents of Social Control," *op. cit.*

tactic of the Black Panther Party which originated in Oakland, perhaps the most significant group to challenge the police role in maintaining the ghetto as a colony. The Panther's later policy of openly carrying guns (a legally protected right) and their intention of defending themselves against police aggression has brought on a series of confrontations with the Oakland police department. All indications are that the authorities intend to destroy the Panthers by shooting, framing up, or legally harassing their leadership —diverting the group's energies away from its primary purpose of self-defense and organization of the Black community to that of legal defense and gaining support in the white community.

There are three major approaches to "police colonialism" that correspond to reformist and revolutionary readings of the situation. The most elementary and also superficial approach sees colonialism in the fact that ghettoes are overwhelmingly patrolled by white rather than by Black officers. The proposal—supported today by many police departments— to increase the number of Blacks on local forces to something like their distribution in the city would then make it possible to reduce the use of white cops in the ghetto. This reform should be supported, for a variety of obvious reasons, but it does not get to the heart of the police role as agents of colonization.

The Kerner Report documents the fact that in some cases Black policemen can be as brutal as their white counterparts. The Report does not tell us who policies the ghetto, but they have compiled the proportion of Negroes on the forces

of the major cities. In some cities the disparity is so striking that white police inevitably dominate ghetto patrols. (In Oakland 31 percent of the population and only 4 percent of the police are Black; in Detroit the figures are 39 percent and 5 percent; and in New Orleans 41 and 4.) In other cities, however, the proportion of Black cops is approaching the distribution in the city: Philadelphia 29 percent and 20 percent; Chicago 27 percent and 17 percent.[32] These figures also suggest that both the extent and the pattern of colonization may vary from one city to another. It would be useful to study how Black communities differ in degree of control over internal institutions as well as in economic and political power in the metropolitan area.

A second demand which gets more to the issue is that police should live in the communities they patrol. The idea here is that Black cops who lived in the ghetto would have to be accountable to the community; if they came on like white cops then "the brothers would take care of business" and make their lives miserable. The third or maximalist position is based on the premise that the police play no positive role in the ghettoes. It calls for the withdrawal of metropolitan officers from Black communities and the substitu-

[32] Report of the National Advisory Commission on Civil Disorders, *op. cit.*, p. 321. That Black officers nevertheless would make a difference is suggested by data from one of the supplemental studies to the Kerner Report. They found Negro policemen working in the ghettoes considerably more sympathetic to the community and its social problems than their white counterparts. Peter Rossi *et al.*, "Between Black and White—The Faces of American Institutions in the Ghetto," *op. cit.*, chap. 6.

tion of an autonomous indigenous force that would maintain order without oppressing the population. The precise relationship between such an independent police, the city and county law enforcement agencies, a ghetto governing body that would supervise and finance it, and especially the law itself is yet unclear. It is unlikely that we will soon face these problems directly as they have arisen in the case of New York's schools. Of all the programs of decolonization, police autonomy will be most resisted. It gets to the heart of how the state functions to control and contain the Black community through delegating the legitimate use of violence to police authority.

The various "Black Power" programs that are aimed at gaining control of individual ghettoes—buying up property and businesses, running the schools through community boards, taking over anti-poverty programs and other social agencies, diminishing the arbitrary power of the police—can serve to revitalize the institutions of the ghetto and build up an economic, professional, and political power base. These programs seem limited; we do not know at present if they are enough in themselves to end colonized status.[33] But they are certainly a necessary first step.

THE ROLE OF WHITES

What makes the Kerner Report a less-than-radical document is its superficial treatment of racism and its reluctance to confront the colonized relationship between Black people and the larger society. The Report emphasizes the attitudes and feelings that make up white racism, rather than the system of privilege and control which is the heart of the matter.[34] With all its discussion of the ghetto and its problems, it never faces the question of the stake that white Americans have in racism and ghettoization.

This is not a simple question, but this paper should not end with the impression that police are the major villains. All white Americans gain some privileges and advantage from the colonization of Black communities.[35] The majority of whites also lose something from this oppression and division in society. Serious research should be directed to the ways in which white individuals and institutions are tied into the ghetto. In closing let me suggest some possible parameters.

1. It is my guess that only a small minority of whites make a direct economic profit from ghetto colonization. This is hopeful in that the ouster of white businessmen may become politically feasible. Much more significant, however, are the private and corporate interests in the land and residential property of the Black community; their holdings

---

[33] Eldridge Cleaver has called this first stage of the anti-colonial movement *community* liberation in contrast to a more long-range goal of *national* liberation. E. Cleaver, "Community Imperialism," Black Panther Party newspaper, 2 (May 18, 1968).

[34] For a discussion of this failure to deal with racism, see Gary T. Marx, "Report of the National Commission: The Analysis of Disorder or Disorderly Analysis," 1968, unpublished paper.

[35] Such a movement is easier to assert than to document but I am attempting the latter in a forthcoming book tentatively titled *White Racism, Black Culture,* to be published by Little, Brown, 1970.

and influence on urban decision-making must be exposed and combated.

2. A much larger minority have occupational and professional interests in the present arrangements. The Kerner Commission reports that 1.3 million non-white men would have to be up-graded occupationally in order to make the Black job distribution roughly similar to the white. They advocate this without mentioning that 1.3 million specially privileged white workers would lose in the bargain.[36] In addition there are those professionals who carry out what Lee Rainwater has called the "dirty work" of administering the lives of the ghetto poor: the social workers, the school teachers, the urban development people, and of course the police.[37] The social problems of the Black community will ultimately be solved only by people and organizations from that community; thus the emphasis within these professions must shift toward training such a cadre of minority personnel. Social scientists who teach and study problems of race and poverty likewise have an obligation to replace themselves by bringing into the graduate schools and college faculties men of color who will become the future experts in these areas. For cultural and intellectual imperialism is as real as welfare colonialism, though it is currently screened behind such unassailable shibboleths as universalism and the objectivity of scientific inquiry.

3. Without downgrading the vested interests of profit and profession, the real nitty-gritty elements of the white stake are political power and bureaucratic security. Whereas few whites have much understanding of the realities of race relations and ghetto life, I think most give tacit or at least subconscious support for the containment and control of the Black population. Whereas most whites have extremely distorted images of Black Power, many—if not most—would still be frightened by actual Black political power. Racial groups and identities are real in American life; white Americans sense they are on top, and they fear possible reprisals or disruptions were power to be more equalized. There seems to be a paranoid fear in the white psyche of Black dominance; the belief that Black autonomy would mean unbridled license is so ingrained that such reasonable outcomes as Black political majorities and independent Black police forces will be bitterly resisted.

On this level the major mass bulwark of colonization is the administrative need for bureaucratic security so that the middle classes can go about their life and business in peace and quiet. The Black militant movement is a threat to the orderly procedures by which bureaucracies and suburbs manage their existence, and I think today there are more people who feel a stake in conventional procedures than there are those who gain directly from racism. For in their fight for institutional control, the colonized will not play by the white rules of the game.

36 Report of the National Advisory Commission on Civil Disorders, *op. cit.*, pp. 253–256.

37 Lee Rainwater, "The Revolt of the Dirty-Workers," *Trans-action,* 5 (Nov., 1967), pp. 2, 64.

These administrative rules have kept them down and out of the system; therefore they have no necessary intention of running institutions in the image of the white middle class.

The liberal, humanist value that violence is the worst sin cannot be defended today if one is committed squarely against racism and for self-determination. For some violence is almost inevitable in the decolonization process; unfortunately racism in America has been so effective that the greatest power Afro-Americans (and perhaps also Mexican-Americans) wield today is the power to disrupt. If we are going to swing with these revolutionary times and at least respond positively to the anti-colonial movement, we will have to learn to live with conflict, confrontation, constant change, and what may be real or apparent chaos and disorder.

A positive response from the white majority needs to be in two major directions at the same time. First, community liberation movements should be supported in every way by pulling out white instruments of direct control and exploitation and substituting technical assistance to the community when this is asked for. But it is not enough to relate affirmatively to the nationalist movement for ghetto control without at the same time radically opening doors for full participation in the institutions of the mainstream. Otherwise the liberal and radical position is little different than the traditional segregationist. Freedom in the special conditions of American colonization means that the colonized must have the choice between participation in the larger society and in their own independent structures.

oil in santa barbara
and power in america*

HARVEY MOLOTCH

More than oil leaked from Union Oil's Platform A in the Santa Barbara Channel—a bit of truth about power in America spilled out along with it. It is the thesis of this paper that this technological "accident," like all accidents, provides clues to the realities of social structure (in this instance, power arrangements) not otherwise available to the outside observer. Further, it is argued, the response of the aggrieved population (the citizenry of Santa Barbara) provides insight into the more general process which shapes disillusionment and frustration among those who come to closely examine and be injured by existing power arrangements.

A few historical details concerning the case under examination are in order. For over thirteen years,

Reprinted from Harvey Molotch, "Oil in Santa Barbara and Power in America," SOCIOLOGICAL INQUIRY 40 (Winter 1969) by permission of the author and publisher.

* This paper was written as Working Paper No. 8, Community and Organization Research Institute, University of California, Santa Barbara. It was delivered at the 1969 Annual Meeting of the American Sociological Association, San Francisco. A shorter version has been published in *Ramparts,* November 1969. The author wishes to thank his wife, Linda Molotch, for her active collaboration and **Robert Sollen,** reporter for the *Santa Barbara News-Press,* for his cooperation and critical comments on an early draft.

Santa Barbara's political leaders had attempted to prevent despoilation of their coastline by oil drilling on adjacent federal waters. Although they were unsuccessful in blocking eventual oil leasing (in February, 1968) of *federal* waters beyond the three-mile limit, they were able to establish a sanctuary within *state* waters (thus foregoing the extraordinary revenues which leases in such areas bring to adjacent localities— e.g., the riches of Long Beach). It was therefore a great irony that the one city which voluntarily exchanged revenue for a pure environment should find itself faced, on January 28, 1969, with a massive eruption of crude oil—an eruption which was, in the end, to cover the entire city coastline (as well as much of Ventura and Santa Barbara County coastline as well) with a thick coat of crude oil. The air was soured for many hundreds of feet inland and the traditional economic base of the region (tourism) was under threat. After ten days of unsuccessful attempts, the runaway well was brought under control, only to be followed by a second eruption on February 12. This fissure was closed on March 3, but was followed by a sustained "seepage" of oil—a leakage which continues, at this writing, to pollute the sea, the air, and the famed local beaches. The oil companies had paid $603,000,000 for their lease rights and neither they nor the federal government bear any significant legal responsibility toward the localities which these lease rights might endanger.

If the big spill had occurred almost anywhere else (e.g., Lima, Ohio; Lompoc, California), it is likely that the current research opportunity would not have developed. But Santa Barbara is different. Of its 70,000 residents, a disproportionate number are upper class and upper middle class. They are persons who, having a wide choice of where in the world they might live, have chosen Santa Barbara for its ideal climate, gentle beauty and sophisticated "culture." Thus a large number of worldly, rich, well-educated persons—individuals with resources, spare time, and contacts with national and international elites— found themselves with a commonly shared disagreeable situation: the pollution of their otherwise near-perfect environment. Santa Barbarans thus possessed none of the "problems" which otherwise are said to inhibit effective community response to external threat: they are not urban villagers (cf. Gans, 1962); they are not internally divided and parochial like the Springdalers (cf. Vidich and Bensman, 1960); nor emaciated with self-doubt and organizational naiveté as is supposed of the ghetto dwellers. With moral indignation and high self-confidence, they set out to right the wrong so obviously done to them.

Their response was immediate. The stodgy *Santa Barbara News-Press* inaugurated a series of editorials, unique in uncompromising stridency. Under the leadership of a former State Senator and a local corporate executive, a community organization was established called "GOO" (Get Oil Out!) which took

a militant stand against any and all oil activity in the Channel.

In a petition to President Nixon (eventually to gain 110,000 signatures), GOO's position was clearly stated:

> . . . With the seabed filled with fissures in this area, similar disastrous oil operation accidents may be expected. And with one of the largest faults centered in the channel waters, one sizeable earthquake could mean possible disaster for the entire channel area. . . .
>
> Therefore, we the undersigned do call upon the state of California and the Federal Government to promote conservation by:
>
> 1. Taking immediate action to have present off-shore oil operations cease and desist at once.
> 2. Issuing no further leases in the Santa Barba Channel.
> 3. Having all oil platforms and rigs removed from this area at the earliest possible date.

The same theme emerged in the hundreds of letters published by the *News-Press* in the weeks to follow and in the positions taken by virtually every local civic and government body. Both in terms of its volume (372 letters published in February alone) and the intensity of the revealed opinions, the flow of letters was hailed by the *News-Press* as "unprecedented." Rallies were held at the beach, GOO petitions were circulated at local shopping centers and sent to friends around the country; a fund-raising dramatic spoof of the oil industry was produced at a local high school. Local artists, playwrights, advertising men, retired executives and academic specialists from the local campus of the University of California (UCSB) executed special projects appropriate to their areas of expertise.

A GOO strategy emerged for a two-front attack. Local indignation, producing the petition to the President and thousands of letters to key members of Congress and the executive would lead to appropriate legislation. Legal action in the courts against the oil companies and the federal government would have the double effect of recouping some of the financial losses certain to be endured by the local tourist and fishing industries while at the same time serving notice that drilling would be a much less profitable operation than it was supposed to be. Legislation to ban drilling was introduced by Cranston in the U.S. Senate and Teague in the House of Representatives. Joint suits by the city and County of Santa Barbara (later joined by the State) for $1 billion in damages was filed against the oil companies and the federal government.

All of these activities—petitions, rallies, court action and legislative lobbying—were significant for their similarity in revealing faith in "the system." The tendency was to blame the oil companies. There a muckraking tone to the Santa Barbara response: oil and the profit-crazy executives of Union Oil were ruining Santa Barbara—but once our national and state leaders became aware of what was going on, and were provided with the "facts" of the case, justice would be done.

Indeed, there was good reason for hope. The quick and enthusiastic responses of Teague and Cranston represented a consensus of men otherwise polar opposites in their political behavior: Democrat Cranston was a charter member of the liberal California Democratic Council; Republican Teague was a staunch fiscal and moral conservative (e.g., a strong Vietnam hawk and unrelenting harrasser of the local Center for the Study of Democratic Institutions). Their bills, for which there was great optimism, would have had the consequence of effecting a "permanent" ban on drilling in the Channel.

But from other quarters there was silence. Santa Barbara's representatives in the state legislature either said nothing or (in later stages) offered minimal support. It took several months for Senator Murphy to introduce Congressional legislation (for which he admitted to having little hope) which would have had the consequence of exchanging the oil companies' leases in the Channel for comparable leases in the under-exploited Elk Hills oil reserve in California's Kern County. Most disappointing of all to Santa Barbarans, Governor Reagan withheld support for proposals which would end the drilling.

As subsequent events unfolded, this seemingly inexplicable silence of the democratically elected representatives began to fall into place as part of a more general problem. American democracy came to be seen as a much more complicated affair than a system in which governmental officials actuate the desires of the "people who elected them" once those desires come to be known. Instead, increasing recognition came to be given to the "all-powerful oil lobby"; to legislators "in the pockets of Oil"; to academicians "bought" by Oil and to regulatory agencies which lobby for those they are supposed to regulate. In other words, Santa Barbarans became increasingly *ideological,* increasingly *sociological,* and in the words of some observers, increasingly *"radical."* [1] Writing from his lodgings in the area's most exclusive hotel (the Santa Barbara Biltmore), an irate citizen penned these words in his published letter to the *News-Press:*

> We the people can protest and protest and it means nothing because the industrial and military junta are the country. They tell us, the People, what is good for the oil companies is good for the People. To that I say, Like Hell! . . .
> Profit is their language and the proof of all this is their history (*SBNP* [2], Feb. 26, 1969, p. A-6).

As time wore on, the editorials and letters continued in their bitterness.

THE EXECUTIVE BRANCH AND THE REGULATORY AGENCIES: DISILLUSIONMENT

From the start, Secretary Hickel's actions were regarded with suspicion. His publicized associations with Alaskan Oil interests did his reputation no good in Santa Barbara. When, after a halt to drilling (for "review" of procedures) immediately after the initial eruption, Hickel one day later ordered a resumption of drilling and production (even as the oil continued to gush into the channel), the government's response was seen as unbelievingly consistent with conservationists' worst fears. That he backed down within 48 hours and ordered a halt to drilling and pro-

duction was taken as a response to the massive nationwide media play then being given to the Santa Barbara plight and to the citizens' mass outcry just then beginning to reach Washington.

Disenchantment with Hickel and the executive branch also came through less spectacular, less specific, but nevertheless genuine activity. First of all, Hickel's failure to support any of the legislation introduced to halt drilling was seen as an *action* favoring Oil. His remarks on the subject, while often expressing sympathy with Santa Barbarans [3] (and for a while placating local sentiment) were revealed as hypocritical in light of the action not taken. Of further note was the constant attempt by the Interior Department to minimize the extent of damage in Santa Barbara or to hint at possible "compromises" which were seen locally as near-total capitulation to the oil companies.

Volume of Oil Spillage

Many specific examples might be cited. An early (and continuing) issue in the oil spill was the *volume* of oil spilling into the Channel. The U.S. Geological Survey (administered by Interior), when queried by reporters, broke its silence on the subject with estimates which struck as incredible in Santa Barbara. One of the extraordinary attributes of the Santa Barbara locale is the presence of a technology establishment among the most sophisticated in the country. Several officials of the General

---

[1] See the report of Morton Mintz in the June 29, 1969 *Washington Post*. The conjunction of these three attributes is not, in my opinion, coincidental.

[2] *SBNP* will be used to denote Santa Barbara News Press throughout this paper.

[3] Hickel publicly stated and wrote (personal communication) that the original leasing was a mistake and that he was doing all within discretionary power to solve the problem.

Research Corporation (a local R & D firm with experience in marine technology) initiated studies of the oil outflow and announced findings of pollution volume at a "minimum" of ten fold the Interior estimate. Further, General Research provided (and the *News-Press* published) a detailed account of the methods used in making the estimate (cf. Allan, 1969). Despite repeated challenges from the press, Interior both refused to alter its estimate or to reveal its method for making estimates. Throughout the crisis, the divergence of the estimates remained at about ten fold.

The "seepage" was estimated by the Geological Survey to have been reduced from 1,260 gallons per day to about 630 gallons. General Research, however, estimated the leakage at the rate of 8,400 gallons per day at the same point in time as Interior's 630 gallon estimate. The lowest estimate of all was provided by an official of the Western Oil and Gas Association, in a letter to the *Wall Street Journal*. His estimate: "Probably less than 100 gallons a day" (SBNP, August 5, 1969:A-1).

Damage to Beaches

Still another point of contention was the state of the beaches at varying points in time. The oil companies, through various public relations officials, constantly minimized the actual amount of damage and maximized the effect of Union Oil's cleanup activity. What surprised (and most irritated) the locals was the fact that Interior statements implied the same goal. Thus Hickel referred at a press conference to the "recent" oil spill, providing the impression that the oil spill was over,

at a time when freshly erupting oil was continuing to stain local beaches. President Nixon appeared locally to "inspect" the damage to beaches, and Interior arranged for him to land his helicopter on a city beach which had been cleaned thoroughly in the days just before, but spared him a close-up of much of the rest of the County shoreline which continued to be covered with a thick coat of crude oil. (The beach visited by Nixon has been oil stained on many occasions subsequent to the President's departure.) Secret servicemen kept the placards and shouts of several hundred demonstrators safely out of Presidential viewing or hearing distance.

Continuously, the Oil and Interior combine implied the beaches to be restored when Santa Barbarans knew that even a beach which looked clean was by no means restored. The *News-Press* through a comprehensive series of interviews with local and national experts on wildlife and geology made the following points clear:

(1) As long as oil remained on the water and oil continued to leak from beneath the sands, all Santa Barbara beaches were subject to continuous doses of oil—subject only to the vagaries of wind change. Indeed, all through the spill and up to the present point in time, a beach walk is likely to result in tar on the feet. On "bad days" the beaches are unapproachable.

(2) The damage to the "ecological chain" (a concept which has become a household phrase in Santa Barbara) is of unknown proportions. Much study will be necessary to learn the extent of damage.

(3) The continuous alternating natural erosion and building up of

beach sands means that "clean" beaches contain layers of oil at various sublevels under the mounting sands; layers which will once again be exposed when the cycle reverses itself and erosion begins anew. Thus, it will take many years for the beaches of Santa Barbara to be completely restored, even if the present seepage is halted and no additional pollution occurs.

Damage to Wildlife

Oil on feathers is ingested by birds, continuous preening thus leads to death. In what local and national authorities called a hopeless task, two bird-cleaning centers were established to cleanse feathers and otherwise administer to damaged wild-fowl. (Oil money helped to establish and supply these centers.) Both spokesmen from Oil and the federal government then adopted these centers as sources of "data" on the extent of damage to wild-fowl. Thus, the number of dead birds due to pollution was computed on the basis of number of fatalities at the wild-fowl centers.[4] This of course is preposterous given the fact that dying birds are provided with very inefficient means of propelling themselves to such designated places. The obviousness of this dramatic understatement of fatalities was never acknowledged by either Oil or Interior

[4] In a February 7 letter to Union Oil shareholders, Fred Hartley informed them that the bird refuge centers had been "very successful in their efforts." In fact, by April 30, 1969, only 150 birds (of thousands treated) had been returned to the natural habitat as "fully recovered" and the survival rate of birds treated was estimated as a miraculously high (in light of previous experience) 20 per cent (cf. *SBNP*, April 30, 1969, F-3).

—although noted in Santa Barbara.

At least those birds in the hands of local ornithologists could be confirmed as dead—and this fact could not be disputed by either Oil or Interior. Not so, however, with species whose corpses are more difficult to produce on command. Several observers at the Channel Islands (a national wildlife preserve containing one of the country's largest colonies of sea animals) reported sighting unusually large numbers of dead sea-lion pups—on the oil stained shores of one of the islands. Statement and counter-statement followed with Oil's defenders arguing that the animals were not dead at all—but only appeared inert because they were sleeping. Despite the testimony of staff experts of the local Museum of Natural History and the Museum Scientist of UCSB's Biological Sciences Department that the number of "inert" sea-lion pups was far larger than normal and that field trips had confirmed the deaths, the position of Oil, as also expressed by the Department of the Navy (which administers the stricken island) remained adamant that the sea animals were only sleeping (cf. *Life*, June 13, 1969; July 4, 1969). The dramatic beaching of an unusually large number of dead whales on the beaches of Northern California—whales which had just completed their migration through the Santa Barbara Channel—was acknowledged, but held not to be caused by oil pollution. No direct linkage (or non-linkage) with oil could be demonstrated by investigating scientists (cf. *San Francisco Chronicle*, March 12, 1969:1-3).

In the end, it was not simply Interior, its U.S. Geological Survey and the President which either supported or tacitly accepted Oil's public relations tactics. The regulatory agencies at both national and state level, by action, inaction and implication had the consequence of defending Oil at virtually every turn. Thus at the outset of the first big blow, as the ocean churned with bubbling oil and gas, the U.S. Coast Guard (which patrols Channel waters regularly) failed to notify local officials of the pollution threat because, in the words of the local commander, "the seriousness of the situation was not apparent until late in the day Tuesday and it was difficult to reach officials after business hours" (*SBNP,* January 30, 1969:A-1, 4). Officials ended up hearing of the spill from the *News-Press.*

The Army Corps of Engineers must approve all structures placed on the ocean floor and thus had the discretion to hold public hearings on each application for a permit to build a drilling platform. With the exception of a single *pro forma* ceremony held on a platform erected in 1967, requests for such hearings were never granted. In its most recent handling of these matters (at a point long after the initial eruption and as oil still leaks into the ocean) the Corps changed its criteria for public hearings by restricting written objections to new drilling to "the effects of the proposed exploratory drilling on *navigation or national defense"* (*SBNP,* August 17, 1969:A-1, 4). Prior to the spill, effects on *fish and wildlife* were specified by the Army as possible grounds for objection, but at that time such objections, when raised, were more easily dismissed as unfounded.

The Federal Water Pollution Control Administration consistently attempted to understate the amount of damage done to waterfowl by quoting the "hospital dead" as though a reasonable assessment of the net damage. State agencies followed the same pattern. The charge of "Industry domination" of state conservation boards was levelled by the State Deputy Attorney General, Charles O'Brien (*SBNP,* February 9, 1969:A-6). Thomas Gaines, a Union Oil executive, actually sits as a member on the State Agency Board most directly connected with the control of pollution in Channel waters. In correspondence with complaining citizens, N. B. Livermore, Jr., of the Resources Agency of California refers to the continuing oil spill as "minor seepage" with "no major long-term effect on the marine ecology." The letter adopts the perspective of Interior and Oil, even though the state was in no way being held culpable for the spill (letter, undated to Joseph Keefe, citizen, University of California, Santa Barbara Library, on file).

With these details under their belts, Santa Barbarans were in a position to understand the sweeping condemnation of the regulatory system as contained in a *News-Press* front page, banner-headlined interview with Rep. Richard D. Ottenger (D-NY), quoted as follows: "And so on down the line. Each agency has a tendency to become the captive of the industry that it is to regulate" (*SBNP,* March 1, 1969:A-1).

THE CONGRESS: DISILLUSIONMENT

Irritations with Interior were paralleled by frustrations encountered in dealing with the Congressional establishment which had the responsibility of holding hearings on ameliorative legislation. A delegation of Santa Barbarans was scheduled to testify in Washington on the Cranston bill. From the questions which Congressmen asked of them, and the manner in which they were "handled," the delegation could only conclude that the Committee was "in the pockets of Oil." As one of the returning delegates put it, the presentation bespoke of "total futility."

At this writing, six months after their introduction, both the Cranston and Teague bills lie buried in committee with little prospect of surfacing. Cranston has softened his bill significantly—requiring only that new drilling be suspended until Congress is convinced that sufficient technological safeguards exist. But to no avail.

SCIENCE AND TECHNOLOGY: DISILLUSIONMENT

From the start, part of the shock of the oil spill was that such a thing could happen in a country with such sophisticated technology. The much overworked phrase, "If we can send a man to the moon . . ." was even more overworked in Santa Barbara. When, in years previous, Santa Barbara's elected officials had attempted to halt the original sale of leases, "assurances" were given from Interior that such an "accident" could not occur, given the highly developed state of the art. Not only did it occur, but the original gusher of oil spewed forth completely out of control for ten days and the continuing "seepage" which followed it remains uncontrolled to the present moment, seven months later. That the government would embark upon so massive a drilling program with such

unsophisticated technologies, was striking indeed.

Further, not only were the technologies inadequate and the plans for stopping a leak, should it occur, nonexistent, but the area in which the drilling took place was known to be ulta-hazardous from the outset. That is, drilling was occurring on an ocean bottom known for its extraordinary geological circumstances —porous sands lacking a bedrock "ceiling" capable of containing runaway oil and gas. Thus the continuing leakage through the sands at various points above the oil reservoir is unstoppable, and could have been anticipated with the data *known to all parties involved.*

Another peculiarity of the Channel is the fact that it is located in the heart of earthquake activity in that region of the country which, among all regions, is among the very most earthquake prone.[5] Santa Barbarans are now asking what might occur in an earthquake: if pipes on the ocean floor and casings through the ocean bottom should be sheared, the damage done by the Channel's *thousands* of potential producing wells would be devastating to the entire coast of Southern California.[6]

Recurrent attempts have been made to ameliorate the continuing seep by placing floating booms

[5] Cf. "Damaging Earthquakes of the United States through 1966," Fig. 2, National Earthquake Information Center, Environmental Science Services Administration, Coast and Geodetic Survey.

[6] See Interview with Donald Weaver, Professor of Geology, UCSB, *SBNP*, Feb. 21, 1969, p. A-1, 6. (Also, remarks by Professor Donald Runnells, UCSB geologist, *SBNP*, Feb. 23, 1969, p. B-2.) Both stress the dangers of faults in the Channel, and potential earthquakes.

around an area of leakage and then having workboats skim off the leakage from within the demarcated area.[7] Chemical dispersants, of various varieties, have also been tried. But the oil bounces over the sea booms in the choppy waters; the work boats suck up only a drop in the bucket and the dispersants are effective only when used in quantities which constitute a graver pollution threat than the oil they are designed to eliminate. Cement is poured into suspected fissures in an attempt to seal them up. Oil on beaches is periodically cleaned by dumping straw over the sands and then raking up the straw along with the oil it absorbs.

This striking contrast between the sophistication of the means used to locate and extract oil compared to the primitiveness of the means to control and clean it up was widely noted in Santa Barbara. It is the result of a system which promotes research and development which leads to strategic profitability rather than to social utility. The common sight of men throwing straw on miles of beaches within sight of complex drilling rigs capable of exploiting resources thousands of feet below the ocean's surface, made the point clear.

The futility of the clean-up and control efforts was widely noted in Santa Barbara. Secretary Hickel's announcement that the Interior Department was generating new "tough" regulations to control offshore drilling was thus met with great skepticism. The Santa Barbara

[7] More recently, plastic tents have been placed on the ocean floor to trap seeping oil; it is being claimed that half the runaway oil is now being trapped in these tents.

County Board of Supervisors was invited to "review" these new regulations—and refused to do so in the belief that such participation would be used to provide the fraudulent impression of democratic responsiveness—when, in fact, the relevant decisions had been already made. In previous years when they were fighting against the leasing of the Channel, the Supervisors had been assured of technological safeguards; now, as the emergency continued, they could witness for themselves the dearth of any means for ending the leakage in the Channel. They had also heard the testimony of a high-ranking Interior engineer who, when asked if such safeguards could positively prevent future spills, explained that "no prudent engineer would ever make such a claim" (*SBNP*, February 19, 1969: A-1). They also had the testimony of Donald Solanas, a regional supervisor of Interior's U.S. Geological Survey, who had said about the Union Platform eruption:

> I could have had an engineer on that platform 24 hours a day, 7 days a week and he couldn't have prevented the accident.

His "explanation" of the cause of the "accident": "Mother earth broke down on us" (*SBNP*, February 28, 1969: C-12).

Given these facts, as contained in the remarks of Interior's own spokesmen, combined with testimony and information received from non-Interior personnel, Interior's new regulations and the invitation to the County to participate in making them, could only be a ruse to preface a resumption of drilling. In initiating the County's policy of not responding to Interior's "invitation," a County Supervisor explained: "I think we may be falling into a trap" (*SBNP*, April 1, 1969).

The very next day, the Supervisors' suspicions were confirmed. Interior announced a selective resumption of drilling "to relieve pressures." (*News-Press* letter writers asked if the "pressure" was geological or political.) The new tough regulations were themselves seriously flawed by the fact that most of their provisions specified those measures, such as buoyant booms around platforms, availability of chemical dispersants, etc., which had proven almost totally useless in the current emergency. They fell far short of minimum safety requirements as enumerated by UC Santa Barbara geologist Robert Curry who criticized a previous version of the same regulations as "relatively trivial" and "toothless" [8] (*SBNP*, March 5, 1969: C-9).

On the other hand, the new regulations did specify that oil companies would henceforth be financially responsible for damages resulting from pollution mishaps. (This had been the *de facto* reality in the Union case; the company had assumed responsibility for the clean-up, and advised stockholders that such costs were covered by "more than adequate" insurance.[9]) The liability requirement has been vociferously condemned by the oil companies—particularly by those firms which have failed to make significant strikes on their Channel leases (*SBNP*, March 14, 1969). Several of these companies have now entered suit (supported by the ACLU) against the federal government charging that the arbitrary changing of lease conditions renders Channel exploitation "economically and practically impossible," thus depriving them of rights of due process (*SBNP*, April 10, 1969:A-1).

The weaknesses of the new regulations came not as a surprise to people who had already adapted to thinking of Oil and the Interior De-

---

[8] Curry's criticism is as follows:

"These new regulations make no mention at all about in-pipe safety valves to prevent blowouts, or to shut off the flow of oil deep in the well should the oil and gas escape from the drill hole region into a natural fissure at some depth below the wellhead blowout preventers. There is also no requirement for a backup valve in case the required preventer fails to work. Remember, the runaway well on Union Platform A was equipped with a wellhead blowout preventer. The blowout occurred some 200 below that device.

Only one of the new guidelines seems to recognize the possible calamitous results of earthquakes which are inevitable on the western offshore leases. None of the regulations require the minimization of pollution hazards during drilling that may result from a moderate-magnitude, nearby shallow-focus earthquake, seismic sea wave (tsunami) or submarine landslide which could shear off wells below the surface.

None of the regulations state anything at all about onshore oil and gas storage facilities liable to release their contents into the oceans upon rupture due to an earthquake or seismic sea wave.

None of the new regulations stipulate that wells must be cased to below a level of geologic hazard, or below a depth of possible open fissures or porous sands, and, as such, none of these changes would have helped the present situation in the Santa Barbara Channel or the almost continuous blowout that has been going on since last year in the Bass Straits off Tasmania, where one also finds porous sands extending all the way up to the sea floor in a tectonically active region—exactly the situation we have here."

[9] Letter from Fred Hartley, President of Union Oil, to "all shareholders," dated February 7, 1969.

partment as the same source. There was much less preparation for the results of the Presidential Committee of "distinguished" scientists and engineers (the DuBridge Panel) which was to recommend means of eliminating the seepage under Platform A. Given the half-hearted, inexpensive and primitive attempts by Union Oil to deal with the seepage, feeling ran high that at last the technological sophistication of the nation would be harnessed to solve this particular vexing problem. Instead, the panel—after a two-day session and after hearing testimony from no one not connected with either Oil or Interior—recommended the "solution" of drilling an additional 50 wells under Platform A in order to pump the area dry as quickly as possible. The process would require ten to twenty years, one member of the panel estimated.[10]

The recommendation was severely terse, requiring no more than one and a half pages of type. Despite an immediate local clamor, Interior refused to make public the data or the reasoning behind the recommendations. The information on Channel geological conditions was provided by the oil companies; the Geological Survey routinely depends upon the oil industry for the data upon which it makes its "regulatory"

decisions. The data, being proprietary, could thus not be released. Totally inexplicable, in light of this "explanation," is Interior's continuing refusal to immediately provide the information given a recent clearance by Union Oil for public release of all the data. Santa Barbara's local experts have thus been thwarted by the counter-arguments of Oil-Interior that "if you had the information we have, you would agree with us."

Science was also having its non-neutral consequences on the other battlefront being waged by Santa Barbarans. The chief Deputy Attorney General of California, in his April 7 speech to the blue-ribbon Channel City Club of Santa Barbara, complained that the oil industry

> is preventing oil drilling experts from aiding the Attorney General's office in its lawsuits over the Santa Barbara oil spill (*SBNP*, Aug. 8, 1969).

Complaining that his office has been unable to get assistance from petroleum experts at California universities, the Deputy Attorney General further stated:

> The university experts all seem to be working on grants from the oil industry. There is an atmosphere of fear. The experts are afraid that if they assist us in our case on behalf of the people of California, they will lose their oil industry grants.

At the Santa Barbara Campus of the University, there is little Oil money in evidence and few, if any, faculty members have entered into proprietary research arrangements with Oil. Petroleum geology and engineering is simply not a local specialty. Yet it is a fact that Oil

---

[10] Robert Curry of the geography department of the University of California, Santa Barbara, warned that such a tactic might in fact accelerate leakage. If, as he thought, the oil reservoirs under the Channel are linked, accelerated development of one such reservoir would, through erosion of subterranean linkage channels, accelerate the flow of oil into the reservoir under Platform A, thus adding to the uncontrolled flow of oil through the sands and into the ocean. Curry was not asked to testify by the DuBridge Panel.

interests did contact several Santa Barbara faculty members with offers of funds for studies of the ecological effects of the oil spill, with publication rights stipulated by Oil.[11] It is also the case that the Federal Water Pollution Control Administration explicitly requested a UC Santa Barbara botanist to withhold the findings of his study, funded by that Agency, on the ecological consequences of the spill (*SBNP,* July 29, 1969:A-3).

Except for the Deputy Attorney General's complaint, none of these revelations received any publicity outside of Santa Barbara. But the Attorney's allegation became something of a statewide issue. A professor at the Berkeley campus, in his attempt to refute the allegation, actually confirmed it. Wilbur H. Somerton, Professor of petroleum engineering, indicated he could not testify against Oil

> because my work depends on good relations with the petroleum industry. My interest is serving the petroleum industry. I view my obligation to the community as supplying it with well-trained petroleum engineers. We train the industry's engineers and they help us. (*SBNP,* April 12, 1969, as quoted from a *San Francisco Chronicle* interview.)

[11] Verbal communication from one of the faculty members involved. The kind of "studies" which oil enjoys is typified by a research conclusion by Professor Wheeler J. North of Cal Tech, who after performing a one week study of the Channel ecology under Western Oil and Gas Association sponsorship, determined that it was the California winter floods which caused most of the evident disturbance and that (as quoted from the Association Journal) "Santa Barbara beaches and marine life should be back to normal by summer with no adverse impact on tourism." Summer came with oil on the beaches, birds unreturned, and beach motels with unprecedented vacancies.

Santa Barbara's leaders were incredulous about the whole affair. The question—one which is more often asked by the downtrodden sectors of the society—was asked: "Whose University is this, anyway?" A local executive and GOO leader asked, "If the truth isn't in the universities, where is it?" A conservative member of the State Legislature, in a move reminiscent of SDS demands, went so far as to ask an end to all faculty "moonlighting" for industry. In Santa Barbara, the only place where all of this publicity was occurring, there was thus an opportunity for insight into the linkages between knowledge, the University, government and Oil and the resultant non-neutrality of science. The backgrounds of many members of the DuBridge Panel were linked publicly to the oil industry. In a line of reasoning usually the handiwork of groups like SDS, a *News-Press* letter writer labeled Dr. Du-Bridge as a servant of Oil interests because, as a past President of Cal Tech, he would have had to defer to Oil in generating the massive funding which that institution requires. In fact, the relationship was quite direct. Not only has Union Oil been a contributor to Cal Tech, but Fred Hartley (Union's President) is a Cal Tech trustee. The impropriety of such a man as DuBridge serving as the key "scientist" in determining the Santa Barbara outcome seemed more and more obvious.

TAXATION AND PATRIOTISM: DISILLUSIONMENT

From Engler's detailed study of the politics of Oil, we learn that the oil companies combat local resistance with arguments that hurt: taxation and patriotism (cf. Engler, 1961). They threaten to take their operations elsewhere, thus depriving the locality of taxes and jobs. The more grandiose argument is made that oil is necessary for the national defense; hence, any weakening of "incentives" to discover and produce oil plays into the hands of the enemy.

Santa Barbara, needing money less than most locales and valuing environment more, learned enough to know better. Santa Barbara wanted oil to leave, but oil would not. Because the oil is produced in federal waters, only a tiny proportion of Santa Barbara County's budget indirectly comes from oil, and virtually none of the city of Santa Barbara's budget comes from oil. News-Press letters and articles disposed of the defense argument with these points: (1) oil companies deliberately limit oil production under geographical quota restrictions designed to maintain the high price of oil by regulating supply (2) the federal oil import quota (also sponsored by the oil industry) which restricts imports from abroad, weakens the country's defense posture by forcing the nation to exhaust its own finite supply while the Soviets rely on the Middle East; (3) most oil imported into the U.S. comes from relatively dependable sources of South America which foreign wars would not endanger; (4) the next major war will be a nuclear holocaust with possible oil shortages a very low level problem.

Just as an attempt to answer the national defense argument led to conclusions the very opposite of Oil's position, so did a closer examination of the tax argument. For not only did Oil not pay very much in local taxes, Oil also paid very little in *federal* taxes. In another of its front-page editorials the *News-Press* made the facts clear. The combination of the output restrictions, extraordinary tax write-off privileges for drilling expenses, the import quota, and the 27.5 per cent depletion allowance, all created an artificially high price of U.S. oil—a price almost double the world market price for the comparable product delivered to comparable U.S. destinations.[12] The combination of incentives available creates a situation where some oil companies pay no taxes whatever during extraordinarily profitable years. In the years 1962–1966, Standard of New Jersey paid less than 4 per cent of profits in taxes, Standard of California, less than 3 per cent, and 22 of the largest oil companies paid slightly more than 6 per cent (*SBNP,* February 16, 1969:A-1). It was pointed out, again and again to Santa Barbarans, that it was this system of subsidy which made the relatively high cost deepsea exploration and drilling in the

[12] Cf. Walter J. Mead, "The Economics of Depletion Allowance," testimony presented to Assembly Revenue and Taxation Committee, California Legislature, June 10, 1969, mimeo; "The System of Government Subsidiaries to the Oil Industry," testimony presented to the U.S. Senate Subcommittee on Antitrust and Monopoly, March 11, 1969. The ostensible purpose of the depletion allowance is to encourage oil companies to explore for new oil reserves. A report to the Treasury Department by Consad Research Corp. concluded that *elimination* of the depletion allowance would decrease oil reserves by only 3 per cent. The report advised that more efficient means could be found than a system which causes the government to pay $10 for every $1 in oil added to reserves. (Cf. Leo Rennert, "Oil Industry's Favors," *SBNP,* April 27, 1969, pp. A-14, 15 as reprinted from the *Sacramento Bee.*)

Channel profitable in the first place. Thus, the citizens of Santa Barbara, as federal taxpayers and fleeced consumers were subsidizing their own demise. The consequence of such a revelation can only be *infuriating*.

THE MOBILIZATION OF BIAS

The actions of Oil and Interior and the contexts in which such actions took place can be reexamined in terms of their function in diffusing local opposition, disorienting dissenters, and otherwise limiting the scope of issues which are potentially part of public controversies. E. E. Schattschneider (1960:71) has noted:

> All forms of political organization have a bias in favor of the exploitation of some kinds of conflict and the suppression of others because *organization is the mobilization of bias*. Some issues are organized into policies while others are organized out.

Expanding the notion slightly, certain techniques shaping the "mobilization of bias" can be said to have been revealed by the present case study.

1. *The pseudo-event.* Boorstin (1962) has described the use of the pseudo-event in a large variety of task accomplishment situations. A pseudo-event occurs when men arrange conditions to simulate a certain kind of event, such that certain prearranged consequences follow as though the actual event had taken place. Several pseudo-events may be cited. *Local participation in decision making.* From the outset, it was obvious that national actions vis-à-vis Oil in Santa Barbara had as their strategy the freezing out of any local participation in decisions af-

fecting the Channel. Thus, when in 1968 the federal government first called for bids on a Channel lease, local officials were not even informed. When subsequently queried about the matter, federal officials indicated that the lease which was advertised for bid was just a corrective measure to prevent drainage of a "little old oil pool" on federal property adjacent to a state lease producing for Standard and Humble. This "little old pool" was to draw a high bonus bid of $21,189,000 from a syndicate headed by Phillips (*SBNP,* February 9, 1969:A-17). Further, local officials were not notified by any government agency in the case of the original oil spill, nor (except after the spill was already widely known) in the case of any of the previous or subsequent more "minor" spills. Perhaps the thrust of the federal government's colonialist attitude toward the local community was contained in an Interior Department engineer's memo written to J. Cordell Moore, Assistant Secretary of Interior, explaining the policy of refusing public hearings prefatory to drilling: "We preferred not to stir up the natives any more than possible." [13] (The memo was released by Senator Cranston and excerpted on page 1 of the *News-Press.*)

Given this known history, the Santa Barbara County Board of Supervisors refused the call for "participation" in drawing up new "tougher" drilling regulations, precisely because they knew the government had no intention of creating "safe" drilling regulations. They

[13] Cranston publicly confronted the staff engineer, Eugene Standley, who stated that he could neither confirm or deny writing the memo. (Cf. *SBNP,* March 11, 1969, p. A-1.)

refused to take part in the pseudo-event and thus refused to let the consequences (in this case the appearance of democratic decision-making and local assent) of a pseudo-event occur.

Other attempts at the staging of pseudo-events may be cited. Nixon's "inspection" of the Santa Barbara beachfront was an obvious one. Another series of pseudo-events were the Congressional hearings staged by legislators who were, in the words of a local well-to-do lady leader of GOO, "kept men." The locals blew off steam—but the hearing of arguments and the proposing of appropriate legislation based on those arguments (the presumed essence of the Congressional hearing as a formal event) certainly did not come off. Many Santa Barbarans had a similar impression of the court hearings regarding the various legal maneuvers against oil drilling; legal proceedings came to be similarly seen as ceremonious arrangements for the accomplishing of tasks not revealed by their formally-stated properties.

2. *The creeping event.* A creeping event is, in a sense, the opposite of a pseudo-event. It occurs when something *is* actually taking place, but when the manifest signs of the event are arranged to occur at an inconspicuously gradual and piecemeal pace, thus eliminating some of the consequences which would otherwise follow from the event if it were to be perceived all-at-once to be occurring. Two major creeping events were arranged for the Santa Barbara Channel. Although the great bulk of the bidding for leases in the Channel occurred simultaneously, the first lease was, as was made clear earlier, advertised for bid prior to the others

and prior to any public announcement of the leasing of the Channel. The federal waters' virginity was thus ended with only a whimper. A more salient example of the creeping event is the resumption of production and drilling after Hickel's second moratorium. Authorization to resume *production* on different specific groups of wells occurred on these dates in 1969: February 17; February 21; February 22; and March 3. Authorization to resume *drilling* of various groups of new wells was announced by Interior on these dates in 1969: April 1, June 12, July 2, August 2, and August 16. (This is being written on August 20.) Each time, the resumption was announced as a safety precaution to relieve pressures, until finally on the most recent resumption date, the word "deplete" was used for the first time as the reason for granting permission to drill. There is thus no *particular* point in time in which production and drilling was re-authorized for the Channel—and full resumption has still not been officially authorized.

A creeping event has the consequences of diffusing resistance to the event by holding back what journalists call a "time peg" on which to hang "the story." Even if the aggrieved party should get wind that "something is going on," strenuous reaction is inhibited. Non-routine activity has as its prerequisite the crossing of a certain threshold point of input; the dribbling out of an event has the consequence of making each of the revealed inputs fall below the threshold level necessary for non-routine activity. By the time it becomes quite clear that "something *is* going on" both the aggrieved and the sponsors of the creeping event can ask why there should be a response *"now"* when there was none previously to the very same kind of stimulus. In such manner, the aggrieved has resort only to frustration and a gnawing feeling that "events" are sweeping him by.

3. *The "neutrality" of science and the "knowledge" producers.* I have already dealt at some length with the disillusionment of Santa Barbarans with the "experts" and the University. After learning for themselves of the collusion between government and Oil and the use of secret science as a prop to that collusion, Santa Barbarans found themselves in the unenviable position of having to demonstrate that science and knowledge were, in fact, not neutral arbiters. They had to demonstrate, by themselves, that continued drilling was not safe, that the "experts" who said it was safe were the hirelings directly or indirectly of Oil interests and that the report of the DuBridge Panel recommending massive drilling was a fraudulent document. They had to document that the University *petroleum* geologists were themselves in league with their adversaries and that knowledge unfavorable to the Oil interests was systematically withheld by virtue of the very structure of the knowledge industry. As the SDS has learned in other contexts, this is no small task. It is a long story to tell, a complicated story to tell, and one which pits lay persons (and a few academic renegades) against a profession and patrons of a profession. An illustration of the difficulties involved may be drawn from very recent history. Seventeen Santa Barbara plaintiffs, represented by the ACLU, sought a temporary injunction

against additional Channel drilling at least until the information utilized by the DuBridge Panel was made public and a hearing could be held. The injunction was not granted and, in the end, the presiding federal judge ruled in favor of what he termed the "expert" opinions available to the Secretary of the Interior. It was a function of limited time for rebuttal, the disorienting confusions of courtroom procedures, and also perhaps the desire to not offend the Court, that the ACLU lawyer could not make his subtle, complex and highly controversial case that the "experts" were partisans and that their scientific "findings" follow from that partisanship.

4. *Constraints of communication media.* Just as the courtroom setting was not amenable to a full reproduction of the details surrounding the basis for the ACLU case, so the media in general—through restrictions of time and style—prevent a full airing of the details of the case. A more cynical analysis of the media's inability to make known the Santa Barbara "problem" in its full fidelity might hinge on an allegation that the media are constrained by fear of "pressures" from Oil and its allies; Metromedia, for example, sent a team to Santa Barbara which spent several days documenting, interviewing and filming for an hour-long program—only to suddenly drop the whole matter due to what is reported by locals in touch with the network to have been "pressures" from Oil. Such blatant interventions aside, however, the problem of full reproduction of the Santa Barbara "news" would remain problematic nonetheless.

News media are notorious for the

anecdotal nature of their reporting; even so-called "think pieces" rarely go beyond a stringing together of proximate "events." There are no analyses of the "mobilization of bias" or linkages of men's actions and their pecuniary interests. Science and learning are assumed to be neutral; regulatory agencies are assumed to function as "watchdogs" for the public. Information to the contrary of these assumptions is treated as exotic exception; in the manner of Drew Pearson columns, exception piles upon exception without intellectual combination, analysis or ideological synthesis. The complexity of the situation to be reported, the wealth of details needed to support such analyses require more time and effort than journalists have at their command. Their recitation would produce long stories not consistent with space requirements and make-up preferences of newspapers and analogous constraints of the other media. A full telling of the whole story would tax the reader/viewer and would risk boring him.

For these reasons, the rather extensive media coverage of the oil spill centered on a few dramatic moments in its history (e.g., the initial gusher of oil) and a few simple-to-tell "human interest" aspects such as the pathetic deaths of the sea birds struggling along the oil-covered sands. With increasing temporal and geographical distance from the initial spill, national coverage became increasingly rare and increasingly sloppy. Interior statements on the state of the "crisis" were reported without local rejoinders as the newsmen who would have gathered them began leaving the scene. It is to be kept in mind that, relative to other local events, the Santa Barbara spill received extraordinarily extensive national coverage.[14] The point is that this coverage is nevertheless inadequate in both its quality and quantity to adequately inform the American public.

5. *The routinization of evil.* An oft quoted American cliché is that the news media cover only the "bad" things; the everyday world of people going about their business in conformity with American ideas loses out to the coverage of student and ghetto "riots," wars and crime, corruption and sin. The grain of truth in this cliché should not obfuscate the fact that there are *certain kinds of evil* which, partially for reasons cited in the preceding paragraphs, also lose their place in the public media and the public mind. Pollution of the Santa Barbara Channel is now routine; the issue is not whether or not the Channel is polluted, but *how much* it is polluted. A recent oil slick discovered off a Phillips Platform in the Channel was dismissed by an oil company official as a "routine" drilling by-product which was not viewed as "obnoxious." That "about half" of the current oil seeping into the Channel is allegedly being recovered is taken as an improvement sufficient to preclude the "outrage" that a big national story would require.

Similarly, the pollution of the "moral environment" becomes routine; politicians are, of course, on

[14] Major magazine coverage occurred in these (and other) national publications: *Time* (Feb. 14, 1969); *Newsweek* (March 3, 1969); *Life* (June 13, 1969); *Saturday Review* (May 10, 1969); *Sierra Club Bulletin*; *Sports Illustrated* (April 10, 1969). The last three articles cited were written by Santa Barbarans.

the take, in the pockets of Oil, etc. The depletion allowance issue becomes not whether or not such special benefits should exist at all, but rather whether it should be at the level of 20 or 27.5 per cent. "Compromises" emerge such as the 24 per cent depletion allowance and the new "tough" drilling regulations, which are already being hailed as "victories" for the reformers (cf. *Los Angeles Times,* July 14, 1969:17). Like the oil spill itself, the depletion allowance debate becomes buried in its own disorienting detail, its ceremonious pseudo-events and in the triviality of the "solutions" which ultimately come to be considered as the "real" options. Evil is both banal and complicated; both of these attributes contribute to its durability.[15]

THE STRUGGLE FOR THE MEANS TO POWER

It should (although it does not) go without saying that the parties competing to shape decision-making on oil in Santa Barbara do not have equal access to the means of "mobilizing bias" which this paper has discussed. The same social structural characteristics which Michels has asserted make for an "iron law of oligarchy" make for, in this case, a series of extraordinary advantages for the Oil-government combine. The ability to create pseudo-events such as Nixon's Santa Barbara inspection or controls necessary to bring off well-timed creeping events are not evenly distributed throughout the social structure. Lacking such ready access to media, lacking

the ability to stage events at will, lacking a well-integrated system of arrangements for goal attainment (at least in comparison to their adversaries) Santa Barbara's leaders have met with repeated frustrations.

Their response to their relative powerlessness has been analogous to other groups and individuals who, from a similar vantage point, come to see the system up close. They become willing to expand their repertoire of means of influence as their cynicism and bitterness increase concomitantly. Letter writing gives way to demonstrations, demonstrations to civil disobedience. People refuse to participate in "democratic procedures" which are a part of the opposition's event-management strategy. Confrontation politics arise as a means of countering with "events" of one's own, thus providing the media with "stories" which can be simply and energetically told. The lesson is learned that "the power to make a reportable event is . . . the power to make experience" (Boorstin, 1962:10).

Rallies were held at local beaches; Congressmen and state and national officials were greeted by demonstrations. (Fred Hartley, of Union Oil, inadvertently landed his plane in the midst of one such demonstration, causing a rather ugly name-calling scene to ensue.) A "sail-in" was held one Sunday with a flotilla of local pleasure boats forming a circle around Platform A, each craft bearing large anti-oil banners. (Months earlier boats coming near the platforms were sprayed by oil personnel with fire hoses.) City-hall meetings were packed with citizens reciting "demands" for immediate and forceful local action.

A City Council election in the

---

[15] The notion of the banality of evil is adapted from the usage of Arendt, 1963.

midst of the crisis resulted in the landslide election of the Council's bitterest critic and the defeat of a veteran Councilman suspected of having "oil interests." In a rare action, the *News-Press* condemned the local Chamber of Commerce for accepting oil money for a fraudulent tourist advertising campaign which touted Santa Barbara (including its beaches) as restored to its former beauty. (In the end, references to the beaches were removed from subsequent advertisements, but the oil-financed campaign continued briefly.)

In the meantime, as a *Wall Street Journal* reporter was to observe, "a current of gloom and despair" ran through the ranks of Santa Barbara's militants. The president of Sloan Instruments Corporation, an international R & D firm with headquarters in Santa Barbara, came to comment:

> We are so God-damned frustrated. The whole democratic process seems to be falling apart. Nobody responds to us, and we end up doing things progressively less reasonable. This town is going to blow up if there isn't some reasonable attitude expressed by the Federal Government—nothing seems to happen except that we lose.

Similarly, a well-to-do widow, during a legal proceeding in Federal District Court in which Santa Barbara was once again "losing," whispered in the author's ear:

> Now I understand why those young people at the University go around throwing things. . . . The individual has no rights at all.

One possible grand strategy for Santa Barbara was outlined by a local public relations man and GOO worker:

> We've got to run the oil men out. The city owns the wharf and the harbor that the company has to use. The city has got to deny its facilities to oil traffic, service boats, cranes and the like. If the city contravenes some federal navigation laws (which such actions would unquestionably involve), to hell with it.
>
> The only hope to save Santa Barbara is to awaken the nation to the ravishment. That will take public officials who are willing to block oil traffic with their bodies and with police hoses, if necessary. Then federal marshals or federal troops would have to come in. This would pull in the national news media (*SBNP,* July 6, 1969, p. 7).

This scenario has thus far not occurred in Santa Barbara, although the use of the wharf by the oil industries has led to certain militant actions. A picket was maintained at the wharf for two weeks, protesting the conversion of the pier from a recreation and tourist facility to a heavy industrial plant for the use of the oil companies.[16] A boycott of other wharf businesses (e.g., two restaurants) was urged. The picket line was led by white, middle-class adults—one of whom had almost won the mayorality of Santa Barbara in a previous election. Hardly a "radical" or a "militant," this same man was several months later representing his neighborhood protective association in its opposition to the presence of a "Free School" described by this man (somewhat ambivalently) as a "hippie hotel."

16 As a result of local opposition, Union Oil was to subsequently move its operations from the Santa Barbara wharf to a more distant port in Ventura County.

Prior to the picketing, a dramatic Easter Sunday confrontation (involving approximately 500 persons) took place between demonstrators and city police. Unexpectedly, as a wharf rally was breaking up, an oil service truck began driving up the pier to make delivery of casing supplies for oil drilling. There was a spontaneous sit-down in front of the truck. For the first time since the Ku Klux Klan folded in the 1930's, a group of Santa Barbarans (some young, some "hippie," but many hard-working middle-class adults), was publicly taking the law into its own hands. After much lengthy discussion between police, the truck driver and the demonstrators, the truck was ordered away and the demonstrators remained to rejoice their victory. The following day's *News-Press* editorial, while not supportive of such tactics, found much to excuse—noteworthy given the paper's long standing *bitter* opposition to similar tactics when exercised by dissident Northern blacks or student radicals.

A companion demonstration on the water failed to materialize; a group of Santa Barbarans was to sail to the Union platform and "take it"; choppy seas, however, precluded a landing, causing the would-be conquerors to return to port in failure.

It would be difficult to speculate at this writing what forms Santa Barbara's resistance might take in the future. The veteran *News-Press* reporter who has covered the important oil stories has publicly stated that if the government fails to eliminate both the pollution and its causes "there will, at best be civil disobedience in Santa Barbara and at worst, violence." In fact, talk of "blowing up" the ugly platforms has been recurrent—and is heard in all social circles.

But just as this kind of talk is not completely serious, it is difficult to know the degree to which the other kinds of militant statements are serious. Despite frequent observations of the "radicalization" [17] of Santa Barbara, it is difficult to determine the extent to which the authentic grievances against Oil have generalized to a radical analysis of American society. Certainly an SDS membership campaign among Santa Barbara adults would be a dismal failure. But that is too severe a test. People, especially basically contented people, change their world-view only very slowly, if at all. Most Santa Barbarans go about their comfortable lives in the ways they always did; they may even help Ronald Reagan to another term in the statehouse. But I do conclude that large numbers of persons have been moved, and that they have been moved in the directions of the radical left. They have gained insights into the structure of power in America not possessed by similarly situated persons in other parts of the country. The claim is thus that some Santa Barbarans, especially those with most interest and most information about the oil spill and its surrounding circumstances, have come to view power in America more intellectually, more analytically, more sociologically—more *radically* —than they did before.

I hold this to be a general sociological response to a series of con-

17 Cf. Morton Mintz, "Oil Spill 'Radicalizes' a Conservative West Coast City," *Washington Post*, June 29, 1969, pp. C-1, 5.

comitant circumstances, which can be simply enumerated (*again!*) as follows:

1. *Injustice.* The powerful are operating in a manner inconsistent with the normatively sanctioned expectations of an aggrieved population. The aggrieved population is deprived of certain felt needs as a result.

2. *Information.* Those who are unjustly treated are provided with rather complete information regarding this disparity between expectations and actual performances of the powerful. In the present case, that information has been provided to Santa Barbarans (and only to Santa Barbarans) by virtue of their own observations of local physical conditions and by virtue of the unrelenting coverage of the city's newspaper. Hardly a day has gone by since the initial spill that the front page has not carried an oil story; everything the paper can get its hands on is printed. It carries analyses; it makes the connections. As an appropriate result, Oil officials have condemned the paper as a "lousy" and "distorted" publication of "lies." [18]

3. *Literacy and Leisure.* In order for the information relevant to the injustice to be assimilated in all its infuriating complexity, the aggrieved parties must be, in the larger sense of the terms, literature and leisured. They must have the ability and the time to read, to ponder and to get upset.

My perspective thus differs from

[18] Union Oil's public relations director stated: "In all my long career, I have never seen such distorted coverage of a news event as the *Santa Barbara News-Press* has foisted on its readers. It's a lousy newspaper." (*SBNP,* May 28, 1969, p. A-1.)

those who would regard the radical response as appropriate to some form or another of social or psychological freak. Radicalism is not a subtle form of mental illness (cf. recent statements of such as Bettelheim) caused by "rapid technological change," or increasing "impersonality" in the modern world; radicals are neither "immature," "underdisciplined," nor "anti-intellectual." Quite the reverse. They are persons who must clearly live under the conditions specified above and who make the most rational (and moral) response, given those circumstances. Thus radical movements draw their membership disproportionately from the most leisured, intelligent and informed of the white youth (cf. Flacks, 1967), and from the young blacks whose situations are most analogous to these white counterparts.

THE ACCIDENT AS A RESEARCH METHODOLOGY

If the present research effort has had as its strategy anything pretentious enough to be termed a "methodology," it is the methodology of what could be called "accident research." I define an "accident" as an occasion in which miscalculation leads to the breakdown of customary order. It has as its central characteristic the fact that an event occurs which is, to some large degree, unanticipated by those whose actions caused it to occur. As an event, an accident is thus crucially dissimilar both from the pseudo-event and the creeping event. It differs from the pseudo-event in that it bespeaks of an authentic and an unplanned happening; it differs from the creeping event in its suddenness, its sensation, in the fact that it brings to light a series of preconditions, actions and consequences all at once. It is "news"—often sensational news. Thresholds are reached; attentions are held.

The accident thus tends to have consequences which are the very opposite of events which are pseudo or creeping. Instead of being a deliberately planned contribution to a purposely developed "social structure" (or, in the jargon of the relevant sociological literature, "decisional outcome"), it has as its consequence the revelation of features of a social system, or of individuals' actions and personalities, which are otherwise deliberately obfuscated by those with the resources to create pseudo- and creeping events. A resultant convenience is that the media, at the point of accident, may come to function as able and persistent research assistants.

At the level of everyday individual behavior, the accident is an important lay methodological resource of gossipers—especially for learning about those possessing the personality and physical resources to shield their private lives from public view. It is thus that the recent Ted Kennedy accident functioned so well for the purpose (perhaps useless) of gaining access to that individual's private routines and private dispositions. An accident such as the recent unprovoked police shooting of a deaf mute on the streets of Los Angeles provides analogous insights into routine police behavior which official records could never reveal. The massive and unprecedented Santa Barbara oil spill has similarly led to important revelations about the structure of power. An accident is

thus an important instrument for learning about the lives of the powerful and the features of the social system which they deliberately and quasi-deliberately create. It is available as a research focus for those seeking a comprehensive understanding of the structure of power in America.

FINALE

Bachrach and Baratz (1962) have pointed to the plight of the pluralist students of community power who lack any criteria for the inevitable *selecting* of the "key political decisions" which serve as the basis for their research conclusions. I offer accident as a criterion. An accident is not a decision, but it does provide a basis for insight into whole series of decisions and non-decisions, events and pseudo-events which, taken together, might provide an explanation of the structure of power. Even though the local community is notorious for the increasing triviality of the decisions which occur within it (cf. Schulze, 1961; Vidich and Bensman, 1958; Mills, 1956), accident research at the local level might serve as "micro"-analyses capable of revealing the "second face of power" (Bachrach and Baratz), ordinarily left faceless by traditional community studies which fail to concern themselves with the processes by which bias is mobilized and thus how "issues" rise and fall.

The present effort has been the relatively more difficult one of learning not about community power, but about national power—and the relationship between national and local power. The "findings" highlight the extraordinary intransigence of national institutions in the face of local dissent, but more importantly, point to the processes and tactics which undermine that dissent and frustrate and radicalize the dissenters.

The relationship described between Oil, government, and the knowledge industry does not constitute a unique pattern of power in America. All major sectors of the industrial economy lend themselves to the same kind of analysis as Oil in Santa Barbara. Where such analyses have been carried out, the results are analogous in their content and analogous in the outrage which they cause. The nation's defeat in Vietnam, in a sense an accident, has led to analogous revelations about the arms industry and the manner in which American foreign policy is waged.[19] Comparable scrutinies of the agriculture industry, the banking industry, etc., would, in my opinion, lead to the same infuriating findings as the Vietnam defeat and the oil spill.

The national media dwell upon only a few accidents at a time. But across the country, in various localities, accidents routinely occur—accidents which can tell much not only about local power, but about national power as well. Community power studies typically have resulted in revelations of the "pluralistic" squabbles among local sub-elites which are stimulated by exogenous interventions (cf. Walton, 1968). Accident research at the local level might bring to light the larger so-

cietal arrangements which structure the parameters of such local debate. Research at the local level could thus serve as an avenue to knowledge about *national* power. Sociologists should be ready when an accident hits in their neighborhood, and then go to work.

REFERENCES

ALLEN, ALLAN A.
  1969 "Santa Barbara oil spill." Statement presented to the U.S. Senate Interior Committee, Subcommittee on Minerals, Materials and Fuels, May 20, 1969.

ARENDT, HANNAH
  1963 Eichmann in Jerusalem: A Report on the Banality of Evil. New York: The Viking Press.

BACHRACH, PETER and MORTON BARATZ
  1962 "The two faces of power." American Political Science Review 57 (December): 947–952.

BOORSTIN, DANIEL J.
  1961 The Image. New York: Atheneum Press.

ENGLER, ROBERT
  1961 The Politics of Oil. New York: Macmillan.

FLACKS, RICHARD
  1967 "The liberated generation." Journal of Social Issues 22 (December): 521–543.

GANS, HERBERT
  1962 The Urban Villagers. New York: The Free Press of Glencoe.

MILLS, C. WRIGHT
  1956 The Power Elite. New York: Oxford University Press.

SCHATTSCHNEIDER, E. E.
  1960 The Semisovereign People. New York: Holt, Rinehart & Winston.

SCHULZE, ROBERT O.
  1961 "The bifurcation of power in a satellite city." Pp. 19–81 in

19 I have in mind the exhaustively documented series of articles by I. F. Stone in the *New York Review of Books* over the course of 1968 and 1969, a series made possible, in part, by the outrage of Senator Fulbright and others at the *mistake* of Vietnam.

Morris Janowitz (ed.), Community Political Systems. New York: The Free Press of Glencoe.

VIDICH, ARTHUR and JOSEPH BENSMAN
1958 Small Town in Mass Society. Princeton: Princeton University Press.

WALTON, JOHN
1968 "The vertical axis of community organization and the structure of power." Pp. 353–367 in Willis D. Hawley and Frederick M. Wirt (eds.), The Search for Community Power. Englewood Cliffs, N.J.: Prentice-Hall.

uncle sam's welfare program—for the rich

PHILIP M. STEARN

Most Americans would probably be intensely surprised to find, in their morning newspaper, headlines such as this one:

CONGRESS SETS $16-PER-YEAR WELFARE RATE FOR POOR FAMILIES, $720,000 FOR MULTIMILLIONAIRES

Or this one:

NIXON ASKS $103-BILLION BUDGET DEFICIT, DOUBLING PREVIOUS RED-INK RECORD

The story behind the first of these headlines (the second will be explained later) might read this way:

Reprinted from Philip M. Stearn, "Uncle Sam's Welfare Program—For the Rich," THE NEW YORK TIMES MAGAZINE, April 16, 1972, pp. 27–28, 60ff. Reprinted by permission of The New York Times.

WASHINGTON, April 16—Congress completed action today on a revolutionary welfare program that, reversing traditional payment policies, awards huge welfare payments to the super-rich but grants only pennies per week to the very poor.

Under the program, welfare payments averaging some $720,000 a year will go to the nation's wealthiest families, those with annual incomes of over a million dollars.

For the poorest families, those earning $3,000 a year or less, the welfare allowance will average $16 a year, or roughly 30 cents a week.

The program, enacted by Congress in a series of laws over a period of years, has come to be called the Rich Welfare Program, after its principal sponsor, Senator Homer A. Rich. In a triumphant news conference, Senator Rich told newsmen that the $720,000 annual welfare allowances would give America's most affluent families an added weekly take-home pay of about $14,000. "Or, to put it another way," the Senator said, "it will provide these families with about $2,000 more spending money every day."

The total cost of the welfare program, the most expensive in the nation's history, amounts to $77.3-billion a year.

Political analysts foresee acute discontent not only among the poor, but also among middle-income families making $10,000 to $15,000 a year. For them, welfare payments under the Rich plan will amount to just $12.50 a week, markedly less than the weekly $14,000 paid to the very rich. Reporters asked Senator Rich whether wealthy families would be required to work in order to receive their welfare payments, a common eligibility requirement with many welfare programs. Senator Rich seemed puzzled by the question. "The rich? Work?" he asked. "Why, it hadn't occurred to me." Congressional experts advised newsmen that the program contains no work requirement.

Admittedly, the above "news story" sounds implausible, if not unbelievable. Yet the story is essentially true. The facts and figures in it are real. Such a system is, in fact, part of the law of the land. Only the law isn't called a welfare law. It goes by the name of "The Internal Revenue Code of 1954, as Amended" —the basic income-tax law of the United States.

Who gets how much of the "tax welfare" payments from the major "tax preferences"—the loopholes? Until recently, one could only make, at best, an educated guess. But in January, two tax experts at the Brookings Institution in Washington, D.C., Joseph A. Pechman and Benjamin Okner, made a computer analysis of information from actual tax returns (furnished on computer tape, without taxpayer names, by the

I.R.S.). Using this data, plus other information from economic surveys, they came up with answers that might astound, or even anger, put-upon taxpayers.

On a per-family basis, a breakdown of the average tax savings of Americans—our "tax welfare" program—looks like this:

Yearly Income	Yearly "Tax Welfare"
Over $1,000,000	$720,000
$500–1,000,000	$202,000
$100–500,000	$41,000
$50–100,000	$12,000
$25–50,000	$4,000
$15–20,000	$1,200
$10–15,000	$650
$5–10,000	$340
$3–5,000	$48
Under $3,000	$16

Since a tax law takes money from people, rather than paying money to them, what connection does the tax law have with the topsy-turvy welfare system in the news story? The connection lies in the way Congress has played fast and loose with the 16th Amendment to the Constitution, and with the principle of basing taxes on "ability to pay."

The 16th Amendment, which authorized the first United States income tax, empowered Congress to tax "incomes, *from whatever sources derived.*" (Italics mine.) That expresses the Gertrude Stein-ish notion that a dollar is a dollar is a dollar and that, regardless of its source, the dollar endows its lucky recipient with 100 cents of "ability to pay" for food, shoes for the baby, a fraction of a yacht—or for taxes. Hence, in fairness, all dollars, no matter what their origin, should be taxed uniformly. But Congress has decreed differently. It has decreed that dollars earned in an oil or real-estate venture, in a stock market bonanza, or in interest on a state or local bond, while undeniably effective in buying food, shoes or yachts, are somehow reduced in potency when it comes to paying taxes—for Congress has exempted such dollars, in whole or in part, from taxation.

The American tax system, which stipulates that rates rise as a person's affluence grows, also holds that a billionaire like oilman Jean Paul Getty—with a reported income of $300,000 *a day*—is better "able to pay" taxes than an impoverished Kentucky coal miner. In fact, under the tax rates supposedly applicable to all citizens, Mr. Getty's $100-million annual income endows him with an "ability to pay" about $70-million to the Internal Revenue Service (on the premise that he should be able to make do on the remaining $30-million each year). But since Mr. Getty's dollars come largely from oil ventures, they are not, by Congressional fiat, taxed like other dollars. In consequence, according to what President Kennedy told two United States Senators, Mr. Getty's income tax in the early sixties came nowhere near $70-million. It amounted to no more than a few thousand dollars—just about the amount a middle-income engineer or professor would pay.

Now compare the notion of excusing Jean Paul Getty from paying $70-million in taxes—taxes that an equally wealthy non-oil man would legally have to pay—with the notion that Mr. Getty is receiving a $70-million Federal welfare check. In both cases the consequences are that:

Mr. Getty is $70-million richer.

The United States Treasury is $70-million poorer than if the full tax had been paid.

The rest of the taxpayers are obliged to pay an added $70-million to make up the difference.

Thus the net effect of a "tax forgiveness" is identical to that of a direct Federal handout.

The Brookings study concludes that of the $77.3-billion in tax "handouts," just $92-million goes to the six million poorest families in the nation, while 24 times that amount—$2.2-*billion*—goes to just 3,000 families (those with incomes of more than a million dollars a year). Coincidentally, that $2.2-billion is just the amount Congress voted last year for food stamps for 14.7-million hungry Americans. Moreover, five times that amount in the form of "tax welfare" went to families earning more than $100,000 a year.

The disparity between the "tax welfare" for the wealthy and that granted the poor is even more breathtaking in the case of the "tax preferences" involving so-called "capital gains"—the profits on sales of stocks and bonds, land, buildings and other kinds of property. When a person cashes in such profits during his lifetime, he pays no more than half the usual tax. Even more striking, all the gains in the value of property a person holds until death are not taxed at all. Some $10-billion entirely escapes taxation in that manner every year.

Since to have capital gains you have to own property (i.e., have the surplus cash to buy same), it's not surprising that only one taxpayer in 12 is able to report any gains, and that three-quarters of such gains are enjoyed by the wealthiest 9 per cent of America's taxpayers. Thus, all but the super-rich have a right to be envious, if not startled, by the Brookings figures on the "tax welfare" payments—the average per-family tax savings—granted capital-gains recipients:

Yearly Income	Yearly "Tax Welfare" from Capital Gains
Over $1,000,000	$641,000
$500–1,000,000	165,000
$100–500,000	23,000
$20–25,000	120
$5–10,000	8
$3–5,000	1

These Federal handouts to the wealthy reach the astounding total of nearly $14-billion a year. But even that sum is dwarfed by the tax benefactions that Uncle Sam bestows on all but our poorest citizens the instant they are pronounced man and wife, a happy moment that carries with it the privilege of filing a joint return. The Brookings study reveals, startlingly, that the annual total of this giveaway to married couples comes to $21.5-billion.

Some, noting that the Environmental Protection Agency will only be permitted to spend one-fourteenth that amount next year, have difficulty discerning how this $21.5-billion matrimonial "tax dole" benefits the national welfare. If it is supposed to be an incentive to marriage, it is a strange one indeed, since it shows a total indifference to the marital status of the poor, who derive no financial benefit from this tax giveaway whatever. Instead, it offers increasingly generous benefits the higher a couple's income goes, in brackets where it matters little

whether two can indeed live as cheaply as one. Two-thirds of this marital "tax welfare" goes to taxpayers making more than $20,000 a year, and less than 3 per cent goes to the hardest-pressed married couples—those making less than $10,000 a year. These are the average per-family matrimonial tax savings:

Yearly Income	Yearly "Tax Welfare" to Married Couples
Under $3,000	$0
$3–5,000	72 cents
$5–10,000	$24
$25–50,000	$1,479
$100–500,000	$8,212
Over $1,000,000	$11,062

Dramatically top-heavy tax largess flows to the super-rich via the fiction, in the tax law, that the $5-billion of interest on state and local bonds is totally nonexistent. Not only is such interest income untaxed; it doesn't even have to be reported on tax returns. Ownership of such bonds is, understandably, reserved to financial institutions and wealthy individuals, in part because only they have the spare cash to buy such bonds, and in part because these bonds bear comparatively low interest rates that are attractive only to persons in high tax brackets.

As a result, the per-family tax benefactions from this loophole are almost insultingly low for the unmoneyed: an average of only 80 cents a year for families earning $5,000 to $10,000, and just $24 a year even for those in the $25,000–50,000 bracket. But the financial blessing is handsome indeed for the wealthy—$36,-000 a year for families with incomes of over $1-million—and it is even more spectacular for the big banks. In 1970 this tax feature saved the Bank of America an estimated $58-million.

All these profligate handouts to the unneedy would be far more publicly apparent if the billions lost to the Treasury through the loopholes came to be regarded in the same jealous, penny-pinching way as the direct outlays that the President requests and Congress votes every year. If that had been the case this past January, newspapers might well have carried a news story such as the following:

WASHINGTON, April 16—President Nixon today sent Congress the most startling budget in history, calling for a Federal deficit of no less than $103-billion, more than twice as high as any previous deficit in American history.

This colossal deficit resulted from Mr. Nixon's inclusion in his annual budget, for the first time, of not only direct outlays from the Treasury but also what the President calls "tax expenditures." These are sums the Treasury does not collect because of various exceptions and preferences embedded in the nation's tax laws. For the current year, such sums amounted to more than $77-billion, Mr. Nixon said.

"It is time the American people faced up to the truth," Mr. Nixon said in his budget message. "Every dollar in taxes that some individual or industry is excused from paying is just as much of a drain on the Treasury, and contributes just as much to Federal deficits, as a dollar appropriated by the Congress and spent directly from the Treasury.

"For example," Mr. Nixon said "nearly $10-billion in 'tax expenditures' is granted every year to stimulate home ownership. This sum ought to be part of the budget of the Department of Housing and Urban Development if we are to get an honest picture of how much we, as a nation, are really spending on America's housing problems."

Of course there was no such fiscal candor in Mr. Nixon's January Budget message; nor had there been in those of his predecessors in both parties. But the housing example is a good one, for almost assuredly, few, if any, of the housing specialists in HUD—and few of our elected representatives—are aware that a tax-subsidy program Congress has enacted for homeowners operates in the following manner:

Three families—the Lowlies (who make $7,000 a year), the Comfortables (with a $50,000 income) and the Opulents (they make $400,000 a year)—ask HUD for help in paying the 7 per cent mortgage interest on homes that each family wants to buy. HUD's response is different in each case.

—To the Opulents, HUD replies: "HUD will be delighted to pay 5 per cent mortgage interest for you, so that when you buy your mansion, you only need pay 2 per cent mortgage interest."

—To the Comfortables: "HUD will pay half the interest charges, so you can borrow toward your house at 3.5 per cent."

—To the Lowlies: "We're terribly sorry, but the most we can do is pay 1 per cent interest for you, so if you want to borrow to buy that house, you'll have to pay 6 per cent."

That seemingly inhumane result, which flows from the tax deductibility of mortgage interest payments, is inherent in the nature of any tax deduction in a tax system such as ours where tax rates get higher as income rises. It works this way: say Mr. Opulent has a taxable income of $400,100. This puts him in the top tax bracket of 70 per cent and it means that he has to pay a tax of $70 on the top $100 of his income. Mr. Lowly, on the other hand, has a taxable income of $7,100, placing him in the 19 per cent tax bracket; this imposes a tax of $19 on the top $100 of his more modest income.

Now suppose that each spends $100 on mortgage interest which, being tax-deductible, reduces the taxable income of each by $100. That step lowers Mr. Opulent's tax by $70; that is, $70 that would have gone to Uncle Sam, were it not for the tax deduction, has been diverted to Mr. Opulent's bank account. Uncle Sam has, in effect, footed the bill for $70 of Mr. Opulent's mortgage interest. But in the case of Mr. Lowly, the $100 deduction only lowers his tax by $19. Only $19 is diverted from Uncle Sam to Mr. Lowly's bank account.

Not only does Mr. Opulent get a bigger bang for each tax-deductible buck than Mr. Lowly does, but also Mr. Opulent far outstrips his counterpart in the *number* of bucks he spends yearly for tax-deductible purposes. Mr. Opulent's average annual deductions for mortgage interest, for example, are about 4½ times as large as Mr. Lowly's. According to the Brookings study, the benefits from the various "tax preferences" enjoyed by homeowners (over home renters) come to just 66 cents a year for the least pecunious taxpayers. But the benefits amount to 10,000 times as much—over $6,000 a year—for the nation's wealthiest and best-housed families.

The price tag attached to this in-

verted subsidy program is enormous: $9.6-billion a year. This is more than twice HUD's total budget and more than 50 times HUD's direct outlays for housing assistance. Clearly, if the $9.6-billion were part of HUD's budget, HUD officials would be embarrassed if they tried to justify a program that gave 66 cents of aid to the neediest citizen and $6,000 to the wealthiest. But since the inequity is embedded in the tax laws, involving no visible outlays, HUD, the President and the Congress are all spared the embarrassment of annually accounting for this expensive and irrational subsidy. Instead, the $9.6-billion drain on the Treasury will continue just as long as Congress fails to change the law, and Congressional *inaction* is demonstrably easier to come by than affirmative Congressional action.

The same is true of the tax favors enjoyed by oil companies and investors, which entail an annual "expenditure" of a billion and a half dollars (supposedly to encourage development of our oil resources). But that sum appears nowhere in the Interior Department's natural resources budget. Perhaps if it did, Secretary of the Interior Rogers C. B. Morton would be spurred to cut back or end this huge "outlay," especially since a recent Government-commissioned study showed that the returns on the $1.5-billion were a meager $150-million in additional oil exploration. Any direct subsidy program with a 90 per cent waste factor would hardly warm Congressional hearts when it came up for annual approval; but oil's multibillion-dollar tax subsidy is spared that discomfiture.

Translating tax loopholes into

"tax expenditures" (i.e., treating the revenues that leak out through the loopholes as if they were direct outlays) can make even the most unexceptionable feature of the tax laws seem questionable. Tax expert Stanley Surrey has explained the effect of that most worthy of all tax features, the deduction for contributions to charity:

Suppose that one Horace Pauper writes the Government as follows: "I am too poor to pay an income tax, but the Salvation Army helped me in a time of need and I am contributing $5 to it. Will the Government also make a contribution?" The response: "Dear Mr. Pauper: We appreciate your generosity and sacrifice, but in this situation we cannot make the contribution you request."

Suppose that at the same time, Herman Greenbacks, nouveau millionaire, writes to say that of his $500,000 income, he has decided to send $3,000 to the Society for the Preservation of Hog-Calling in Arkansas. He wants to know if the Government will help. Reply: "We will be delighted to be of assistance and are at once sending a Government check for $7,000 to the Hog-Calling Society."

Here again, this strange situation results from the fact that when a taxpayer in the 70 per cent bracket such as Mr. Greenbacks gives $10,000 to charity, it reduces his tax by $7,000 —i.e., it diverts $7,000 from the United States Treasury to the charity. But for Horace Pauper, who has no taxable income to be affected by his generous deduction, there is no tax saving and the Government's role is zero.

As if the Greenbacks-Pauper contrast weren't irrational enough, the charitable-deduction feature of the tax law could even give rise to a third situation. Let us say that Roger Croesus, heir to the huge Croesus fortune, writes the Government to say that he is selling $2-million in stocks inherited from his grandfather, since he wants to raise cash to pay his taxes and also to buy a yacht. Croesus adds that he feels the Antique Car Society of America is a worthy institution, and that while he has decided not to contribute to the Society himself, he is writing to inquire if the Government has any interest in doing so. In this case, the Government writes as follows:

"Dear Mr. Croesus: We will be delighted to send a $2-million contribution to the Antique Car Society and we will be glad to say that the contribution is in your name. Moreover, in appreciation of your thoughtfulness in suggesting this fine idea to us—and confident that your new yacht will need outfitting—we are sending you a check for $100,000, tax-free, of course."

That unbelievable feat could be accomplished if Mr. Croesus, a taxpayer in the 70 per cent bracket, were to give to the cause of antique cars $2-million of stock that was virtually valueless when he inherited it. His tax saving (i.e., the Treasury's contribution) includes $1,400,000 of income tax from the deduction, plus the avoidance of $700,000 in capital gains tax, for a total of $2,100,000— or, $100,000 more than his $2-million gift. The result: even after the Treasury has, in effect, paid for his entire contribution, he still enjoys a $100,000 cash profit.

But such quirks in the tax law are overshadowed by the even more gaping tax loopholes we've already discussed, as revealed in the Brookings Institution study. During the coming months, the Brookings findings will take on immense importance if, as expected, the Nixon Administration proposes major revenue-raising through a so-called "value-added tax," or VAT. The VAT is a tax on the "value added" to any product, at each stage of its manufacture or distribution, as that product makes its way to the consumer through various middlemen. Since the VAT is, in essence, a hidden national sales tax, it tends to place a relatively heavy share of the burden on lower- and middle-income taxpayers—a far heavier share than would be the case if the same amount of revenue were raised by closing existing loopholes in the tax law. The Brookings study documents that fact in dramatic fashion.

For example, the $13-to-$16-billion in additional revenue the Administration is reportedly considering raising from a VAT coincides almost exactly with the 13.7-billion the Brookings study estimates would be raised by ending the favored taxation on capital gains. Tax reformers can offer a battery of arguments for ending this tax preference, which wholly bypasses 11 out of 12 taxpayers. First, it violates the Basic American Virtues, not to mention elementary standards of fairness, by rewarding the "work" done by *money* vastly more than the work done by men. Why should an already-wealthy multimillionaire pay less tax on, say, a million-dollar stock-market profit—for which he did not an iota of work—than does an industrious professional person who earns a fraction of that amount by personal ingenuity, talent and plain sweat?

Second, capital gains represent by far the most gaping escape hatch for the very rich, allowing them to pay, on the average, only half what the Federal tax rates indicate they should. Third, ending the capital-gains preference would at one stroke narrow, or close, a variety of tax escape-routes available to only a few selected taxpayers guided by ingenious tax lawyers. Examples of such escape routes are corporate executives' stock options, and tax shelters for high-salaried doctors and other professional men who invest in—but usually never see—cattle farms, or kiwi-nut groves, and the like.

Finally, the dire predictions about the drying up of capital that invariably greet any proposal to alter the taxation of capital gains are, at the least, greatly exaggerated. This is evidenced by the economy's apparently tremorless adjustment to a 10 per cent increase in the capital gains tax enacted in 1969, as well as by the fact that 95 per cent of corporations' capital needs are met through plowed-back profits and borrowings, and only 5 per cent from stock issues.

The search for alternatives to the VAT is also likely to increase pressure to end or modify the tax exemption of state and local bonds (it's part of Edmund Muskie's otherwise-moderate tax-reform program, for example). While zealously cherished by hard-pressed governors and mayors as an inexpensive means of public borrowing (the tax-free status allows these bonds to carry below-average interest rates), the tax exemption is a grossly inefficient means of subsidizing state and local borrowing costs. Students of the subject calculate that about half this annual $1.2-billion "tax expenditure" is, in effect, wasted, and that both tax justice and governmental economy would be served by replacing the tax exemption with a direct-subsidy program.

The inefficiency of the bond-interest exemption is typical of such "tax expenditures," which, ironically, are spared the traditional scrutiny for "efficiency" that pinchpenny Congressmen usually require of direct-spending programs. For example, in 1971, in enacting multibillion-dollar tax "incentives" for corporate exports and plant investment, Congress wastefully granted the incentives to exports and to plant outlays that most corporations would have made anyway—rather than confining the benefits to *increases* in those activities. Thus, those tax subventions are windfalls to corporations that merely export or invest as usual. Similarly, the oil-depletion allowance, supposedly designed to reward risk-taking, not only goes to the venturesome oil driller but also is freely dispensed to the fortunate landowner—who permits a successful well to be drilled on his property, but who risks absolutely nothing in doing so.

Tax favors granted to the lowly as well as to the mighty often produce both inequity and inefficiency. Take, for example, the additional $750 personal exemption that Congress has voted the aged and the blind. For nonagenarian Charles Stewart Mott, who is said to be worth more than $300-million, that exemption allows him a saving of $525 a year. But for a retiree in St. Petersburg who qualifies for the lowest tax bracket, it saves only $105. And the exemption gives no relief whatsoever to, say, an ancient and impoverished sharecropper whose meager income would not be taxable anyway.

That same perversity applies to the regular exemption available to each taxpayer and his dependents. While its supposed purpose is to spare poor families from being taxed on what they need to meet "some minimum essential living costs," the exemption nonetheless confers some $4-billion in tax handouts to families making over $15,000 a year. Some Congressional reformers have proposed replacing the exemption with a flat $150 cut in *taxes* for each dependent. This would be applicable equally to the St. Petersburg benchsitter and to the nonagenarian multimillionaire. That step alone—which would increase the taxes of those who earn $10,000 or more, while reduction the taxes of those who are less affluent—would increase Federal revenues by nearly $2-billion a year.

Other long-standing "loopholes for the many" are rarely examined with a critical eye, even though they represent immense "tax expenditures" justified by little rhyme or reason. For example, about $10-billion in interest accruing on life-insurance policies is exempt from taxation; this annual "tax expenditure" amounts to $2.7-billion. Nonbusiness personal itemized deductions (for major-medical expenses, charitable contributions, taxes, interest and the like) excuse another $10-billion from taxation, and the price tag for this is over $4-billion annually. Another rarely discussed but major untaxed item is the return on a homeowner's investment in his own house; this takes the form of rent the homeowner is spared paying to a landlord, rent which the homeowner, in effect, pays to himself. The total of this untaxed "income" amounts to an estimated $15.5-billion annually; failure to tax it represents an unconscious decision on the part of Congress to "spend" more than $4-billion annually on aid to homeowners—with, as usual, far more comfort to mansion-dwellers than to Levittowners.

The basic question raised by the Brookings study is whether the unreviewed annual "tax welfare" of over $77-billion makes sense in a time of budgetary deficits averaging $30-billion a year, and in a time when we are plagued with "social deficits" (in housing, health and the like) of vastly greater proportions. The Brookings experts propose an essentially preference-free, or "no-loophole," tax system. That would open up some choices that the present sieve-like system forbids: it would make it possible to raise added revenues that could be applied to the nation's social needs. Or it could make possible a massive tax-rate reduction; Drs. Pechman and Okner say that in a no-loophole system, the present levels of Federal revenues could be collected with tax rates ranging from 7 to 44 per cent, instead of the present 14 to 70 per cent. Or there could be a combination of both revenue-raising and rate-reduction. But whatever the choice, a preference-free system would put an end to irrational multibillion-dollar "tax expenditures" that continue to be perpetuated as long as Congress fails to act. It would also put an end to a tax system that is highly manipulable by the well-to-do (such as the 112 people with incomes over $200,000 who contrived to pay no tax whatever in 1970, despite the supposed Congres-

sional effort in 1969 to stop such taxlessness) but that leaves largely helpless the vast majority of taxpayers whose taxes are withheld from their paychecks and whisked away before they even see the money.

What are the prospects for significant tax reform? On a strictly nose-count basis, the cause should be a popular one, especially when it comes to ending such preferences as capital gains (from which just one taxpayer in 12 benefits), or the multibillion-dollar tax favors to large corporations. But past loophole-closing efforts have provoked concentrated lobbying pressure on Congress while generating little public enthusiasm. So, as the Brookings study shows, the tax system is clearly not based on a popular nose count.

Some reformers, however, believe that the tactic President Nixon seems ready to pursue in support of his value-added tax—holding out the bait of using the VAT proceeds to relieve hard-pressed property-taxpayers—may at long last create the vocal "constituency" that could prod Congress into genuine reforms. Offering the proceeds of loophole-closing to reduce property taxes could, in effect, steal Mr. Nixon's bait. Indeed, the prospect of the value-added tax has prodded some legislators who were not heretofor enlisted under the reform banner to search for popular alternatives to the VAT.

Reportedly, under pressure from apparent Democratic successes with the tax-reform issue in the early Presidential primaries, Mr. Nixon is considering sweeping reforms instead of the value-added tax. But if he does propose a VAT, it could set off the most basic debate about the tax system in many years and, ironically—despite Treasury Secretary Connally's openly expressed indifference to tax reform ("It leaves me cold")—he and the Nixon Administration might inadvertently give the reform cause the biggest boost it has had in many years.

Deviance and
Social Control

6

For centuries, social theorists have speculated on deviance and criminal behavior; traditionally, the central focus of these efforts could be captured in the question, "Why do they do it?" The "cause" for, or explanation of, wrongdoing was sought. Sometimes personality or psychological factors were put forth as the reason why some individuals strayed from the path of tradition and convention. Biological explanations have been resurrected from time to time. Often, conditions related to the culture or the society as a whole are invoked—such as poverty, blocked aspirations, or a general state of alienation and normlessness. Regardless of which of these "causes" is selected, all involve the view that it is deviance that is problematic; any departure from the norm is seen as puzzling, anomalous, and in need of an explanation. In these early writings on deviant behavior, there was no sense that any normal or completely free individual would actually *choose* to violate the norms. Certainly there was little or no effort to *appreciate* deviance as a worthwhile activity; a moralistic condemnation was more the rule than the exception. Generally, older conceptions of deviance almost never saw it as a *viable* form of behavior; it was viewed as, either, in its most extreme form, pathological, or, in a more patronizing vein, as an understandable but essentially makeshift adjustment to an unpleasant situation.

Newer sociological conceptions have approached deviance and crime from a quite different perspective; this change can be summed up by the following emphases:

(1) Contemporary sociological perspectives on deviance tend to stress the deviant act or experience *from the deviant actor's point of view.* This constitutes a change from: What problems does the deviant cause for conventional society? to: What problems does mainstream society cause for the deviant? Adopting the actor's perspective also involves attempting to grasp, from a firsthand point of view, the *subjective* features of the deviant experience.

(2) Recent work in deviance and crime has stressed the *arbitrariness* of norms and laws. This is not to say that they are all necessarily "wrong," or that any necessarily is. What it does mean is that they are not dictated by logic or reason. Laws are not passed and enforced because they outlaw behavior which threatens society with some "objective" harm or damage; they are passed and enforced because the behavior in question upsets and angers powerful (or many) members of society. People do not express moral outrage at a deviant act because they think that the act is dangerous by some abstract set of standards; quite simply, they think that the act is evil and immoral. Any conceivable forms of behavior have been thought immoral; contrarily, any conceivable acts—even killing—have been condoned and praised.

Some questions along these lines come to mind. Why is one form of behavior (let us say, recreational and illegal drug use) condemned and criminalized, while another, which is similar to it in many ways (drinking alcohol) accepted and tolerated? Why were laws against homosexuality passed, and why are they occasionally enforced? In what areas are police resources deployed? And why? How are laws passed in the first place? By whom? What is the connection between the mores and laws? What is the nature of the socialization process which inculcates attitudes relating to deviance and the mores? What is the interaction process which occurs when a conventional member of society confronts someone whose behavior he believes violates the norms?

(3) A third recent emphasis in this area has been on what might be called the *dramaturgy* of deviance. All people deviate from the rules of their society to some degree; thus, in a formal sense, *everyone* is a deviant. All people violate laws—some of them obscure, trivial, obsolete, and never enforced—so that in the formal sense, again, everyone is a criminal. The issue, then, is how do *certain* infractions become observed, and classified as deviant or criminal, and how do those who commit these acts become classified as deviant or criminal—that is, the *kind of person* who would perform such acts? What this means is that it is important to look at the subtle and complex *reading* process conventional members of society, and agents of social control (such as the police, psychiatrists, teachers, parents) give to those whose behavior violates certain standards. The behavior itself is not the sole criterion of deviancy; the same behavior, committed by two different individuals, may earn one the label of a deviant, while the behavior of the other will be ignored.

(4) A fourth current theme in sociological writings on deviance has been that society's attempts at social control often *further* deviant behavior and *increase* commitment to a deviant way of life.   Many attempts to "reform" the criminal have not only failed—they have actually boomeranged.   Attempting to criminalize many drug-related activities has had the consequence of increasing the severity of the drug problem.   The police and the courts often "create" juvenile delinquents by treating young boys who misbehave (from the police and the courts' point of view) *as if they were* actually delinquent.   The drop in maternal deaths in New York State subsequent to de-criminalizing abortion emphasizes the fact that laws often create more problems than they solve—and social control often actually *manufactures* deviance.

This emphasis on the *manufatcure* of deviance by social control, and its impact on the individuals classified as deviant, emerges clearly in our three selections.   Past views have emphasized that the transgressor was *factually* incorrect in this behavior—it is dangerous when he thinks that it is not, it harms others when he thinks that it does not, it blocks other values and achievements when the deviant thinks otherwise.   A kind of wisdom was assumed to society's position; the moral and the medical and scientific spheres were supposedly accurate reflections of one another.   Recent views have called this perspective into question.   Much of what was presumed to be a matter of simple fact actually turns out to be, upon examination, to be deeply rooted in sentiment and prejudice.

Richard Quinney's selection stresses the arbitrariness built into the criminal code.   Most of us look upon crime as an offense against nature, as well as against the whole society.   Quinney argues that crime is an arbitrary definition, made by powerful elements in society, about the behavior of those who are less powerful.   The criminal code is a crystallization of a specific moral and ideological interpretation—as well as of certain political and economic interests.   Certainly large segments of society might be harmed by one or another form of behavior which has been defined as criminal, but this is an incidental feature of the law.

Morality in the guise of medicine is the theme of the selection by psychiatrist Seymour Halleck, who illustrates the principle of the crystallization of prejudice into psychiatric judgement by examining several issues and groups that have been evaluated negatively by psychiatrists.   The majority of psychiatrists insist, for example, that homosexuality is a kind of illness.   The writings of psychiatrists have "helped to provide a rationale for keeping women in a subservient position."   Psychiatrists have traditionally been unable to relate to the poor and the Black—evaluating their behavior in terms of an ethnocentric white, middle-class value system—and have ignored the problems of the elderly.   As a consequence of Halleck's discussion, we begin to see "abnormality" as an evaluation of one group by another—based on sentiment, prejudice, and emotion—and not a natural, medical, or psychiatric state.   Deviance, in short, is manufactured—it does not just exist.   It is a judgment, not simply a fact.

a theory of the social reality of crime

RICHARD QUINNEY

THEORY: THE SOCIAL REALITY OF CRIME

The theory contains six propositions and a number of statements within the propositions. With the first proposition I define crime. The next four are the explanatory units. In the final proposition the other five are collected to form a composite describing the social reality of crime. The propositions and their integration into a theory of crime reflect the assumptions about explanation and about man and society outlined above.

PROPOSITION 1 (DEFINITION OF CRIME)

Crime is a definition of human conduct that is created by authorized agents in a politically organized society.

This is the essential starting point in the theory—a definition of crime —which itself is based on the concept of definition. Crime is a *definition* of behavior that is conferred on some persons by others. Agents of the law (legislators, police, prosecutors, and judges), representing segments of a politically organized society, are responsible for formu-

From THE SOCIAL REALITY OF CRIME, *by Richard Quinney, pp. 15– 23, 32–42. Copyright © 1970 by Little, Brown and Company (Inc.). Reprinted by permission of the publisher and author. [footnotes omitted]*

lating and administering criminal law. Persons and behaviors, therefore, become criminal because of the *formulation* and *application* of criminal definitions. Thus, *crime is created.*

By viewing crime as a definition, we are able to avoid the commonly used "clinical perspective," which leads one to concentrate on the quality of the act and to assume that criminal behavior is an individual pathology. Crime is not inherent in behavior, but is a judgment made by some about the actions and characteristics of others. This proposition allows us to focus on the formulation and administration of the criminal law as it touches upon the behaviors that become defined as criminal. Crime is seen as a result of a process which culminates in the defining of persons and behaviors as criminal. It follows, then, that *the greater the number of criminal definitions formulated and applied, the greater the amount of crime.*

PROPOSITION 2 (FORMULATION OF CRIMINAL DEFINITIONS)

Criminal definitions describe behaviors that conflict with the interests of the segments of society that have the power to shape public policy.

Criminal definitions are formulated according to the interests of those *segments* (types of social groupings) of society which have the *power* to translate their interests into *public policy.* The interests—based on desires, values, and norms—which are ultimately incorporated into the criminal law are those which are treasured by the dominant interest groups in the society. In other words, those who have the ability to have their interests represented in public policy regulate the formulation of criminal definitions.

That criminal definitions are formulated is one of the most obvious manifestations of *conflict* in society. By formulating criminal law (including legislative statutes, administrative rulings, and judicial decisions), some segments of society protect and perpetuate their own interests. Criminal definitions exist, therefore, because some segments of society are in conflict with others. By formulating criminal definitions these segments are able to control the behavior of persons in other segments. It follows that *the greater the conflict in interests between the segments of a society, the greater the probability that the power segments will formulate criminal definitions.*

The interests of the power segments of society are reflected not only in the content of criminal definitions and the kinds of penal sanctions attached to them, but also in the *legal policies* stipulating how those who come to be defined as "criminal" are to be handled. Hence, procedural rules are created for enforcing and administering the criminal law. Policies are also established on programs for treating and punishing the criminally defined and for controlling and preventing crime. In the initial criminal definitions or the subsequent procedures, and in correctional and penal programs or policies of crime control and prevention, the segments of society that have power and interests to protect are instrumental in regulating the

behavior of those who have conflicting interests and less power. Finally, law changes with modifications in the interest structure. When the interests that underlie a criminal law are no longer relevant to groups in power, the law will be reinterpreted or altered to incorporate the dominant interests. Hence, *the probability that criminal definitions will be formulated is increased by such factors as (1) changing social conditions, (2) emerging interests, (3) increasing demands that political, economic, and religious interests be protected, and (4) changing conceptions of the public interest.* The social history of law reflects changes in the interest structure of society.

PROPOSITION 3 (APPLICATION OF CRIMINAL DEFINITIONS)

Criminal definitions are applied by the segments of society that have the power to shape the enforcement and administration of criminal law.

The powerful interests intervene in all stages in which criminal definitions are created. Since interests cannot be effectively protected by merely formulating criminal law, enforcement and administration of the law are required. The interests of the powerful, therefore, operate in *applying* criminal definitions. Consequently, crime is "political behavior and the criminal becomes in fact a member of a 'minority group' without sufficient public support to dominate the control of the police power of the state." Those whose interests conflict with the interests represented in the law must either change their behavior or possibly find it defined as "criminal."

The probability that criminal definitions will be applied varies ac-

cording to the extent to which the behaviors of the powerless conflict with the interests of the power segments. Law enforcement efforts and judicial activity are likely to be increased when the interests of the powerful are threatened by the opposition's behavior. Fluctuations and variations in the application of criminal definitions reflect shifts in the relations of the various segments in the power structure of society.

Obviously, the criminal law is not applied directly by the powerful segments. They delegate enforcement and administration of the law to authorized *legal agents,* who, nevertheless, represent their interests. In fact, the security in office of legal agents depends on their ability to represent the society's dominant interests.

Because the interest groups responsible for creating criminal definitions are physically separated from the groups to which the authority to enforce and administer law is delegated, local conditions affect the manner in which criminal definitions are applied. In particular, communities vary in the law enforcement and administration of justice they expect. Application is also affected by the visibility of acts in a community and by its norms about reporting possible offenses. Especially important are the occupational organization and ideology of the legal agents. Thus, the *probability that criminal definitions will be applied is influenced by such community and organizational factors as (1) community expectations of law enforcement and administration, (2) the visibility and public reporting of offenses, and (3) the occupational organization, ideology, and actions of the legal agents to whom the au-*thority *to enforce and administer criminal law is delegated.* Such factors determine how the dominant interests of society are implemented in the application of criminal definitions.

The probability that criminal definitions will be applied in *specific situations* depends on the actions of the legal agents. In the final analysis, a criminal definition is applied according to an *evaluation* by someone charged with the authority to enforce and administer the law. In the course of "criminalization," a criminal label may be affixed to a person because of real or fancied attributes: "Indeed, a person is evaluated, either favorably or unfavorably, not because he *does* something, or even because he *is* something, but because others react to their perceptions of him as offensive or inoffensive." Evaluation by the definers is affected by the way in which the suspect handles the situation, but ultimately their evaluations and subsequent decisions determine the criminality of human acts. Hence, *the more legal agents evaluate behaviors and persons as worthy of criminal definition, the greater the probability that criminal definitions will be applied.*

PROPOSITION 4 (DEVELOPMENT OF BEHAVIOR PATTERNS IN RELATION TO CRIMINAL DEFINITIONS)

Behavior patterns are structured in segmentally organized society in relation to criminal definitions, and within this context persons engage in actions that have relative probabilities of being defined as criminal.

Although behavior varies, all behaviors are similar in that they represent the *behavior patterns* of segments of society. Therefore, all persons—whether they create criminal definitions or are the objects of criminal definitions—act according to *normative systems* learned in relative social and cultural settings. Since it is not the quality of the behavior but the action taken against the behavior that makes it criminal, that which is defined as criminal in any society is relative to the behavior patterns of the segments of society that formulate and apply criminal definitions. Consequently, *persons in the segments of society whose behavior patterns are not represented in formulating and applying criminal definitions are more likely to act in ways that will be defined as criminal than those in the segments that formulate and apply criminal definitions.*

Once behavior patterns are established with some regularity within the respective segments of society, individuals are provided with a framework for developing *personal action patterns.* These patterns continually develop for each person as he moves from one experience to another. It is the development of these patterns that gives his behavior its own substance in relation to criminal definitions.

Man constructs his own patterns of action in participating with others. It follows, then, that *the probability that a person will develop action patterns that have a high potential of being defined as criminal depends on the relative substance of (1) structured opportunities, (2) learning experiences, (3) interpersonal associations and identifications, and (4) self-conceptions.* Throughout his experiences, each person creates a conception of himself as a social being. Thus prepared, he behaves according to the anticipated consequences of his actions.

During experiences shared by the criminal definers and the criminally defined, personal action patterns develop among the criminally defined because they are so defined. After such persons have had continued experience in being criminally defined, they learn to manipulate the application of criminal definitions.

Furthermore, those who have been defined as criminal begin to conceive of themselves as criminal; as they adjust to the definitions imposed upon them, they learn to play the role of the criminal. Because of others' reactions, therefore, persons may develop personal action patterns that increase the likelihood of their being defined as criminal in the future. That is, *increased experience with criminal definitions increases the probability of developing actions that may be subsequently defined as criminal.*

Thus, both the criminal definers and the criminally defined are involved in reciprocal action patterns. The patterns of both the definers and the defined are shaped by their common, continued, and related experiences. The fate of each is bound to that of the other.

PROPOSITION 5 (CONSTRUCTION OF CRIMINAL CONCEPTIONS)

Conceptions of crime are constructed and diffused in the segments of society by various means of communication.

The "real world" is a social construction: man with the help of others creates the world in which he lives. Social reality is thus the world a group of people create and believe in as their own. This reality is constructed according to the kind of "knowledge" they develop, the ideas they are exposed to, the manner in which they select information to fit the world they are shaping, and the manner in which they interpret these conceptions. Man behaves in reference to the *social meanings* he attaches to his experiences.

Among the constructions that develop in a society are those which determine what man regards as crime. Wherever we find the concept of crime, there we will find conceptions about the relevance of crime, the offender's characteristics, and the relation of crime to the social order. These conceptions are constructed by communication. In fact, *the construction of criminal conceptions depends on the portrayal of crime in all personal and mass communications.* By such means, criminal conceptions are constructed and diffused in the segments of a society. The most critical conceptions are those held by the power segments of society. These are the conceptions that are certain of becoming incorporated into the social reality of crime. In general, then, *the more the power segments are concerned about crime, the greater the probability that criminal definitions will be created and that behavior patterns will develop in opposition to criminal definitions.* The formulation and application of criminal definitions and the development of behavior patterns related to criminal definitions are thus joined in full circle by the construction of criminal conceptions.

PROPOSITION 6 (THE SOCIAL REALITY OF CRIME)

The social reality of crime is constructed by the formulation and application of criminal definitions, the development of behavior patterns related to criminal definitions, and the construction of criminal conceptions.

These five propositions can be collected into a composite. The theory, accordingly, describes and explains phenomena that increase the probability of crime in society, resulting in the social reality of crime.

Since the first proposition is a definition and the sixth is a composite, the body of the theory consists of the four middle propositions. Each proposition is related to the others forming a theoretical system of developmental propositions interacting with one another. The phenomena denoted in the propositions and their relationships culminate in what is regarded as the amount and character of crime in a society at any given time, that is, in the social reality of crime.

FROM SOCIOLOGICAL JURISPRUDENCE TO SOCIOLOGY OF CRIMINAL LAW

Law is not merely a complex of rules and procedures; Pound taught us that in calling for the study of "law in action." For some purposes it may be useful to think of law as autonomous within society, developing according to its own logic and proceeding along its own lines. But law also simultaneously reflects society and influences it, so that, in a social sense, it is both social product and social force. In Pound's juristic approach, however, law represents the consciousness of the total society. This *consensus* model of (criminal) law has been described in the following way: "The state of criminal law continues to be—as it should—a decisive reflection of the social consciousness of a society. What kind of conduct an organized community considers, at a given time, sufficiently condemnable to impose official sanctions, impairing the life, liberty, or property of the offender, is a barometer of the moral and social thinking of a community." Similarly, Pound, formulating his theory of interests, felt that law reflects the needs of the well-ordered society. In fact, the law is a form of "social engineering" in a civilized society:

> For the purpose of understanding the law of today, I am content to think of law as a social institution to satisfy social wants—the claims and demands involved in the existence of civilized society—by giving effect to as much as we may with the least sacrifice, so far as such wants may be satisfied or such claims given effect by an ordering of human conduct through politically organized society. For present purposes I am content to see in legal history the record of a continually wider recognizing and satisfying of human wants or claims or desires through social control; a more embracing and more effective securing of social interests; a continually more complete and effective elimination of waste and precluding of friction in human enjoyment of the goods of existence—in short, a continually more efficacious social engineering.

Thus, the interests Pound had in mind would maintain and, ulti-

mately, improve the social order. His was a *teleological* as well as consensus theory of interests: men must fulfill some interests for the good of the whole society; these interests are to be achieved through law. In Pound's theory, only the right law can emerge in a civilized society.

Jurisprudence has generally utilized a *pluralistic* model with respect to law as a social force in society. Accordingly, law regulates social behavior and establishes social organization; it orders human relationships by restraining individual actions and by settling disputes in social relations. In recent juristic language, law functions "first, to establish the general framework, the rules of the game so to speak, within and by which individual and group life shall be carried on, and secondly, to adjust the conflicting claims which different individuals and groups of individuals seek to satisfy in society." For Pound, the law adjusts and reconciles conflicting interests:

> Looked at functionally, the law is an attempt to satisfy, to reconcile, to harmonize, to adjust these overlapping and often conflicting claims and demands, either through securing them directly and immediately, or through securing certain individual interests, or through delimitations or compromises of individual interests, so as to give effect to the greatest total of interests or to the interests that weigh most in our civilization, with the least sacrifice of the scheme of interests as a whole.

In Pound's theory of interests, law provides the general framework within which individual and group life is carried on, according to the postulates of social order. Moreover, as a legal historian has written, "The law defines the extent to which it will give effect to the interests which it recognizes, in the light of other interests and of the possibilities of effectively securing them through law; it also devises means for securing those that are recognized and prescribes the limits within which those means may be employed." In the interest theory of sociological jurisprudence, then, law is an instrument that controls interests according to the requirements of social order.

Pound's theory of interests included a threefold classification of interests, including the individual, the public, and the social:

> Individual interests are claims or demands or desires involved immediately in the individual life and asserted in the title of that life. Public interests are claims or demands or desires involved in life in a politically organized society and asserted in the title of that organization. They are commonly treated as the claims of a politically organized society thought of as a legal entity. Social interests are claims or demands or desires involved in social life in a civilized society and asserted in the title of that life. It is not uncommon to treat them as the claims of the whole social group as such.

Pound warned that the types are overlapping and interdependent and that most can be placed in all the categories, depending upon one's purpose. He argued, however, that it is often expedient to put claims, demands, and desires in their most general form; that is, into the category of social interests.

Surveying the claims, demands, and desires found in legal proceedings and in legislative proposals, Pound suggested that the most important social interests appears to involve security against actions that threaten the social group. Others are interest in the security of domestic, religious, economic, and political institutions; morals; conservation of social resources; general progress, including the development of human powers and control over nature to satisfy human wants; and individual life, especially the freedom of self-assertion. According to Pound, any legal system depends upon the way in which these interests are incorporated into law.

My theoretical perspective on criminal law departs from the general tradition of the interest theory of sociological jurisprudence in a number of ways. First, my perspective is based on a special conception of society. Society is characterized by diversity, conflict, coercion, and change, rather than by consensus and stability. Second, *law is a result of the operation of interests,* rather than an instrument that functions outside of particular interests. Though law may control interests, it is in the first place *created* by interests. Third, *law incorporates the interests of specific persons and groups;* it is seldom the product of the whole society. Law is made by men, representing special interests, who have the power to translate their interests into public policy. Unlike the pluralistic conception of politics, *law* does not represent a compromise of the diverse interests in society, but *supports some interests at the expense of others.* Fourth, the theoretical perspective of criminal law is devoid of teleological connotations. The social order may require certain functions for its maintenance and survival, but such functions will not be considered as inherent in the interests involved in formulating substantive laws. Fifth, the perspective proposed here includes a conceptual scheme for analyzing interests in the law. Finally, construction of the perspective is based on findings from current social science research.

LAW IN POLITICALLY ORGANIZED SOCIETY

Authority relations are present in all social collectivities: some persons are always at the command of others. As order is established in a society, several systems of control develop to regulate the conduct of various groups of persons. Human behavior is thus subject to restraint by varied agencies, institutions, and social groupings—families, churches, social clubs, political organizations, labor unions, corporations, educational systems, and so forth.

The control systems vary considerably in the forms of conduct they regulate, and most provide means for assuring compliance to their rules. Informal means, spontaneously employed by some persons, such as ridicule, gossip, and censure, may ensure conformity to some rules. Control systems may, in addition, rely upon formal and regularized means of sanction.

The *legal system* is the most explicit form of social control. The law consists of (1) specific rules of conduct, (2) planned use of sanctions to support the rules, and (3) designated officials to interpret and enforce the rules. Furthermore, law becomes more important as a system of control as societies increase in complexity. Pound wrote that "in the modern world law has become the paramount agent of social control. Our main reliance is upon force of a politically organized state."

Law is more than a system of formal social control; it is also a body of specialized rules created and interpreted in a *politically organized society,* or the state, which is a territorial organization with the authorized power to govern the lives and activities of all the inhabitants. Though other types of organized bodies may possess formal rules, only the specialized rule systems of politically organized societies are regarded here as systems of law.

Law, as a special kind of institution, again is more than an abstract body of rules. Instead of being autonomous within society and developing according to its own logic, law is an integral part of society, operating as a force in society and as a social product. The law is not only that which is written as statutes and recorded as court opinions and administrative rulings, but is also a method or *process* of doing something. As a process, law is a dynamic force that is continually being *created* and *interpreted.* Thus, law in action involves the making of specialized (legal) decisions by various *authorized agents.* In politically organized society, human actions are regulated by those invested with the authority to make specified decisions in the name of the society.

Furthermore, law in operation is an aspect of politics—it is one of the methods by which public policy is formulated and administered for governing the lives and activities of the state's inhabitants. As an act of politics, law and legal decisions do not represent the interests of all persons in the society. Whenever a law is created or interpreted, the values of some are necessarily assured and the values of others are either ignored or negated.

THE INTEREST STRUCTURE

Modern societies are characterized by an organization of differences. The social differentation of society, in turn, provides the basis for the state's political life. Government in a politically organized society operates according to the interests that characterize the socially differentiated positions. Because varied interests are distributed among the positions, and because the positions are differently equipped with the ability to command, public policy represents specific interests in the society. Politically organized society, therefore, may be viewed as a differentiated *interest structure.*

Each *segment* of society has its own values, its own norms, and its own ideological orientations. When these are considered to be important for the existence and welfare of the respective segments, they may be defined as *interests.* Further, interests can be categorized according to the ways in which activities are generally pursued in society; that is, according to the *institutional orders* of society. The following may then serve as a definition of interests: *the institutional concerns of the segments of society.* Thus, interests are grounded in the segments of society and represent the institutional concerns of the segments.

The institutional orders within which interests operate may be classified into fairly broad categories. For our use, these may be called: (1) *the political,* which regulates the distribution of power and authority in society; (2) *the economic,* which regulates the production and distribution of goods and services; (3) *the religious,* which regulates the relationship of man to a conception of the supernatural; (4) *the kinship,* which regulates sexual relations, family patterns, and the procreation and rearing of children; (5) *the educational,* which regulates the formal training of the society's members; and (6) *the public,* which regulates the protection and maintenance of the community and its citizens. Each segment of society has its own orientation to these orders. Some, because of their authority position in the interest structure, are able to have their interests represented in public policy.

The segments of society differ in the extent to which their interests are organized. The segments themselves are broad statistical aggregates containing persons of similar age, sex, class, status, occupation, race, ethnicity, religion, or the like. All these have *formal interests;* those which are advantageous to the segment but which are not consciously held by the incumbents and are not organized for action. *Active interests,* on the other hand, are manifest to persons in the segments and are sufficiently organized to serve as the basis for representation in policy decisions.

Within the segments, groups of persons may become aware of and organize to promote their common interests; these may be called *interest groups.* Public policy, in turn, is the result of the success gained by these groups.

The interest structure is characterized by the unequal distribution of *power* and *conflict* among the segments of society. It is differentiated by diverse interests and by the ability of the segments to translate their interests into public policy. Furthermore, the segments are in continual conflict over their interests. Interests thus are structured according to differences in power and are in conflict.

Power and conflict are linked in this conception of interest structure. Power, as the ability to shape public policy, produces conflict among the competing segments, and conflict produces differences in the distribution of power. Coherence in the interest structure is thus ensured by the exercise of force and constraint by the conflicting segments. In the conflict-power model, therefore, politically organized society is held together by conflicting elements and functions according to the coercion of some segments by others.

The conflict-power conception of interest structure implies that public policy results from differential distribution of power and conflict among the segments of society. Diverse segments with specialized interests become so highly organized that they are able to influence the policies that affect all persons in the state. Groups that have the power to gain access to the decision-making process are able to translate their interests into public policy. Thus, the interests represented in the formulation and administration of public policy are those treasured by the dominant segments of the society. Hence, public policy is created because segments with power differentials are in conflict with one another. Public policy itself is a manifesta-tion of an interest structure in politically organized society.

FORMULATION AND ADMINISTRATION OF CRIMINAL LAW

Law is a form of public policy that regulates the behavior and activities of all members of a society. It is *formulated* and *administered* by those segments of society which are able to incorporate their interests into the creation and interpretation of public policy. Rather than representing the institutional concerns of all segments of society, law secures the interests of particular segments, supporting one point of view at the expense of others.

Thus, the content of the law, including the substantive regulations and the procedural rules, represents the interests of the segments of society that have the power to shape public policy. Formulation of law allows some segments of society to protect and perpetuate their own interests. By formulating law, some segments are able to control others to their own advantage.

The interests that the power segments of society attempt to maintain enter into all stages of legal administration. Since legal formulations do not provide specific instructions for interpreting law, administration of law is largely a matter of discretion on the part of *legal agents* (police, prosecutors, judges, juries, prison authorities, parole officers, and others). Though implementation of law is necessarily influenced by such matters as localized conditions and the occupational organization of legal agents, the interest structure of politically organized society is responsible for the general design of the administration of criminal justice.

Finally, the formulation and administration of law in politically organized society are affected by changing social conditions. Emerging interests and increasing concern with the protection of various aspects of social life require new laws or reinterpretations of old laws. Consequently, legal changes take place within the context of the changing interest structure of society.

INTERESTS IN CONTEMPORARY SOCIETY

Interests not only are the principal forces behind the creation and interpretation of law, but they are changing the very nature of government. For centuries the state was the Leviathan, protector, repository of power, main source of the community's economic and social life. The state unified and controlled most of the activities of the society. In recent times, however, it is apparent that some groups and segments of society have taken over many of the state's functions:

> The question must be raised in all seriousness whether the "overmighty subjects" of our time—the giant corporations, both of a commercial and non-commercial character, the labor unions, the trade associations, farmers' organizations, veterans' legions, and some other highly organized groups—have taken over the substance of sovereignty. Has the balance of pressures and counter-pressures between these groups left the legal power of the State as a mere shell? If this is a correct interpretation of the social change of our time, we are witnessing another dialectic

process in history: the national sovereign State—having taken over effective legal political power from the social groups of the previous age—surrenders its power to the new massive social groups of the industrial age.

Some analysts of the contemporary scene have optimistically forecasted that checks of "countervailing power" will adequately balance the interests of the well organized groups. This pluralistic conception disregards the fact that interest groups are grossly unequal in power. Groups that are similar in power may well check each others' interests, but groups that have little or no power will not have the opportunity to have their interest represented in public policy. The consequence is government by a few powerful private interest groups.

Furthermore, the politics of private interests tends to take place outside of the arena of the public governmental process. In private politics, interest groups receive their individual claims in return for allowing other groups to press for their interests. Behind public politics a private government operates in a way that not only guarantees rewards to well organized groups but affects the lives of us all.

If there be any check in this contemporary condition, it is in the prospect that the "public interest" will take precedence over private interests. Interest groups, if for no other reason than their concern for public relations, may bow to the commonweal. Optimistically, the public interest may become an ideal fulfilled, no matter what the source of private power.

But the fallacy in any expectation

of the achievement of the public good through the "public interest" is that the government which could foster such a condition will become again in a new age an oppressive interest in itself. That age, in fact seems to be upon us. Increasingly, as Reich has argued, "Americans live on government largess—allocated by government on its own terms, and held by recipients subject to conditions which express 'the public interest.'" While the highly organized, scientifically planned society, governed for the social good of its inhabitants, promises the best life that man has ever known, not all of our human values will receive attention, and some may be temporarily or permanently negated.

In raw form we cannot hold optimistically to either government by private interests or public interest by government largess. The future for individual man appears to lie in some form of protection from both forms of government. Decentralized government offers some possibility for the survival of the individual in a collective society. But more immediately, that protection must be sought in procedural law, a law that must necessarily be removed from the control of either the interests of private groups or public government. The challenge for law of the future is that it create an order providing fulfillment for individual values that are now within our reach, values that paradoxically are imminent because of the existence of interests from which we must now seek protection. A new society is indeed coming: Can a law be created apart from private interests which assures individual fulfillment within a good society?

the uses
of abnormality

SEYMOUR L. HALLECK

The psychiatrist is granted more power than the ordinary man to influence the standards of conduct

Reprinted from Seymour L. Halleck, THE POLITICS OF THERAPY, *pp. 99–117 (New York: Science House, 1971) by permission of the author and publisher.*

within his community. To begin with, he is allowed to certify the abnormality of certain people by making them become patients. As the one who decides who is to be a patient, the psychiatrist can comment liberally on what constitutes normal or abnormal behavior within his community. The psychiatrist's prestige as a doctor of medicine is such that the public is likely to take his pronouncements seriously.

The power to define standards of normality can be used either to change or stabilize the society. Some psychiatrists feel that community standards are overly restrictive; they are likely to encourage their patients and the public to believe that greater freedom in all areas of life is synonymous with mental health. Probably at least a few psychiatrists believe that community standards are not rigid enough; they will encourage their patients and the society to accept greater discipline and control. Most psychiatrists, however, define mental health, or normality, in terms of acceptable community standards. In their practice and in their public postures they tend to stabilize those institutions that are currently popular and acceptable to the majority of citizens.

By the very nature of his work the psychiatrist learns to equate deviation from community norms with abnormality or sickness. Sociologists and psychiatrists have long recognized that people who behave differently from their neighbors are more likely to become psychiatric patients than those who behave conventionally, but this relationship has never been satisfactorily explained.[1] Perhaps it exists because those who behave unconventionally are inherently unhappy people; perhaps they would be unhappy in any environment. Or, perhaps the socially deviant become patients because society imposes so many restrictions on them that they become unhappy. Or, conceivably, those who view the world a little differently from their neighbors are simply more accepting of the role of psychiatric patient. Whatever the reasons for the correlation, the psychiatrist regularly encounters and treats people who are both unhappy and different. Because he views his patient's unhappiness as a form of illness, he eventually learns to think of his patient's "difference" as a manifestation of illness.

The general impact of the psychiatrist's work with deviant individuals and his public pronouncements about them tends to be in the direction of negating the kinds of changes probably desired by those who are different. As I have noted previously, the patient role deprives one of power. To the extent that those who might initiate change in the society become patients, society is stabilized. Unfortunately, other repressive consequences also follow whenever the medical practitioner has the power to influence community morality. Some people suffer deeply as a result of being defined as abnormal by the psychiatrist. Even when he doesn't label people, his attitudes and public pronouncements may still contribute to keeping in a state of subjugation deviant individuals and groups who are already oppressed.

Again, the psychiatrist's political influence isn't restricted to his role in what Szasz calls "institutional psychiatry,"[2] since he can influence both voluntary and involuntary patients; for that matter his posture on moral issues can affect many who will never become his patients.

---

[1] Mechanic, D. *Mental Health and Social Policy*. Englewood Cliffs, N.J.: Prentice-Hall, 1969.

[2] Szasz, T. *The Manufacture of Madness*. New York: Harper & Row, 1970.

THE OPPRESSION OF A LABEL

For the most part, the psychiatrist preaches the values of tolerance, permissiveness, and humane treatment in dealing with deviant individuals. However, he sometimes contributes to their oppression directly or indirectly. By virtue of his power to label deviant people as mentally ill, he can take away the freedom of those who are different by putting them in a hospital. The process of labeling also contributes to the oppression of deviant groups in a more subtle manner by strengthening the community's beliefs that those who are different are somehow dangerous or inferior. These issues have been discussed in detail by other psychiatrists such as Thomas Szasz,[3] Ronald Leifer,[4] and Karl Menninger,[5] but they are important enough to review briefly here.

In controlling people who are violent and whose violence seems irrational, the community may have good reason to treat them as if they were sick. But most deviant individuals, however irrational they may be judged, are not violent. Deviant behavior usually does not threaten the safety of others, but it may threaten the community by affronting standards of dignity or propriety or by appearing to reject the existing social order. When nonviolent deviant individuals are labeled as sick, however, the public tends to view them as if they were violent. The community is also likely to re-

[3] Szasz, T. *Law, Liberty and Psychiatry.* New York: Macmillan, 1963.
[4] Leifer, R. *In the Name of Mental Health.* New York: Science House, 1969.
[5] Menninger, K. A. *The Vital Balance.* New York: Viking Press, 1967.

strict them in the same harsh way as those who are violent.

When an individual is given a medical label, society is encouraged to believe that his behavior cannot be controlled; a nonmedical label, on the other hand, leads society to assume that an individual can control his behavior. Thus, a heavy drinker may be thought of as imprudent or obnoxious; however, once we call him an alcoholic, we assume that he cannot control his drinking. If a grown man becomes sexually intimate with a fourteen-year-old girl, we may think that he is gross, insensitive, or stupid. However, once we call him a pedophiliac, we fear that he cannot restrain himself from attacking small children. The movement from a moral to a medical or psychological evaluation of an individual's behavior has both positive and negative consequences. On the one hand, society treats the person who cannot seem to help himself with considerable solicitousness, but it also fears him because presumably he is unable to contain his impulses. Society views him as an inferior person who is dangerous because he lacks the autonomy and control that normal people have. Thus, the community feels justified in imposing restrictions upon him and in rejecting or ignoring whatever he might try to say.

There is, of course, considerable value to diagnosis in ordinary medical practice. Putting people into diagnostic categories makes it convenient for doctors to communicate with one another and enables research to be done. Frequently the diagnosis dictates treatment and enables the physician to prognosticate the patient's fate. In psychiatry, however, diagnostic categories such as schizophrenia, paranoia, psychopathy, or alcoholism are not sufficiently precise so that the doctor can have a clear idea of desirable treatment or prognosis. A schizophrenic may be treated in a variety of ways, all of which can be justified by some theoretical orientation; the diagnosis of schizophrenia tells the doctor little about how long or how severely the patient will suffer. Similar considerations apply to most psychiatric labels.

On the basis of a rather vague concept of what schizophrenia actually is, thousands of Americans are so labeled by psychiatric physicians. (Europeans are a little more fortunate in this regard, for their psychiatrists will diagnose schizophrenia only if certain behaviors are clearly observable. In America there is a tendency for psychiatrists to infer the presence of schizophrenic thinking or propensities on the basis of very little evidence and the diagnosis is loosely applied to many people whose behavior does not markedly deviate from the norm.) Once an individual is designated a schizophrenic he becomes a pariah: he is approached with a mixture of awe, distrust, and sometimes fear by both the doctor and the general public. Employment, particularly in sensitive or important jobs, may be denied to him. The patient's pride and self-confidence are often shattered; he may view himself as afflicted with a disease that makes him incapable of controlling his most undesirable impulses. The very word "schizophrenia" strikes fear in the hearts of many people. I have seen patients who are severely depressed, suicidal, and living in severe states of mental agony, but who seemed to find a perverse kind of reassurance

when I told them that they were not schizophrenic.

The diagnostic term "paranoid" has taken on an almost totally pejorative meaning. The term is not restricted to those who behave strangely, are overly suspicious, or tend to blame their failings on others; professionals insensitively apply it to many people who take unusual or deviant positions on social issues, and even nonprofessionals bandy it about loosely. To accuse one's adversary of being paranoid has become a kind of trump card, a powerful weapon for negating the opponent's position.

Consider also the diagnosis of psychopathy. A number of chronically antisocial individuals are believed to be suffering from psychopathy or sociopathy These individuals are assumed to have a personality defect, an organic defect, or some kind of psychological malfunction that produces their antisocial behavior. Psychiatrists have a great deal of difficulty defining the term "psychopath." Sometimes it is applied to only a few offenders, sometimes to the mass of offenders, and sometimes to any person whose behavior seems offensive. Although the term doesn't have a precise meaning, its social implications are profound; just the concept itself leads the public to believe that many of those who are antisocial are plagued with uncontrollable impulses and must, therefore, be harshly restrained in order to protect "normal" people.

In the area of drugs, a man who uses alcohol or other drugs to excess may be overwhelmed with all sorts of personal and social difficulties and still maintain a respectable role in society. However once he is labeled an alcoholic or addict, he is cast into an entirely different social role—he is viewed as a person who is diseased. Some people will pity him, but a sizable number will fear or scorn him. Under certain circumstances he could lose many of his rights, even though his use of drugs doesn't hurt anyone but himself.

We do not usually think of people who behave so peculiarly that they are labeled "schizophrenic," "paranoid," "psychopathic," or "addicted" as would-be reformers of the social order. Yet, much of the behavior that psychiatrists consider symptomatic is at least partly an effort on the part of an individual to communicate with others in order to change something in his environment. The psychiatric label allows those whom the patient might wish to influence to ignore the content of his message and to focus instead on his dangerousness or defectiveness.

It is unlikely that psychiatry can advance scientifically unless its members continue to search for scientific means of classifying deviant behavior. Psychiatrists could help society immeasurably, however, if they would frankly admit that current diagnostic categories do not have much scientific meaning—that they are largely arbitrary. Then society might be able to confront rationally and humanely the moral questions raised by those who behave differently.

Even if the physician uses psychological rather than medical terms to describe his patients, his judgment of the normality of any given behavior has important social consequences. When used by a doctor, terms such as "emotionally disturbed," "conflicted," or "immature"

have almost the same social impact as medical expressions. The repressive power of psychological—as opposed to medical—labeling is readily obvious in the area of sexual behavior. The Western world has long been dominated by the Judeo-Christian ethic which emphasizes the immorality of certain sexual practices. Masturbation, oral-genital relations, and other kinds of sexual gratification that do not lead to intercourse are often considered immoral. The same is true of any sexual relationships outside of marriage. The psychiatric profession has never labeled these practices as immoral, nor has it, in recent years at least, labeled them as evidence of illness. It has, however, repeatedly said that some of these behaviors indicate emotional disturbance or immaturity.[6] If an individual happens to enjoy an unconventional variety of sexual gratification and then hears a psychiatrist say that it is a sign of immaturity, he will wonder about the propriety of his activities and perhaps feel ashamed or guilty. Admittedly, the psychiatric profession has become much more tolerant of diversity in sexual behavior than it used to be, but psychiatrists are still shaming people into abiding by conventional behavior. They have the power to inhibit many kinds of behavior by describing it in psychological terms that have basically the same pejorative meaning as medical terms.

It is hard to imagine how anyone could practice psychiatry without some idea of what behavior is good for people and what is not. There

6 Freud, S. "Three Essays on the Theory of Sexuality." In the standard edition of the *Complete Psychological Works of Sigmund Freud*, edited by J. Strachey. London: Hogarth Press, 1953.

must be some standard of normality in order to decide whether a given person needs treatment, how he should be treated, and what should be the treatment goals. This standard can be based on biological norms, social utility, or prevailing community mores. The problem here is that the psychiatrist is not required to, nor does he usually go to the trouble to, spell out his standards of normality. The community often believes that his definitions of normality are based on medical facts, while frequently he is only echoing the mores of the majority. Because they determine what is abnormal, psychiatrists can significantly affect the social order; therefore, they should critically reexamine their criteria for making such determinations. They should make these criteria known to their patients, and, when their public pronouncements touch on the question of normality, they should also reveal them to the public.

THE JUSTIFICATION OF OPPRESSION

A number of social institutions in our country allow certain groups to hold power, while other groups are kept powerless. Many of these institutions came into existence at a time when they served some social or economic need. Laws and customs restricting nonreproductive sexual activity possibly helped to increase the labor force at some past time. The practice of slavery or the establishment of institutions to subjugate women or children may also have produced economic efficiency at some previous time. When social and economic conditions change, however, it becomes difficult to just-

ify the oppression of selected groups on the basis of social utility. Yet, those who hold power are reluctant to give it up. One way in which they can retain power is to develop and perpetuate belief systems that reassure the oppressors (and sometimes convince the oppressed) that the subjugated are somehow dangerous or inferior. Such belief systems or, perhaps more correctly, myths serve to justify oppression.

The psychiatric profession has often loaned its talents to perpetuate unsubstantiated belief systems or myths. Through public pronouncements or attitudes toward patients, psychiatrists have attributed characteristics to oppressed groups that helped convince the rest of society that these people really were dangerous, inferior, or didn't mind being treated as inferior. Again, the psychiatrist has inadvertently used his position to deter society from confronting and dealing with inequities in the distribution of power.

THE HOMOSEXUAL

Acts of physical love with a member of the same sex sometimes bring harsh or brutal punishment in the United States. While other unconventional sexual behavior may engender attitudes of similar repressiveness, persecution of the homosexual has become quite common. The community, of course, will want to control the homosexual who attacks or molests children or who seeks his gratification in public. But most homosexuals are more discreet than heterosexuals and are far less predatory and violent. Persecution of the homosexual not only hurts those who have nonconventional sexual tastes, but indirectly helps to keep most males preoccupied with the need to appear virile and to engage in a somewhat aggressive form of heterosexuality.

When an increase in the population was economically desirable, there was probably some justification for imposing restrictions on those who sought sexual gratification through non-reproductive activities. With our present overpopulated world, however, such restrictions seem outmoded and detrimental. Oppression of the homosexual today is primarily maintained by the irrational fear that homosexuality threatens the stability of the society and by the irrational belief that tolerating homosexuality implies weakness.

While most psychiatrists have made repeated pleas for tolerance of homosexuality, their professional attitudes toward homosexual behavior have probably not helped the homosexual's plight. Psychiatrists insist that homosexuality should be treated as an illness,[7] yet there is no convincing evidence that the homosexual differs in any profound biological or psychological manner from the heterosexual. To assert that the homosexual is ill helps to convince both the individual and the public that he cannot control his behavior; this has a detrimental effect on both parties. The homosexual who believes that he is ill feels more driven and less responsible, and the public comes to assume that at any time he can be overwhelmed by a monstrous lust. Both parties are victims of a myth because the homosexual urge is no more powerful or irresistible than the heterosexual urge.

[7] Socarides, C. *The Overt Homosexual.* New York: Grune & Stratton, 1968.

Describing the homosexual as sick has other repressive consequences. When placed in a medical category, the homosexual is usually diagnosed as a sexual deviate, the same category that applies to rapists, child molesters, and sadists. Since the public tends to view all sex deviates as violent, it assumes that the homosexual is potentially violent. Thus, the psychiatric diagnosis leads to restrictions being placed on the homosexual that may be as severe as those placed on the rapist or murderer.

Psychiatrists should frankly acknowledge that they have no way of knowing whether homosexual behavior has enough biological or genetic determinants to justify calling it a disease. Nor is there any justification, even in terms of social expediency, for thinking of consenting adult homosexuality as an illness. The most that psychiatrists can say is that homosexuals, either because of their biological makeup or because of an eccentric learning experience, have failed to develop sustaining sexual attachments to members of the opposite sex and may be attracted to members of the same sex. This behavior should be considered a problem only if the homosexual wants to see it as a problem. The homosexual who is not predatory, who does not bother children, and who is discreet should never be described as a sick person. He should only be thought of as a potential patient if he wants to be a patient.

OPPRESSION OF WOMEN

Women generally have second-class status in the United States, as well as elsewhere. There is no way of knowing if there is something in woman's psychological nature that makes her content to take a passive or submissive position vis-à vis men, or if she has been forced into this role because of social needs or circumstances. At one time there was a rationale for confining women to a secondary position. When the ability to secure food and provide shelter were largely dependent upon physical strength, men could contribute more to the community than women. But in our modern technological society physical strength has become a relatively unimportant factor in survival, and there is no apparent rational purpose served by keeping women in a repressed condition.

The tendency of men to enjoy dominating women is quite understandable. So long as women are discouraged from establishing themselves in the business, academic, or political world, men are guaranteed an advantageous position from which to accumulate power and wealth. But men also have psychological reasons for fearing women as equals. If a man is to enjoy the sex act, he must have a sense of security that he is not being called upon to perform at a certain level and that he is not being judged as to his sexual abilities. Without this security he may have difficulty maintaining an erection. So long as women are viewed as second-class citizens, the male need not be too preoccupied with his potency. But if women are equal partners in sexual and other social relations, the male, particularly if he is insecure about his own status, is likely to feel on trial during the sex act. His fear of impotency is especially great at the present time because scientific research has shown that women are capable of enjoying sex as much as,

and sometimes even more than, men. It is not too surprising, therefore, to find that even males who are committed to many other forms of human liberation are not too sympathetic toward women's attempts at liberation.

The writings and teachings of psychiatry have helped to provide a rationale for keeping women in a subservient position. The founders of psychoanalysis saw women as basically masochistic and passive—as needing a certain degree of masculine domination in order to feel comfortable and whole. Many outstanding psychiatrists still refer to women in terms of their needs for passivity, to be companions to men, or to be mothers; [8] little mention is made of their need to be active contributors to the larger society. A woman who enters psychotherapy will usually be exposed to a system of values that emphasizes the virtues of passivity; if she rejects these values her therapist may interpret her attitude as immature.

Sometimes the psychiatric view of the psychological needs of women seems to be suspiciously formulated on the assumption of male superiority.[9] For years most psychiatrists and psychoanalysts rigidly held to the doctrine that there was a major difference between clitoral and vaginal orgasms. It was assumed that a woman could not enjoy a vaginal orgasm until she was mature and that her maturity could not be evidenced by her willingness to be submissive and passive. Although the research of Masters and Johnson

[8] Fenichel, O. *Psychoanalytic Theory of the Neuroses.* New York: Norton, 1945.
[9] Koedt, A. "The Myth of the Vaginal Orgasm." *The Radical Therapist* 1 (1970): 6–7.

showed that there is no biological difference between a vaginal and a clitoral orgasm, the teachings of psychiatrists still significantly affect society.[10] Even today some women who experience powerful orgasms through clitoral manipulation but infrequent orgasms during intercourse worry that they may be defective or inadequate.

The repressive attitude of psychiatrists toward women is also apparent in their views on multiple orgasms. For many years, psychiatrists doubted that women could have more than one orgasm during an ordinary period of lovemaking, but when Kinsey reported that some of his subjects frequently experienced multiple orgasms, they insisted that his subjects were either emotionally ill or lying.[11] Not until Masters and Johnson conclusively demonstrated that normal women commonly experience multiple orgasms did psychiatrists reluctantly concede that women (at least in their capacity to experience orgasm) were sexually more powerful than men.[12] Perhaps if male psychiatrists had listened to their patients (or their wives), they would have known better.

We do not really know if women are better off psychologically if they take a secondary role to man or if they have a role as an equal. Unfortunately, psychiatrists have not helped to clarify the situation; by accepting prevailing belief systems of the community and by strengthening them with psychological interpretations, psychiatrists have deterred society from examining this issue objectively. Perhaps, as Freud has suggested,[13] "anatomy is destiny" and women will always be unhappy if they are not at last partially dominated by men. But if he does not wish to be an oppressor himself, the psychiatrist should be willing to allow his women patients a fair chance to experiment with more aggressive and, conceivably, more fulfilling patterns of behavior.

THE POOR AND THE BLACK

Oppression of the poor and the black is one of the tragic realities of American life. At first glance the psychiatric profession's record in dealing with these groups looks good: with rare exceptions psychiatrists have emphasized that social discrimination and prejudice—rather than innate weakness or illness—are the main causes of the unhappiness of both groups. However, the profession has also taken an implied negative stand toward these people by ignoring their mental health needs. By failing to uncover, dramatize, or treat the problems of poverty-stricken or minority groups, the psychiatrist has made it easier for society to ignore their problems. Furthermore, even with a growing awareness of the susceptibility of oppressed groups to emotional disorders, psychiatrists still tend to assume that these people cannot be helped with

[10] Masters, W. H., and Johnson, V. E. *Human Sexual Response.* Boston: Little, Brown, 1966.

[11] Kinsey, A. C.; Pomeroy, W. B.; Martin, C. E.; and Gebhard, P. H. *Sexual Behavior in the Human Female.* Philadelphia: Saunders, 1953.

[12] Brecher, R., and Brecher, E. *An Analysis of Human Sexual Response.* Boston: Little, Brown, 1966.

[13] Freud, S. *Some Psychological Consequences of the Anatomical Distinction Between the Sexes.* Collected Papers, vol. 5, edited by J. Strachey. London: Hogarth Press, 1950.

the most highly valued varieties of psychiatric treatment. It is deplorable enough that psychiatrists do not offer the poor the same quality of treatment that they offer the affluent; [14] it is even worse when, in situations where ability to pay is not a crucial factor, psychiatrists tend to offer more prestigious (and perhaps more liberating) treatments, such as psychotherapy, to middle- or upper-class people and to use potentially repressive treatments, such as drug and other somatic therapy, to lower-class people. This practice is reinforced by the psychiatrist's tendency to label lower-class people as schizophrenic—a diagnosis that reflects hopelessness, that implies the patient cannot communicate rationally, and that can be used to justify treatments that do not require much doctor-patient communication.

Psychiatrists who are well educated and have been raised in middle- or upper-class environments will obviously have some difficult communicating with a relatively uneducated client. This probably accounts for much of their reluctance to treat the poor person with therapies that require verbal interaction and expansion of awareness. Many psychiatrists seem to have a subtle kind of prejudice toward lower-class persons, which increases the probability that they will treat such patients with nonverbal techniques. It is sometimes alleged that lower-class people are too impulsive, too eager for immediate gratification, or too simple-minded for psychotherapy; therefore, psychiatrists are more likely to talk *to* rather than *with*

these people. There is an implied assumption of class superiority here. In dealing with the poor, the psychiatrist tends to assume the authoritarian role of the patrician or benefactor (a role more common to the non-psychiatric physician), rather than the egalitarian role he usually adopts with patients of his own class.

The psychiatrist often has similar attitudes toward black patients; he rarely selects them for psychotherapy, and he is more likely to give them a diagnosis that will allow him to treat them with repressive therapies and keep them at a distance. Recently it has been fashionable to classify delinquent youth on the basis of whether sociological or psychological factors seem to be the main determinants of their antisocial behavior.[15] The so-called social delinquent is assumed to need education and a change in his value systems, whereas the neurotic delinquent is usually assumed to be under great psychological stress and to need some kind of psychotherapy. Implied in this classification is the belief that the neurotic delinquent is more unhappy and more fragile than the social delinquent. In my work in institutions for delinquent children I have noted an insidious tendency to view black children as social delinquents far more often than white children. In fact, in some institutions it is still extremely rare for a black child to be given psychotherapy, even though white children from the same socioeconomic background are more readily given such tratment. As in the case of the poor, much of this discrimina-

---

14 Hollingshead, A. B., and Redlich, F. C. *Social Class and Mental Illness.* New York: Wiley, 1958.

15 Jenkins, R. "Adaptive and Maladaptive Delinquency." *The Nervous Child* 11 (1955): 9–11.

tion can be accounted for because of communication difficulties between blacks and whites. But in their attitudes and practices, psychiatrists seem to accept and perpetuate the myth that black children do not suffer as much as white children.

Psychiatrists should try to learn more about the problems of those who are oppressed because of poverty or skin color and stop perpetuating the myth that these people are unresponsive to certain forms of treatment. They should try to understand the poor and the black and treat them at least as well as the affluent white. If white psychiatrists who were raised in middle-class homes are unable to provide psychotherapy to those with markedly different origins and upbringings, they should help train therapists from poor or black families who can identify with and treat the problems of these groups.

THE ELDERLY

Because of modern medicine and public health measures, the number of people who are living beyond their sixth decade has greatly increased. Millions of Americans who are now retired have few responsibilities except to keep themselves alive and entertained as they approach the certainties of illness and death. It would seem that our country would want to treat these people with special kindness, but this is not the case. There is no role for older people in our rapidly changing society, no work, no sense of usefulness, and little dignity.

Those who are both old and poor are among the most wretched: nearly isolated and bored, they are practically hidden in our ghettoes and rural communities. Even those with money face formidable stresses: many people who reach a certain age and can afford to do so go to live in a retirement community, which may be of great wealth or of limited comfort. In either case, it is an isolated community; a visit to such a community or even to certain sections of a retirement state such as Florida or Arizona can be rather depressing. One sees thousands of old people with nothing to do and with no sense of purpose. Deprived of close contact with their families, they seem to wander through a series of aimless distractions as they await death.

The psychiatrist who interprets the misery of the elderly as an illness helps to perpetuate a vicious form of oppression. It is commonly assumed that people will naturally become more depressed as they grow older. Failing strength, illness, and the fear of death—all of which are associated with aging—are indeed formidable stresses, but there is absolutely no evidence that these stresses inevitably cause depression. If the elderly person has an important place in society, he can live with grace and dignity. To assume that aging is itself a major cause of depression may well be a social myth. But if the psychiatrist treats the unhappiness of the older person as an illness, he may help to justify society's unwillingness to treat that person decently.

The association of aging with illness has almost come to be taken for granted. A recent advertisement in a medical journal pictured a sad-faced elderly man and noted that he was about to go to a party to celebrate his retirement. The ad said that retirement was a great moment for this man, even though he would probably not sleep well that night and might frequently be depressed in the days to come, and it advised the physician of the importance of proper medication at such a crucial point in a patient's life. This advertisement illustrates the destructive manner in which medical treatment is used to justify oppression: the ad does not suggest that the psychiatrist or physician has any responsibility to help his patient find a more acceptable social role during his retirement, nor does it criticize or recognize the oppressiveness of a society that allows its elderly citizens to become useless and lonely.

Instead of merely treating the depression of elderly citizens, perhaps the psychiatrist should try to identify those factors that contribute to a decent and happy old age and those that help to make old age a nightmare. He should feel obligated not only to care for the victims of a brutal process, but to prevent this process from becoming worse.

A FURTHER NOTE ON THE USE OF PSYCHIATRIC PRONOUNCEMENTS

Just about anything a psychiatrist says publicly can be used for moral or political purposes; in fact, he makes certain pronouncements for their political effect. Psychological analyses of the motivations of political figures, for example, are often designed to support or criticize a given political viewpoint. A researcher's comments about the personality of a political figure may imply a judgment of the worthiness of the causes he advocates. Most of these analyses have only a limited influence if the political figure is dead;

the researcher generally does a scholarly job of trying to understand his subject,[16] but his studies are not widely read and probably influence only a small, academically oriented audience.

The really significant psychiatric analyses deal with living political figures. Although some psychiatrists have been willing to comment on the motivations and emotional stability of such a person, their comments are usually not based on a scholarly examination of the person's life or on a careful study of his writings or public statements; most often they are based on the psychiatrist's own political biases. Perhaps the most unfortunate political use of psychiatry occurred during the 1964 presidential campaign. Psychiatrists were polled by popular magazines and asked whether one of the candidates was emotionally fit to be president. A large number of psychiatrists went on record to say the candidate was either fit or unfit. It seems that these psychiatrists were willing to use their position to influence the election even if it meant forgoing their scientific mandate to examine a patient before diagnosing him. Many psychiatrists expressed alarm over the willingness of some of their colleagues to make quasi-medical judgments on the basis of political prejudices; in this case, their alarm seems justified.

Up to this point my description of the psychiatrist's political influence can be viewed as an inevitable consequence of his effort to help patients. While that influence is important, it arises from benevolent and humanitarian motivations. If

16 See, for example, Erikson, E. H. *Gandhi's Truth.* New York: Norton, 1969.

psychiatrists lost their political power, many patients would be hurt. However, an entirely different situation arises when political figures who are not seeking and would not be likely to receive psychiatric help are analyzed by psychiatrists who would not even want to help them. These psychiatrists are exhibiting no humanitarian purpose; they are merely exploiting their medical position without even a pretense of helpfulness. It might, of course, be argued that some political figures might become so disturbed (for example, Adolf Hitler) that the psychiatrist would have a moral mandate to publicize that disturbance. But in a sophisticated society where information is generally accessible, such professional intervention would probably not be necessary. Gross disturbances in public figures could be detected by ordinary citizens as well as by psychiatrists who had not examined them.

Even if the psychiatrist is not aware of his political or moral motivations, his public pronouncements may still have a significant impact upon the status quo. Groups advocating a particular political or moral position will use any kind of psychiatric statement, written or spoken, to support their viewpoint. Several years ago I wrote a paper comparing the virginity rates in college girls who were psychiatric patients with those who were not.[17] I found that the girls who were patients were far less likely to be virgins than those who were not, and I speculated on the meaning of this relationship. In the course of my theorizing, I noted

17 Halleck, S. L. "Sex and Mental Health on the Campus." *Journal of the American Medical Association* 200 (1967): 684–690.

some of the potential psychological hazards of female promiscuity. The popularity of my paper has somewhat dismayed me. I have received thousands of requests for reprints; many teachers have asked for permission to use the article in sex education courses. It has also been reproduced in several journals and books. Not surprisingly, however, only certain people were enthusiastic about the contents of the article. These were usually people who had a strong commitment to premarital chastity. Yet it was not my intention to advocate premarital chastity; I was only trying to present information and raise certain questions. In this instance, I unwittingly became an agent of the status quo. To my extreme embarrassment and outrage, the article has even been used by religious leaders in my own state who are fighting to maintain laws that deny birth control information to unmarried women. These leaders believe that supplying women with contraceptive information would lead to promiscuity, and they insist that I have provided scientific evidence that promiscuity leads to mental illness. Therefore, they conclude that disseminating birth control information will increase the amount of mental illness in our country.

It is likely that comments by psychiatrists on a wide variety of issues such as sex, youth, the rights of women, or even war and peace have been used to strengthen or undermine political positions. It doesn't seem to make much difference whether the psychiatrists are aware of their political motivations or not. One critical area in which psychiatry is having an increasing influence is the issue of youthful unrest. Psychiatric and medical journals are now filled with articles that describe the psychological weaknesses of rebellious youth. Although these articles are written by men who are sympathetic to their patients, their statements are interpreted by defenders of the status quo as evidence that dissent is being generated by only a small number of abnormal individuals. Even as I was writing this chapter, a band of young hippies was charged with the spectacular murder of some prominent entertainers. The crime received considerable publicity. Predictably, physicians were called in to comment upon the hippie violence, and some of them said that the hippie style of life was conducive to violence. Many people who resent the fact that hippies question our standards of morality were delighted with these analyses; they will certainly use them as ammunition to justify oppression of even the most peaceful hippie groups.

Because any psychiatric statement inherently touches on social issues, it can be used for moral or political purposes. Since the public statements of psychiatrists necessarily involve social issues, psychiatrists need to be as well informed as possible on their topic. They can serve society best by being as honest as possible in their public presentations, by describing their political intentions wherever appropriate, and by rigorously noting the evidence upon which their opinions are based. They should be careful to explain which opinions are based on biological and social data and which are based on their community's or their own moral position.

notes on the enforcement of moral crimes

ERICH GOODE

INTRODUCTION: LAW, POWER AND SUBCULTURES

The basic nature of society has been debated hotly for millenia, and still a central question in this debate is the tension between society as an integrated unit and society as a mosaic

Previously unpublished.

of disparate units. While Enlightenment philosophers posited a "natural harmony of interests," Marx and later marxist thinkers held that capitalist society was composed of classes whose interests were inherently antagonistic, that society was split apart by a radical dissensus in ideology, world outlook, culture, and interest-group formation. Although a generation ago sociologists of a structural-functionalist persuasion emphasized society's unity through "common values" and concentrated mainly on the cohesive and integrative "functions" of man's social behavior, today's social theorists accept a more fractious view of the character of society's subunits. Although it is a truism (and perhaps a tautology) that at least some minimal degree of cohesion is necessary for a society to survive, it is an empirical question, therefore testable, as to how much actually obtains. Moreover, it is necessary to spell out some of the alternate modes of keeping society together, if a high degree of value consensus is lacking. For instance, an early Italian sociologist, Vilfredo Pareto—curiously, one of the fathers of the functionalist school—assumed that society's heterogeneous character minimized legitimacy, and posited force and fraud as the principal methods of governing.

Every society is in varying degrees made up of disparate subcultures with competing versions of reality; the larger and more complex the society, the greater the corresponding diversity of subcultures in that society. Yet power is never distributed in any society randomly; members of some subcultures will always have more than members of others. And, *although power over someone is by definition linear and hierarchical* (Aristotelian, as it were), *subcultures are mosaic and incommensurable.* Given the diversity of subcultures, some sort of effort has to be made to neutralize effectively power challenges from members of one or another group not in power, or to legitimize the validity of one special definition of reality.

Knowing that (1) subcultural definitions of reality are largely a matter of taste, and (2) subcultures have differential access to power and social control, gives us powerful entree into the workings of the legal machinery of any society. Marx held that law and the state in capitalist society are nothing more than devices to protect the economic interests of the bourgeoisie, the ruling classes. This is a somewhat simpleminded conception of how things work, and for several reasons. Differential power and its exercise represent attempts at *moral hegemony,* rather than protection and extension of economic interests. Society is chasmically rent by large groups of individuals who simply see right and wrong in radically different ways. And many individuals have a powerful *emotional investment* in the dominance of one particular subcultural point of view. These are the "moral entrepreneurs," [1] the cultural imperialists who wish to extend their way of life to all members of society, regardless of the validity of that way of life for the others.

Moral entrepreneurs, of course, think of their work as protective in nature. They see their task as protecting society from the damaging effects of the criminal behavior, and protecting the individual committing the criminal acts from damaging himself. There is the attempt, then, to go beyond a simple prohibition of an act because it is "immoral" within the confines of a specific moral code; there is the further assertion that the act causes objec-

[1] Howard S. Becker, *Outsiders* (New York: Free Press, 1963), chs. 7 and 8.

tively agreed-upon damage to the individual transgressor himself, as well as to society at large. Yet the very perception of the act as immoral structures one's perceptions concerning the actual occurrence of the "objectively agreed-upon" damage.[2] He who believes marijuana smoking to be evil (a strictly moral premise) will also believe that it has effects on the body and mind which all will agree are damaging (an empirically verifiable statement); no one argues with the noxiousness of death, insanity, or automobile accidents, but many will question marijuana's causal role in these phenomena. There are, in addition, vast areas where total disputation will prevail over the noxiousness or benefit of certain effects of an act—such as marijuana's reputed impact on "reality distortion," or sexuality.

Subordinates in any society or social system invariably view the world in a radically different manner from the way in which the superordinates who have power over them see it. In a sense, then, hierarchies form miniature subcultures. Yet, at the some time, hierarchies are inherently distributions of power. There is, in any organization, society, or social grouping, a "hierarchy of credibility."[3] That is, those at the top—in terms of prestige and designated authority—are taken more seriously than those at the bottom, who are subject to their power. A prisoner and a prison guard have radically different conceptions of the prison

system, but in the hierarchy of credibility, the guard's version will be accepted as impartial, while the prisoner's will be viewed as exaggerated, fanciful, and biased. A patient and a psychiatrist, a child and a parent, a confessor and a priest, a pupil and a teacher, are all implicated in the web of credibility, and society has decided in advance whose definition of the situation it will give greater weight. It is taken for granted that certain status-occupants or individuals in any society or organization "have a right" to tell others about the nature of the universe which they both inhabit. Yet this world vision inculcation is of a specific perspective, the acceptance of which will invariably advantage those in power, to the detriment of their subordinates.

DIFFERENTIAL LAW ENFORCEMENT

Although their public stance toward most moral crimes is characteristically punitive in private, law enforcement officers will not infrequently claim that they have no special stake in the execution of these laws; they enforce them because they would be remiss in their duties if they did not. It is the voter, after all, and not the policeman, who is responsible for the prevailing situation, since he elected the present lawmakers who keep the illegal status of the activity on the books. This plea is unacceptable as it stands, however, and for a number of powerful empirical reasons. (The *moral* argument, that a man must act only as his conscience dictates, and must refuse to participate in any activities which are morally repug-

[2] For a detailed discussion of this point, see Erich Goode, "Marijuana and the Politics of Reality," *Journal of Health and Social Behavior* 10 (June, 1969).

[3] Howard S. Becker, "Whose Side Are We On?" *Social Problems* 14 (Winter, 1967), 239–47.

nant to him—Eichmann, after all, presented the same defense as our hypothetical law-enforcement officer —is compelling, but irrelevant for our present purposes.) Law enforcement in regard to any moral crime is largely purposeful. The formal legal machinery of a given society, law as it obtains "on the books," exists only as a potentiality for actual effective sanctioning. Laws prevail which are never activated, and, conversely, punishment is administered by the agencies of social control where no law has been breached. The relationship between law and sanction is systematic, not random, but it obeys a logic of nonrational custom, rather than blind justice. The translation of formal law into living sanction is a problematic execution, but it is one which obeys definite sociological laws. The breach of some laws engenders widespread moral outrage; the *enforcement* of others incurs that same public wrath—although the personnel of the latter public will differ from that of the former.

To begin with, some laws are rarely or never invoked. To mention only a few unenforced sex laws in the United States, in Indiana and Wyoming, it is criminal to *encourage* a person to masturbate. In forty-five states, adultery is illegal, and Connecticut calls for a five year imprisonment upon prosecution. Mere fornication is a crime in thirty-eight states, and a breach of this law theoretically brings forth a fine of $500 or two years imprisonment, or both.[4] Many states dictate the manner in which one may make love to one's

spouse—cunnilingus and fellatio, for instance, are criminalized in more than a few legal jurisdictions.[5] In view of the near-universality of the first of these activities—at least, among men—and the fact that a majority of all couples marrying today have engaged in premarital intercourse, the virtual absence of any prosecution for these crimes is remarkable. Although sanctioning all crimes without victims entails severe logistical detection problems, with adultery at least, a fertile field exists for detection—divorce suits. In New York State, where until very recently adultery was the only legitimate grounds for divorce, thousands of divorces have been filed and granted in the past few years, yet no one is ever prosecuted for the crime of adultery.[6] (The penalty in New York State is $250 in fine or 6 months in prison, or both.)

In fact, it might be fruitful to look at police arrests in terms of the "arrest potential" of the citizen. Clearly, there inhere in the citizen— as a result of the reading process applied by the policeman—a number of characteristics, or factors, which pertain to the likelihood of his be-

[4] For these penalties, see Samuel G. Kling, *Sexual Behavior and the Law* (New York: Bernard Geis and Random House, 1965), pp. 251, 15–17, 26–28.

[5] In partial contradiction to the general point concerning differential enforcement, *Playboy* magazine publishes large numbers of letters from men in prison who were convicted of these crimes; our surprise at their legal status is surpassed only by our discovery that anyone has ever been sanctioned for them.

[6] Even the occasional exceptions illustrate our points. A recent case in a rural area of Vermont involving alleged adultery between a married Black man and a divorced white woman demonstrates the need of a community to punish an activity which is legal (interracial socializing) in the guise of invoking an illegal activity (adultery). For the case, see *Life* 66 (April 4, 1969), 62–74.

ing arrested. One of these factors obviously pertains to the commission of a crime; law-breakers are more likely to be arrested than those who do not break the law, and those who break the law often increase their chances correspondingly. But since all of us are law-breakers, in that we have all committed some serious offense at some time in our lives, this factor is minor. Far more significant is the role of what might be called "ancillary characteristics." Certain kinds of citizen characteristics are more likely to *attract arrest* than others. The Black man is always and everywhere under greater suspicion than the white; the police are differentially alerted to offenses along racial lines. What is read as an offense by a Black will often be ignored if committed by a white. Crime involves the intervention of a perceptual screen. Crimes are not committed—their very existence is called into being by being selectively perceived. *Crimes are created by the perception process.* In order to know about the nature of crime, we must know at least as much about the characteristics of the agents of social control as about the citizens from who, supposedly, crimes spring.

Thus, one of the key elements in the selective reading process of the legality or illegality of a man's behavior—in the *criminalization* of the behavior of others—lies in the face-to-face interaction between policeman and citizen. Regardless of the *formal* legal status of the citizenry's behavior, the policeman is primed to react *differentially* to the *same* behavior from different representatives of the citizenry. In one man's gestures, the police read "probable cause" for investigation; the same

gesture from a different man elicit only indifference. The statement made to the civil rights lawyer, Paul Chevigny by a policeman, referring to hippies, "I wish one of these characters would make a false move, so I could plug him," [7] illustrates the differential response potential of the law enforcement agencies to behavior of the same kind from actors of a variable composition. A more formal phrasing of the same principle underscores our point: "Does not a furtive movement in one part of town constitute probable cause, where the same movement would not in another?" "Can we afford to structure the system to protect persons living in ambiguous situations?" [8] The tactical issues aside, it is clear that an elaborate "reading" process occurs whereby the behavior of certain segments of the citizenry is more closely scrutinized, and criminal potential is interpreted in their ambiguous behavior, whereas the same behavior is ignored if enacted by different segments of the populace.

The possibility of law enforcement officers detecting an illegal act in private involves both legal and logistical questions. Yet the sociological factors in the equation are at least as consequential. Not only do the police operate within a context of "probable cause"; they also take into consideration probable *consequence*. As any account of police work makes clear, many arrests fol-

[7] Paul Chevigny, *Police Power: Police Abuses in New York City* (New York: Pantheon, 1969), p. 173.

[8] These statements were made by Professor Edward Barrett, and quoted by Skolnick, in *Justice Without Trial* (New York: John Wiley, 1966), p. 219.

low police violations of strict due process of law.[9] Police willingness to violate due process is dependent on a variety of factors. Some are clearly related to the nature of the offense—the more serious the offense, the greater the risk the officer is willing to take, and the more that the public will tolerate such violations; others are tied in with the likelihood that a specific suspect has committed the crime in question. But another set of variables encompasses the characteristics of the suspect, rather than the nature of his crime. The less the power of the suspect to retaliate, the more likely the police are to violate due process in making an arrest. For instance, homosexuals are especially vulnerable to harassment, and therefore represent a fertile locus for such violations.[10] Describing a specific case of unlawful entry, Chevigny writes:

> It is apparent that . . . the police felt less compunction about breaking into a party of obvious homosexuals than they would have felt about intruding upon another party. When outcasts are involved, the restraints on police action begin to weaken, not only those against assault, but those against unlawful entry and search as well.[11]

An equally problematic "reading" process is involved in the concept of "law and order."[12] When the cry of "law and order" is invoked, a very specific *version* of adherence to the legal code is meant, a highly *selective* conception which includes formally legal and illegal behavior alike and, conversely, excludes many forms of illegal behavior. When a political conservative calls for law and order, he understands that to mean an end to rioting and looting. He is not talking about income tax evasion or illegal monopolies, false advertising or violation of anti-discrimination statutes. He is talking about the need for respect toward policemen and law enforcement agencies, even if the duly constituted authorities are corrupt and are themselves engaged in illegal activities. The Chicago riots during the summer of 1968 illustrate this selective perception process precisely. Reference to the "lawlessness and disorder" in Chicago is automatically understood by different parties, each with his own respective political ideology, in totally different ways. Many groups, from the ACLU to *Life* magazine, labelled the riots "police riots," and held the police to be the lawbreakers. Those of a more conservative persuasion see the lawlessness located with the dissenters—most of whom, according to all reports, were violating no known law. *The perception of law-breaking is a highly contingent event, dependent on the social characteristics of the perceiver, and can in no way be taken for granted.*

---

[9] Both the Chevigny and the Skolnick books document dozens of such cases.

[10] For some peculiar reason, the police seem to find homosexuals particularly repugnant. One study showed that next to "cop fighters," the police most dislike homosexuals. See Arthur Niederhoffer, *Behind the Shield: The Police in Urban Society* (New York: Doubleday, 1967), p. 123.

[11] *Ibid.*, p. 123.

[12] To compound the confusion, "law" and "order" are not the same thing, and could conceivably vary independently. Skolnick points out that bohemians may be law-abiding but disorderly, while another group (say, members of the Mafia) may be orderly, but lawless.

The question, "Why do some people break the law?" then, must be supplemented with a number of queries concerning the implementation of the law. We must also ask, "Why are certain laws enforced, and not others?" and "What is it about the nature of a society that chooses to enforce certain kinds of laws and not others?" and "What is distinctive about the nature of those laws which are not enforced?" It should be clear, then, that law enforcement is problematic, and is itself an area which should be explored empirically.

LAW AS A RESOURCE IN MORAL HEGEMONY

Although laws exist merely as a potentiality for sanctioning, and many laws are dead in the sense that transgressors are rarely if ever punished for their breach, nonetheless, the mere fact that a norm, regardless of whether it has any general community support, has been formally crystallized into law makes a great deal of difference as to whether any given individual will be penalized for a breach of the law. Since each subculture has differential access to the formal agencies of social control, a norm can have lost legitimacy for a majority of the citizenry, and yet there will be some individuals in a position to determine and define the legal process, who continue to regard the law as just and legitimate, and are therefore able to sanction in the absence of general societal licitness. Laws and formal agencies of social control may be thought of as a *resource* in the hands of one subculture to enforce their beliefs on other, disagreeing subcultures. So powerfully is this the case that

members of a group may be punished, ostensibly for an act which is in fact illegal, but in reality for an act which is not formally illegal, but which the wielders of social control find repugnant. One clear-cut example may be found in the arena of marijuana use. Known political radicals are often arrested by evangelistic law enforcement officers who are frustrated because most forms of politically radical activity are not formally illegal.[13]

Clearly, however, most of the laws which are enforced have a high degree of moral legitimacy. But legitimacy is a matter of degree; the more widespread and deeply-held a given norm is, the greater the likelihood that its transgression will be effectively sanctioned. The moral legitimacy of a given norm can be looked at as another resource in the hands of moral entrepreneurs in punishing dissident groups.

It is of course highly relevant to consider *who* accepts the norm. The ability to translate infractions into

13 The "yippie" ideologue, Jerry Rubin, recently arrested on a marijuana possession charge by officers who emphatically acknowledged their solely political concern in the arrest, reconstructs questions directed at him by the policemen: "Why do you hate America?" "Why did you go to Cuba when your government told you not to?" "Hey don't you have any patriotic magazines, any American magazines?" In concluding his article, Rubin writes, "My case will show cops whether or not it is easy to get away with political persecution disguised as drug busts." Cf. Jerry Rubin, "The Yippies Are Going to Chicago," *The Realist*, 82 (September, 1968), 1, 21–23. See also: Don McNeil, "LBJ's Narco Plan: Lining Up the Big Guns: Crackdown on the Way?" *Village Voice* (March 14, 1968), pp. 11ff, and Irving Shusnick, "Never Trust a Man With a Beard," *East Village Other* (January 12–19, 1968), p. 4. All of these journals favor legalizing marijuana.

sanctions is differentially distributed throughout the social structure. Among some subgroups in a given society there will be a closer correspondence between their own norms and the law. Norms apply more heavily to subgroup and subculture members, but laws generally apply to all. It is likely that those groups which exhibit the greatest identity between norms (their own) and the laws are specifically those groups which have the greatest power to effect sanctions.

POLICE ENFORCEMENT OF MORAL CRIMES

The illegalization of "crimes without victims," written into formal law and implemented by arrests and prosecutions, is an effort to legislate morality. Whatever one's attitude toward legal attempts at controlling such behavior, there obtain a number of empirical sequelae of such attempts. The most obvious is, of course, that *detection* is rendered extremely difficult. There is no victim and no complainant, so that systematic surveillance techniques inherently involve a certain degree of loss of civil liberties. The success of any police venture is ringed about by various *situational* features having to do with the kinds of crimes which they are attempting to detect. For instance, it is obvious that acts conducted by two consenting adults who have a long-term relationship with one another, and who have no incentive to punish or discredit one another, conducted in privacy, are highly unlikely to be detected and sanctioned. On the other hand, acts perpetrated on many people by one person, previously unknown to them, in public, which they define as nega-

tive and hurtful, are highly likely to be detected, and the perpetrator punished for his act. Marijuana use, for instance, is clearly at the former pole of this spectrum. It is generally conducted among intimates or semi-intimates, all of whom are compliant, in private; moreover, it rarely incurs negative consequences, at least in the microcosm of the single act of smoking during a single evening.

Whenever any of the following conditions is violated, the likelihood of a moral crime coming to the attention of the police rises: (1) it takes place among individuals who are previously unknown to one another, (2) it takes place in public, (3) evidences of its use become manifest to strangers, (4) negative consequences ensue use: a fight, a psychotic episode, an automobile accident, and the possibility to trace use prior to the consequence, (5) it is forced upon someone unwilling to participate, (6) a large number of individuals are involved either simultaneously or in the same social group during the same period.

Now, given these logistic circumstances, the law enforcement agencies face a choice of sorts: the complete suppression of certain moral crimes would involve in invasion of privacy heretofore unseen in American society, but doing nothing, or maintaining a constant surveillance level in the face of rising occurrences, entails capitulation to a large-scale and serious "problem" (defined as such in police and political terms). Here is a genuine dilemma. To imagine the enormity of the chasm between a laissez-faire attitude toward infractions and one of complete suppression, let us for the moment suppose that law enforcement agencies were suddenly interested in enforcing all of the laws which actually exist concerning sodomy, cunnilingus, fellatio, and so on, between consenting adults. The surveillance demands of such a job would rival those of *1984*.

Another consequence of the "criminalization of the environment" —as Skolnick labels efforts to control conventional morality [14]—is that there is more work for the police to do.[15] The greater the number and range of activities that are defined as criminal, the more crime there will be. Laws may be looked at as the formal "cause" of crime. Without laws, crime does not exist.[16]

Further, with widespread laws against mortality, the police will view their environment as hostile and threatening.[17] The greater the scope of the law, the greater the number and range of activities that are defined as illegal, the greater the disagreement in society on the legitimacy of the legal status of a given activity, and the greater the diversity of the citizenry of a given population, the more difficult the policeman's task as he sees it, the more uncertain and defensive he will be about performing it, and the greater the psychological discomfort he will suffer from it. Enforcing a law which lacks legitimacy for large segments of the population can only create paranoia and self-righteousness in those whose task it is to enforce it. The police see "symbolic assailants" as abundant in their environment.[18]

The desire on the part of public and police to prosecute what they view as moral "undesirables" creates pressure to skirt certain legal procedures designed to protect unpopular minorities. Chevigny writes:

Morals legislation enhances the tendency of the policeman to regard members of any outcast group as potential and perhaps actual criminals. Furthermore, the simple increase in the number of crimes and the problems of controlling them strengthens the temptation to look for such shortcuts in enforcement as systematic arrest and search. Finally, the policeman is convinced by the public outcry for such legislation that the press and the citizens care less for the lawful conduct of law enforcement than for the control of antisocial behavior. Policemen . . . know that the impulse to control morality through punishment runs directly against the increasingly rigid protection of due process of law by the courts, and they recognize that any lingering public demand for due process, as compared with the de-

---

[14] Jerome H. Skolnick, *Justice Without Trial* (New York: John Wiley, 1966), p. 206.

[15] In a recent testimony to the House of Representatives, the Associate Director of the Bureau of Narcotics and Dangerous Drugs, Henry L. Giordano, explained that with the recent upsurge of marijuana use, the Bureau had to divert manpower from the enforcement of the heroin traffic to marijuana details; he requested, therefore, a larger staff and budget. See House of Representatives, Ninetieth Congress, First Session, "Extracts From Treasury-Post Office Departments and Executive Office Appropriations for 1968: Bureau of Narcotics," *Hearings Before a Subcommittee of the Committee on Appropriations* (Washington, D. C.: U. S. Government Printing Office), February 8, 1967, p. 406.

[16] Although this proposition sounds strange to the individual densely imbedded in the moral and legal norms of his society, it nonetheless has a long tradition in sociology. See, for instance, Willard Waller, "Social Problems and the Mores," *American Sociological Review*, 1 (December, 1936), 922–33.

[17] Skolnick, *op. cit.*, p. 205.

[18] *Ibid.*, pp. 45–48, 105–9, 217–18.

mand for a crime cleanup, must be largely hypocritical. Every new sumptuary crime creates a new class of criminals, and the public as well as the police believe that they must be controlled by harassment.

Also, it must be remembered that *services* are supplied in many morals crimes, services which are highly valued by some segments of the populace. For some of these services, the demand is quite inflexible —as with an addicting drug, such as heroin—which means that daring and innovative criminals willing to take the necessary risk will *inevitably* supply what is necessary. For other services, public attitude is ambivalent, as with prostitution, which is compatible with both a conservative and a permissive sexual ideology. Wherever valued goods and services are outlawed, given sufficient demand, an organization or group of individuals will supply them. The greater the amount of money involved, and the greater the similarity in background and ideology between police and suppliers, the greater the likelihood of police cooperation and and corruption.

Efforts at controlling morality also provide unlimited opportunities for police corruption. Where public demand for enforcement is perceived as being largely rhetorical, where a few massive and highly visible "clean-up campaigns" are sufficient to quell the public outcry for the implementation of morality laws, and where the public is unable to perceive breaches of morality laws, the police will experience a wide disjunction between their efforts at enforcement and public pressure. That is, there will be a scant relationship between arrest—the police

"doing their job"—and public perception thereof. The police may be flexible about enforcement, yet few negative sanctions will flow from their laxness. The more consistent the public's attitude is about the need for the enforcement about a given law, and the more in line with the policeman's own moral code— the less the police will take advantage of the possibilities for corruption.

ARREST AS A STATUS TRANSFORMATION

Legal *agencies* have the power to define legal *reality*. They can, of course, create laws and immediately "create" criminals *de novo*. But in a narrower sense, *the legal process is successful to the extent that* it either (1) compels the individual to accept society's version of himself as *in fact* criminal, i.e., criminal in more than a technical sense, a person *deserving* of society's scorn and punishment, or (2) discredits the individual in all important areas of life, illegitimates the validity of his trustworthiness, moral rectitude, and integrity, to many members of society. An arrest is able to do at least the latter. There are, of course, those for whom an arrest is a mark of honor, or at least has no moral significance. (They are in the minority, even among marijuana smokers.) But public exposure is often unavoidable in an arrest. Consequently, one's private life is subject to public scrutiny. Small minds classify your deed and the quality of your life in their terms. A search of one's premises destroys the paper-thin illusion that "A man's home is his castle." Private letters, journals, one's diary, are read for criminal implications—and one's naked soul is exposed, twitching, to the judgement of ignorant philistines. Surveillance involves encroachments of privacy.[19] Policemen rarely make the fine distinctions between uncovering necessary evidence and a wholesale invasion of privacy. In fact, they often use their legitimate monopoly on the ability to invade the privacy of a suspect (or even of an individual or individuals who are sufficiently unusual in society's eyes that a formal objection to the abuse of police powers would be futile) for their own self-interested ends.

In any case, being suspected of committing a crime, being under surveillance, having one's dwelling and/or person searched, being arrested, booked, brought to trial, and (if it comes to that) convicted, not to mention the nature of one's experiences in a penitentiary, all serve as *public degradation ceremonies.*[20]

The legal apparatus has immense power to determine the nature of a felon's *public and private presenta-*

19 In "On Being Busted at Fifty," Leslie A. Fiedler describes electronic surveillance devices being used during the ceremony of his Passover Seder. Cf. *The New York Review* (July 13, 1967), p. 12.

20 See Harold Garfinkel, "Conditions of Successful Degradation Ceremonies," *American Journal of Sociology*, 61 (March, 1956).

tion. Although this is a variable and not a constant, in all likelihood, he sees himself as a man who has done something which is technically against the law, but which in no way qualifies him for a criminal status, for "true" criminality. He may not see himself as being "a criminal." Nor does society, not knowing about his crimes. Marijuana users often state that they "don't think of marijuana use as a crime." But going through the legal procedure impresses in the mind of the offender the view that one powerful segment of society (and perhaps, by extension, society in general) has of his activity's legality; he cannot, after that, view it in the same blithe light.

In other words, the elaborate legal procedure, and its attendant social implications, serve as a kind of *dramaturgic rite de passage,* which serves to transform the transgressor publicly into a criminal, into "the kind of person who would do such a thing." Although many going through the ritual will reject the definition of them imposed by the process, it nonetheless leaves its impress, particularly the more broadly the representatives of the legal machinery interpret their role and the greater the power and discretion they are permitted.

Students and
the Youth Culture

7

As the tranquil fifties gave way to the turbulent sixties, Joe College and his classmates around the industrialized world became involved in national and international politics more so than ever before in this century. Their interests shifted from intra-mural sports to international relations, from the dating, rating, mating game to the dissent, disobedience, confrontation game, from Greek letter societies, to societies run by unlettered Greeks, from phone numbers in little black books, to sayings in little red books. All this, quite unexpected, quite without warning, but quite undeniable. Unexpected because conditions which politicize student consciousness and promulgate revolt were absent, and conditions which inhibit them, were present.

On the absent list were the following: (1) students should see themselves as the future elite of their country, (2) their education should be philosophically broad, not vocationally specific so they cannot be easily integrated into the economy, (3) their universities should be vanguards of modern consciousness and turn them against worn-out institutions, and (4) they should experience, in their own lives, the new direction of their societies as it is reflected in their own move from a traditional extended kinship system, based on an etiquette of particularism, to a modern, segmented university, based on an etiquette of universalism.

Of course, the opposite is more nearly the case. Students do not see themselves as the future governing elites of their country. Universities provide vocational, technical, professional training to the neglect of inquiries into broader, normative issues; the atmosphere they generate is anything but conducive to progressive, critical, and radical consciousness. And, the traditional extended kinship system lost its pre-eminence well over a generation ago. So, the historical conditions which foster revolt were absent. Moreover, the structural conditions which inhibit revolt were present.

For example, student status is of short duration, thus a consistent organizational base is lacking; students are young and short on political skills and experience; they lack financial resources, do not enjoy the full measure of civil rights accorded adults, have virtually no informal access to decision-makers, and offer no strategic services which can be withheld in strike action. From every point of view, students are weak on resources. Yet student consciousness is high and there has been, and probably will continue to be, student revolt. Why? How?

Prominent among the immediate causes of revolt, at least according to Richard Flacks and Philip Slater, is the startling clarity with which the students see the difference between the reality that *is* and the reality that *could be*. They see an abundance of wealth coupled with an ideology of scarcity—an ideology based on an obsolete premise which nevertheless encourages competition, possessiveness, status aggrandisement, alienated labor, and an impoverished sensual and aesthetic life. They see an official legitimization of structured inequality, the priority of property over life, and the accumulation of dead possessions concomitant with the trivialization of live relationships. They see a culture they cannot relate to. In consequence, bourgeois students revolt against a bourgeois society which, in its own terms, works.

But even if students see the disparity between what is and what could be, what prepared them to see things this way? How did students come to define the society they live in as inimical to the interests of its members? The answer, at least as Flacks formulates it, is less than dramatic. Simply put, children learn from their parents, so it all depends on who the student's parents are.

The leaders of student protests in America turn out to be academically gifted people who attend the very best schools and come from financially secure families. Their parents are highly educated, politically alert, and hold jobs outside the mainstream business economy. They raised their children to have a strong commitment to intellectuality, culture, education, self-development, political liberalism, social responsibility and active citizenship. They taught them to be skeptical about middle-class attitudes, life style, religion, sexual repressiveness, materialism, status striving, etc. With this kind of upbringing, the children did not adjust easily to conventional peer group relationships or excessively rigid classrooms. Uneasy in, and rebuffed by, these conventional institutions, the young began the long march down the road to the counterculture. They and their culture emerged full-blown on the campus in the early sixties.

Yet, despite the upbringing which sharpened their perception, and the counterculture which implemented it, how did they launch their protest, given a nonexistent set of material resources?   The sense one gets from A. Belden Field's analysis of this anomaly is that the students turned their weaknesses into strengths.   Transitory student status, coupled with lack of political and organizational skills, gave rise to a strategy of decentralized, non-bureaucratized spontaneity—a strategy that a centralized, bureaucratized officialdom could cope only with in a manner that would disclose its monopoly on fire power.   The students capitalized on the only resource they could depend upon—their own bodies.   The students *reacted* to massively inept governmental policy by direct confrontation of officials.   Officials reacted with force, students were beaten, non-student segments of the population sympathized with them, and an incipient anti-regime attitude began to crystallize.   An air of unrest produced dissension within the regime; officials were fired, responsibilities shifted, and top people isolated within their own ranks.   Outside the regime the political unrest affected international relations and stock markets; large investors, bankers, and corporations put pressure on the regime to "cool it."   The regime modified those policies which were in direct violation of the formal values of the society and which brought the students out in the first place.

Although this scenario is not refined, it does seem to fit the French, German, and American experiences.   It is a strategy which makes a strength of weakness and exacts a very high price from its proponents—their bodies. Apparently the cost does not appear to them excessive.   Its major virtue is that it works; and there is no greater incentive for future repetition than past success.   To the degree that government regimes realize that the students have a winning strategy, perhaps it will work as a deterrent.   Perhaps massively stupid policies will be sifted out before their operationalization places the entire regime in jeopardy.   Neither DeGaulle nor Johnson understood the strategy they were up against, or, if they did, they could not beat it. Both lost their regimes when neither had to.

social and cultural meanings of student revolt: some informal comparative observations

RICHARD FLACKS

The phenomenon of student rebellion has in the past few years come to appear international in scope. During this period, student demonstrations and strikes have paralyzed universities and shaken the political systems in societies as far apart, culturally and geographically, as Japan and France, Mexico and West Germany, Italy and Brazil, Czechoslovakia and the United States.

The simultaneity of these outbursts and the similarities in style and tactics of the student movements have led many observers to assume that there is a world-wide revolt of the youth, which is new historically, and which derives from a single set of causes.

It is obvious, however, that student movements, acting in opposition to established authority, are not at all new. For example, student revolutionary activity was a constant feature of Russian life during the 19th century. It played a major role in the revolution of 1848 in Central Europe. The communist movements in China and Vietnam grew out of militant student movements in those countries. In Latin America, student movements have been politically crucial since the early part of this century. Youth and student movements were a dramatic feature of life in pre-World War Germany; the Zionist movement among European Jews had its roots in the German youth movement. Since World War II, student movements have helped bring down regimes in Asia and Latin America. It is clear that the events of recent months are in certain respects merely further expressions of a long tradition of student rebelliousness (Cf. Altbach, 1967, for an overview of this tradition).

But just as it would be a mistake to think that the student revolts are historically new, it would also be an error to uphold the conventional wisdom which asserts that youth are "naturally" rebellious, or idealistic. There are, of course, good reasons for believing that some segments of the youth are likely to be particularly disposed to revolt, particularly attracted to new ideas, particularly prepared to take direct action in behalf of their ideals. But it is by no means true that rebellious, experimental, or idealistic behavior is a general characteristic of young people—indeed, it is probably the case that in any historical period the majority of the young, as Bennett Berger has remarked, are not "youthful." Moreover, it is even less true that youthful impulses in support of

Reprinted from Richard Flacks, "Social and Cultural Meanings of Student Revolt: Some Informal Comparative Observations," SOCIAL PROBLEMS, 17 (Winter, 1970) by permission of the author and the Society for the Study of Social Problems.

radical change inevitably take the form of distinct, autonomous political movements against the established political system. For instance, such movements have been quite rare in the U.S. and other advanced Western countries until the present decade. Although significant minorities of students and other young people have been active participants in movements for social change in the U.S., Britain, France, and the smaller capitalist democracies, these societies have not had movements created by and for youth, independent of adult organizations, containing a strong element of rebellion not only against injustice but against the authority of the older generation. The feeling that there is something new about generational revolt is not accurate in global terms; but it is substantially correct for societies like our own.

There is a need for a theoretical framework to account for the emergence of oppositional movements among youth—a framework which can embrace the fact that such movements have become a feature, not only of developing pre-industrial societies, but of apparently stable advanced industrial nations as well. In searching for such a framework, two classical theoretical perspectives might be expected to provide some help. One would be Marxian theory, which, after all, was created in an effort to account for the rise of revolutionary movements in contemporary society. But Marxism, since it emphasizes the role of classes as revolutionary agencies, has a difficult time assimilating student revolutionary action. First, students do not themselves constitute a class. Second, students do occupy class positions, but these are typically privi-

leged ones. Indeed, one fact about the American student movement is that participation in it tends to be associated with high family status and income (Westby and Braungart, 1966; Flacks, 1970), and the same pattern may be found in other countries as well. Thus, a problem for Marxian theory of revolution would be to account for the mass defection of students from their families' class, and for the tendency of privileged youth to identify with the plight of the dispossessed in their society. This is particularly problematical in the advanced industrial societies: here we have a situation in which at the present time organized political and cultural opposition to capitalism appears to be more extensive and militant among students than among workers. There is no straightforward way to derive this fact from the body of Marxian theory.

A second theoretical perspective which one might find useful is that of Parsons. Indeed, one of the few theories about the conditions giving rise to generational conflict is that of Eisenstadt (1956) whose perspective flows directly from Parsons (Cf. Parsons, 1962, for a recent formulation).

This perspective focusses less on the revolutionary thrust of student and youth movements than on their functional character. What is most salient to Parsons and Eisenstadt is the formation of distinctive groups or movements among persons at the same stage in the life-cycle. The appearance of such groupings among youth is seen as a consequence of the differentiation of the family from the occupational structure, resulting in a sharp discontinuity between the values and role-expectations operative within the family and those prevailing in the larger society. As youth move out of the family and experience such discontinuities, major problems of socialization are created by the necessity for them to successfully orient toward occupational roles. Such problems are not manageable within the family, nor within the institutions of formal schooling. What is needed are institutions which can combine some of the features of family life with those of the occupational structure. Youth groups, youth cultures, and youth movements serve this function of aiding the transition to adulthood by combining relations of diffuse solidarity with universalistic values.

This perspective predicts that the sharper the disjunction between family values and those in the larger society, the more distinctive and oppositional will be the youth culture. In particular, one would expect that students in societies undergoing a rapid breakdown of traditional authority, and in which new bases of legitimation had not yet been established, would most acutely experience problems of achieving adult status and would be most likely to form autonomous, oppositional movements. By the same token, young people in the advanced, stable, industrial, democratic societies, although experiencing marked discontinuity between familial and occupational roles, would not experience the same intense cultural dislocation found in developing countries. For, although familial and occupational roles are disjunctive in advanced industrial countries, families in these societies tend to be congruent in their values and expectations with other institutions. Thus the industrialized societies would exhibit distinctive youth cultures, but these

implicitly support other socializing agencies in identity formation and orientation toward adulthood. In short, the Parsons-Eisenstadt perspective leads us to expect student movements in societies where traditional authority is disintegrating under the impact of industrialization, Western ideas, and modernizing trends, and where families continue to adhere to traditional culture. Depicting industrial societies as ones in which both parental and political authority support modernity and change, this perspective leads us to expect a distinctive youth culture, but not an "alienated" oppositional, revolutionary one in societies like our own (Eisenstadt, 1956; Parsons, 1962).

As I have suggested, this perspective was a viable one—until this decade. Now each passing year makes it less and less easy to assume the stability of the developed western societies, less and less safe to adopt the view that the U.S. represents some culmination point in cultural development, or that there is a fundamental congruence among socializing, political and economic institutions and the values which prevail within them in our society.

A comparative perspective on student movements and generational revolt leads us to seek a theoretical framework which transcends the Marxism view of the sources of revolutionary impulse in capitalist society, and the Parsonian view that such impulses are not characterisic of advanced industrial society. If such a framework existed it would undoubtedly constitute a synthesis of Eisenstadt's insight that student movements are a symptom of cultural disintegration and the Marxian insight that capitalism and its culture are themselves unstable and capable of being negated.

II

If recent events lead us to discard the view that student movements are characteristic only of societies in which traditional culture and authority are breaking down, we nevertheless ought to be able to specify why such movements have been endemic under such conditions. The Parsons-Eisenstadt hypothesis provides us with at least a partial answer: the university student in an agrarian society is someone who is compelled to abandon the values with which he was raised, who is exposed to a set of new cultural influences, but who is becoming an adult in an historical period in which the new values have not been clarified, new roles have not been created, new authority has not been established or legitimated. The student movement, with its diffuse, fraternal interpersonal life, its identification with the masses of the people, its disdain for privilege and authority—combined with a commitment to rationalism, democracy, nationalism and other "modern" values —enables them to develop the political skills and motives which may be necessary to challenge the established elites, enables them to undergo the personal transition which is an aspect of the historical transition through which the whole society is going.

In addition to this hypothesis, which locates the sources of "strain" in the cultural and psychological consequences of modernization, there are additional and equally powerful factors at work in such societies which make such movements extremely likely. (A summary of such factors appears in Lipset, 1968.)

There is, for example, the widely remarked fact that typically in developing countries there is an "overproduction" of educated youth—the available jobs for university graduates often are not commensurate with the training or aspirations they have as a result of their educational attainment. Prospective or actual unemployment, and the frustration of aspiration, is presumably a politicizing experience for many educated youth in such societies.

Another politicizing and radicalizing feature of these societies is the backwardness and authoritarianism of political authority. Political authority in these societies plays a paradoxical role for students; on the one hand, it sponsors the formation and expansion of a university system in order to promote technical progress, while simultaneously it resists the political, social, and cultural transformations which such progress requires. In this situation, students inevitably come into conflict with the state and other established elite institutions. The more intransigent the established elites are with respect to nationalist, democratic, and modernizing aspirations, the more likely it is that the student movement becomes the breeding ground for a "counter-elite" and the spearhead of revolutionary politics (Ben-David and Collins, 1967).

Still another factor likely to generate discontent is the quality of life in the universities of these societies. Living and working conditions are likely to be extremely impoverished. The schools are likely to be overflowing; the quality of instruction and facilities for study are likely to be totally inadequate; and material poverty among students is likely to be substantial.

If cultural disintegration, overproduction of the educated, reactionary regimes, and university conditions generate discontent leading to politicization and radicalism, additional factors promote the emergence and growth of autonomous student movements in developing nations. For example, the autonomous character of student movements in these countries is facilitated by the absence of other oppositional forces. To the extent that peasants, workers and other strata are poorly organized or passive or suppressed, students, with their high degree of interaction and their sophistication may become the only group in a society capable of initiating oppositional activity. Moreover, students may have a degree of freedom for political action which is not available to other opposition forces. This freedom may in part be due to the fact that many student activists are the offspring of elite or upper status families, in part because of the recognition of the fact that students are indispensable to the future of the society, in part because of an established tradition of university autonomy which makes it illegitmate for police power to invade the campus. Given the relative leniency toward students and the ambivalence of authorities toward them, instances of repressive action taken against students are likely to be especially discrediting to the regime. Thus, the weakness of other oppositional forces, the wide opportunities for intensive interaction available to students, the large numbers of students likely to be concentrated in particular locales, and the special freedom for political expression which they are likely to have all combine to foster the growth of a student movement as an independent oppositional movement.

The conditions we have been describing may be regarded as the "classic" pattern presaging the emergence of students as a revolutionary force. Put another way, these conditions help us understand why student oppositional movements have been a regular feature of developing societies.

III

Our analysis has suggested that the classical student movement is a symptom of marked cultural incoherence, of political stagnation, and of severe problems of identity for educated youth in the face of the social and technological changes associated with the process of "modernization." Because this analysis emphasizes that student movements are an aspect of the modernization process, it appears to be quite inadequate for accounting for the rise of student movements in societies like our own, which are not agrarian, which are not dominated by traditional culture and authority, which are not struggling to achieve national identity and independence, where democratic, rationalistic and egalitarian values prevail, where families orient their offspring toward active achievement in a technological society, where the freedom to organize political opposition is available and used. At least at first glance one would be led to believe that the advanced industrial capitalist societies of the West would provide the least hospitable soil for a revolt of educated youth.

Yet a student movement has grown up over the past decade in American society. Over these years, it has become increasingly radicalized, and indeed now includes an avowedly revolutionary wing. Like the classical movements, it contains a strong component of generational revolt—that is, of implicit and explicit hostility to the authority of older generations, and an emphasis on the moral superiority of the young as such and on their capacity to be an agency of social transformation. Like the classical movements, the student movements of the West are intensely anti-authoritarian, egalitarian, and populist. They also resemble the classical type in being completely independent of other, "adult" political groups.

Are there any ways to comprehend the appearance of such a movement in American society that will account for its comparability with classical student movements?

The most parsimonious hypothesis, perhaps, would focus on possible similarities between the immediate situation of the student in the advanced industrial societies and in the developing countries. For example, it seems plausible that the rapid expansion of higher education and the great influx of young people to the universities has led to a devolution in the quality of educational institutions and of student life in the U.S. and Western Europe. It is also plausible that the rapid growth in the numbers of educated youth has produced the same kind of sectional unemployment of the educated which is present in the developing nations.

There may be considerable valid-ity to these hypotheses; indeed, much of the commentary on the French student revolt has emphasized these factors as crucial ones. But it is much harder to see how they can be applied to the American case. For instance, data on the distribution of student protest on American campuses quite clearly show that the student movement had its origins at the highest quality state universities and prestigious private universities and colleges, that the movement continues to have its widest following on such campuses, and that it has only recently spread to schools of lower prestige and quality (Peterson, 1966; 1968). There is, in short, a negative correlation between the quality of an institution and the proportion of its student body which is activist, and between the selectivity of an institution and the radicalism of its student body.

It is equally hard to make a case that the student movement in the U.S. originates in overproduction of educated youth. In the first place, there is no dearth of opportunity for college graduates. Still, one might hypothesize that students who are attracted to the movement experience "relative deprivation"—for example, they may be students who cannot hold their own in academic competition. However, the data on student protesters indicate otherwise, there is, in fact, a tendency for activists to have above average academic records in high school and college, and most of the several studies on student protesters indicate they include a disproportionate underrepresentation of students with poor academic records (Flacks, 1967; 1970). Student protesters come from families with high income and occupational status; they tend to be most prevalent at the top schools; they have above average aptitude for academic work, and perform at above average levels. If there is an overproduction of educated youth in this society at this time, it is hard to see how this would affect the structure of opportunities available to the academic elite from which activists tend to be recruited.

It seems clear that any effort to explain the rise of a student movement in the U.S. must take account of the fact that the movement originated among highly advantaged students, that it did not begin as a revolt against the university, and that its active core contains many students whose aptitudes, interests, values, and origins suggest a strong orientation to intellectual and academic life.

Indeed, one of the most striking findings about American activists has to do with their intellectualism. I refer here not only to the variety of studies which find activists exhibiting intellectual interests and achievements superior to those of the student body as a whole. More persuasive and more sociologically relevant are findings concerning the socioeconomic backgrounds of participants in protest activity. These findings may be briefly summarized as follows: activists are disproportionately the sons and daughters of highly educated parents; in a large proportion of cases, their parents have advanced graduate and professional degrees; a very high percentage of activists' mothers are college graduates; the parents tend to be in occupations for which higher education is a central prerequisite: professions, education, social service, public service, the arts; both businessmen and blue and white collar workers tend to be underrepresented among the parents of activists; family interests—as they are expressed in recreation, or in dinner-table conversation, or in formal interviews—tend to be intellectual and "cultural" and relatively highbrow; these are families in which books were read, discussed, and taken seriously, in which family outings involved museums and concert-halls rather than ball-parks and movies, etc. They were families in which "values" were taken seriously—conventional religion and morality were treated with considerable skepticism, while at the same time strong emphasis was placed on leading a principled, socially useful, morally consistent life. They were, finally, families in which education was regarded with considerable reverence and valued for its own sake, rather than in utilitarian terms.

In short, the student movement originated among those young people who came out of what might be called the "intellectual" or "humanist" subculture of the middle class. In the last two years, it has become considerably more heterogeneous, but it was created almost exclusively by offspring of that particular stratum. (A more detailed review of these findings appears in Flacks, 1970.)

At first glance, it would seem that nothing could be more incomparable than the situation of these middle class American youth and the situation of educated youth in underdeveloped countries. The former, as we have said, can look forward to an array of high status occupational opportunities. Their lives as students are well-subsidized, comfortable, and intellectually rich. Their parents are highly "modern" people, playing central cultural roles, well-informed about and sympathetic with the latest cultural developments. All of this is especially true in comparison with the position of educated youth in developing countries, whose futures are extremely uncertain, whose lives as students are likely to be meager and oppressive, whose families are likely to be locked into traditional ways and attitudes and stand as positive hindrances to the emancipation of their children.

These contrasts are striking, but they may be quite superficial. What I want to do is to restate some of the major factors which we have seen to be central in accounting for the appearance of classical student movements—and try to determine whether comparable factors are at work in American society, especially in relation to the situation of students who come out of the educated middle class.

1. We have said, after Eisenstadt, that a central determinant of the appearance of youth and student movements is sharp discontinuity between values embodied in the family and those emerging in other institutional contexts. From this perspective, as we have suggested, the student movement serves as a "secondary institution"—a way of reestablishing family-like solidarity to ease the achievement of independent adult identities and role-orientations. For youth in developing countries, discontinuity arises because of the fundamental conflict between the traditional orientation of the family and the modernizing orientations encountered in the university and the cosmopolitan community associated with it.

This kind of discontinuity could not be one exeperienced by the off-spring of the educated middle class in America—if anything, students from this stratum are likely to experience less disjunction between familial and university values than any other groups of students. But there are grounds for feeling that humanist youth in America do experience a kind of discontinuity between family and larger society that may have comparable implications for the establishment of identity.

Our studies (cf. Flacks, 1967) of the parents of student activists show that these parents differ from others in the middle class in the following respects:

First, as mentioned above, there is a strong commitment to intellectuality and "culture" and a considerable disdain for mass culture and mass leisure. Their children were expected to be intellectually aware and serious, artistically creative or at least appreciative, serious about education and self-development.

Second, these parents were unusual in their political awareness and their political liberalism. Although they were not necessarily politically active, they tended to stress to their children the necessity for social responsibility and service, and active citizenship, and encouraged their children to support racial equality, civil liberties, and other liberal political goals. In this respect, these families were likely to see themselves, correctly, as different from the vast majority of politically passive or conservative families in their community.

Third, these parents were overtly skeptical about conventional middle-class values, life-styles, and religious orientations. Most of these parents were explicitly secular; those who were actively religious tended to belong to particularly liberal religious denominations or to have a strong social gospel kind of religious commitment. Many of these parents were articulate critics of conventional middle-class mores—by which, in particular, they had in mind sexual repressiveness, materialism, status-striving, and strict methods of rearing children. Many were quite explicit in hoping that their children would be more successful than they had been in leading self-fulfilling, socially responsible lives rather than participating in the "rat race," the "suburban way of life," the "commercial world."

Finally, these parents tended to express these values implicitly through the structure of the family and the styles of child rearing which they adopted. These were parents who encouraged "self-expressive" and "independent" behavior in their children, who interacted with each other and with their children in relatively "democratic" ways, who refused to impose conventional stereotypes of masculine and feminine conduct on their children (e.g., they tended to foster aesthetic and intellectual interests in their boys and assertive behavior on the part of their girls). It was not that these parents were unusually "permissive" or over-indulgent—for instance, their very explicit expectations about intellectuality and social responsibility indicate that they did not adopt a "laissez-faire" attitude toward their children. But they rather consciously organized family life to support anti-authoritarian and self-assertive impulses on the part of their children and rather clearly instructed them in attitudes favoring skepticism toward authority, egalitarianism and personal autonomy

(Flacks, 1967, 1970; Keniston, 1968b).

Now what happens when these intellectual, anti-authoritarian, socially conscious, somewhat unconventional children move on to school and street and peer group? I think it is clear that they are likely to experience a considerable discontinuity between the values they encounter in these settings and the values which which they were raised. They are likely to find authority in school to be petty, arbitrary, repressive. They are likely to feel considerable isolation from the conventional culture of their peers. They are likely to be particularly sensitive to the hypocrisies, rigidities, and injustices of particular institutions and of the society as a whole as they experience it.

Most American youth experience some dislocation as they move from their families into the larger society, if for no other reason than that the rapidity of social change prevents any family from adequately preparing its offspring for the world as it actually is developing, and because proper, moral behavior for children in the American family is inescapably different from proper, moral behavior in the competitive, impersonal society beyond. The existing primary and secondary institutions —school and youth culture—which Parsons and others have expected to be serviceable in easing the transition to adulthood, have failed to incorporate humanist youth, who were in fact raised to question many of the fundamental premises of these institutions. As more and more such youth have entered upon the scene, they have tended to find each other and to create a kind of counter-culture, much as Black urban youth, similarly unincorporated, have created theirs. This new humanist youth culture embodies norms concerning sex-role behavior, worthwhile activity, and personal style which are quite opposed to those which prevail in conventional adolescent society; it expresses values which seem quite subversive of conventional middle-class aspirations, and an attitude toward adult authority which is quite clearly defiant. The American student movement is an expression of that new youth culture, although by no means the only one.

In a peculiar sense, then, the appearance of a student movement and a rebellious youth culture in American society in recent years supports the Eisenstadt hypothesis that such phenomena are rooted in sharp discontinuities between family values and values in the larger society. It is a peculiar kind of support for that hypothesis because, unlike the classical case, the discontinuities we refer to do not have to do with incongruence between a traditional family and a modernizing culture. If anything, the reverse may be the case.
2. As we have suggested, a second major factor contributing to the rise of classical student movements has been the "overpopulation" of educated youth—a factor which appears to be largely absent in the American situation. Nevertheless, there are severe problems for humanist youth with respect to vocation. These problems have to do, not with the scarcity of opportunity, but with the irrelevance of the opportunities which do exist. One of the most characteristic attributes of students in the movement (and an attribute which they share with a large number of apolitical students) is their inability to decide on a career or a vocation. This indecision is less the result of the wide range of choices available, than of the unsatisfactory quality of those choices. What is repellent about the existing opportunities is not their incompatibility with the status or financial aspirations of these youth—but that they are incompatible with their ideals. Business careers are rejected outright as acquisitive, self-seeking, and directly linked to that which is defined as most corrupting in American society. Careers in government or conventional politics are regarded as either self-deluding or "selling out." Professional careers—particularly such established professions as law and medicine—are attractive to some, but only if one can become a doctor or lawyer outside of the conventional career lines; otherwise such careers are regarded as just as acquisitive as business. Teachers and social workers are seen as agents of social control; a few are attracted to scholarship or science, but with profound anxiety. To take an ordinary job is to give up any chance for leading a free life. In general, embarking on a career within the established occupational structure is regarded as morally compromising because it leads to complicity with established interest or because it requires abandoning personal autonomy or because it draws one away from full commitment to radicalism or because it signifies acceptance of the norms and standards of bourgeois society or because it means risking corruption because of material comfort and security.

Although some of these attitudes are undoubtedly the result of participation in the movement rather than a determinant of such participation, it is clear that an underlying revulsion with conventional adult roles and established, institutionalized careers pre-dates movement involvement for many students. One reason for believing that it does is the fact that such revulsion is observable among young people who do not become political activists; indeed, a widespread restlessness about becoming committed to conventional careers and life-styles is evident on the American campus. This has been particularly surprising for those of us who remember the decade of the Fifties and the prevailing feeling of that era—namely, that affluence was producing a generation which would be particularly conformist, complacent, status-conscious, and bourgeois.

It now appears that the opposite may be equally true. Although people with high status and material security may typically be motivated to maintain their position, it is also the case that being born into affluence can foster impulses to be experimental, risk-taking, open to immediate experience, unrepressed. For some at least, growing up with economic security in families of secure status can mean a weakening of the normal incentives of the system and can render one relatively immune to the established means of social control, especially if one's parents rather explicitly express skepticism about the moral worth of material success. Post-war affluence in our society then has had the effect of liberating a considerable number of young people from anxieties about social mobility and security, and enabled them to take seriously the quest for other values and experiences. To such youth, established careers and adult roles are bound to

be unsatisfying. What is the sense, after all, of binding oneself to a large organization, of submitting to the rituals, routines and disciplines of careerism, of postponing or foregoing a wide range of possible experience—when there is little chance of surpassing one's father, when the major outcome of such efforts is to acquire goods which one has already had one's fill of, when such efforts mean that one must compromise one's most cherished ideals?

In newly-industrializing societies, students become revolutionaries, or bohemians, or free intellectuals and artists, because established careers commensurate with their education had not been created. In our society, large numbers of students do the same, not because opportunities for conventional achievement are absent but because they are personally meaningless and morally repugnant. We began with the proposition that a blockage of economic opportunity for the educated is a determinant of student movements. Our comparative analysis leads us to a reformulation of this proposition —any condition which leads to a weakening of motivation for upward mobility increases the likelihood of student rebellion—such conditions can include either blocked opportunity *or* high levels of material security. In short, when numbers of youth find occupational decisions extremely difficult to make, their propensity for collective rebellion is likely to increase.

3. What we have so far been discussing may be described as a kind of cultural crisis—the emergence of a sector of the youth population which finds its fundamental values, aspirations, and character structure in sharp conflict with the values and

practices which prevail in the larger society. We have said that, in certain respects, this conflict is similar to that experienced by youth in societies undergoing rapid transition from traditional to "modern" culture; and in both cases, we find these youth responding to their crisis by banding together in movements of opposition to the older generations and attempting to generate what amounts to a counter-culture.

In some ways, this kind of crisis is not new in American society. For more than a century, at least, small groups of intellectuals have expressed their revulsion with industrial capitalism, and the commercialism, philistinism, and acquisitiveness they saw as its outcome. By the turn of the century, what had largely been an expression of genteel criticism was supplanted by a more vigorous and intense revolt by some educated youth—expressed through bohemianism and through a variety of political and social reform movements. Indeed, opposition to Victorian morality and business culture has been characteristic of American intellectuals in this century (Hofstadter, 1966); and the emergence of large numbers of humanist youth out of relatively intellectual families is an indication of the impact this opposition has had on the society. What was once the protest of tiny pockets of intellectuals and artists has become a mass phenomenon, in part because the ideas of these earlier critics and reformers were taken up in the universities and became part of the world-view of many members of the educated middle class. These ideas influenced not only sentiments regarding commercialism, material success and intellectuality, they also had a direct bearing on the treatment of women and the raising of children, since an important element of anti-bourgeois thinking had to do with the emancipation of women and the liberation of the child from repressive and stultifying disciplines.

What is new in this decade is, first of all, the degree to which this cultural alienation has become a mass phenomenon—an extensive, rooted subculture on the campus and in major cities, with a wide and steadily growing following. Equally important, the present movement is new in the degree to which it has expressed itself through political opposition—an opposition which has become increasingly revolutionary, in the sense that it has increasingly come to reject the legitimacy of established authority and of the political system itself.

As we have previously pointed out, political rebellion by students in other countries has largely been a response to authoritarian, reactionary regimes—regimes which were incapable of or unwilling to adapt to pressures for modernization, and which tended to meet such pressures by attempting to repress them. Thus, classical student movements tend to arise out of the cultural crisis created by the processes of modernization, and tend to go into active political opposition when the political system stands against those processes.

It is perhaps hard for American social scientists to understand why American students should undergo a similar reaction to the American political system. After all, many of them have spent years demonstrating that the system was pluralist, democratic, egalitarian, and highly flexible; thus, while it may be rational for Russian, Chinese, or Latin-

American students to have become revolutionary in the face of tsars, war-lords, and dictators, it is, for them, irrational for students in the U.S. and other Western countries to adopt revolutionary stances against liberal, democratic regimes. (For one example cf. Glazer, 1968.)

To understand why the cultural alienation of intellectual youth in America has become politicized and radicalized requires an historical analysis—the details of which are beyond the scope of this paper. Without attempting such an analysis we can, I think, at least point to some of the most relevant factors.

The first point would be that culturally alienated intellectuals in America have not historically been revolutionary. They have, instead, either been anti-political or have placed their hopes in a variety of progressive, reform movements. In part they have been sustained by the view that the national political system, whatever its flaws, had progressive potential because of its democratic character. They have also been sustained by comparisons between the American system and the rest of the world.

During the New Deal and World War II period, a kind of culmination was reached in the formulation of an ideological perspective for the educated class in America. At the heart of this perspective was the view that inequality, injustice, and business culture could be controlled and offset by effective political and social action through the Federal government. The rise of labor as a political force, the passage of social legislation, and the subsidization of reform by the government would create the conditions for a just and humane society. Not incidentally,

the expansion of the public sector would also create vast view vocational opportuities for educated people with humanitarian concerns—in education, in social service, in public health, mental health, child care, public planning, and all the rest. Thus the creation of the welfare state and an American version of social democracy was crucial for the exanded intelligentsia, not only because it provided a solution to the social ills that contributed to their alienation, but also because it offered a way to realize themselves vocationally outside of the business economy and in terms of their values. It is perhaps important to mention that it was in this ideological milieu that the parents of the present generation reached maturity.

In the past twenty years, however, two things have been happening simultaneously: on the one hand, the ranks of the educated middle class have greatly expanded, due in considerable degree to government support of higher education and of public sector types of occupations which required advanced education; on the other hand, the social benefits anticipated from this development have not been forthcoming—that is, liberal politics have not eradicated gross social inequality, have not improved the quality of public life, and perhaps above all have not created a pacific, internationalist global posture on the part of the American government. Instead, the educated middle-class person is likely to see his society as increasingly chaotic and deteriorating, to feel that enormous waste of material and human resources is taking place, and to believe that his nation is not a liberalizing force internationally, but perhaps the reverse.

The offspring of this stratum, as they began to throng the nation's universities in the early Sixties, entered political involvement at just the point where their parents had begun to experience disillusionment with progressive ideology. But the early phase of the student movement tended to continue traditional middle-class faith in the democratic process. The New Left, in its beginnings, rejected all received ideology; for fairly obvious reasons, it found neither social democracy, nor Marxism-Leninism, nor liberalism at all adequate foundations for renewing radical politics. Indeed, in an early age, many New Leftists would not have attempted to create a youth-based radicalism at all; they would instead have found their way into one or another established radical or reform movement. It is important to realize that the exhaustion of existing ideologies in post-war Europe and America meant that young people with radical impulses had to start afresh. The starting point in the U.S. was to take democratic ideals seriously; to try to make the system work, by participating in and catalyzing grass-roots protest against glaring injustice—particularly against segregation and the threat of nuclear holocaust. Such an outlook included a fairly explicit expectation that the creation of protest and ferment from below would provide an impetus for major change at the top—on the part of the Federal government (in behalf of the constitutional rights of Negroes, for example) and on the part of established agencies of reform such as the churches, the universities, the labor movement. Until about 1964, this political model seemed to be working to a considerable extent—civil

rights laws were passed, the Kennedy Administration was moving toward detente with the Soviet Union, a war on poverty was declared, and a spirit of social renovation seemed to be taking hold in the society. In this situation, the SDS and other student radicals retained a considerable willingness to operate within the conventional political system; it is well to remember for example that in the election campaign of 1964, SDS adopted the slogan, "Part of the Way with LBJ."

The escalation of the war in Vietnam marked a turning point for radical students—it began a process of progressive disillusionment with the political system, a process which, for many, has culminated in a total rejection of its legitimacy. I cannot here recount in any adequate way the series of events which contributed to this process; but it is clear that the war itself was crucial to it, as was the use of the draft to prosecute that war and to "channel" young man educationally and occupationally, as was the failure of the war on poverty (a failure directly experienced by many young activists as they tried to work in poverty areas), as was the transformation of the black movement from a struggle for integration to a far more radical struggle for "liberation" and economic equality, as was the revelation that many universities actively contributed to the war effort and military research, as was the increasing use of the police to suppress protest demonstrations in the streets and on the campuses, as was the failure of the political parties to recognize their liberal, doveish constituencies. In short, for young people who identified with the cause of racial equality, who despised war and militarism, and who had hoped to construct lives based on humane, intellectual, and democratic ideals, by 1968 American society did seem largely reactionary, authoritarian, and repressive. (A more detailed review of this history appears in Skolnick, 1969: 87–105.)

This perception is heightened and reinforced by other, more fundamental beliefs. For example, it is very difficult to accept the amount of squalor, inequality, and misery in this society if one is aware of the fact that the society has the material resources to guarantee a decent private and public life to the whole population. It is very difficult to accept war and the arms race and the expansion of militarism when one is convinced that these institutions have the capacity to destroy the human race. And, finally, it is very difficult to maintain a calm long-run perspective, if one believes that the society has the capacity—in its technology, in its large-scale organizational structure, and in the character structure of millions of its members —to obliterate personal autonomy, individuality, and free expression. Many radical students, in other words, have a profound pessimism about the chances for democracy, personal freedom and peace (for an empirical demonstration of this pessimism, cf. Westby and Braungart, 1970); this pessimism, however, leads toward activism rather than withdrawal because many are convinced that the probable future is not a necessary one. The events of the past four or five years have overwhelmingly confirmed their sense of the main social drift, but what has sustained the impulse to act has been the rapid growth of resistance among many in their generation.

Briefly, then, our argument to this point has been something like the following: the expansion of higher education in our society has produced a social stratum which tends to rear its children with values and character structures which are at some variance with the dominant culture. Affluence and secure status further weaken the potency of conventional incentives and undermine motivations for upward mobility. The outcome of these processes is a new social type or subculture among American youth—humanist youth. Such youth are especially sensitized to injustice and authoritarianism, are repelled by acquisitive, militaristic, and nationalistic values, and strive for a vocational situation in which autonomy and self-expression can be maximized. They have been politicized and radicalized by their experiences in relation to the racial and international crises, and by the failure of established agencies of renewal and reform, including the universities, to alleviate these crises. They also sense the possibility that opportunities for autonomy and individuality may be drying up in advanced technological societies. One of the reasons that their political expression has taken generational form is that older ideologies of opposition to capitalism and authoritarianism have failed in practice.

We have also been saying that, although it is clear that the situation of these youth is enormously different from the situation of educated youth in underdeveloped countries, there are important analogies between the two. Both groups of youth confront the problem of discontinuity between family tradition and the values of the larger society. Both confront major problems of vocation and adult identity. Both confront political systems which are stagnated and repressive, and find new resources and allies external to themselves as they attempt to change the system.

There is a final issue in the comparative analysis of student movements that I want to raise. In our discussion of the classical movements, we suggested that the appearance of such movements was a clear sign that processes of fundamental social and cultural change were at work, and that these movements were not simply the result of certain pressures operating on a particular group of young people in a society but more importantly were indications that traditional, agrarian society was being transformed by processes of industrialization and modernization. It is clearly important to ask whether the appearance of student movements in advanced industrial societies are similarly signs that a new social and cultural era is struggling to emerge.

There are those who believe that the current crop of student revolutionaries is not the vanguard of a new social order, but rather, in the words of Daniel Bell, "the guttering last gasps of a romanticism soured by rancor and impotence" (Bell, 1968). In this view, student unrest in industrial societies is regarded as analogous to the protests of the first waves of industrial workers who resisted their uprooting by the machine. Now, it is argued, high-status intellectually and artistically inclined youth resist their incorporation into large-scale organizations —an incorporation which, nevertheless, is as inevitable as was the imposition of the factory on the rural lower classes.

Such a view does implicitly recognize that a major social transformation may be in the making. What I find objectionable in it is the implication that the new radicalism of the young is irrelevant to the nature of that transformation.

An alternative view would emphasize the possibility that large scale social, political, and cultural changes are occurring, that these are reflected in the social origins and focal concerns of student rebels, and that the existence of student rebellion may be a determining feature of this process of change.

First, at the cultural level, the student movement and the new alienated youth culture appear to reflect the erosion, if not the collapse, of what might be called the culture of capitalism—that cluster of values which Max Weber labelled the "Protestant Ethic"—a value system which was appropriate for the development of capitalism and the entrepreneurial spirit but which has lost its vitality under the impact of the bureaucratic organization of the economy, the decline of entrepreneurships, and the spread of affluence. The erosion of this culture is reflected in the transformation of family structure and childrearing practices, in the changing relations between the sexes, in the replacement of thrift with consumership as a virtue. As Schumpeter (1950) predicted many years ago, bourgeois culture could not survive the abundance it would generate. Thus, the cultural crisis experienced very sharply and personally by humanist youth really impinges on the whole society. It is a crisis because no coherent value system has emerged to replace what has deteriorated; but it is hard not to believe that the anti-authoritarian, experimental, un-repressed, and "romantic" style of the youth revolt does in fact represent the beginnings of the effort to create a workable new culture, rather than the "last gasps" of the old. Such a view gains support when one observes the degree to which the youth revolt has affected popular culture and attracted the interest, if not the total involvement, of large numbers of young people in this country and abroad.

A second major social change which underlies the student movement is the rise of mass higher education. If the student movement is any indication of the possible effects of higher education, then one might have the following expectations about the coming period. First, the number of people in the middle class with critical attitudes toward the dominant culture will rapidly rise. In my view, critical feelings about capitalist culture—particularly negative attitudes toward symbols and ideology which support competitive striving, acquisitiveness, narrow nationalism, and repressive moral codes—are enhanced by exposure to higher education. Such feelings are further reinforced by entrance into occupations which are structurally not bound into the private, corporate economy—for example, occupations associated with education, social service, social planning, and other intellectual or human service work. These occupations embody values which tend to be critical of the culture and of the going system and tend to have an ethic which emphasizes collective welfare rather than private gain. It is important to recognize that the current student activists were born into the social stratum defined by these occupa-tions, and many students with activist sympathies end up in these occupations. Data collected by Lubell (1968) show a general tendency for students oriented toward such occupations to move toward the left, politically. In a certain sense, then, the student movement may be seen as an outgrowth of a new level of occupational differentiation, i.e., the development of a distinct stratum organized around these occupations. This stratum is one of the most rapidly growing occupational sectors, and its political impact can already be seen, not only on the campus, but in such developments as the "new politics" movement during the recent elections. I am not arguing that this "new middle class" of intellectuals, professionals, upper white-collar workers, technical workers, public employees, etc., is politically homogeneous, or class-conscious, or radical. Indeed, it contains many antagonisms, and its participants are hardly ready for massive collective action, much less the barricades. But it does seem to me that the student movement, with its opposition to nationalism and militarism, its identification with egalitarian ideals, and particularly its opposition to bureaucratic and rigid authority in the university represents a militant version of the kinds of attitudes which are increasingly likely to prevail in the stratum to which I am referring. It seems particularly likely that the spread of mass higher education will mean increasing pressure against bureaucratic forms of authority and for "participatory democracy" within the institutions in which the newly educated work. The political trajectory of the educated class will, in large measure, be a function of the responsiveness of the political and economic system to their demands for more rational domestic and international policies, more personal autonomy and participation in decision-making, and a more authentic and humane cultural and public life. More Vietnams, more racial turmoil, more squalor in the cities, more political stagnation, more debasement of popular culture—in short, more of the status quo is likely to increase the availability of members of this stratum for radical politics.

One may continue at great length to enumerate other cultural and social changes which seem to be implied by the appearance of a student movement in our society. For example, it clearly signifies a process of change in the position of youth in the society—a change which involves protest against the subordination of youth to rigid and arbitrary forms of authority in the school system and in the general legal system, and which also may involve an extension of youth as a stage of life beyond adolescence (Keniston, 1968a). The student movement may also signify a general decline in the legitimacy of military authority and nationalist ideology—a decline associated with rising education levels, with changing character structure, and with the impact of mass communications.

My point in mentioning all of these potential cultural and social transformations is not to stake a claim as a prophet, but rather to urge that we take seriously the possibility that the appearance of student movements in advanced industrial societies really does signify that a new social and cultural stage is in the process of formation. A comparative perspective leads us to that

hypothesis, because the classical student movements were, as we have suggested, just such signs. If we were to take the student movement in our own country seriously in this sense, then we would, I believe, be less likely to assume the stability of our social and political order and the cultural system sustaining it, less likely to dismiss campus unrest as a momentary perturbation or a romantic last gasp, less likely to focus on particular tactics and bizarre outcroppings of the youth revolt. Instead, we would open up the intellectual possibility that our kind of society can undergo major transformation, that it can generate, as Marx anticipated, its own "internal contradictions" and "negations," and that the future need not be like the present only more so.

REFERENCES

ALTBACH, P.
  1967 "Students and politics." Pp. 175–187 in Seymour Martin Lipset (ed.), Student Politics. New York: Basic Books.

BELL, DANIEL
  1968 "Columbia and the new left." The Public Interest. (Fall): 61–101.

BEN-DAVID, J., and R. COLLINS
  1967 "A comparative study of academic freedom and student politics." Pp. 148–195 in S. M. Lipset (ed.), Student Politics. New York: Basic Books.

EISENSTADT, S. N.
  1956 From Generation to Generation. Glencoe: The Free Press.

FLACKS, R.
  1967 "The liberated generation: An exploration of the roots of student protest." Journal of Social Issues 23 (July): 52–75.

1970 "Who protests: The social bases of the student movement." Pp. 134–157 in J. Foster and D. Long (ed.), *Protest! Student Activism in America.* New York: William Morrow and Company.

GLAZER, N.
1968 "Student power at Berkeley." *The Public Interest.* (Fall): 61–101.

HOFSTADTER, R.
1966 *Anti-intellectualism in American Life.* New York: Vintage.

KENISTON, K.
1968a "Youth as a stage of life." New Haven: Yale University (mimeo).
1968b *Young Radicals,* New York: Harcourt, Brace and World.

LIPSET, S. M.
1968 "Students and politics in comparative perspective." *Daedalus* 91: 97–123.

LUBELL, S.
1968 "That 'generation gap'." *The Public Interest.* (Fall): 52–60.

PARSONS, T.
1962 "Youth in the context of American society." *Daedalus* 91: 97–123.

PETERSON, RICHARD F.
1966 *The Scope of Organized Student Protest in 1964–65.* Princeton: Educational Testing Service.
1968 *The Scope of Organized Student Protest in 1967–1968.* Princeton: Educational Testing Service.

SCHUMPETER, J.
1950 *Capitalism, Socialism and Democracy.* New York: Harper and Bros.

SKOLNICK, JEROME
1969 *The Politics of Protest.* New York: Simon and Schuster.

WESTBY, D. and R. G. BRAUNGART
1966 "Class and politics in the family backgrounds of student political activists." *American Sociological Review* 31 (October): 690–692.
1970 "Activists and the history of the future." Pp. 154–183 in J. Foster and D. Long (ed.), *Protest! Student Activism in America.* New York: William Morrow and Company.

the effects of student activism in industrialized countries

Some Comparative Reflections on France and the United States

A. BELDEN FIELDS

La jeunesse n'a pas toujours raison. Mais la société qui la frappe a toujours tort.—François Mitterand [1]

INTRODUCTION

When I first agreed to present this paper I was convinced that it would be almost impossible to talk intelligently about the effects of student activism without discussing its causes and the nature or characteristics of the activism. I still think that this is true but, in the interest of time and space allotments, compromises have to be made. Still I am very bothered by the unsystematic picking and choosing of variables to explain student activism and by some of the polemics which have issued out of the pens of social scientists with the main intent of proving how

A. Belden Fields, "The Effects of Student Activitism in Industrialized Countries," paper presented at the annual meeting of the American Political Science Association in September 1971. Reprinted by permission of the author and the American Political Science Association. (Later published in Perucci and Pilisuk, eds., THE TRIPLE REVOLUTION EMERGING: SOCIAL PROBLEMS IN DEPTH, *pp. 585–603. New York: Little, Brown and Company, 1971.)*

[1] Cited in Alain Ayache (ed.), *Les Citations de la Révolution de Mai* (Paris: Jean-Jacques Pauvert, 1968), p. 32.

evil and dangerous the most active individuals really are. In both France and the United States there is a complex cluster of variables which are mutually reinforcing. While they can be dealt with intellectually in isolation, none of them suffices alone as a total explanation of behavior. Moreover, the nature and situational contexts of activism vary on some very important dimensions. The limitations imposed upon this presentation did not permit me to deal with these questions in the systematic way that I would have liked to.

This is particularly disquieting to me because, as I am sure the reader will detect, I am convinced that the material with which we are dealing involves the most important social and political phenomena facing us today. While this paper is an attempt at accurate social analysis, the writer is not dispassionate about the conclusions and would regard it as a great tragedy if the audience remained dispassionate. Critical, the more the better. But dispassionate, no. The stakes are too high.

In the long run I am optimistic as to the effects of student activism. I find hope in aspects of what I refer to as the "counter-culture" of American youth. In the short term I fear for that youth and for all of us who share its humanitarian concerns. If our political system and leaders are capable of positive responses to those concerns, then they had better offer some demonstrative proof very soon.

I will be discussing two kinds of effects. First, there is the question of effects upon specific policy outputs and/or the personnel responsible for making decisions. While in the United States we must differentiate between university policy and personnel and general governmental policy and personnel, in France basic education policy had been determined by the government in Paris until 1968. This pattern provided one target for positive demands and negative expressions of disapproval on both educational questions and general political issues.

Second, there is the question of more basic systemic change. By more basic systemic change is meant fundamental changes in social relationships which involve redistribution of rights, power, or resources. Basic change can be either immediate (corresponding to the traditional use of the term "revolution") or longer term. My intention here is to suggest succinctly certain characteristics of the situation as indicators of future basic change. The admittedly important question of strategies by which students might become a conscious and coordinated force to affect the tempo and direction of such change is not dealt with in this essay.

EFFECTS ON SYSTEM OUTPUTS AND PERSONNEL

A number of attributes attached to the status of student work against students exercising power in indus-

trialized societies the way some of the more successful categories of people do. Stated a little differently, students are deprived of the kind of resource base which has been translated into power by these groups.

First, there is the short duration of the student status in the life of any given individual. This creates difficulties when students attempt to organize. There are rapid shifts in leaders, constituencies, attitudes, and policies. Not only are decision-makers kept off-guard (this may be an asset) but so are potential or real allies.

Second, students tend to be unfamiliar with the exercise of political skills. Engagement in politics as a student is often the first engagement in politics and there is considerably less time for in-group training than there is among many other categories.

Third, students generally lack financial and material resources that other groups have. Students are often dependent upon parents, the government, universities, or poorly paying part-time or summer jobs for their money. When students do engage in large-scale organization or campaigns that involve high financial costs, they run the risk of losing independence to their benefactors.

Fourth, a good proportion of the student population does not enjoy full civil rights. France, like most industrialized countries, permits only those who have reached their twenty-first year to vote. This situation changed last year in Britain when the voting age was reduced to eighteen. This year eighteen-year-olds were given the right to vote in national elections in the United States and a constitutional amendment which would extend this to all elections is in the ratification process.[2] Thus, while the situation may be remedied in the United States, in both France and the United States students have been able to pose an electoral threat only indirectly through publicity campaigns aimed at the general voting population. They have no voting block of their own to speak of.

Fifth, students lack informal channels of access to decision-makers based upon friendship ties, socio-economic similarity, or lateral shifts in institutional affiliations—e.g., between government, business, and the military.

Sixth, in industrial societies, students do not hold the same strategic position which some other groups enjoy in terms of being able to have an immediate and direct impact upon the political or economic life of a country. The withholding of services by labor, business, or the military is much more immediately felt than is a student strike.

It is this problem of a weak resource base in comparison with other categories which have exerted power that gives the phrase "student as a nigger" some measure of truth. And just as in the case of other minorities which must contend with a weak resource base, one variable of extreme importance is the degree to which decision-makers are predisposed to act in accordance with student demands despite this weak resource base. A positive attitude toward students can be the result of a favorable image which the decision-makers themselves have of students or the perception on the part of the decision-makers that the students enjoy a favorable image and widespread support within the body politic and that acquiescing to or anticipating student sentiments and demands is politically expedient or at least acceptable.

France, during the Fourth Republic, provides us with a case of students exerting considerable political influence because of indulgent attitudes among both the general public and government decision-makers. In both sectors there existed a veritable cult of youth. Youth was viewed as something important because the future of French culture and civilization was in its hands.

In more concrete terms, the subsidy which had first been granted to the national student union (UNEF) as an organization of public service during the Third Republic was continued throughout the Fourth Republic. UNEF enjoyed very good relations with the Education Committee of the Chamber of Deputies and generally enjoyed good relations with the Ministry of Education. The students obtained a student insurance program which was administered by students themselves and very important representation on the body which controlled student services. That students should have these services and should bear responsibility for decision-making and administration was viewed as perfectly appropriate by both political

---

[2] Even if the constitutional amendment should pass, the question of where students will be permitted to vote is a crucial one. Local registrars in my community are in the habit of refusing students the right to register even if they are twenty-one on the grounds that they should register where their parents vote—even if they never reside with their parents! They do not want "outsiders" upsetting the local conservative political apple cart. And an Illinois state legislator has introduced a one-sentence bill that would deny students the right to vote in a university area unless they resided there before attending the university.

leaders and the general population.[3]

The situation changed with the fall of the Fourth Republic and the coming to power of the Gaullists. Even before UNEF took a stand against the Algerian War, there was conflict with the Gaullist regime. But once the organization did decide to take a position on the war in 1960, UNEF felt the full fury of the government. The subsidy was suspended and punitive measures were attempted against at least one of the national leaders. Nevertheless, the organization continued to demonstrate against the war and to spur other labor and teachers' unions to come together in syndical solidarity against it. The students were both the catalysts and the vanguard of the antiwar movement. And while other factors undoubtedly came into play —i.e., de Gaulle's conviction that the French could not win, his conviction that a settlement which would permit good relations in the future was the optimal policy, and problems with army discipline and the OAS (particularly after the 1961 attempted coup)—there is little doubt that the tension which the students were creating in metropolitan France and the clashes between demonstrators and police and the right and left played an important role in the government's decision to give up the ghost and stop the war in 1962.

Until 1968, however, this was the one positive victory to which the students could at least make partial claim during the Fifth Republic. While the general image of the students among the population at large remained favorable, the Gaullists

3 See my book, *Student Politics in France: A Study of the Union Nationale des Etudiants de France* (New York: Basic Books, 1970), especially Chapter III.

continued a hard line after the war. This experience revealed how important a resource the positive attitude of decision-makers during the Fourth Republic had been. The students were thrown completely on the defensive. UNEF's subsidy was restored for a brief period and then canceled again; its access to decision-makers was terminated; student representation on the body determining policy regarding student benefits was drastically reduced; and students were physically beaten off the streets when they attempted to publicly demonstrate their grievances. The government simply continued to make and enforce policies, like the Fouchet university reforms, which were generally repugnant to the students.

As an observer of all this it was very difficult to see what UNEF or any other student organization could do to reassert its influence on the policy process. At the same time one had the feeling that the government was taking prerogatives which certainly reflected its ability to make decisions and have them stick in the short term but which also might involve serious costs for the regime sometime in the future. Bitterness and alienation from the regime ran deep and wide within the student milieu. And this was more important than the more visible indices of the proliferation of anti-regimist organizations and the ideological fragmentation.

Even so, what could the students do? We had hypothesized before the 1968 revolt that when faced with a resistant set of governmental decision-makers there are three conditions which must be met before students can emerge victorious: (1) they must be prepared to engage in revolutionary activity or convince the decision-makers that they are; (2) there must be a high degree of political instability; and (3) they must enjoy the support of powerful non-student forces.[4]

These conditions were particularly inspired by the cases of the overthrow of the Rhee regime in South Korea and the Sukarno regime in Indonesia. But the 1968 revolt in France taught us how slight a hold we have on problems of stability and instability in industrialized countries.

Some have contended that the student revolt was worse than a failure for the students, that it backfired. Professor Lipset has written: "In France, the student revolt has had one obvious political consequence; it has given France its first majority party government in history, one which is right wing."[5] This argument, I maintain, is misleading. First, while it is of statistical interest that the Gaullists won a majority in the National Assembly, power relationships were not really changed. The Gaullists were perfectly capable of accomplishing everything in the previous Assembly that they were with their absolute majority.

Second, the revolt did indeed result in important victories for the students, victories which they were unsuccessful in obtaining before the particular set of events that occurred in 1968. The Fouchet reforms were scrapped and reforms that were more acceptable to the students were substituted. These involved decentrali-

zation of the university system and the provision for considerable student representation on university governing bodies. This was indeed a very radical shift in policy. There was also the immediate removal of those cabinet members who had been primarily responsible for the Gaullist hard-line policy: Peyrefitte, Fouchet, and Joxe. Another key hard-liner, Debré, was removed from responsibility in domestic policy by being transferred to the Ministry of Foreign Affairs. Amnesty was granted to students who had been involved in clashes with the police in May. And, almost one year after the revolt itself, the man whom many claimed that the student revolt had ensured unlimited tenure as President of France, General de Gaulle himself, fell from power. And, as we have previously indicated, while some maintain that de Gaulle needlessly put himself in a precarious position over the referendum, the facts are that he did do it and that his decision to do it and the French electorate's loss of faith in him were determined by the revolt.

The first important characteristic of the revolt was, thus, that it brought about important successes in terms of system outputs and personnel. There are two other characteristics of extreme significance. First, the students did indeed pose a threat to the very existence of a political regime in an industrialized country. They themselves created a condition of political instability by their own activity which touched off an imitative response on the part of the workers. They injected a stimulus which rendered the government incapable of performing almost all of its functions. The productive and distributive processes of the country

4 *Ibid.*

5 Seymour Martin Lipset, "The Possible Effects of Student Activism on International Politics" in Seymour Martin Lipset and Philip G. Altbach (eds.), *Students in Revolt* (Boston: Houghton Mifflin, 1969), p. 515.

were simply brought to a halt. By posing a credible threat to the existence of the political system, they rendered the costs of a continuation of alienating policies excessive to decision-makers.

Second, the revolt was spontaneous. The dynamism unleashed in 1968 was severe alienation transformed into human energy and activity by action on the part of decision-makers which pushed people beyond the brink. It could not have been channeled through organizations. Indeed, the revolt was the result of the failure of organizational activity to achieve anything at all. This was a "movement" of alienated, frustrated, and angry people.

This is not to imply that the revolt was entirely negative. While there was no single highly structured ideology that united the participants, they were united around several themes. First, there was the libertarian theme. The revolt was seen as opening up the possibility of a permanent and effective challenge to social institutions which were viewed as being extremely hierarchical and authoritarian. In place of the ubiquitous "forbidden" signs was scribbled, "it is forbidden to forbid." There was the theme of equalitarianism and the hope that the revolt might lead to a system based upon humanitarian and cooperative norms rather than one dominated by egoistic and exploitative social relationships as the present system was viewed. And there was the theme of decentralization and participation which accompanied the widespread disenchantment with representative democracy à la de Gaulle. During the revolt new structures, "action committees" and "occupation committees" were created, first in the universities and then in factories, and even professional institutions. They represented a search for new modes of participation which would maximize the above values. They were admittedly experimental, they were in many cases cumbersome, they were often ill coordinated, and those that exercized effective power did so for a relatively short period. But for many they represented a real advance, a real political education, in what cannot be expected to be a one-shot process of the transformation of institutions.

What can we say about the ability of students to affect system outputs and changes of personnel in the United States? As opposed to pre-1968 France, American students have had to deal with a plurality of decision-makers. American universities themselves are "political" systems within which is wielded a good deal of power. Faculty bodies, administrators, and boards of trustees must be contended with if students are to attain certain goals. State political systems exert control over state university budgets, to a greater or lesser extent they may intrude into internal university governance, and they make laws that regulate the behavior of students. And then there is the national government which must be contended with if students want to affect the broader questions of resource allocation, racial injustice, poverty, and Vietnam. In this sense, one would expect a lesser degree of national cohesion and organizational facility than in France where all students had to confront only one set of decision-makers.

We are sorely lacking in systematic studies of the comparative politics of student activism within American universities which focus on the incidence and conditions of success or failure that students have had in extracting concessions from university decision-makers. Until we have such studies, which ought to be treated just as seriously and rigorously as any other work of comparative politics (it is amazing how lightly and carelessly some scholars tread when it comes to the subject of students—something they would not dare to do if dealing with labor, the business community, or other more powerful sectors), we are all going to be tempted to generalize from our own most immediate experience or from those situations that receive the most publicity. Largely from my own experience at the University of Illinois and from what I have read and heard about several other campuses, I would offer the following tentative generalizations.

First, while there is a greater tendency than in the past to include students on committees, there is very little commitment on the part of most administrators and faculty members to the proposition that students should wield real power and responsibility as existed in France during the Fourth Republic. Indeed, in France public opinion and political figures were far more convinced of the proposition than those immediately involved in the academic community and the students were able to make no headway in strictly academic areas of governance (as opposed to student services and benefits) even during the Fourth Republic. Where students are gaining access to such committees there is generally great care taken to structure the situation so that their power will be minimized. This is done either by making sure that students

are a minority on committees or by posing external checks upon the powers of the committees on which they sit. The student perceptions of attempts at "cooptation" tend thus to be quite correct.

Second, there are two mutually reinforcing sources of the fear of student power within the university community. These are traditional prerogative and fear of political radicalism. In terms of traditional prerogative, administrators and faculty members tend to be most sensitive to different challenges. For the administrators, control over expenditures, facilities, and programs is crucial. For the faculty, the most serious challenges are in hiring and retention of faculty members and course content and pedagogy. While students generally have not been permitted to participate formally in the latter matters, they do exercise some power by refusing to take certain professors or courses and by publishing course critiques. In terms of their fear of political radicalism, administrators and faculty members run neck and neck. SDS is the *bête-noire* which is responsible for all their difficulties with the students. Indeed, some of our most well-known social scientists on university faculties have engaged in the most simplistic of analyses. The comparison of the new left or SDS with the Nazis or Fascists or somehow implicitly making distinctions that permit repressive behavior toward the "hard-core" or "leaders" but not others is too frequent a theme of these presentations.[6]

6 I would include here Professor Edward Shils' article, "Dreams of Plentitude, Nightmares of Scarcity," in Lipset and Altbach's *Students in Revolt, op. cit.,* in which he accuses activists bent on confrontation of

Third, student governments or their equivalents at most major universities have indeed turned their attention toward general political and social issues as well as the more constricted issues of student participation. This is entirely normal behavior, as we have seen in France, when the general society is being torn asunder by divisive issues. Moreover, it is not a question of choice. It is based on a realistic assessment of the university operating as a control mechanism in conjunction with external political institutions.

Fourth, in some cases outputs and personnel have been affected through the use of disruptive tactics. At Berkeley, the 1964 revolt did indeed result in loosening up restrictions on speech and the ouster of President Kerr. At Columbia, it took a major conflict with the police in 1968 to bring about a division between faculty and administration, the appoint-

contriving all issues other than Vietnam (p. 26) and contends that "the Nazi abuse of the Weimar 'system' " and "the frequent denunciations of the 'system' " by student radicals in France, Germany, and the United States "bespeaks an affirmity of outlook" (note 7, p. 30). I would also include Professor Daniel Bell's article "Columbia and the New Left" in *The Public Interest,* No. 13 (Fall 1968), which is basically a tirade against the SDS. A sample: "The administration above all failed to understand the *dynamics* of the student protest: That whatever reason there may have been for early police action, when the buildings were seized by hard-core SDS members, the subsequent surge of political support on the part of 500 other students—most of them liberal, moderate, pacifist, and not members of SDS—effectively changed the *political* character of the situation. The failure to make the necessary distinctions between these students and SDS, and then to understand that these students were not wreckers but were now trying to express their inchoate grievances against the university, permitted SDS to call the tune. . ." (p. 95).

ment of the Cox Commission, and an open admission that the internal governance of the university was indeed repressive and that that fact might just have had something to do with the university being torn apart. There too, the president of the university, who had been resistant to change, was displaced. But where the French revolt resulted in victories for French students generally, victories won through disruption on American campuses have been restricted to the particular university where the battle was fought. Students at other universities must contend within their own little political systems. And faculties and administrators on other campuses seem all too often to have drawn the conclusion that there wasn't enough control exerted at Berkeley and Columbia.

Fifth, these confrontations can involve costs. To some extent the events at the University of California undoubtedly aided reactionary forces in gaining control of the executive branch of the state. And most, if not all, of the student activists are not Reagan or Rafferty fans. It is all to fashionable, however, to blame the students exclusively for these costs. Administrators and faculty members who resist all efforts at change and who engage in what students feel to be repressive practices, but who also disapprove of what they feel to be the repressiveness of outside political forces, must bear heavy responsibility for bringing this cost upon themselves. Because one's own interests and prerogatives always seem so reasonable and one is always convinced that one is doing good for other people, it is difficult for these administrators and faculty members to see the parallel between repressive external political forces and repressive university governance which is evident to many students.

Sixth, the decline of *in loco parentis* on most large campuses in the United States is due less to the exercise of student power than to the impossibility of enforcement within the huge university environment. However, while surveillance and control over student life in this regard is diminishing, it is frighteningly increasing in the areas of drug usage and political expression and behavior. In these areas, as opposed to the case of *in loco parentis,* university security offices (often staffed by former local law-enforcement officers or by ex-FBI men who belong to the FBI Association) and ever-expanding university police forces (on the campus at which I work we now have a force of seventy officers) work in conjunction with federal and state authorities.

On the general political level, students apepar to have had very little positive impact upon policy-making or makers within the state legislatures. Indeed, at the present time we are witnessing an unprecedented vindictiveness directed toward students from state legislatures because of what their members feel is unwarranted disruptive and destructive tactics. At least in Illinois, the legislature has narrowed the prerogatives of administrators in dealing with people who are defined as disruptive or destructive.

At the national level the major issues have been civil rights and racial equality and foreign policy, especially Vietnam. Let us take these issue areas and assess the impact which students have had and might have in the future.

It is often forgotten that accompanying the movement for civil rights for the black population of the South were two other causes of students in the early 1960s, the Fair Play for Cuba movement and the movement against the tactics of the House Un-American Activities Committee (HUAC). That committee was determined to seek out Communists and/or "subversives" and expose them to the public. And it decided that the pickings were especially good within the academic community in the Bay area of California. HUAC's visit to California resulted in demonstrations and confrontations which the committee claimed impeded it from effectively performing its function. And, in order to counterattack, it made the very serious error of making and distributing what was one of the most patently stupid and radicalizing films of all time, "Operation Abolition." Due to the confrontation of the students, and some courageous faculty members it must be acknowledged, what was once an effective group of political witch hunters and intimidators was forced into the open. Through the distribution of the film, particularly on campuses, HUAC made itself look ridiculous. This marked the end of its reign of political terror.

The other major civil-rights battle was fought in the South. This was the combined struggle of the Student Non-Violent Coordinating Committee and white civil-rights workers (the Freedom Riders) from northern campuses for equal political rights for black people in the South. While the Brown versus Board of Education decision had marked the interest of the federal government in equal education in the South, the government did not interject itself seriously into the problem of political rights before the agitation began in 1960. Again, using confrontation tactics of a nonviolent variety, SNCC and the Freedom Riders, along with the Southern Christian Leadership Conference, focused national and worldwide attention on the oppression of the black in the American South. At a cost of life and physical injury to the activists, some gains were made in the form of national legislation covering voting rights and equal accommodations. However, very little was accomplished in terms of a shift in power relationships or resource distribution. And it soon became very clear to the activists that when one thinks in these terms, the problem of racism is not a regional but a national one. The legislative gains thus turned out to be largely symbolic. And despite the continued interest of black and white student activists in racism throughout the American institutional structure, about the only real gain has been in opening up some of the larger universities and colleges more to minority groups than they have been in the past. Moreover, alliances between black and white student groups have been made very difficult by a shift toward a separatist position on the part of the blacks. The Panthers are an exception but even among the Panthers there is a suspicion that most of the white activists would not be prepared to take up guns when the chips were down as the Panthers are prepared to do. Thus while the theme of racism is still raised in white-student activists circles, action has recently been centered around other issues.

Student interest in the cold war and foreign policy has a postwar history that antedates the Vietnam war. Immediately after the Second World War, in 1947, the United States National Student Association was formed. Up to 80 percent of the yearly budget of this organization was supplied covertly by the Central Intelligence Agency. And a small group of national leaders which changed each year were aware of the source of funds and performed intelligence functions for the Agency at international meetings. In 1950, they cooperated with the Agency in forming the International Student Conference which was to be the American cold-war rival to the communist-dominated International Union of Students. Until the 1960s the student role in international politics was a small group of leaders of NSA serving the CIA and its cold-war efforts either because they were in tune with the efforts or, a little later, because they were under the threat of prosecution under the National Security Act. At the mass level students either were genuinely not interested in international politics or feared the repercussions if they should speak out in a critical manner during the McCarthy period. Such interest as did exist could be channeled through safe enterprises like international relations clubs and mock United Nations meetings. These were characterized by a low intensity of commitment to most issues. The Arab-Israeli conflict was the notable exception.

In 1959 and 1960, the first really critical approach to American foreign policy which involved a commitment to political action was taken by the Fair Play for Cuba groups. They were immediately branded as communists or dupes of the communists. But students were now less intimidated by this kind of attack as would be soon indicated by the confrontation with HUAC. The issue of Cuba was crucial. For some, Kennedy's attacks on the Republicans for permitting communism to exist ninety miles off of our shores in the television debates with Nixon and his Bay of Pigs and missile decisions were convincing proof that the United States was suffering from a cold-war anti-communist mania which transcended parties and personalities. While Kennedy was successful in appealing to many young people who were attracted by his sophisticated and intellectual style, his peace-corps program, and his obvious concern for the race and poverty issues, the Cuban and Vietnamese policies and the development of the general counterinsurgency strategy were crucial steps in the process which was to alienate so many American students from the political system.

The next fateful steps were taken by President Johnson in 1965: the large-scale expansion of the war in Vietnam and the intervention in the Dominican Republic. In the election campaign of 1964 Johnson had differentiated himself from the more aggressive Goldwater and promised that he would not commit American boys to a land war in Asia. And we students (I was a student then) were impressed and if of voting age voted for him. Not only did Johnson expand the war but he did so on the most implausible of pretexts: the so-called Pleiku incident; the so-called Gulf of Tonkin incident; and that lovely pamphlet distributed by the State Department entitled "Aggres-

sion from the North." The collective behavioral response to this was the first mass march on Washington to protest the war in April 1965.

Following on the heels of the national antiwar march was the intervention in the Dominican Republic and an attempted justification of this which informed us whose uncles were communists down there by the same publishing house which had brought us "Aggression from the North." It was as if the government was trying to clear things up for those who might have missed the point and viewed Vietnam as an aberration or a mistake. Cuba, Vietnam, and the Dominican Republic were part of a systematic response process of this nation which was to stifle any attempt at social change in a more equalitarian direction wherever it thought it could get away with it.

From 1965 to the present, Vietnam has been the major area of concern for student activists. And a number of tactics have been attempted. There was the "teach-in," the effect of which was confined within academic communities. National and local demonstrations were continued and the largest demonstrations in the history of the nation assembled. The electoral process was attempted in the form of the McCarthy primary races and the electoral races of other peace candidates. The rates of draft resistance and desertion from the armed forces swelled. ROTC, military and industrial recruiters with defense contracts, and university relations with the Defense Department were challenged. And lately industrial, commercial, financial, and military establishments which are being blamed for American policies have been the subject of bombing attacks numbering in the thousands per year.[7]

In 1968 the antiwar movement was having an important effect upon public opinion. Immediately after the polls reported a new low in confidence in Johnson's handling of the war, the President announced that he would not serve another term. He admitted that it would take someone else to bring any unity to the people. Of the four major contenders for the Democratic nomination—McCarthy, Kennedy, Humphrey, and McGovern—three were peace candidates. And before the assassination of Kennedy it looked as though the nomination might be decided in negotiations or combat between the Kennedy and McCarthy forces. But Kennedy was assassinated and the Democratic Party decided to commit suicide both inside and outside its convention hall.

Both Nixon and Humphrey felt the necessity to run on a program that called for withdrawal from Vietnam. Nixon claimed to have a plan which he could not reveal and, in retrospect, he could not have revealed it. The Nixon strategy has been twofold. Attempt to defuse the peace movement by announcing a policy of phased withdrawal, by introducing a draft lottery and the intention to go to a completely voluntary army, by announcing that there will be no more Vietnams, and by getting people interested in other issues like pollution. The other aspect to the strategy has been the attempt to suppress and intimidate those who persist in the peace move-

ment through activities of the FBI, military intelligence, and prosecution in the courts. The performance of the intimidation function (we should add that to Almond's list) has been shifted from the legislature and HUAC to the executive.

Despite the downfall of President Johnson and the Democratic Party and the promises of Nixon to end the war and the draft and not to engage in more Vietnams, the war did in fact continue. The aim of the peace movement became total and immediate withdrawal without gimmicks like "Vietnamization." There was an attempt to exert further pressure by reviving the technique of the national demonstration and combining it with a cessation of normal activity. This took the form of the several "Moratoria" held during the academic year 1969–1970. By the spring of 1970, the National Mobilization Committee found that it was impossible to maintain the momentum of the October moratorium in the face of no visible impact on policy and went out of business, ostensibly to work at the grass roots. With the exception of a minority of the most alienated who were willing to take large personal risks and a minority of the most tenacious who were willing to continue antiwar publicity campaigns and work within the system, the antiwar movement was demoralized. There was a brief mass transfer of energy and activity over to the pollution issue. After all, the government seemed to be on the side of the angels here and one could even get in a few licks at big business. And maybe one could forget the war.

In reality few were kidding themselves. The frustration over the war issue had been accumulated to a

7 On the rate of bombing in New York City (368 from January 1969 through May 1970), see the *New York Times* (July 17, 1970), p. 1.

point where the transfer would not work. The attitude toward the war and the government within the student milieu was similar to the hostility which the Gaullists had managed to generate against themselves in France. And having observed the ravaged state in which the Algerian War had left France and the Gaullists continued to push people to the brink, it was incredible to watch the Nixon Administration, which talked withdrawal, the end of the draft, and deescalation of the conflict at home out of one side of its mouth, feed the alienation by taking the offensive against the dissidents. In many instances even the language used by the Vice-President, the Attorney General, and the President himself was the very same as that used by French hard-liners. While I had been convinced for some time that the Vice-President's speech writers had been going over old French texts, the expression "carnival in the streets," an echo of President de Gaulle's characterization of the French student revolt two years previously, and "effete intellectual snobs," reminiscent of Minister of Algerian Affairs Lacoste's "exhibitionists of the heart and mind" remark made during the Algerian War in a speech to a group of war veterans, did at least raise the possibility of an international conspiracy.

In good Gaullist tradition, the Nixon Administration not only fed the alienation by pursuing the obnoxious policies and by taking the offensive against the antiwar movement but, in ordering the Cambodian invasion, also provided a catalyst which set off an explosion of spontaneous responsive activity.

The Gaullists and the French students have provided us with an example of political behavior and outcomes when decision-makers pursue policies which highly alienate the student population. Up to this point in time, the behavior of the decision-makers and the behavior of the students in the United States bear such a similarity to France between the end of the Algerian War and the 1968 revolt that we may well have a model which can be generalized to such conflict when it arises in industrialized societies. We may also be able to extend the model to cover other groups deprived of resource bases within these societies.

The model takes the form of a scenario in which time and memory play key roles. The starting point is policies which violate the formal values of the society. Students view them as immoral and refuse to rationalize them. Although UNEF had been politically active since its inception and had shifted its concern after World War II from exclusive attention to educational issues (1945–46) to both educational and general issues (1946–50) and back again to exclusive concern with educational issues (1950–56), in both France and the United States the policies which began the process of alienation did not have to do with education. They were "environmental," the Algerian War in France and civil rights and the Vietnam War in the United States. In both cases, however, the initial response of the students was to work through organizations to influence these specific policies and to conduct political education both within and without the student milieu. There is great similarity in the relative moderation of UNEF throughout the Algerian War (the war ended two years after UNEF took a position) and in the early positions of SNCC, SDS, and the *ad hoc* committees on Vietnam. This is what I refer to as the "apple pie" stage.

The government resists the demands for change. The students do not possess the resources to compel change or even to open up direct channels of access to decision-makers. In the absence of such resources students turn to direct-action techniques, such as peaceful demonstrations, in order to demonstrate the intensity of their feeling to the government and to public opinion. They attempt to include nonstudent allies in these demonstrations of sentiment.

The government has a low degree of tolerance for such public demonstrations. It uses bans, unacceptable restrictions, violence, threats, and actual prosecutions to discourage such behavior. The students persist. Some might even attempt to fight back in the streets but, because of the disparity of resources, the students lose there also. And the government attempts to place the blame upon the students for whatever violence occurs.

Disaffection from the government transcends the original issue or issues. There develops a general antiregimist sentiment which spreads to a much larger group than the activists. In fact, as the antiregimism spreads it is accompanied by a sentiment of powerlessness and frustration. Activist groups diminish in size and fragment according to narrow ideological interpretations. This is a stage of sectarianism.

A small minority forms activist guerrilla groups. While the groups might engage in open confrontation initially, as in The Weatherman's 1968 Days of Rage, in short order they are forced underground.[8] Some participants see this activity as literally the vanguard of a coming revolution. Others view it as the only possible hope for effective disruption. Some see it as the only way to take a stand on the moral issue regardless of the probable effect on the system. Most of those involved in activism at an earlier stage, however, doubt the feasibility of such activity and are unwilling to engage in activities for which serious criminal penalties might be incurred.

At some point, however, the government overestimates its power and pushes too far. It supplies a catalyst which the student population regards as so outrageous that the normal incentive system upon which the government relies for control is rendered ineffective. The underlying discontent and alienation blow up in spontaneous action.

The spontaneous action may or may not pose a real and immediate threat to the existence of the regime. The key variables will be how far the students are willing to go in terms of running risks (a function of the spread and depth of the alienation and the degree to which the catalyst is viewed as "outrageous") and how the explosion is responded to by decision-makers, other groups in the society, and public opinion.

In France, the attitude of the hard-liners during the early stages of the revolt was rejection of all demands and the ordering of police

---

8 The government has not been as effective in tracking down members of these groups as many, including myself, had thought they would be. At any point in time there is a tremendous base of support for these people among those who are alienated but who are not willing to engage in guerrilla activities themselves.

charges. On the night of May 10–11, the "Night of the Barricades," the students broke with the normal incentive system. They did not flee from the barricades. They stood their ground and fought a night-long pitched battle with the police and paramilitary CRS.[9]

Public opinion, which had been favorable to the demands of the students in the area of education before the revolt, reacted with indignation against the behavior of the government and police. The students had the continuing support of the largest teachers' union and the small *Parti Socialiste Unifié*. On May 13, all of the major labor unions protested the action of the government by calling a twenty-four-hour strike and by participating in a march and demonstration in which between one-half and one million people took to the streets of Paris. The most threatening action for the government, however, was the long wild-cat strike of between nine and ten million workers.

The situation is obviously different in the United States. The response to the Cambodian invasion provided some very interesting data. Even though lines of communication among American campuses are much weaker than in France, American students can act in unison. The mind-sets at major American universities and colleges are sufficiently in tune that a political stimulus can set off similar spontaneous responses.

The President was obviously surprised and frightened although it was reported that he had been warned of the possible repercussions on the campuses by his advisors.

9 See my "The Revolution Betrayed: The French Student Revolt of May–June 1968" in Lipset and Altbach, *op. cit.*, pp. 127–166.

Unable to sleep in the predawn hours, he aroused his valet who drove him to the Lincoln Memorial where he subjected young protestors who were trying to sleep to what they described as disjointed and incoherent rambling.

Although the American students were generally not prepared to fight the kind of pitched battle that the French students had fought, the reaction of locally controlled police and National Guard units was more brutal than that of the French police. Four students lay dead at Kent State and two at Jackson State. This was consistent with the previous pattern of a much greater propensity among American police to use bullets on demonstrators or dissidents (e.g., the Alameda County Sheriff's office in 1969, the murders of Fred Hampton and Mark Clark, and numerous killings of black Panthers and students in the South) than is the case in France. During the entire revolt in France, I could not document one shooting by law-enforcement officers.

In the United States, the Administration has invested a great deal of energy in attempting to polarize opinion against the dissidents and public opinion has tended to be negative. While a couple of liberal labor leaders were stirred to expressions of open opposition to the war, the Executive Council of the AFL-CIO approved of the President's Cambodian action. In several cities, construction workers formed violent vigilante groups and/or launched counter demonstrations.

There were, however, more favorable responses from the students' point of view. Bureaucrats charged with the execution of policy in both HEW and the State Department openly expressed their strong opposition to the President's policies. The Commissioner of Education attacked the Cambodian adventure. He was fired. The Secretary of the Interior accused the President and his political associates of being insensitive to the concerns of youth and he too was subsequently dismissed. It appeared that the President and his most right-wing associates, Mr. Mitchell and Mr. Agnew, were being isolated within their own executive branch.

The Senate was clearly impressed. This was indicated by the passage of the Cooper-Church Amendment. Thus both within the executive and legislative branches the student action of May stimulated some very bold antiwar behavior. But the behavior of the bureaucrats, upon whom the execution of policy depends, was the more interesting. And that the President seems to have perceived the danger to his position is reflected in the shift of some responsibilities from State to Defense and in both the threat of dismissal and actual dismissal of dissidents.

From the point of view of the students, the reaction of investors was also favorable. Economists admit that the most important determinant of the direction of the stock market is psychological. The student revolt in France cost that country a fortune and necessitated a devaluation in the franc. The comparatively mild action of the American students wreaked havoc with the market. After all is said and done, it may well be that the most potent support which the student movement will generate on the war issue will not come from other powerless anti-establishment forces like ghetto blacks but from within the establishment itself, particularly from government bureaucrats and market investors.

Less important in terms of potential effect but important in symbolic terms was the support generated within the academic community. More faculty members than ever before became active participants in the events of May. In general, the faculty became much more honest with themselves and their students over what was happening. A permanent antiwar lobby of academics in Washington was formed. And even some administrators who had opposed any political commitment on the part of the university broke their silence under pressure.

The French case demonstrates that there is always a danger of instability in any political system when the government insensitively attempts to push beyond the effectiveness of the incentive system. I know of no one who considered the French political system before May 1968 to be unstable. All of the usual indices which have been used by social scientists to measure stability were there —it was an industrialized country, there was inflation but the economy was not in trouble from the point of view of investors and financiers, de Gaulle had been in power for a full decade, the extreme right was virtually nonexistent, the Communist Party was playing within the system, and the dissident student organizations had been immobilized by the government at every turn. In very short order the students changed all that.

The major lesson of both the French and American cases is the futility of traditional organizational efforts to bring about specific policy changes when students are faced with a government in a relatively "efficiently" operating industrialized society which is determined to resist their demands. Such organizational efforts are inherently conservative and are viable mechanisms only for those categories that already possess greater resource bases. In order for the students to emerge victorious they must clearly indicate to the government that they are prepared to incur the serious risks involved in breaking through the system's incentive structure. In other words, they must show that they are prepared to engage in disruptive behavior despite costs to themselves which will involve costs to the system which decision-makers do not want to incur. The ultimate cost would be, of course, the termination of the regime. But there are also intermediate costs—both political and economic—which the government will not wish to incur. All political decision-makers are eager to foster the impression that they can keep things under control in the streets, provide efficient policy execution and services, and maintain a favorable climate for economic growth.

The 1968 uprising in France and the reaction to the Cambodian invasion in the United States may well indicate that the only way that such disruptive behavior which is not easily "managed" can come about under the above conditions is through spontaneous action. There is some room for strategic maneuvering on the part of students—i.e., the maintenance of a certain level of political consciousness within their own ranks and in the ranks of potential allies and of a certain level of tension or threat. But the structuring of the situation must be done by the government itself. The government must act according to the scenario. It must develop alienation through resistance to demands and repressive responses and it must provide the catalyst that makes possible the mass transcendance of the incentive structure upon which it relies for effective control. Once this has been accomplished, once spontaneity has been experienced on a mass scale, a new state of mind or consciousness and a new political context has been created. The Gaullists learned this the hard way. All at once, concessions to the students on specific issues and personnel seemed a reasonable price to preserve power. But by this point most of the activists are no longer just thinking in terms of changing specific policies or office holders. They are thinking in terms of basic systemic change.

BASIC SYSTEMIC CHANGE

On numerous occasions the question is raised as to whether or not we are experiencing a phenomenon which is significantly different from left-wing student activism in American universities in the 1930s. There is usually an implicit assumption and question behind this. The assumption is that the activism of the 1930s either faded away as the participants aged or was absorbed by the war and the New Deal without having significant impact upon the political system. The question is: will the same fate not befall contemporary student activism?

I am cognizant of Professor Lipset's criticism of Professor Andrew Hacker and Mr. William Braden for "their ahistoricism, their exaggeration of the uniqueness of the contemporary." [10]   Nevertheless, I will argue that student activism today is different from student activism in the 1930s in that it is occurring within the context of a "counterculture."

Of course, I am not the first one to put forward the idea of a counterculture. It runs through the writings of Herbert Marcuse. Theodore Roszak, in his *The Making of a Counter Culture,* discusses the counterculture but actually devotes almost all of his attention to the technocracy which he sees as responsible for its growth.[11]   In his very recent book, Philip E. Slater speaks of

> two separate cultures in America . . . the opposition between the old scarcity-oriented technological culture that still predominates and the somewhat amorphous counterculture that is growing up to challenge it.   At times this distinction may seem synonymous with old-versus-young, or radical-versus-conservative, but the overlap is only approximate.   There are many young people who are dedicated to the old culture and a few old people dedicated to the new.[12]

Margaret Mead argues that the generation gap is worldwide and that we are now entering a new and universal anthropological stage which she calls "prefigurative culture." [13]

[10] Seymour Martin Lipset, "The Banality of Revolt," *Saturady Review* (July 18, 1970), p. 34.

[11] Theodore Roszak, *The Making of a Counter Culture* (Garden City, N.Y.: Anchor, 1969).

[12] Philip E. Slater, "America's Changing Culture," *Current* (June 1970), p. 15.

[13] Margaret Mead, *Culture and Commitment: A Study of the Generation Gap* (Garden City, N.Y.: Natural History Press/Doubleday, 1970).

In prefigurative culture young people learn from their peers rather than from their elders.   Thus cumulative patterns of political socialization are broken by peer-group interaction. In 1967, Kenneth Keniston argued that there were really two kinds of youth dissent in the United States, the "romantic-alienated" (the culturally oriented) and that "universalistic-activist" (the politically oriented), that these were going in different directions, and that the tension between them would probably increase.[14]   I argue, and Keniston now agrees, that these are aspects of the same phenomenon and that they are mutually reinforcing.

Let me be more explicit in regard to the differences with the 1930s. While I shall deal elsewhere in more detail and in a more rigorous comparative fashion with these characteristics, here space permits little more than a brief enumeration.

First, we now have a differentiation running along generational lines in regard to language, dress, art, drugs, and sex.   Attitudes and behavior in regard to these phenomena are very different in the new youth culture from what they are in the dominant culture.

Second, the youth culture exhibits far greater spread than it did in the 1930s.   It is widely spread within the university student milieu wherein we find the children of those especially rewarded during the postwar period of economic abundance,[15] it is affect-

[14] Kenneth Keniston, "The Sources of Student Dissent," *Journal of Social Issues,* **23** (1967), pp. 108–137 reprinted in his *Young Radicals: Notes on Committed Youth* (New York: Harcourt, Brace, and World, 1968).

[15] However, students are now rapidly finding themselves economically deprived by the spiraling unemployment.   This will

ing people who come into constant contact with students like faculty members (some of whom were students themselves only a short time ago), it is being carried by graduating students in the various professional areas of life, and, most importantly, it is spreading downward into high schools, junior high schools, and even grammar schools at a rapid rate. Over the past five years each freshman class has been more deeply touched than the previous one. It is through this downward spread that the counterculture is affecting young people who will not go into universities or the professions but into the blue-collar labor force.

Third, there is a high degree of political separatism or the shunning of traditional political structures. The student activism of the 1930s tended to be centered around either establishment parties or adult-controlled anti-establishment parties like the Communist or Socialist parties. Neither the establishment parties nor these anti-establishment parties have much attraction for today's students.

Fourth, we have the rise and fragmentation of ideological organizations and movements which goes well beyond the fragmentation of the left-wing parties of the 1930s. Moreover, the fragmentation stems from the base as opposed to the 1930s in which the lines of fragmentation followed disaffection at the leadership level. I would argue that the present fragmentation indicates a higher degree of alienation and frustration than existed in the 1930s.

And, *fifth,* we have the progressive escalation in the use of direct-action

techniques which was more characteristic of the labor movement than of student activism in the 1930s.

It is generally argued that the counterculture is a result of technological growth and the attendant increase in impersonality and hierarchical control. Margaret Mead sees prefigurative culture as a universal phenomenon. While I would agree that the revolt against impersonality and hierarchical control transcends national boundaries and is probably found in all industrialized societies in greater or lesser intensity, I would argue that there are differences in the nature of the challenges. The second through fifth characteristics which we have attributed to the American counterculture would apply in France as well. While formulated in more rigorous Marxian theoretical terms in France, the two youth milieux also share in a negative attitude toward capitalism. But in France, the expression of political differentiation and alienation is not reinforced by differentiations in language, dress, art, sex, and drugs as it is in the United States.

At this point I would advance two propositions. First, despite the difference in manifestation of the challenges to the dominant system, I would contend that basic systemic change is inevitable in France and the United States as in all of the industrialized countries. For within the youth milieux there is a new "mind-set." Culture is composed of mind-sets. They are both cognitive and normative, both prescriptive ideas and ways of perceiving the world. They are based upon felt human needs and, in the long run, are the crucial variables in political change. And, some of the work on American political socialization not-

---

act as a further radicalizing factor as it has in France since 1963.

withstanding, at critical points in history they are not simply the result of cumulative political socialization extending in a linear direction from the family through the work experience.

We are now in a period in which the requisites of Weber's impersonal hierarchical organizations no longer conform to the felt needs of the individuals who are subjected to them. Hierarchy and impersonal authority have simply gone beyond the point of diminishing returns. Just as Marx, at least in his later writings, went too far when he attempted to demystify Hegel by substituting materialism and economic determinism for idealism, so Weber and the sociologists influenced by him fall into a similar error by asserting the absolute primacy of the requirements of systems of production, distribution, and control over all other determinants. Thus I would expect that the more dehumanizing and authoritarian aspects of industrialized societies will be minimized as the new mind-sets replace the old ones presently dominant.[16]

The second proposition is that because of the mutually fortifying impact of the political and more broadly cultural aspects of the youth and student counterculture in the

[16] Here, of course, I am in agreement with Professor Flacks in his critique of Professor Bell's contention that the increasingly militant tactics of students are simply the "guttering last gasps of a romanticism soured by rancor and impotence." This interpretation might save the end-of-ideology thesis but I do not think that it conforms to the reality "out there" either in France or the United States. See Daniel Bell, *op. cit.*, p. 100; and Richard Flacks, "Social and Cultural Meanings of Student Revolt: Some Informal Comparative Observations," *Social Problems,* **17**:3 (Winter 1970), pp. 354–357.

United States, change will be even more basic and more rapid in this country than in France.

The question remains, however— what about the short term? If our analysis is correct, if the only way that students can hope to change policy in the face of a resistant government is by disruption, does this not threaten a change in the system toward more repression and a drastic reduction in civil liberties?

I do not think that anyone, even within the youth culture, takes this prospect lightly. The older generation too has a mind-set and is in control of tremendous resources. Philip E. Slater has written:

If the issue is left to generational confrontation, with new culture adherents attempting simply to push their elders out of the way and into the grave, the results will probably be catastrophic. The old culture will not simply fall of its own weight. It is not rotten but wildly malfunctioning, not weak and failing but strong and demented, not a sick old horse but a healty runaway. It no longer performs its fundamental task of satisfying the needs of its adherents, but it still performs the task of feeding and perpetuating itself. Nor do the young have the knowledge and skill successfully to dismantle it. If the matter is left to the collision of generational change it seems to me inevitable that a radical-right revolution will occur as a last-ditch effort to stave off change.[17]

If we are correct, then the choice obviously comes down to dropping one's goals or running the risk of the shift to the right which Slater talks about. Several points need to be made. *First,* since the goals relate

[17] Slater, *op. cit.*, p. 16.

to deeply felt needs and commitments, the goals will not be dropped. Students will continue to oppose the unconscionable Vietnam War in which they or their friends or husbands must participate or opt for prison or exile. And once we are out, if indeed we will ever be out, they will continue to oppose racism, poverty, the cold-war mentality, and the impersonalization and authoritarianism of social institutions.

Second, it is widely believed in the counterculture that we are either already in a state of fascism or inevitably and rapidly moving toward it. Therefore, while action might indeed hasten the process, it is also seen as the only possibility for resistance. And if enough people act, it might, *just might,* be possible to reverse the trend.

Third, it is the establishment, not the counterculture, that has structured the situation. While there is romanticism in the counterculture, there is also anguish and fear. Indeed, it is the government that is attempting to play on the danger of backlash and to use it as a resource. The rhetoric of the Administration, and particularly that of Mr. Agnew, seems to be consciously designed to this end.

Our governmental decision-makers thus bear the responsibility for the situation they have structured. But if men like Nixon, Agnew, and Mitchell are not terribly concerned about a shift to the right and are willing to play on it, those of us who share or pretend to share many of the aspirations of the students—e.g., an end to the war, to racism, to poverty—ought to be concerned. Yet too often university administra-

tors and academics have served the cause of the reaction. Too often serious analysis of the causes and nature of student activism has been replaced by denunciations that conjure up images of a totally destructive fascist-like radical student movement, denunciations that can only contribute to public panic rather than understanding. Too often have men who claim to agree with the goals of the students criticized them for their tactics without offering viable alternatives and without active engagement themselves on the vital issues. And too often have those "liberal" administrators who advance the concept of institutional "neutrality" justified and participated with federal and state authorities in turning universities into virtual totalitarian police states replete with spies, informers, and files. They seem to have forgotten the lesson of McCarthyism, when there were no activist students to blame, that no social institution escapes general repression unless it resists it.

Up to this point the French example has provided a model offering a high degree of predictability for the behavior of both the political system and its youthful dissidents. Like the French, the American system seems determined to force the younger generation to choose between their most deeply felt needs and humanitarian instincts and attachment to the system itself. And, like the French system, it thereby loses the most potent binding force and its very *raison d'être.* There is no greater sign of social degeneration than a general policy of infanticide. Both at home and in Vietnam that seems to be our choice.

half slave, half free

PHILIP E. SLATER

We shall be able to rid ourselves of many of the pseudo-moral principles which have hag-ridden us for two hundred years, by which we have exalted some of the most distasteful of human qualities into the position of the highest virtues.
> KEYNES

Consider the lilies of the field, how they grow; they toil not, neither do they spin: and yet I say unto you, that even Solomon in all his glory was not arrayed like one of these.
> MATTHEW 6:28–29

Don't you know that it's a fool
Who plays it cool
By making his world a little colder.
> LENNON AND MC CARTNEY

And what's the point of revolution
Without general copulation.
> WEISS

In the new there is always an admixture of the old, and this is true of the protean counterculture now burgeoning in the United States. This makes it very difficult, as we saw in the last chapter, to tell what is a true counterculture and what is simply a recruiting outpost for the old culture. But the mere fact that the old culture tries to gobble up something new does not invalidate the potential revolutionary impact of this novelty. As some point a devourer always overreaches himself, like the witch or giant in folk tales who tries to drink up the sea and bursts, or like the vacuum monster in *Yellow Submarine* who ultimately devours himself and disappears. This seems to me the most probable future for the old culture in America.

When I talk of two separate cultures in America I do not mean rich and poor, or black and white (or science and humanism), but rather the opposition between the old scarcity-oriented technological culture that still predominates and the somewhat amorphous counterculture that is growing up to challenge it. At times this distinction may seem synonymous with old-versus-young, or radical-versus-conservative, but the overlap is only approximate. There are many young people who are dedicated to the old culture and a few old people attracted to the new;

Reprinted from Philip E. Slater, THE PURSUIT OF LONELINESS, *Chapter 5, "Half Slave, Half Free," pp. 96–118. Copyright © 1970 by Philip E. Slater. Reprinted by permission of Beacon Press.*

while as to politics, nothing could be more old-culture than a traditional Marxist.

I speak of two cultures, first because each is in fact a total system with an internal logic and consistency: each is built upon a set of assumptions which hangs together and is viable under some conditions. Second, I wish to emphasize a fact which has escaped the liberal-centrist group that plays so dominant a role in America: that they are no longer being wooed so fervently by those to the left and right of them. The seduction of the center is a phenomenon that occurs only in societies fundamentally united. This has in the past been true of the United States and most parliamentary democracies, but it is true no longer. I speak of two cultures because we no longer have one. Mixing the two that exist does not add up to the American way of life. They cannot be mixed. From two opposing systems—each tightly defined—can only come a collision and a confusion. No meaningful compromise can be found if the culture as a whole is not articulated in a coherent way. American centrists—liberal university presidents are the best example —are still operating under the illusion that all Americans are playing by the same rules, an assumption which puts the centrists into the advantageous position of mediators. But this is not the case. Indeed, the moderates are increasingly despised by both radicals and conservatives as hypocritical, amoral, and opportunistic—people who will take no stand and are only interested in their own careers.

What we see instead are two growing absolutistic groups with a shrinking liberal one in between, a condition that will probably obtain until some new cultural structure emerges which is more widely shared. The left attacks the middle most vigorously, since its equivocating stances and lack of conviction make it morally the most vulnerable. Times of change are times when the center is crushed in this way—when it is regarded as the least rather than the most valid, when it is an object of contempt rather than a court of appeal. As the new culture settles in, a new center will grow in strength— become dominant and sure, acquire moral conviction.

So long as our society had a common point of moral reference there was a tendency for conflicts to be resolved by compromise, and this compromise had a moral as well as practical basis. Today this moral unity is gone, and the *only* basis for compromise is a practical one. Whenever moral sentiments are aroused, the opposing groups are pulled in opposite directions, and mere expedience is usually too weak a consideration to counteract this divergence.

For the older generation, the ultimate moral reference group is the far right—authoritarian, puritanical, punitive, fundamentalist. Such views are of course considered extreme, impractical, and "moralistic," but they are accorded an implicit and unquestioned *moral* validity. The liberal majority generally feel uncomfortable and awkward defining issues in moral terms, but when it becomes inescapable it is this brand of morality that they tend to fall back upon. They are practical and "realistic" as long as possible, but when accused of moral flabbiness or being too compromising they feel called upon to pay homage to a kind of Bible Belt morality. They tend to view their position as one of sensible men mediating between hypermoralistic conservatives and amoral radicals, bending the rigid rules of the former to accommodate and indulge the latter.

For middle-class college students the ultimate moral reference group tends increasingly to be the New Left, with its emphasis on equalitarianism, radical democracy, social justice, and social commitment. Once again the moderate majority among the young tend to view the proponents of their moral code as extreme, moralistic, and fanatic. They regard the militant activistis as pursuing a course which is too pure and demanding to be realistic. Allowances must be made for human frailty—the narcissistic needs of those in power, resistance to change, and so on. They, too, see themselves as mediating, but this time between hypermoralistic radicals and amoral conservatives.

So long as the two sides do not feel that a significant moral issue is at stake they can reach a compromise, and the illusion of a unitary culture can be maintained. But sooner or later a moral issue *is* at stake, and negotiations then break down. This is because each side feels it has to justify itself to its moral reference group—to prove that it is not merely giving in out of weakness and cowardice—to prove that it is willing to stand up for some principle. But instead of being common principles, shared by the vast central majority of the society, with each side attempting to show that they are closer to this central morality, the principles are at opposite poles, pulling the sides apart. Today expedience is the *only* unifying force in campus confrontations; no morally based unity is possible.

This may have something to do with the peculiar obtuseness that seems to afflict college presidents, who appear to learn nothing from each other's mistakes or even their own. They are unwilling to face the absence of an even minimal value consensus and keep trying to manufacture one ("the preservation of the university," "the maintenance of free expression and rational discourse," etc.). They talk of "outside agitators" and "a small disruptive minority" and, acting on their own rhetoric, soon find themselves confronted with a hostile majority. They shrink from facing the fact that an ever increasing number of students (for despite the deliberate attempts of admissions officers to prevent it, each entering class is more radical than the last) reject the legitimacy of the established order. The legal monopoly of violence is being challenged by students—they see the crimes of "legitimate" order as demanding extra-legal countermeasures: "An opposition which is directed . . . against a given social system as a whole, cannot remain legal and lawful because it is the established legality and the established law which it opposes." Since the crimes of the soceity are defended and protected by legal techniques they can only be attacked by extra-legal means. Since the forces of law and order fail to comply with their own standards their "betrayed promises are, as it were, 'taken over' by the opposition, and with them the claim for legitimacy."

What all this means is that the university is no longer one society with shared norms of proper behavior, fair play, tolerance and so on, as university administrators try to pretend. Students are not simply challenging an authority they fundamentally accept. Campus confrontations are warfare, with neither side accepting the validity of occupation and control by the other. Students who take over a building hold the same view of this act as police do of wiretapping: the enemy is too dangerous to give them the benefit of the doubt; their crimes require emergency measures.

THE OLD CULTURE AND THE NEW

There are an almost infinite number of polarities by means of which one can differentiate between the two cultures. The old culture, when forced to choose, tends to give preference to property rights over personal rights, technological requirements over human needs, competition over cooperation, violence over sexuality, concentration over distribution, the producer over the consumer, means over ends, secrecy over openness, social forms over personal expression, striving over gratification, Oedipal lover over communal love, and so on. The new counterculture tends to reverse all of these priorities.

Now it is important to recognize that these differences cannot be resolved by some sort of compromise or "golden mean" position. Every cultural system is a dynamic whole, resting on processes that must be accelerative to be self-sustaining. Change must therefore affect the motivational roots of a society or it is not change at all. An attempt to introduce some isolated element into such a system produces cultural redefinition and absorption of the novel element if the culture is strong, and deculturation if it is suceptible. As Margaret Mead points out, to introduce cloth garments into a grass- or bark-clad population, without simultaneously introducing closets, soap, sewing, and furniture, merely transforms a neat and attractive tribe into a dirty and slovenly one. Cloth is part of a complex cultural pattern that includes storing, cleaning, mending, and protecting—just as the automobile is part of a system that includes fueling, maintenance, and repair. A fish with the lungs of a land mammal still will not survive out of water.

Imagine, for example, that we are cooperation purists attempting to remove the invidious element from a foot race. We decide, first of all, that we will award no prize to the winner, or else prizes to everyone. This, we discover, brings no reduction in competitiveness. Spectators and participants alike are still preoccupied with who won and how fast he ran relative to someone else now or in the past. We then decide to eliminate even *announcing* the winner. To our dismay we discover that our efforts have generated some new cultural forms: the runners have taken to wearing more conspicuous identifying clothing—bright-colored trunks or shirts, or names emblazoned in iridescent letters—and underground printed programs have appeared with names, physical descriptions, and other information facilitating this identification. In despair we decide to have the runners run one at a time and we keep no time records. But now we find that the sale of stopwatches has become a booming enterprise, that the underground printed programs have expanded to include voluminous statistics on past time records of participants, and that private "timing services," comparable to the rating services of the television industry, have grown up to provide definitive and instantaneous results for spectators willing to pay a nominal sum (thus does artificial deprivation facilitate enterprise).

At this point we are obliged to eliminate the start and finish lines —an innovation which arouses angry protest from both spectators and participants, who have evinced only mild grumbling over our previous efforts. "What kind of a race can it be if people begin and end wherever they like? Who will be interested in it?" To mollify their complaints and combat dwindling attendance, we reintroduce the practice of having everyone run at the same time. Before long we observe that the runners have evolved the practice of all starting to run at about the same time (although we disallow beginning at the same place), and that all of the races are being run on the circular track. The races get longer and longer, and the underground printed programs now record statistics on how many laps were run by a given runner in a given race. All races have now become longevity contests, and one goes to them equipped with a picnic basket. The newer fields, in fact, do not have bleachers, but only tables at which drinks are served, with scattered observation windows through which the curious look from time to time and report to their tables the latest news on which runners are still going. Time passes, and we are increasingly subjected to newspaper attacks concerning the corrupt state

into which our efforts have fallen. With great trepidation, and in the face of enormous opposition from the ideologically apathetic masses, we inaugurate a cultural revolution and make further drastic alterations in racing rules. Runners begin and end at a signal, but there is no track, merely an open field. A runner must change direction every thirty seconds, and if he runs parallel with another runner for more than fifteen seconds he is disqualified. At first attendance falls off badly, but after a time spectators become interested in how many runners can survive a thirty-minute race without being eliminated for a breach of these rules. Soon specific groups become so skilled at not running parallel that none of them are ever disqualified. In the meantime they begin to run a little more slowly and to elaborate intricate patterns of synchronizing their direction changes. The more gifted groups become virtuosi at moving parallel until the last split second and then diverging. The thirty-second rule becomes unnecessary as direction changes are voluntarily frequent, but the fifteen-second rule becomes a five-second one. The motions of the runners become more and more elegant, and a vast outpouring of books and articles descends from and upon the university (ever a dirty bird) to establish definitive distinctions between the race and the dance.

The first half of this parable is a reasonably accurate representation of what most liberal reform amounts to: opportunities for the existing system to flex its muscles and exercise its self-maintaining capabilities. Poverty programs put very little money into the hands of the poor because middle-class hands are so much more gifted at grasping money —they know better where it is, how to apply for it, how to divert it, how to concentrate it. That is what being middle class means, just as a race means competition. No matter how much we try to change things it somehow ends as merely a more complex, intricate, bizarre, and interesting version of what existed before. A heavily graduated income tax somehow ends by making the rich richer and the poor poorer. "Highway beautification" somehow turns into rural blight, and so on.

But there is a limit to the amount of change a system can absorb, and the second half of the parable suggests that if we persist in our efforts and finally attack the system at its motivational roots we may indeed be successful. In any case there is no such thing as "compromise": we are either strong enough to lever the train onto a new track or its stays on the old one or it is derailed.

Thus it becomes important to discern the core motivational logic behind the old and the new cultures. Knowing this would make rational change possible—would unlock the door that leads most directly from the old to the new.* For a prolonged, unplanned collision will nullify both cultures, like bright pigments combining into gray. The transition must be as deft as possible if we are to minimize the destructive chaos that inevitably accompanies significant cultural transformations.

* This of course makes the assumption that some kind of drastic change is either desirable or inevitable. I do not believe our society can long continue on its old premises without destroying itself and everything else. Nor do I believe it can contain or resist the gathering forces of change without committing suicide in the process.

The core of the old culture is scarcity. Everything in it rests upon the assumption that the world does not contain the where-withal to satisfy the needs of its human inhabitants. From this it follows that people must compete with one another for these scarce resources—lie, swindle, steal, and kill, if necessary. These basic assumptions create the danger of a "war of all against all" and must be buttressed by a series of counternorms which attempt to qualify and restrain the intensity of the struggle. Those who can take the largest share of the scarce resources are said to be "successful," and if they can do it without violating the counternorms they are said to have character and moral fibre.

The key flaw in the old culture is, of course, the fact that the scarcity is spurious—man-made in the case of bodily gratifications and man-allowed or man-maintained in the case of material goods. It now exists only for the purpose of maintaining the system that depends upon it, and its artificiality becomes more palpable each day. Americans continually find themselves in the position of having killed someone to avoid sharing a meal which turns out to be too large to eat alone.

The new culture is based on the assumption that important human needs are easily satisfied and that the resources for doing so are plentiful. Competition is unnecessary and the only danger to humans is human aggression. There is no reason outside of human perversity for peace not to reign and for life not to be spent in the cultivation of joy and beauty. Those who can do this in the face of the old culture's ubiquity are considered "beautiful."

The flaw in the new culture is

the fact that the old culture has succeeded in hiding the cornucopia of satisfactions that the new assumes—that a certain amount of work is required to release the bounty that exists from the restraints under which it is now placed. Whereas the flaw in the old culture has caused it to begin to decompose, the flaw in the new culture has produced a profound schism in its ranks—a schism between activist and dropout approaches to the culture as it now exists. We will return to this problem a little later.

It is important to recognize the internal logic of the old culture, however absurd its premise. If one assumes scarcity, then the knowledge that others want the same things that we have leads with some logic to preparations for defense, and, ultimately (since the best defense is offense), for attack. The same assumption leads to a high value being placed on the ability to postpone gratification (since there is not enough to go around). The expression of feelings is a luxury, since it might alert the scarce resources to the fact that the hunter is near.

The high value placed on restraint and coldness (which, as the Beatles observe in the epigraph for this chapter, creates even greater scarcity) generates in turn another norm: that of "good taste." One can best understand the meaning of such a norm by examining what is common to those acts considered to be in violation of it, and on this basis the meaning of "good taste" is very clear. "Good taste" means tasteless in the literal sense. Any act or product which contains too much stimulus value is considered to be "in bad taste" by old-culture adherents. Since gratification is viewed

as a scarce commodity, arousal is dangerous. Clothes must be drab and inconspicuous, colors of low intensity, smells nonexistent ("if it weren't for bad taste there wouldn't be no taste at all"). Sounds should be quiet, words should lack affect. Four-letter words are always in bad taste because they have high stimulus value. Satire is in bad taste if it arouses political passions or creates images that are too vivid or exciting. All direct references to sexuality are in bad taste until proven innocent, since sexual arousal is the most feared result of all. The lines in old-culture homes, furnishings, and public buildings are hard and utilitarian. Since auditory overstimulation is more familiarly painful than its visual counterpart, brilliant, intense, vibrant colors are called "loud," and the preferred colors for old-culture homes are dull and listless. Stimulation in any form leaves old-culture Americans with a "bad taste" in their mouths. This taste is the taste of desire—a reminder that life in the here-and-now contains many pleasures to distract them from the carrot dangling beyond their reach. Too much stimulation makes the carrot hard to see. Good taste is a taste for carrots.

In the past decade, however, this pattern has undergone a merciless assault from the new culture. For if we assume that gratification is easy and resources plentiful, stimulation is no longer to be feared. Psychedelic colors, amplified sound, erotic books and films, bright and elaborate clothing, spicy food, "intense" (i.e., Anglo-Saxon) words, angry and irreverent satire—all go counter to the old pattern of understimulation. Long hair and beards provide a more "tactile" appearance than the bland, shaven-and-shorn, geometric lines of the fifties. Even Edward Hall's accusation that America is a land of "olfactory blandness" (a statement any traveler will confirm) must now be qualified a little, as the smells of coffee shops, foreign cooking, and incense combine to breathe a modicum of sensation even into the olfactory sphere. (Hall is right, however, in the sense that when America is filled with intense color, music, and ornament, deodorants will be the old culture's last-ditch holdouts. It is no accident that hostility to hippies so often focuses on their olfactory humanity.) The old culture turned the volume down on emotional experience in order to concentrate on its dreams of glory, but the new culture has turned it up again.

New-culture adherents, in fact, often display symptoms of *under*-sensitivity to stimuli. They say "Wow!" in response to almost everything, but in voices utterly devoid of either tension or affect. They seem in general to be more certain that desire can be gratified than that it can be aroused.

This phenomenon probably owes much to early child-rearing conditions. Under ordinary circumstances a mother responds to her child's needs when they are expressed powerfully enough to distract her from other cares and activities. Mothers who overrespond to the Spockian challenge, however, often try to anticipate the child's needs. Before arousal has proceeded very far they hover about and try several possible satisfactions. Since we tend to use these early parental responses as models for the way we treat our own impulses in adulthood, some new-culture adherents find themselves

moving toward gratification before need arousal is clear or compelling. Like their mothers they are not altogether clear which need they are feeling. To make matters worse they are caught in the dilemma that spontaneity automatically evaporates the moment it becomes an ideology. It is a paradox of the modern condition that only those who oppose complete libidinal freedom are capable of ever achieving it.

Another logical consequence of scarcity assumptions is structured inequality. If there is not enough to go around then those who have more will find ways to prolong their advantage, and even legitimate it through various devices. The law itself, although philosophically committed to equality, is fundamentally a social device for maintaining structured systems of inequality (defining as crimes, for example, only those forms of theft and violence in which lower class persons engage). One of the major thrusts of the new culture, on the other hand, is equality: since the good things of life are plentiful, everyone should share them: rich and poor, black and white, female and male.

It is a central characteristic of the old culture that means habitually become ends, and ends means. Instead of people working in order to obtain goods in order to be happy, for example, we find that people should be made happy in order to work better in order to obtain more goods, and so on. Inequality, originally a consequence of scarcity, is now a means of creating artificial scarcities. For in the old culture, as we have seen, the manufacture of scarcity is the principal activity. Hostile comments of old-culture adherents toward new-culture forms ("people won't want to work if they can get things for nothing," "people won't want to get married if they can get it free") often reveal this preoccupation. Scarcity, the presumably undesired but unavoidable foundation for the whole old-culture edifice, has now become its most treasured and sacred value, and to maintain this value in the midst of plenty it has been necessary to establish invidiousness as the foremost criterion of worth. Old-culture Americans are peculiarly drawn to anything that seems to be the exclusive possession of some group or other, and find it difficult to enjoy anything they themselves have unless they can be sure that there are people to whom this pleasure is denied. For those in power even life itself derives its value invidiously: amid the emptiness and anesthesia of a power-oriented career many officials derive reassurance of their vitality from their proximity to the possibility of blowing up the world.

The centrality of invidiousness offers a strong barrier to the diffusion of social justice and equality. But it provides a *raison d'être* for the advertising industry, whose primary function is to manufacture illusions of scarcity. In a society engorged to the point of strangulation with useless and joyless products, advertisements show people calamitously running out of their food or beer, avidly hoarding potato chips, stealing each other's cigarettes, guiltily borrowing each other's deodorants, and so on. In a land of plenty there is little to fight over, but in the world of advertising images men and women will fight before changing their brand, in a kind of parody of the Vietnam war.

The fact that property takes precedence over human life in the old culture also follows logically from scarcity assumptions. It possessions are scarce relative to people they come to have more value than people. This is especially true of people with few possessions, who come to be considered so worthless as to be subhuman and hence eligible for extermination. Many possessions, on the other hand, entitle the owner to a status somewhat more than human. But as a society becomes more affluent these priorities begin to change—human life increases in value and property decreases. New-culture adherents challenge the high relative value placed on property, although the old priority still permeates the society's normative structure. It is still considered permissible, for example, to kill someone who is stealing your property under certain conditions. This is especially true if that person is without property himself—a wealthy kleptomaniac (in contrast to a poor black looter) would probably be worth a murder trial if killed while stealing.*

A recent sign of the shift in values was the *Pueblo* courtmartial. While the Navy, standing firmly behind old-culture priorities, argued that the Commander of the spy ship should have sacrificed the lives of ninety men to prevent the loss of "expensive equipment" to the enemy, the public at large supported his having put human life first.

---

* A more trivial example can be found in the old culture's handling of noise control. Police are called to prevent distraction by the joyous noises of laughter and song, but not to stop the harsh and abrasive roar of power saws, air hammers, power mowers, snow blowers, and other baneful machines.

Much of the intense legal upheaval visible today—expressed most noticeably in the glare of publicity that now attaches to the activities of the U.S. Supreme Court—derives from the attempt to adapt an old-culture legal system to the changing priorities that render it obsolete.

It would not be difficult to show how the other characteristics of the old culture are based on the same scarcity assumptions, or to trace out in detail the derivation of the new culture from the premise that life's satisfactions exist in abundance and sufficiency for all. Let us instead look more closely at the relationship that the new culture bears to the old —the continuities and discontinuities that it offers—and explore some of the contradictions it holds within itself.

First of all it should be stressed that affluence and economic security are not in themselves responsible for the new culture. The rich, like the poor, have always been with us to some degree, but the new culture has not. What is significant in the new culture is not a celebration of economic affluence but a rejection of its foundation. The new culture is concerned with rejecting the artificial scarcities upon which material abundance is based. It argues that instead of throwing away one's body so that one can accumulate material artifacts, one should throw away the artifacts and enjoy one's body. The new culture is not merely blindly reactive, however, but embodies a sociological consciousness. In this consciousness lies the key insight that possessions actually generate scarcity. The more emotion one invests in them the more chances for significant gratification are lost—the more committed to them one becomes the

more deprived one feels, like a thirsty man drinking salt water. To accumulate possessions is to deliver pieces of oneself to dead things. Possessions can absorb an emotional cathexis, but unlike personal relationships they feed nothing back. Americans have combined the proliferation of possessions with the disruption, circumscription, and trivialization of most personal relationships. An alcoholic becomes malnourished because drinking obliterates his hunger. Americans become unhappy and vicious because their preoccupation with amassing possessions obliterates their loneliness. This is why production in America seems to be on such an endless upward spiral: every time we buy something we deepen our emotional deprivation and hence our need to buy something. This is good for business, of course, but those who profit most from this process are just as trapped in the general deprivation as everyone else. The new-culture adherents are thus not merely affluent—they are trying to substitute an adequate emotional diet for a crippling addiction.

The new culture is nevertheless a product of the old, not merely a rejection of it. It picks up themes latent or dormant or subordinate in the old and magnifies them. The hippie movement, for example, is brimming with nostalgia—a nostalgia peculiarly American and shared by old-culture adherents. This nostalgia embraces the Old West, Amerindian culture, the wilderness, the simple life, the utopian community—all venerable American traditions. But for the old culture they represent a subordinate, ancillary aspect of the culture, appropriate for recreational occasions or fantasy representation—a kind of pastoral relief from everyday striving—whereas for the new culture they are dominant themes. The new culture's passion for memorabilia, paradoxically, causes uneasiness in old-culture adherents, whose future-oriented invidiousness leads to a desire to sever themselves from the past. Yet for the most part it is a question of the new culture making the old culture's secondary themes primary, rather than simply seeking to discard the old culture's primary theme. Even the notion of "dropping out" is an important American tradition—neither the United States itself nor its populous suburbs would exist were this not so.

Americans have always been deeply ambivalent about the issue of social involvement. On the one hand they are suspicious of it and share deep romantic fantasies of withdrawal to a simple pastoral or even sylvan life. On the other hand they are much given to acting out grandiose fantasies of taking society by storm, through the achievement of wealth, power, or fame. This ambivalence has led to many strange institutions—the suburb and the automobile being the most obvious. But note that both fantasies express the viewpoint of an outsider. Americans have a profound tendency to feel like outsiders—they wonder where the action is and wander about in search of it (this puts an enormous burden on celebrities, who are supposed to know, but in fact feel just as doubtful as everyone else). Americans have created a society in which they are automatically nobodies, since no one has any stable place or enduring connection. The village idiot of earlier times was less a "nobody" in this sense than the mobile junior executive or academic. An American has to "make a place for himself" because he does not have one.

Since the society rests on scarcity assumptions, involvement in it has always meant competitive involvement, and, curiously enough, the theme of bucolic withdrawal has often associated itself with that of cooperative, communal life. So consistently, in fact, have intentional communities established themselves in the wilderness that one can only infer that society as we know it makes cooperative life impossible.

Be that as it may, it is important to remember that the New England colonies grew out of utopian communes, so that the dropout tradition is not only old but extremely important to our history. Like so many of the more successful nineteenth century utopian communities (Oneida and Amana, for example) the puritans became corrupted by involvement in successful economic enterprise and the communal aspect was eroded away—another example of a system being destroyed by what it attempts to ignore. The new culture is thus a kind of reform movement, attempting to revive a decayed tradition once important to our civilization.

In stressing these continuities between the new culture and the American past, I do not mean to imply a process unique to our society. One of the most basic characteristics of all successful social systems—indeed, perhaps all living matter as well—is that they include devices that serve to keep alive alternatives that are antithetical to their dominant emphases, as a kind of hedge against change. These latent alternatives usually perisist in some encapsulated and imprisoned form ("break glass in case of fire"), such as myths, festivals, or specialized roles. Fanatics continually try to expunge these circumscribed contradictions, but when they succeed it is often fatal to the society. For, as Lewis Mumford once pointed out, it is the "laxity, corruption, and disorder" in a system that makes it viable, considering the contradictory needs that all social systems must satisfy. Such latent alternatives are priceless treasures and must be carefully guarded against loss. For a new cultural pattern does not emerge out of nothing —the seed must already be there, like the magic tricks of wizards and witches in folklore, who can make an ocean out of a drop of water, a palace out of a stone, a forest out of a blade of grass, but nothing out of nothing. Many peoples keep alive a tradition of a golden age, in which a totally different social structure existed. The Judeo-Christian God, patriarchal and omnipotent, has served in matrifocal cultures to keep alive the concept of a strong and protective paternal figure in the absence of real-life examples. Jesters kept alive a wide variety of behavior patterns amid the stilted and restrictive formality of royal courts. The specialized effeminate roles that one finds in many warrior cultures are not merely a refuge for those who fail to succeed in the dominant pattern—they are also a living reminder that the rigid "protest masculinity" that prevails is not the only conceivable kind of behavior for a male. And conversely, the warrior ethos is maintained in a peaceful society or era by means of a military cadre or reserve system.

These phenomena are equivalent to (and in literate cultures tend increasingly to be replaced by) written records of social practices. They are like a box of seldom-used tools, or a trunk of old costumes awating the proper period-play. Suddenly the environment changes, the tolerated eccentric becomes a prophet, the clown a dancing-master, the doll an idol, the idol a doll. The elements have not changed, only the arrangement and the emphases have changed. Every revolution is in part a revival.

Sometimes societal ambivalence is so marked that the latent pattern is retained in a form almost as elaborated as the dominant one. Our society, for example, is one of the most mobile (geographically, at least) ever known; yet, unlike other nomadic cultures it makes little allowance for this fact in its patterns of material accumulation. Our homes are furnished as if we intended to spend the rest of our lives in them, instead of moving every few years. This perhaps represents merely a kind of technological neurosis—a yearning for stability expressed in a technological failure to adapt. Should Americans ever settle down, however, they will find little to do in the way of readjusting their household furnishing habits.

Ultimately it seems inevitable that Americans must either abandon their nomadic habits (which seems unlikely) or moderate their tendency to invest their libido exclusively in material possessions (an addiction upon which the economy relies rather heavily). The new culture is of course pushing hard to realize the second alternative, and if it is successful one might anticipate a trend toward more simply furnished dwellings in which all but the most portable and decorative items are permanent installations. In such a case we might like or dislike a sofa or bed or dresser, but would have no more personal involvement with it than we now do with a stove, furnace, or garage. We would possess, cathect, feel as a part of us, only a few truly personal and portable items.

This tendency of human societies to keep alternative patterns alive has many biological analogues. One of these is *neoteny*—the evolutionary process in which foetal or juvenile characteristics are retained in the adult animal. Body characteristics that have long had only transitional relevance are exploited in response to altered environmental circumstances (thus many human features resemble foetal traits of apes). I have not chosen this example at random, for much of the new culture is implicitly and explicitly "neotenous" in a cultural sense: behavior, values, and life-styles formerly seen as appropriate only to childhood are being retained into adulthood as a counterforce to the old culture.

I pointed out earlier, for example, that children are taught a set of values in earliest childhood—cooperation, sharing, equalitarianism—which they begin to unlearn as they enter school, wherein competition, invidiousness, status differentiation, and ethnocentrism prevail. By the time they enter adult life children are expected to have largely abandoned the value assumptions with which their social lives began. But for affluent, protected, middle-class children this process is slowed down, while intellectual development is speeded up, so that the earlier childhood values can become integrated into a conscious, adult value system centered around social justice. The same is true of other characteristics of childhood: spontaneity, hedonism, candor, playfulness, use of the senses for pleasure rather than utility, and so on. The protective, child-oriented, middle-class family allows the child to preserve some of these qualities longer than is possible under more austere conditions, and his intellectual precocity makes it possible for him to integrate them into an ideological system with which he can confront the corrosive, life-abusing tendencies of the old culture.

When these neotenous characteristics become manifest to old-culture adherents the effect is painfully disturbing, for they vibrate feelings and attitudes that are very old and very deep, although long and harshly stifled. Old-culture adherents have learned to reject all this, but since the learning antedated intellectual maturity they have no coherent ideological framework within which such a rejection can be consciously understood and thoughtfully endorsed. They are deeply attracted and acutely revolted at the same time. They can neither resist their fascination nor control their antipathy. This is exemplified by the extravagant curiosity that hippie communes attract, and by the harassment that so often extinguishes them. It is usually necessary in such situations for the rote-learned abhorrence to discharge itself in persecutory activity before the more positive responses can be released. This was true in the case of the early Christians in Rome, with whom contemporary hippies are often compared (both were communal, utopian, mystical, dropouts, unwashed; both were viewed as dangerous, masochistic, ostentatious, the cause of their own troubles; both existed in societies in which the exclusive pursuit of material advantages had reached some kind of dead end), and seems equally true today. The absorption of this persecution is part of the process through which the latent values that the oppressed group protects and nurtures are expropriated by the majority and released into the mainstream of the culture.

Up to this point we have (rather awkwardly) discussed the new culture as if it were an integrated, monolithic pattern, which is certainly very far from the case. There are many varied and contradictory streams feeding the new culture, and some of these deserve particular attention, since they provide the raw material for future axes of conflict.

The most glaring split in the new culture is that which separates militant activism from the traits we generally associate with the hippie movement. The first strand stresses political confrontation, revolutionary action, radical commitment to the process of changing the basic structure of modern industrial society. The second involves a renunciation of that society in favor of the cultivation of inner experience and pleasing internal feeling-states. Heightening of sensory receptivity, commitment to the immediate present, and tranquil acceptance of the physical envioronment are sought in contradistinction to old-culture ways, in which the larger part of one's immediate experience is overlooked or grayed out by the preoccupation with utility, future goals, and external mastery. Since, in the old culture, experience is classified before it is felt, conceptualization tends here to be forsworn altogether. There is also much emphasis on aesthetic expression and an overarching belief in the power of love.

This division is a crude one, and there are, of course, many areas of overlap. Both value systems share an antipathy to the old culture, both share beliefs in sexual freedom and personal autonomy. Some groups (the Yippies, in particular) have tried with some success to bridge the gap in a variety of interesting ways. But there is nonetheless an inherent contradiction between them. Militant activism is task-oriented, and hence partakes of certain old-culture traits such as postponement of gratification, preoccupation with power, and so on. To be a competent revolutionary one must possess a certain tolerance for the "Protestant Ethic" virtues, ond the activists' moral code is a stern one indeed. The hippie ethic, on the other hand, is a "salvation now" approach. It is thus more radical, since it remains relatively uncontaminated with old-culture values. It is also far less realistic, since it ignores the fact that the existing culture provides a totally antagonistic milieu in which the hippie movement must try to survive in a state of highly vulnerable parasitic dependence. The activists can reasonably say that the flower people are absurd to pretend that the revolution has already occurred, for such pretense leads only to severe victimization by the old culture. The flower people can reasonably retort that a revolution based to so great a degree on old-culture premises is lost before it is begun, for even if the militants are victorious they will have been corrupted by the process of winning.

The dilemma is a very real one and arises whenever radical change is sought. For every social system attempts to exercise the most rigid control over the mechanisms by which it can be altered—defining some as legitimate and others as criminal or disloyal. When we examine the characteristics of legitimate and nonlegitimate techniques, however, we find that the "legitimate" ones involve a course of action requiring a sustained commitment to the core assumptions of the culture. In other words, if the individual follows the "legitimate" pathway there is a very good chance that his initial radical intent will be eroded in the process. If he feels that some fundamental change in the system is required, then, he has a choice between following a path that subverts his goal or one that leads him to be jailed as a criminal or traitor.

This process is not a Machiavellian invention of American capitalists, but rather a mechanism which all viable social systems must evolve spontaneously in order to protect themselves from instability. When the system as it stands is no longer viable, however, the mechanism must be exposed for the swindle that it is; otherwise the needed radical changes will be rendered ineffectual.

The key to the mechanism is the powerful human reluctance to admit that an achieved goal was not worth the unpleasant experience required to achieve it. This is the basic principle underlying initiation rituals: "if I had to suffer so much pain and humiliation to get into this club it must be a wonderful organization." The evidence of thousands of years is that the mechanism works extremely well. Up to some point, for example, war leaders can count on high casualties to increase popular commitment to military adventures.

Thus when a political leader says to a militant, "why don't you run for political office (get a haircut, dress conservatively, make deals, do the dirty work for your elders) and try to change the system in that way"— or the teachers says to the student, "wait until you have your Ph.D. (M.D., LL.B.) and then you can criticize our program," or the white man says to the black man, "when you begin to act like us you'll receive the same opportunities we do"—there is a serious subterfuge involved (however unconscious it may be) in that the protester, if he accepts the condition, will in most cases be automatically converted by it to his opponent's point of view.

The dilemma of the radical, then, is that he is likely to be corrupted if he fights the *status quo* on its own terms, but is not permitted to fight it in any other way. The real significance of the New Left is that it has discovered, in the politics of confrontation, as near a solution to this dilemma as can be found: it is always a bit problematic whether the acts of the new militants are "within the system" or not, and substantial headway can be made in the resulting confusion.

Yet even here the problem remains: if an activist devotes his life to altering the power structure, will he not become like old-culture adherents—utilitarian, invidious, scarcity-oriented, future-centered, and so on? Having made the world safe for flower people will he be likely to relinquish it to them? "You tell me it's the institution," object the Beatles, "you'd better free your mind instead." But what if all the freed minds are in jail?

The dilemma is particularly clear for blacks. Some blacks are much absorbed in rediscovering and celebrating those characteristics which seem most distinctively black and in sharpest contrast to white Western culture: black expressiveness, creativity, sensuality, and spontaneity being opposed to white constrictedness, rigidity, frigidity, bustle, and hypocrisy. For these blacks, to make too great a commitment to the power game is to forsake one's blackness. Power is a white hangup. Yet the absence of power places rather severe limits on the ability of blacks to realize their blackness or anything else.

There is no way to resolve this dilemma, and indeed, it is probably better left unresolved. In a revolutionary situation one needs discipine and unity of purpose, which, however, leads to all kinds of abuses when the goal is won. Discipline and unity become ends in themselves (after the old-culture pattern) and the victory becomes an empty one. It is therefore of great importance to have the envisioned revolutionary goals embodied in a group culture of some kind, with which the acts of those in power can be compared. In the meantime the old culture is subject to a two-pronged attack: a direct assault from activists—unmasking its life-destroying proclivities, its corruption, its futility and pointlessness, its failure to achieve any of its objectives—and an indirect assault by the expansion of expressive countercultures beyond a tolerable (i.e., freak) size.

Closely related to the activist-hippie division is the conflict over the proper role of aggression in the new culture. Violence is a major theme in the old culture and most new-culture adherents view human aggression with deep suspicion.

Nonviolence has been the dominant trend in both the activist and hippie segments of the new culture until recently. But more and more activists have become impatient with the capacity of the old culture to strike the second cheek with even more enthusiasm than the first, and have endorsed violence under certain conditions as a necessary evil.

For the activists the issue has been practical rather than ideological: most serious and thoughtful activists have only a tactical commitment to violence. For the dropout ideologues, however, aggression poses a difficult problem: if they seek to minimize the artificial constriction of emotional expression, how can they be consistently loving and pacific? This logical dilemma is usually resolved by ignoring it: the love cult typically represses aggressive feelings ruthlessly—the body is paramount only so long as it is a loving body.

At the moment the old culture is so fanatically absorbed in violence that it does the work for everyone. If the new culture should prevail, however, the problem of human aggression would probably be its principal bone of contention. Faced with the persistence of aggressiveness (even in the absence of the old culture's exaggerated violence-inducing institutions), the love cult will be forced to reexamine its premises, and opt for some combination of expression and restraint that will restore human aggression to its rightful place as a natural, though secondary, human emotion.

A third split in the new culture is the conflict between individualism and collectivism. On this question the new culture talks out of both sides of its mouth, one moment pitting ideals of cooperation and community against old-culture competitiveness, the next moment espousing the old culture in its most extreme form with exhortations to "do your own thing." I am not arguing that individualism need be totally extirpated in order to make community possible, but new-culture enterprises often collapse because of a dogmatic unwillingness to subordinate the whim of the individual to the needs of the group. This problem is rarely faced honestly by new-culture adherents, who seem unaware of the conservatism involved in their attachment to individualistic principles.

It is always disastrous to attempt to eliminate any structural principle altogether; but if the balance between individualistic and collective emphases in America is not altered, everything in the new culture will be perverted and caricatured into simply another bizarre old-culture product. There must be continuities between the old and the new, but these cannot extend to the relative weights assigned to core motivational principles. The new culture seeks to create a tolerable society within the context of persistent American strivings—utopianism, the pursuit of happiness. But nothing will change until individualism is assigned a subordinate place in the American value system—for individualism lies at the core of the old culture, and a prepotent individualism is not a viable foundation for any society in a nuclear age.